1985	GBE	Gen Sir Frank Kitson
	KCB	Maj Gen R.A. Pascoe
	KCVO	Lt Gen Sir David House
	CBE	Maj Gen C.E.W. Jones
	TD	Lt Col E.I. Williamson

Operational Awards
Northern Ireland:
MID Maj P.D. Browne, Rfn P.A. Ross, Col C.B.Q. Wallace

1986	CBE	Brig C.L.G.G. Henshaw
	OBE	Lt Col S.D.G. McKinley, Lt Col G.F. Smythe
	MBE	Maj W.J. Taylor
	BEM	CSgt J.E.C. Clifton, CSgt B. Edwards, CSgt M.J. O'Hara

Operational Awards
Northern Ireland:
MID Lt Col Gde V.W. Hayes, Maj S.R. Stanford-Tuck

1987	Life Peerage	
		FM Sir Edwin Bramall
	GCB	Gen Sir Roland Guy
	KCB	Maj Gen D.J. Ramsbotham
	BEM	CSgt K.G. Cox
	TD	Maj P.C. Clifford
	TA Efficeincy Medal	
		Rfn Fisher, Cpl French, Sgt Hollingsworth, CSgt Purvis

Operational Awards
Northern Ireland:
MBE Maj R.A. Churcher

1988	KCVO	Col R.A.StG. Martin
	BEM	Sgt T. Evans, Sgt J.J.V. McEvoy, CSgt G. Morrish, CSgt J.H.A. Needham, CSgt G.B. Ternent

Operational Awards
Northern Ireland:
MBE Maj N.J. Mangnall
MID Lt Col R.J. Rimmer

1989	OBE	Lt Col D.J. Innes, Lt Col N.A. Johnson
	BEM	Sgt C.M. Cooper

Operational Awards
Northern Ireland:
QGM Sgt A.R. Hoare
MID Lt Col J.S. Carter, Lt Col S.C. Hearn

1990	KCB	Maj Gen G.D. Johnson
	BEM	Sgt C.F. Branson, CSgt J.D.S. Humphrey

Operational Awards
Northern Ireland:
OBE Lt Col N.J. Cottam
MID CSgt E.V. Baker, CSgt M.J. Keating, Lt Col A.M.D. Palmer

1991	CBE	Col A.R.D. Pringle, Brig C.G.C. Vyvyan
	MBE	Maj J.H. Gordon
	BEM	CSgt P. Palmer

Operational Awards
Northern Ireland:
MID Capt E.A. Butler
Operation Granby:
CB Maj Gen J.P. Foley
DCM Sgt S.B. Mitchell
MID Cpl W.B. Tyson

1992	MBE	Maj H. Babbington-Smith, Sgt P. Flaherty, WO2 J. Pickford

Operational Awards
Northern Ireland:
OBE Lt Col J.M.J. Balfour, Lt Col N.J. Mangnall, Lt Col M. Smith
MBE Maj N.R.G. Chavasse
MID Rfn S.G. Fairs, Maj N.R. Haddock, Capt N.J. Hyslop, Capt J.L. Mann, Lt Col C.E.M. Snagge, Maj D.M. Tobey

1993	MBE	Maj M.F.J. Gleeson, WO2 M.F. Godbold

Operational Awards
Northern Ireland:
OBE Lt Col A.J.R. Jackson
MBE Maj A.E.H. Worsley
MM LCpl M.J. Fryer
MID Capt J.R.D. Bryson, Col N.J. Cottam, LCpl D.R.W. Ware

1994	KCB	Maj Gen J.P. Foley

Operational Awards
Northern Ireland:
MBE Maj J.I.S. Plastow, WO2 E.T. Hughes
MID Cpl M.E. Downard, Lt M.A. Hughes
Former Republic of Yugoslavia:
CBE Brig Gde V.W. Hayes
MC Capt A.M.F. Carleton-Smith

1995	CBE	Brig M.C.H. Manners-Smith, Brig A.M.D. Palmer
	OBE	Col J.A. Daniell, Lt Col R.C.J. Martin, Lt Col R.J. Rimmer
	MBE	Maj N.A.C. Baverstock, WO2 M.J. Keating
	QCVS	Lt Col C.E.I. Beattie

Operational Awards
Former Republic of Yugoslavia:
QCVS Maj Gen A.R.D. Pringle

1996	OBE	Col S.C. Hearn
	MBE	Maj N.P. Carter, Maj J.H. Gordon, WO2 E.L. Jones

1997	KBE	Lt Gen C.B.Q. Wallace
	MBE	Maj E.A. Butler, Lt Col P.J.F. Schofield

Operational Awards
Northern Ireland:
MBE Cpl B.K. Brown
QCVS Cpl A. Moodie

1998	MBE	Maj N.J.R. Haddock, Maj P.J. Proctor

Operational Awards
Northern Ireland:
CBE Col M. Smith
Former Yugoslavia:
QCVS Maj E.A. Butler, Maj Gen A.R.D. Pringle

1999	QCB (Posthumous)	
		Rfn R.S. Blackledge

Operational Awards
Former Yugoslavia:
MBE Maj T.H. Emck, WO2 K.T. Oxby
QCVS Lt Col N.P. Carter

2000	CB	Maj Gen A.R.D. Pringle
	MBE	Lt Col N.W. Fox, WO1 A.F. Hands, WO2 M.J. Morgan

Operational Awards
Former Yugoslavia:
OBE Col N.P. Carter
MID Cpl M. Harris, Sgt G. Miller, Maj S. Plummer
QCB LCpl J. Rooney
QCVS Capt I.R. Moodie, Maj M.R. Winsloe

2001	Meritorious Service Medal WO2 A.S. Watson

Operational Awards
Northern Ireland:
CBE Brig J.M.J. Balfour
MBE WO2 R.E. Keys
QCVS Cpl J.P.B. Becker, Lt Col J.I.S. Plastow

2002	MBE	CSgt M. Pashby

Operational Awards
Sierra Leone:
CBE Brig N.R. Parker
Former Yugoslavia:
QCVS Brig J.M.J. Balfour, Capt R.G. Streatfield, Lt Col A.E.H. Worsley

2003	MBE	Maj S.P. Plummer, Maj T. Roper
	QVRM	WO2 C. Percival

Operational Awards
Iraq:
DSO Lt Col E.A. Butler
QCVS Maj J.C.W. Maciejewski
Afghanistan:
  Sgt S.M. McNiff
Northern Ireland:
QCB WO2 C.L. Nufer
QCVS Col J.I.S. Plastow

2004	MBE	WO1 S. Hopgood

Operational Awards
Afghanistan:
QCVS Brig N.P. Carter
Iraq:
OBE Lt Col P.N.Y.M. Sanders
MID Sgt S.M. McNiff
Former Yugoslavia:
MBE Maj R.H.S. Shaw
QCVS Rfn S.P. Staley

2005	CB	Lt Gen A.M.D. Palmer
	OBE	Col J.C.C. Schute
	MBE	Lt Col J.C.W. Maciejewski, Capt M.R. Robson, Maj R.J. Thomson

Operational Awards
Sierra Leone:
QCVS Lt Col E.A. Butler
Afghanistan:
DSO Lt Col E.A. Butler

2006	QVRM	Capt S.L. Ellis

Operational Awards
Afghanistan:
CBE Brig E.A. Butler
MBE Capt M.J. Dicks
Northern Ireland:
  Brig J.H. Gordon
Democratic Republic of Congo:
OBE Col R.P. Winser

2007	CBE	H.C.G. Willing

Operational Award
Iraq:
MID Maj M.E. Foster-Brown

SWIFT AND BOLD:

A Portrait of
THE ROYAL GREEN JACKETS

1966–2007

With a Foreword by
FIELD MARSHAL THE LORD BRAMALL
KG GCB OBE MC

Editor's Note
Andrew Pringle

This book, as its name suggests, is a portrait not a history, painted in words and pictures. The end result is I hope a passable likeness of the Regiment. It is not definitive, and the major challenge has been not what to include but what to leave out. One day if anyone cares to write a history of The Royal Green Jackets a mound of information will be found on which to draw. The annual Royal Green Jackets *Chronicle* is a year-by-year record of the doings of the Regiment. Much information has been gleaned from the *Chronicle*, and from the Archives and Regimental Museum at Winchester, and a number of riflemen of all ranks have contributed articles and photographs on which we have drawn.

The idea of compiling a book on the Regiment has been around for some time. A number of false starts were made, and in 2001 I agreed to pull together a book, written by riflemen, which would attempt to capture something of the flavour of The Royal Green Jackets. I am grateful to those who assisted me in drafting chapters of the book: The Evolution of the Regular Battalions, Mark Scrase-Dickins; Inside the Regiment, Michael Dewar; The Contribution to the Wider Army, Vere Hayes; The Royal Green Jackets – Volunteers, Neil Johnson and Geoffrey Pattie; Royal Green Jackets Cadets, David Innes; Counter Insurgency, Christopher Dunphie; Northern Ireland, Charles Vyvyan; the Cold War, Vere Hayes; Soldiering Around the World, Vere Hayes; Into the Future: Rifles Once More, Nick Parker, Nick Cottam and Jamie Balfour; Operations in Iraq, Quentin Naylor, Alex Baring, Patrick Sanders and Tom Copinger-Symes.

I am grateful to the many others, too numerous to mention by names, who have helped in all areas, from providing articles for insertion in the chapters, conducting research, proof reading and corrections, to ensuring that the Green Jacket family has been kept fully abreast of progress via the various regimental websites that have proved an invaluable means of communication.

Thanks are also due to many others who have given help and advice, including Ron Cassidy and Ken Gray from the Archives and the Museum; Bert Henshaw, who willingly made available his extraordinary photographic archive of The Royal Green Jackets; Christopher Wallace for permission to use material and pictures from his two recent publications: 'The King's Royal Rifle Corps … the 60th Rifles. A Brief History: 1755 to 1965 – From Royal Americans to Royal Green Jackets' and 'Focus on Courage', published jointly with Ron Cassidy describing the 59 VCs awarded to members of the antecedent regiments; Chris McDonald, Chairman of the Australasian Branch of The Royal Green Jackets Association; and Julian Calder for permission to use some of his excellent photographs of The Royal Green Jackets in his book on The London Regiment.

As editor I thank especially Vere Hayes for all the help so freely given, not only in compiling chapters but also in taking on a myriad of tasks that meant, working together with Chris Fagg, Matt Wilson and Bonnie Murray from Third Millennium Publishing, we were able to pull the book together and meet our publication date. As editor I accept responsibility for any errors or omissions.

This then is the portrait of the Regiment, enough I hope to capture something of the ethos and spirit of The Royal Green Jackets and to describe something of what we hand on to The Rifles, where all that was best in The Royal Green Jackets will be melded with the best of the other merging regiments to provide an intoxicating mix that will ensure the best possible start for The Rifles.

Contents

	Foreword: Field Marshal the Lord Bramall	4
01	The Origins, Characteristics and Ethos of The Royal Green Jackets	6
02	The Evolution of the Regular Battalions of The Royal Green Jackets: A Story of Continual Change	20
03	The Green Jacket Approach to Leadership	32
04	Inside the Regiment	40
05	The Green Jackets' Contribution to the Wider Army	70
06	The Royal Green Jackets – Volunteers	78
07	The Royal Green Jackets Cadets	92
08	Counter-Insurgency: From Green Jackets Brigade to Royal Green Jackets	98
09	Northern Ireland 1969–2007	110
10	Germany and the Cold War Years	124
11	Soldiering Around the World	146
12	Into the Future: Rifles Once More	166
13	Operations in Iraq: The Royal Green Jackets to The Rifles – 'Forged Under Fire'	174

FOREWORD

FIELD MARSHAL THE LORD BRAMALL OF BUSHFIELD, KG GCB OBE MC

As one of the first Commanding Officers of The Royal Green Jackets, 41 years ago, I am proud and delighted to write the foreword to *Swift and Bold* – a portrait of The Royal Green Jackets from 1966 to 2007, when it merged with a number of others to form a new Rifle Regiment.

Never can a single regiment have acquired and maintained such a distinguished reputation in such a short time. It is true that the Regiment started with a very fine pedigree, being itself a union of three famous regiments – the Oxfordshire and Buckinghamshire Light Infantry (43rd/52nd), the King's Royal Rifle Corps (60th Rifles) and the Rifle Brigade (the 95th), all of which had won renown, in bygone days, as light troops and skirmishers, and in more recent times as airborne troops, motorised and mechanised infantry, and as doughty and skilful fighters in both the desert and the jungle. This got the Regiment off to a very good start.

Since that union, however, the single Regiment has served all over the world in almost every continent and theatre of operations, and won high praise and recognition for its fighting spirit, its initiative and ability to innovate and improvise (so essential in modern conflict operations) and for its propensity for forward thinking, both tactically and in the leadership of men.

The Regiment's record in higher command has also been exceptional – uniquely so, having produced in its short life, two Field Marshals and Chiefs of the General Staff, five Adjutant Generals, three Quartermaster Generals and six Commanders-in-Chief, all of whom have left their mark on the way the British Army has developed and carried out its duty.

Throughout the Regiment's lifespan, the British Army has been almost continuously engaged on warlike operations somewhere in the world with notable success; this wide experience, when you add the restrained, impressive and also successful Aid to the Civil Power over the 40 years of the serious troubles in Northern Ireland, and the ongoing hard battling in Iraq and Afghanistan, makes the British Army the most respected army in the world. Members of The Royal Green Jackets at every rank have played a notable and distinctive part in all of this, and *Swift and Bold* tells something of their story.

It also closes an historic chapter in the Army's history as The Royal Green Jackets merges still further in an even wider grouping of Infantry to form yet another single, but this time much larger, regiment with five regular battalions and two Territorial Army battalions. Since this new regiment – The Rifles – will by its uniform and accoutrements, its drill and military music and, above all, its ethos, be in every sense a Rifle Regiment, even accepting the same motto, which forms the title of this book, the legacy of The Royal Green Jackets has certainly not been lost but is at this very moment being carried forward with confidence in this twenty-first century.

It is indeed a splendid portrait of a fine Regiment, and I hope you will enjoy reading it and savouring something of the very special contribution that The Royal Green Jackets brought to our military affairs.

ROLL OF HONOUR

The Royal Green Jackets

Rfn A.C. Kelway	31 Mar 1966	2RGJ	Borneo
Rfn R.M.T. Webster	31 Mar 1966	2RGJ	Borneo
Cpl R. Bankier	22 May 1971	1RGJ	Northern Ireland
Rfn D. Walker	12 Jul 1971	1RGJ	Northern Ireland
Rfn J.C.E Hill	16 Oct 1971	2RGJ	Northern Ireland
Maj T.E.F. Taylor	7 Nov 1971	Sultan's Armed Forces	Muscat, Oman
Maj R.N.H. Alers-Hankey	30 Jan 1972	2RGJ	Northern Ireland
Rfn J.W. Taylor	20 Mar 1972	2RGJ	Northern Ireland
Rfn J. Meredith	26 Jun 1972	2RGJ	Northern Ireland
LCpl D.N. Card	04 Aug 1972	1RGJ	Northern Ireland
Cpl I.R. Morrill	28 Aug 1972	3RGJ	Northern Ireland
Rfn D. Griffiths	30 Aug 1972	3RGJ	Northern Ireland
Rfn J.R. Joesbury	08 Dec 1972	3RGJ	Northern Ireland
Pte R.B. Roberts	02 Jul 1973	3RGJ	serving with the LI in NI
Rfn M.E. Gibson	29 Dec 1974	1RGJ	Northern Ireland
Cpl W.J. Smith	31 Aug 1977	1RGJ	Northern Ireland
Lt Col I.D. Corden-Lloyd	17 Feb 1978	2RGJ	Northern Ireland
Rfn N.W. Smith	04 Mar 1978	2RGJ	Northern Ireland
Rfn C.J. Watson	19 Jul 1980	3RGJ	Northern Ireland
LCpl G. Winstone	19 May 1981	1RGJ	Northern Ireland
Rfn M.E. Bagshaw	19 May 1981	1RGJ	Northern Ireland
Rfn A. Gavin	19 May 1981	1RGJ	Northern Ireland
Rfn J.W. King	19 May 1981	1RGJ	Northern Ireland
Drv P. Bulman	19 May 1981	RCT attached to 1RGJ	Northern Ireland
LCpl G.T. Dean	16 Jul 1981	2RGJ	Northern Ireland
Rfn D.R. Holland	25 Mar 1982	2RGJ	Northern Ireland
Rfn N.P. Malakos	25 Mar 1982	2RGJ	Northern Ireland
Rfn A.M. Rapley	25 Mar 1982	2RGJ	Northern Ireland
Cpl R.E. Armstrong	19 May 1982	1RGJ	seconded to 22 SAS Falklands
Cpl E.T. Walpole	19 May 1982	3RGJ	seconded to 22 SAS Falklands
WO2 G. Barker	20 Jul 1982	1RGJ	Regent's Park London
Cpl R.A. Livingstone	20 Jul 1982	1RGJ	Regent's Park London
Cpl J.R. McKnight	20 Jul 1982	1RGJ	Regent's Park London
Bdsm C.J. Mesure	20 Jul 1982	1RGJ	Regent's Park London
Bdsm K.J. Powell	20 Jul 1982	1RGJ	Regent's Park London
Bdsm L.K. Smith	20 Jul 1982	1RGJ	Regent's Park London
Bdsm J. Heritage	1 Aug 1982	1RGJ	Regent's Park London
Gnr T.P. Utteridge	19 Oct 1984	1RHA attached to 3RGJ	Northern Ireland
Rfn D.A. Mulley	18 Mar 1986	1RGJ	Northern Ireland
LCpl T.W. Hewitt	19 Jul 1987	1RGJ	Northern Ireland
Cpl E.R.P. Jedruch	31 Jul 1987	1RGJ	Northern Ireland
Cpl M.C. Maddocks	14 Nov 1991	2RGJ	Northern Ireland
Cpl M. Phillips	27 Jan 2002	1RGJ	Sierra Leone
Rfn I.J. Coman	27 Jan 2002	1RGJ	Sierra Leone
Rfn V.C. Windsor	21 Jan 2004	2RGJ	attached to 1LI Iraq

The Royal Green Jackets' Roll of Honour records the names of all those, including attached personnel and those seconded to other regiments, who have died as a direct result of enemy action, in the act of conducting operations against the enemy or as a result of acts of terrorism since 1966. The names of all those serving in the Regiment who have died as a result of accidents, illness, during training or from other causes are recorded in the Book of Remembrance, the Light Division Chapel, Sir John Moore Barracks, Winchester.

The Rifles
(Formerly The Royal Green Jackets)

Rfn D.L. Coffey	Feb 2007	2Rifles	Iraq
Rfn A. Lincoln	Apr 2007	2Rifles	Iraq
Rfn P. Donnachie	Apr 2007	2Rifles	Iraq
Cpl J. Brookes	May 2007	4Rifles	Iraq
Cpl R. Wilson	Jun 2007	4Rifles	Iraq
Maj P. Harding	Jun 2007	4Rifles	Iraq
Cpl J. Rig	Jun 2007	4Rifles	Iraq
Rfn E. Vakabua	Jul 2007	4Rifles	Iraq

The Origins, Characteristics and Ethos of The Royal Green Jackets

The Green Jacket approach to soldiering stemmed directly from the characteristics and ethos of the antecedent regiments of The Royal Green Jackets. The immediate antecedents were the Oxfordshire and Buckinghamshire Light Infantry (43rd & 52nd), The King's Royal Rifle Corps (60th Rifles) and The Rifle Brigade. Each of these distinguished regiments had a lengthy lineage. The 43rd Regiment, as it became, was raised in 1741 as Thomas Fowke's Regiment of Foot, regiments taking their colonels' name until the numbering system was introduced in 1747 when the Regiment was ranked as the 54th of Foot. In 1751, following the disbandment of a number of lower numbered regiments, the 54th of Foot was renumbered the 43rd of Foot.

Right: Private, 60th or Royal American Regiment of Foot, 1758.

The 52nd regiment, coincidentally also raised in 1755 as the 54th of Foot, was renumbered the 52nd in 1756 when two further regiments, the 50th and 51st, were struck off. The 62nd or Royal American Regiment of Foot was also raised in 1755 and renumbered 60th in 1756 for the same reason. The 95th was raised in 1800 as the Experimental Corps of Riflemen, numbered in 1802 as the 95th (Rifle) Regiment of Foot, and in 1816 removed from the numbered Regiments of the Line to be styled the Rifle Brigade, the only instance in the history of the British Army that such a distinction has been conferred on a regiment.

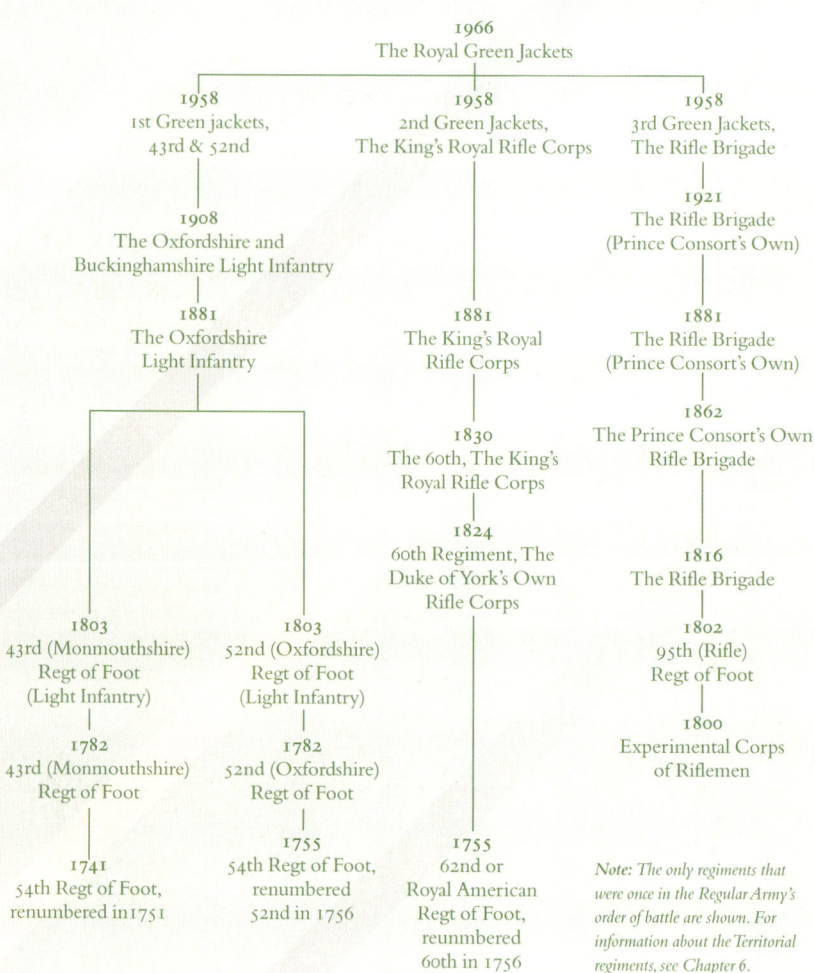

The Royal Green Jackets Family Tree

1966 — The Royal Green Jackets

- **1958** 1st Green Jackets, 43rd & 52nd
  - **1908** The Oxfordshire and Buckinghamshire Light Infantry
  - **1881** The Oxfordshire Light Infantry
  - **1803** 43rd (Monmouthshire) Regt of Foot (Light Infantry)
  - **1782** 43rd (Monmouthshire) Regt of Foot
  - **1741** 54th Regt of Foot, renumbered in 1751
  - **1803** 52nd (Oxfordshire) Regt of Foot (Light Infantry)
  - **1782** 52nd (Oxfordshire) Regt of Foot
  - **1755** 54th Regt of Foot, renumbered 52nd in 1756

- **1958** 2nd Green Jackets, The King's Royal Rifle Corps
  - **1881** The King's Royal Rifle Corps
  - **1830** The 60th, The King's Royal Rifle Corps
  - **1824** 60th Regiment, The Duke of York's Own Rifle Corps
  - **1755** 62nd or Royal American Regt of Foot, reunmbered 60th in 1756

- **1958** 3rd Green Jackets, The Rifle Brigade
  - **1921** The Rifle Brigade (Prince Consort's Own)
  - **1881** The Rifle Brigade (Prince Consort's Own)
  - **1862** The Prince Consort's Own Rifle Brigade
  - **1816** The Rifle Brigade
  - **1802** 95th (Rifle) Regt of Foot
  - **1800** Experimental Corps of Riflemen

Note: The only regiments that were once in the Regular Army's order of battle are shown. For information about the Territorial regiments, see Chapter 6.

Grenadier 43rd Regiment of Foot, c.1776.

Grenadier 52nd Regiment of Foot, c.1775.

The 43rd and the 60th fought together at Quebec in 1759, in General Wolfe's small force of 4,500 men which was landed by the Royal Navy, scaled the cliffs and defeated the French on the Plains of Abraham. The 43rd and the 52nd fought together at Bunker Hill in 1775 and several times again during the American War of Independence. But it was in Portugal, on 21 August 1808 at the Battle of Vimiera, that all four regiments – the 43rd Light Infantry, 52nd Light Infantry, 5th Battalion 60th and the 95th Rifles, as they had each become – fought together for the first time. It was the beginning of a long and happy association between the regiments, steeped in mutual respect and forged through comradeship in battle. Captain Sir John Kincaid of the 95th Rifles wrote about the 43rd Light Infantry and its sister regiment the 52nd Light Infantry during the Peninsular War:

Wherever we were they were; and although the nature of our arm generally gave us more employment in the way of skirmishing, yet, whenever it came to a pinch, independent of a suitable mixture of them among us, we had only to look behind to see a line, in which we might place a degree of confidence almost equal to our hopes in heaven; nor were we ever disappointed. There never was a corps of riflemen in the hands of such supporters!

Lieutenant Blackiston of the 43rd Light Infantry showed similar regard when he wrote of Kincaid's 95th Rifles:

I never saw such skirmishers as the 95th. They could do the work much better and with infinitely less loss than any of our best light troops. They possessed an individual boldness, a mutual understanding, and a quickness of the eye in taking advantage of the ground, which taken altogether, I never saw equalled. They were in fact as much superior to the French voltigeurs as the latter were to our skirmishers in general. As our regiment was often employed in supporting them I am fairly well qualified to speak of their merits.

Chapter 2 describes how these regiments united on 1 January 1966 to become The Royal Green Jackets, but in the late eighteenth and early nineteenth centuries each of the antecedent regiments had played its own leading role in developing radical and new ideas about soldiering. Significantly, those ideas – now no longer novel or radical in the British Army – represent what had always been the essential nature of how the Green Jackets had sought to do things: a traditional ethos handed down from generation to generation.

Top: 'Sharp Shooters in Ambush', The Rifle Corps 1803.

Left: Rifleman 95th Rifles, Rifleman 5/60th Rifles, Private 43rd Light Infantry, Private 52nd Light Infantry – Peninsular War, 1808–14.

Bottom left: 52nd Light Infantry – capturing the guns at Waterloo, 1815.

Left: Bunker Hill, 17 June 1775, 43rd Regiment of Foot and 52nd Regiment of Foot fight together.

The Origins, Characteristics and Ethos of The Royal Green Jackets

Above: Lieutenant General Sir John Moore.

Bottom right: Henry Bouquet, c.1756.

Below: Francis, Baron de Rottenburg, c.1800.

For some fifty years before 1800 it had been the practice for infantry regiments of the line to include a light company of picked men, usually the more intelligent and agile ones, for tasks that required rapidity of action and individual initiative. These men were equipped more lightly than standard infantrymen and taught to move swiftly. In 1803 this development was taken a step further when the 43rd Regiment and the 52nd Regiment (later to be united as The Oxfordshire and Buckinghamshire Light Infantry) were chosen to form the first Corps of Light Infantry. The corps was trained together with the 95th Rifles (later The Rifle Brigade) to form the élite Light Brigade then undergoing specialist training at Shorncliffe camp under the command of the forward-thinking Sir John Moore, who had previously been appointed colonel of the 52nd by King George III.

The fourth regiment from which The Royal Green Jackets drew its identity, the 60th (later The King's Royal Rifle Corps), had its formative years in America. Founded in 1755 as the 62nd (Royal American) Regiment, it was renumbered the 60th within a year of formation. The 60th played a key role in pioneering new tactics with which to fight the French and their American Indian allies in the forests and up and down the waterways of North America. The 60th's founders, among whom was Henry Bouquet, an innovative Swiss soldier of fortune who commanded the 1st Battalion, regarded the rigid, unthinking 'pipe clay and drill' discipline of the British Army at large to be incompatible with the tactics required for success against the French and the Indians: open-order skirmishing and deep patrolling, moving on foot through the forests and mountains, and using boats to navigate along the waterways, which required individual initiative, self-reliance, self-discipline and marksmanship. This sort of warfare demanded a different form of discipline from that practised in the rest of the British Army, including highly professional officers and soldiers and a much closer relationship between officers and men. Camouflaged clothing – initially based on the functional dress worn by the woodsmen, hunters and trappers, and developed later in the form of the green jacket – was adopted as a practical measure. Companies were trained to act independently of each other, which fostered a high degree of independence and autonomy amongst the company commanders. In many ways the 60th could be described in this period as the first 'special forces' ever formed in the British Army.

In December 1797 the 60th Regiment added a fifth battalion, drawn initially from German troops serving as 'mounted riflemen' in Hompesch's Corps. Formed at Cowes on the Isle of Wight, Hompesch's *Jäger* – German troops trained as riflemen and serving the British crown – were subsequently merged with other German units to bring the new battalion up to full strength. Francis, Baron de Rottenburg was given command, training the men as a rifle battalion and the first one in the British Army officially to be equipped as riflemen (using a German weapon first introduced into the British Army in 1794). The free-thinking principles of Henry Bouquet were officially recognised in formal Army Dress Regulations when the battalion became the first regular one in the British Army to be dressed in a green jacket, which was to become the hallmark of the rifleman. To be a 'green jacket' rather than a 'red coat' was to be something special, and something to be proud of – a green jacket set one aside from the mass. With their obvious differences in dress and equipment, culture and training, a special ethos began to evolve in the 60th, which was continued in those regiments trained as the Light Brigade by Sir John Moore and other like-minded officers.

During the Napoleonic Wars these four regiments came to be seen as an answer to French shock tactics based on massed columns of conscript soldiers preceded by picked sharpshooters. Riflemen, armed with the new and accurate Baker rifle, which offered far greater range and accuracy than the smooth-bore musket, were taught to shoot at selected targets. Their bottle green uniforms afforded concealment, and the men were taught to move and attack in open, loose formations, responding to orders sounded on bugle-horns. While the Light Brigade (or, from spring 1810, the Light Division) operated as a cohesive formation, independent

The Royal Green Jackets

companies of the 5th Battalion 60th (5th/60th) served throughout Wellington's army during the Peninsular War. Attached to separate brigades and working with many different regiments as specialist skirmishers and snipers, the riflemen were characterised by their independence of mind and initiative. Many a French officer, specially targeted, met his end as a result of their marksmanship. This was of particular concern to Marshal Soult, commander-in-chief of the French Army in Spain, who wrote to the Minister of War in Paris:

The loss in prominent and superior officers is so disproportionate to that of the rank and file that I have been at pains to discover the reason. There is in the English Army a battalion of the 60th armed with a short rifle; the men are selected for their marksmanship; they perform the duties of scouts, and in action are expressly ordered to pick off the officers, especially Field and General Officers. Thus it has been observed that whenever a superior officer goes to the front, either for purpose of observation or to lead and encourage the men, he is usually hit. This mode of making war is very detrimental to us; our casualties in officers are so great that after a couple of actions the whole number are usually disabled. I saw yesterday a regiment whose officers had been disabled in the ratio of one officer to eight men. I also saw battalions which were reduced to two or three officers although less than one-sixth of their men had been disabled. You can imagine that if these casualties should recur, it would be very difficult to provide for the replacement of officers even though the nominations were made beforehand.

Above: Marksmanship – Riflemen were trained to hit selected targets at ranges up to 300 yards (275m).

Above left: 60th Royal Americans, Fort William Henry, 1763.

Below: Rifleman Tom Plunkett kills French General Colbert at Cacabelos, retreat to Corunna, 1809.

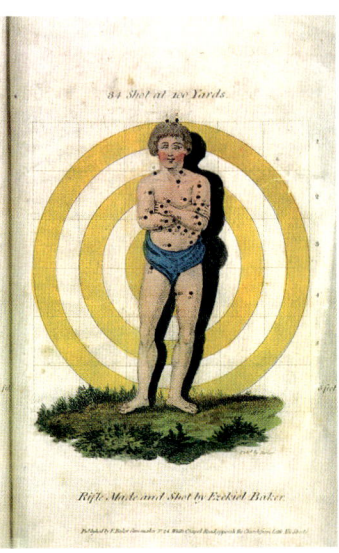

The Origins, Characteristics and Ethos of The Royal Green Jackets

This was warfare conducted by thinking riflemen. Their specialist role and its revolutionary methods of training encouraged a special and close relationship between officers and riflemen, which helped put into effect certain tactical requirements. The Royal Green Jackets' distinctive way of doing things had its origins in these early days when its forebears were pioneering new tactics. The new principles insisted on then remain just as pertinent in the modern era:

First, that it was necessary to have the officers efficient before the men, and to require of the officers real knowledge, good temper and kind treatment of the men. Second, that power should be delegated to officers commanding companies, the men to be taught to look up to them in matters alike of drill, food, clothing, rewards and most punishments. Third, that all officers and non-commissioned officers were to understand that it was their business to prevent rather than to punish crime. The whole system was one of developing, not of repressing intelligence, of making the development of the man contribute to the effective unity of the whole, of enlisting the zeal of the private as much as of the officer in perfecting the whole.

Left: Rifleman, 95th (Rifle) Regiment.
Below: Rifleman, 5th Battalion 60th.

The leadership of such distinguished officers as Henry Bouquet, Francis, Baron de Rottenburg, Coote Manningham, William Stewart, Kenneth McKenzie, the respected (if not loved) 'Black Bob' Craufurd, John Colborne and Sir John Moore generated a succession of advanced ideas, much later to be adopted as ideals by the rest of the British Army: open-order tactics and mobility in place of rigid drills and ponderous movement; camouflage and concealment in place of serried ranks of red coats; individual marksmanship in place of massed musket fire; and intelligence and self-reliance in place of blind obedience instilled by the fear of brutal punishment. As Richard Holmes has put it: 'There was a palpable tension between the light infantry ethos, with its emphasis on practical uniform, individual skills and relaxed discipline, and the older notion of unthinking obedience.'

During the early years many progressive and modernising officers gravitated towards these new regiments, and they proceeded to create an élite fighting force that operated in a way that was culturally and physically markedly different from the norm found in the rest of the British Army.

Many of the officers serving with the 60th Regiment had either served in the French Army or had taken pains to understand how it worked. At a time when British soldiers trained along traditional Prussian lines with an absolute focus on blind obedience and rigid discipline, it was the early commanding officers of the 60th Regiment – such as Henry Bouquet and Francis, Baron de Rottenburg, who later led the 5th Battalion of the 60th – who changed the emphasis in order to place particular importance on the cultivation of the intelligence and initiative of each individual soldier.

Bouquet himself was born in Switzerland in 1719. He served with the Swiss Guard of the Prince of Orange, which included time spent in the north Italian Alps, and his varied experiences provided him with a wider perspective on which to reflect on his profession. In 1756 Bouquet was appointed the first commanding officer of the 1st Battalion, the then 62nd (Royal American) Regiment, serving in North America. The regiment had an international flavour because of many foreigners in its ranks, including German mercenaries, Polish adventurers and French royalist émigrés who had fled the revolution. Under Bouquet the regiment became the first regular unit to shed the red coat and adopt light inconspicuous clothing instead. The official and formal attire of the regiment remained a red coat (devoid of lace, to emphasise that it would be operating primarily in the bush and forests), but it was normally only on parade or in barracks that they would turn out in it. When campaigning, the regiment preferred backwoods dress and backwoods tactics. As Colonel Bouquet's own regulations put it: 'The clothing of a soldier for the campaign should consist of a short jacket of brown cloth, a strong tanned shirt, short trousers, leggings, moccasins, a sailor's hat, a knapsack for provisions and an oiled surtout against the rain.'

Francis de Rottenburg was born in Danzig in 1757. He served with several armies, including the 77th Regiment of the then royalist French Army, which he left at the outbreak of the revolution. He then helped to reorganise the forces of the kingdom of Naples. He fought against the Russians in the Polish rebellion of 1794, subsequently entering the service of the British Crown and rising to

Right: Lieutenant Colonel Robert Craufurd (later Major General), as a Major in Hompesch's Chasseurs. He transferred from Hompesch's Regiment to the 60th on 30 December 1797, later to earn both fame and notoriety commanding the Light Brigade and subsequently the Light Division in the Peninsular War.

Far right: Lieutenant Colonel The Hon William Stewart, Organiser and Trainer of the Rifle Corps 1800.

The Royal Green Jackets

Left: The Rifle Corps 1800, firing positions.

Right: Statue of John Colborne (and inset), Baron Seaton, Peninsula Barracks, Winchester. Colborne commanded the 52nd Light Infantry from 1811 during the Peninsular War and at Waterloo 1815, leading the charge of the 52nd that finally repulsed the French Imperial Guard.

Bottom: Colonel Coote Manningham, the Founder of The Rifle Corps, 1800.

the rank of lieutenant colonel in Hompesch's *Jäger* Regiment, with which he saw considerable service in North America. He wrote a textbook on the training of light troops, both riflemen and light infantry, and many of his ideas were picked up and developed by Manningham, Stewart, McKenzie and Moore.

Coote Manningham was already a veteran light infantry officer and had commanded with distinction native light infantry troops in various campaigns in the West Indies. William Stewart had been attached to the Austrian army in Italy in 1799 where he was struck by the utility of light troops, particularly riflemen, in fighting the French. Mackenzie had seen lengthy service as a light infantry officer in the West Indies. He had won fame at the Battle of Aboukir when he had fought under Moore, and in 1803 Moore summoned him to Shorncliffe to command the 52nd. Mackenzie was instrumental in the drill and tactics adopted and codified by Moore. Sir John Moore was also a seasoned veteran, having seen service in America, Corsica, the West Indies and Ireland – he had survived being shot in the face by a French *tirailleur* at the Battle of Egmont-op-Zee in 1799 during the campaign in Holland and went on to play a prominent part in the Egypt campaign of 1801. All these battle-experienced officers shared a professional interest in the use of specially trained light troops and were determined to see the culture and ethos deemed so essential for the proper training and employment of such specialist troops adopted more widely in the British Army.

Manningham and Stewart in particular sought to drive a new approach to soldiering at the end of the eighteenth century, drawing heavily on Bouquet's work of some forty years earlier and

Lieutenant Colonel McCleod leads the 43rd Light Infantry into the breach at Badajos, Peninsular War, 1812.

de Rottenburg's innovative training of the 5th/60th. Together these two made a formal representation to the military authorities on the importance of having in the general order of battle a regiment armed with the newly approved Baker rifle and trained in the special duties and tactics of riflemen. (At the time the 5th/60th was serving in North America, having been raised specifically for duty overseas. The battalion was recalled from the West Indies to Europe in 1806.)

In January 1800 the adjutant general invited the commanding officers of fourteen different regiments to send two sergeants and thirty privates to be trained to serve in a newly forming Experimental Corps of Riflemen. Each regiment was also to request a captain, a lieutenant and an ensign to volunteer, self-selecting themselves as able to meet the rigorous and demanding requirements of this new form of soldiering – only eight, just over half, of each rank would be selected to serve in The Rifle Corps. Therefore, from its inception the unit was to be a *corps d'élite* of chosen men. In a similar vein, when the 43rd and 52nd regiments joined The Rifle Corps for training as the Light Brigade, Sir John Moore hand-picked selected officers. His choice to train the 52nd to become the first officially designated light infantry regiment in the British Army was Lieutenant Colonel Kenneth McKenzie, who had used de Rottenburg's ideas and skirmishing tactics to transform the 90th (Perthshire Volunteers) Regiment into a light corps in all but name.

Seen in this historical light, The Royal Green Jackets was the product of innovative tactical thinkers – officers deeply interested in their profession, with wide and varied operational experiences (many in foreign armies) to draw on, who were able to adapt to the new requirements of campaigns conducted in the forests of North America and to the French tactics that had conquered Europe by seeking to conduct military business in a different way. These officers had noticed the utility of light infantrymen and riflemen, and they believed that the rank and file should be specially selected to be able to cope with the new demands that would be placed upon

The rifle, designed by Ezekiel Baker, and sword – the first weapons of The Rifle Corps.

The Rear Guard – Brigadier General Robert Craufurd with the Light Brigade, 2nd Battalion 95th Rifles, 1st Battalion 43rd Light Infantry, 2nd Battalion 52nd Light Infantry in the retreat to Corunna, 1808.

them. As training progressed, those officers and men deemed not up to the special mental and physical pressures of the Light Brigade were weeded out. Many commanding officers tried to palm off their misfits to the new unit rather than give up their best men, but those found to be below standard were quickly returned. However, given the raw material from which the bulk of the ranks of the British Army was formed – often illiterate men, lacking in self-discipline, with many addicted to alcohol – it is remarkable how the regiments of the Light Brigade were honed into such a formidable fighting machine, let alone one based on the very qualities that were so conspicuously absent at large, namely self-discipline and individual initiative. It is perhaps a reflection on what it was possible to achieve when soldiers were treated in a humane way, given a sense of pride and self-respect and encouraged to think for themselves. Of course, the training was undertaken by deeply professional, independent-minded officers and non-commissioned officers from whom only the highest standards were deemed acceptable. Sir Charles Napier, one of the founders of The Rifle Corps, wrote of Lieutenant Colonel Stewart, the commanding officer: 'Stewart makes it a rule to strike at the heads. With him the field-officers must first be steady and then he goes downwards: hence the privates say, "We had better look sharp if he is so strict with the officers".'

But the enthusiasm for light troops was by no means universal. There were many traditionalists who thought that an undue importance had been put on these new tactics, learned largely in North America and perfected especially by the 60th. Others thought that the extended order and loose formations adopted by light troops would be a threat to discipline and steadiness. The more conservative preferred to see light troops in general, and especially riflemen, remain the preserve of those foreigners who had traditionally served the British Army in that more specialist capacity in various campaigns – a description that fitted the 5th/60th perfectly. Generally regarded as 'irregulars and misfits', light troops were described in 1789 by Major General David Dundas as 'in danger of putting grenadiers out of fashion'. New ideas and ways of thinking, almost by their nature, went against the accepted and traditional wisdom of the day. Officers with a love of soldiering and no time for humbug who were prepared to take the risk of being seen to be different in their approach managed to foster a fresh ethos and spirit amongst the light troops and not a little envy and hostility from the old guard. Dundas complained: 'This showy exercise, the airy dress, have caught the minds of young officers, and made them imagine that that these ought to be general and exclusive.' Dundas, of course, was an advocate of the Prussian principles espoused by

The Royal Green Jackets

Frederick the Great, a doctrine that formed the basis of infantry training in many armies at the time, including the British Army, and one designed to 'educate the soldier only in a machine-like manner, to do nothing in accordance with his likes, and to regard soldiers as automata that have no thought but only physical movements'.

The objective in the training of light troops was quite different, being to replace a rigid system of unthinking subordination with one of two-way trust and mutual respect between the ranks. Dundas had spoken out for the grenadiers: 'But for the 95th it was almost an insult to call someone a grenadier, for they used that term to evoke a picture of pipeclay, parade-ground formalism and pedantry which belonged firmly in the previous century.'

Mindless shouting, bawling and foot-stamping have never been the ways of the rifle regiments:

Every inferior, whether officer or soldier shall receive the lawful commands of his superior with deference and respect, and shall execute them to the best of his power. Every superior in his turn, whether he be an officer or non-commissioned officer, shall give his orders in the language of moderation and of regard to the feelings of the individual under his command; abuse, bad language or blows being positively forbid in the Regiment.

Officers and individual riflemen were trained to act on their own or in small groups, a concept markedly different to the rest of the British Army, where initiative was regarded as irrelevant, if not dangerous. As Arthur Bryant put it:

The training was based on treating riflemen not as rigid drill automata, but as human beings capable of individual initiative and self-improvement. The goal was 'the thinking, fighting man'. Officers were encouraged to get to know their men as individuals, to study their particular attributes, to bring out the best of which each was capable and teach them to think for themselves. Wherever possible, they were to be shown the why and wherefore of things; to be put in the picture; to understand their orders, instead of merely obeying them blindly out of fear or mechanical routine. Punishment, particularly of the curse, hang and flog kind that robbed a man of his dignity, was discouraged. Its place was taken by a discipline of example and encouragement whose object was the prevention rather than the punishment of crime.

The distinctive characteristic of The Royal Green Jackets was a sense of personal responsibility and initiative based on a clear explanation and understanding of the 'reason why', existing within an elastic, but clearly defined structure of command. It is a sentiment now readily recognisable in British Army doctrine today. Underpinning all of this was a pride in professional standards rather than amateurism and a concentration on operational effectiveness. This concept was encapsulated by the The Royal Green Jackets in the term 'the thinking fighting rifleman', which all recruits were encouraged to emulate. But simple, brutish, raw fighting ability, whilst plainly important for any infantryman, was never considered sufficient on its own. All riflemen – officers, non-commissioned officers and ranks – were expected to live up to the 'thinking and fighting' concept; an ethos well captured for the modern era's media-literate riflemen in the eponymous hero of the novel series created by Bernard Cornwell, Sharpe's Rifles.

Captain Sir John Kincaid, a veteran of the Peninsular War, Quatre Bras and Waterloo, commented on the system when writing

Left: General Sir David Dundas, known to the Army as 'Old Pivot' from his martinet's addiction to the drill book, appointed Colonel in Chief of the 95th Rifles in 1809 on Coote Manningham's death, had never been a Rifleman, and stood for almost everything the Regiment opposed.

The Origins, Characteristics and Ethos of The Royal Green Jackets

Above: Military General Service Medals displaying Peninsular War clasps, Royal Green Jackets Museum, Winchester.

Right: The Rifles Company, 1st Mounted Infantry, organised and trained at Aldershot for the Boer War.

Below: Mounted Rifleman, Kings Royal Rifle Corps, Boer War South Africa, 1900.

some years after his service in the 95th Rifles had come to an end: 'Splendid as was their appearance, it was the least admirable part about them, for the beauty of their system of discipline consisted in their doing everything that was necessary, and nothing that was not, so that every man's duty was a pleasure to him, and the esprit de corps was unrivalled.'

'To do everything that is necessary and nothing that is not' encapsulates the way the modern successor regiment conducts its business. Tented camps are not outlined with white-washed stones. guy-ropes are not wrapped in white tape, riflemen do not stand rigidly to attention in front of an officer and ask permission to speak, and endless hours spent drilling on the square are abhorred as so much time wasted. When the regiment has to conduct ceremonial parades it will practise just hard enough for the event, perfecting the unique pace and drill movements carried out to the sounding of the bugle with the minimum of shouting and foot-stamping. Invariably there is less time than is desirable to prepare for such events, and invariably the regiment is confident enough to believe that 'it will be alright on the day' without getting unduly fussed about it – and it usually is because the riflemen's panache can be relied upon. Kit and equipment will be polished and clean, but hours spent at 'spit and polish' are deemed unnecessary. Once ceremonial duties are over the regiment will revert to more productive training such as fieldcraft, tactics and marksmanship.

A sense of style and a forward-looking ethos have always been important to a regiment whose founders took pride in being at the sharp end of developments in the military profession. The regiment played a prominent role in the development of mounted infantry by forming a complete battalion, 25th Mounted Infantry, during the Boer War, and in 1926 the 2nd Battalion The King's Royal Rifle Corps was selected for mechanisation, experimenting until 1932 with trucks and prototype half-tracks and carriers mounting medium machine guns. Subsequently, in 1937 both The King's Royal Rifle Corps and The Rifle Brigade were selected to provide the motor battalion infantry of the new armoured divisions as the nation prepared for the Second World War. This role involved 'motor companies', under the command of affiliated armoured regiments, tasked to ensure the mobility and protection of the tanks in all terrain by day and night. Writing about the conversion to

The Royal Green Jackets

motorised infantry, the official history recorded: 'The new mobile role was not inappropriate to a regiment which had fought with such distinction in the Light Division. For the qualities of quickness and independence of thought, of mobility and of individual initiative were just those which were required by Sir John Moore and established in the 95th throughout the Peninsular campaigns.' Meanwhile, the 2nd Batallion The Oxfordshire and Buckinghamshire Light Infantry (which still referred to itself as the 52nd Light Infantry) was selected to join the new airborne formation as a glider-borne battalion, winning immortal fame as the first Allied troops to land in France on D-Day, capturing Pegasus Bridge in a brilliant coup-de-main operation.

Above: Carden-Loyd carrier and trailer of the Machine Gun Platoon, 2KRRC, Tidworth, 1930.

Recruiting Poster, 1936.

The Origins, Characteristics and Ethos of The Royal Green Jackets

The Royal Green Jackets never allowed tradition to deaden its sense of the present nor its vision of the future, but it always drew strength and inspiration from its past, which its successor The Rifles continues to do.

But, as we have seen, the greatest of the regiment's assets, and the source from which its qualities sprang, was the unique responsibility that was given to the officers for the genuine and proper well-being of their men. This remained at the heart of Green Jacket soldiering, and it accounted for the special attention that the regiment always placed on the selection of its officers. In Arthur Bryant's book, *Jackets of Green*, he states that: 'From the start riflemen came to respect their officers, and model themselves on their standards. Chivalry, forbearance, consideration for others and a refusal to put oneself forward before one's comrades and the regiment, were the indispensable qualities of a good officer and had to be learnt by everyone who aspired to be one.'

The Royal Green Jackets' ethos was based on the systems pioneered, developed and passed on by its antecedent regiments. It was one that was always primarily about officers and non-commissioned officers who really knew and cared for their riflemen; a leadership style that was based on professionalism, self-discipline, mutual trust and loyalty; a spirit of self-reliance embodied in the historic tradition of the 'thinking fighting rifleman'; a forward-looking attitude; an expectation of a high level of competence and military effectiveness; and the knowledge that all of this came about only through hard work and attention to detail, without making an undue fuss about it. Within the regiment it was sometimes joked that to act in a rifleman-like way was akin to the behaviour of the mallard – black and green and serenely calm on top, but paddling like fury below!

Below: Pegasus Bridge, D Day, 6 June 1944, from a display in The Royal Green Jackets Museum, Winchester.

Above: Airborne soldier of the 2nd Battalion Oxfordshire and Buckinghamshire Light Infantry (52nd).

19

The Evolution of the Regular Battalions of The Royal Green Jackets: A Story of Continual Change

The story of the evolution of The Royal Green Jackets echoed that of the changing shape of the British Army as a whole in the second half of the twentieth century – it was a tale of post-war reductions, Cold War tensions and imperial withdrawals, as well as Northern Ireland duties and the quest for peace dividends. Although the end of the Cold War seemed to set superpower rivalries aside, it was followed by the realisation that the new era created new and unforeseen demands on the military. This is a story of continual organisational adaptation, which meant change upon change for The Royal Green Jackets, with hardly one reorganisation having taken place before yet another was required.

Below: 43rd & 52nd, KRRC, Rifle Brigade.

Below middle: Green Jackets Brigade.

Bottom: Royal Green Jackets.

In 1957 the British government announced the decision to form an all-regular army by 1962, bringing National Service to an end. The infantry was to be reduced and reorganised. After considering the recommendations of the Infantry Committee, the Army Council accepted in principle that the infantry should be organised into groups of four regiments, or in some cases three, with a combined depot serving each group; that each group of regiments should be termed a brigade; that as far as possible regimental identities and titles should be preserved; and that all regiments in a brigade should wear some form of common emblem.

On 7 March 1957 the Chief of the Imperial General Staff (CIGS), Field Marshal Sir Gerald Templer, established the Whistler Committee, chaired by General Sir 'Bolo' Whistler. Its task was to make recommendations for reducing the infantry from seventy-seven to sixty battalions. In trying to achieve this, it was to take into consideration regimental seniority, the recruiting potential of regiments and of brigade areas, territorial affiliations and the standard of officers. In due course the committee recommended that any reductions should be made through the amalgamation of regiments rather than their disbandment.

So, how were three separate regiments brought together to form The Royal Green Jackets? The King's Royal Rifle Corps (KRRC), or the 60th as its members preferred to describe it, and The Rifle Brigade (RB) had a long history of working closely together, including a shared depot at Winchester since 1858. The committee judged their standard of officers to be high and their regular recruiting to be very strong. In addition, due to their long association, they cooperated closely at all levels, and better than other infantry regiments, with the exception, perhaps, of the Brigade of Guards. Of course, as rifle regiments they were more similar to one another than to the rest of the infantry. However, one more like-minded regiment was required to make a brigade of a minimum workable size, since the Winchester depot could not be expanded further to accommodate a four-regiment brigade. Three regiments were problematic enough due to a lack of space for suitable indoor training areas and accommodation, and that problem got worse when The Light Infantry's depot at Shrewsbury, where the Green Jackets boy soldiers were also trained, was closed and everyone was moved to Winchester. In considering the future Light Infantry Brigade, the committee had the task of reducing the existing six light infantry regiments to a workable brigade of four regiments. The committee judged the officers of The Oxfordshire and Buckinghamshire Light Infantry (43rd & 52nd) to be of a high standard, though the regiment's regular recruiting was well below average. Given the close historical links described in the previous chapter, the 43rd & 52nd emerged as the obvious choice to make up the Green Jackets to a three-regiment brigade.

In this way a sensible coming together was achieved; it was one rooted in strong historical links and a common ethos. Although the changes laid down earlier – such as a common cap-badge, the potential for posting individuals between regiments of the brigade and the formation of the

The Evolution of The Royal Green Jackets

Above: The Rifle Depot, Winchester.

Below: The Rifle Depot, Peninsula Barracks, Winchester, 1975.

brigade depot – were readily accepted, the Colonels Commandant, taking the long view, decided voluntarily to go a little further. By recommending certain modifications in regimental titles, dress and drill they wished to emphasise the unity of the new Green Jackets Brigade and to be prepared for any future organisational developments. In implementing the changes needed, the Colonels Commandant considered that the views of serving officers, who would have to make the new organisation work, should be taken into account. A meeting of the commanding officers of the three regiments – lieutenant colonels Peter Young, Hugh Hope and Paddy Boden (each with a deputy) – was held in London, the War Office having agreed to fly them home from Cyprus, North Africa and Malaya. This meeting was successful and, with Colonel (later General) Tony Read of the 43rd & 52nd in the chair, within twenty-four hours the team had decided what was required. The only subject that generated a slightly heated exchange of views was deciding to retain the ball buttons of the 60th for officers. Although not all the recommendations of the officers were accepted by the Colonels Commandant, there is no doubt that the unanimity and speed of their decision-making helped in arriving at a satisfactory solution. After referring some matters back for further deliberation, the Colonels Commandant put the whole plan to the three respective regimental club committees, before finally submitting their proposals to the War Office in December 1957 (having first obtained the full agreement of the respective royal colonels-in-chief – Her Majesty (HM) the Queen, for The King's Royal Rifle Corps, and His Royal Highness (HRH) The Duke of Gloucester, for The Rifle Brigade).

There remained the issue of what to call the new brigade. Some thought it a little odd to give it the same name as the regimental cricket club of the two rifle regiments, the 60th and The Rifle Brigade, which since its formation had been termed 'The Green Jackets Club'. There was no desire on the part of the Army Board to change regimental titles. However, whilst having no intention of losing the separate identities of the three regiments, the Colonels Commandant were determined that the three become part of one single and unified organisation – The Green Jackets. The wish was to underline to all, especially new recruits, that this was a brigade with common and identical interests.

The final solution for regimental and battalion titles emerged as:

- 1st Green Jackets, 43rd & 52nd
- 2nd Green Jackets, The King's Royal Rifle Corps
- 3rd Green Jackets, The Rifle Brigade

Initially, there was some confusion over these names. The word 'battalion' was omitted and each title represented that of the then still separate regiments. In the unlikely event of an additional battalion being added to one of the regiments at some stage in the future, it would be titled, for example, 2nd/3rd Green Jackets

The Royal Green Jackets

(The Rifle Brigade). An equally important decision concerned the choice of the brigade cap-badge. The final design resulted from the Colonels Commandant's proposals, which were as follows:

The brigade cap-badge requires little explanation. It incorporates the 'stringed bugle horn' which is common to all three regiments and intended to be as prominent as possible. It also has the word 'PENINSULA' which is a common battle honour with a great tradition in all three regiments. The badge also includes the Maltese Cross, a common feature to both The King's Royal Rifle Corps and The Rifle Brigade, surmounted by a crown to denote the royal favour which we have enjoyed and hope will continue. The whole is enclosed in a laurel wreath, as in The Rifle Brigade badge, and this denotes unity. We hope this badge will be considered a simple, sensible and practical expression of our past tradition and future purpose. We propose that it should be made in white metal.

In fact, the badge for The Rifle Brigade contained the symbol of the Order of the Bath rather than a Maltese Cross, but the new design was received with general satisfaction by the three regiments. Commonality of dress was introduced with the continuation of the black cross belt, with silver accoutrements, for commissioned officers and Warrant Officers First Class (WO1) in the 60th and The Rifle Brigade, and its adoption, instead of the double Sam Browne, or 'braces belt', for the 43rd & 52nd. There were simple differences between the Number One Dress of the three regiments (red piping round the collar for the 60th and a gorget cord on the collar for the 43rd & 52nd, for example), which could easily be adjusted when an individual was attached to another regiment in the brigade. In service dress and battle dress, all distinctive badges of rank, whistlecords and suchlike were retained. In battle dress an embroidered shoulder title of 'Green Jackets' in scarlet on green was worn. (This caused some dismay in The Rifle Brigade, which had never worn any form of red, except in its earliest days for the sashes of commissioned officers.) Equally, there was concern initially in the 43rd & 52nd at privates becoming 'riflemen' and the loss of items of red such as mess dress and the sashes of non-commissioned officers (NCOs). Black buttons were to be worn by all three regiments. The brigade depot (or Rifle Depot as it was more commonly known) was formed without difficulty at Winchester, together with the regimental headquarters. Cross-posting of individuals between the regiments was nothing new. Indeed 2 KRRC, or 2nd 60th, had for the last few years been half provided by The Rifle Brigade.

On 7 November 1958 the new Green Jackets Brigade was officially formed, with the three separate regiments assuming their new titles. On the previous day HRH the Duke of Gloucester, attended by the Colonels Commandant, took a parade at the depot to mark the occasion and the new brigade cap-badge and shoulder flash were seen on parade for the first time. Nine platoons of recruits from the depots at Winchester and Oxford took part. The new brigade's rifle drill and words of command, a combination of practices from the three regiments, were also seen and heard for the first time.

On 1 January 1959 the Winchester depot assumed its new title as the Green Jackets Brigade Depot, and officers and NCOs from the 43rd & 52nd began taking their places on the establishment pending the final closing of the old Oxfordshire and Buckinghamshire Light Infantry Depot at Cowley Barracks, Oxford, on 31 March 1959.

However, it was not long before further changes were being discussed in the War Office. The 'large regiment' concept was being pursued in order to increase the flexibility and ways of managing the varying size and shape of the infantry, particularly in order to be able to make further cuts to individual regiments with less pain. Although the possibility of such cuts was not made public, it was widely understood in the infantry because the Army Council had

Left: Michael Haines inspecting a Rfn at a Passing Out Parade, c.1961 – note the Green Jackets shoulder flash.

Bottom left: Green Jackets Brigade cap-badge, 1958.

Below: Field Marshal HRH the Duke of Gloucester, Colonel-in-Chief The Rifle Brigade, accompanied by Major J.H. Hanscombe OC Training Company inspects recruits at the Rifle Depot, November 1958, on the formation of the Green Jackets Brigade.

The Evolution of The Royal Green Jackets

Above: HRH the Duke of Gloucester, Colonel-in-Chief The Rifle Brigade and the Colonels Commandant at the inauguration parade of The Green Jackets Brigade, November 1958. L–R: General Sir Euan Miller, Colonel Commandant 60th Rifles, General Sir George Erskine, GOC-in-C, Southern Command (60th Rifles), HRH The Duke of Gloucester, General Sir Montagu Stopford, Retiring Colonel Commandant The Rifle Brigade, Major General Sir T.J.W. Winterton, Colonel 43rd and 52nd and General Sir Francis Festing, who took over as Colonel Commandant The Rifle Brigade on the following day.

Top right: General Sir George 'Bobby' Erskine, Col Comdt 2nd Green Jackets, KRRC.

Top far right: Field Marshal Sir Francis Festing, Col Comdt 3rd Green Jackets, The Rifle Brigade.

Right: General Sir Gerald Lathbury, Col Comdt 1st Green Jackets, 43rd & 52nd.

Below: The recruits double past demonstrating the new Green Jackets Brigade rifle drill.

decided that the infantry should be reorganised into regiments which 'shall at no time contain less than three battalions each'. The Bower Committee, chaired by Lieutenant General Sir Roger Bower, was formed in early 1962 to advise how this reorganisation should be carried out. The committee's aim was to ensure that, with the minimum disturbance, the number of regular battalions (still sixty at the time) might be varied as required – ranging from a reduction to fifty or an expansion to seventy battalions.

When the committee issued its report later that year it recommended that the 'large regiment' should be introduced in two phases. Phase one was to regroup the existing brigades and regiments to form a 'large regiment' with the battalions numbered consecutively within the regiment. During the first phase battalions could retain their old title in brackets after their new title, as subsidiaries. Phase two would be implemented as and when it became necessary to reduce the number of battalions in any particular regiment. This would, in effect, involve the dropping of subsidiary titles. Any regiment wishing to implement this second phase could do so at any time. The report also addressed the question of how regiments might be selected, stating:

> A feeling may exist that those large regiments which consist of only three battalions may not be required to accept reductions as they would not then be viable. Although this is true today it may not be so in the future if viability changes. The selection of large regiments to accept reductions must depend on the many factors obtaining at

> the time reductions are called for. Nevertheless those regiments which have been re-grouped under this plan will require more time to settle down than those which have not. We recommend that those regiments which have been re-grouped under this plan should not be selected to bear part of any early reductions.

The Army Council Instruction that authorised the introduction of the 'large regiment' added: 'The adoption of the large regiment concept will in no way make the regiments concerned more liable to be selected for making reductions.'

By the end of 1964 the Colonels Commandant were unanimous that the moment had arrived to form a new regiment. There were many pros and cons, but the Colonels Commandant (General Sir Gerald Lathbury of the 43rd & 52nd, General Sir Bobby Erskine of the 60th Rifles and Field Marshal Sir Francis Festing of The Rifle

The Royal Green Jackets

25 July 1967: Colonel-in-Chief Visit

On 25 July 1967 the new regiment was visited for the first time by the Colonel-in-Chief, Her Majesty the Queen. It was a day that stirred the heart of every serving rifleman, every Old Comrade, and all those connected with the regiment. The Colonel-in-Chief arrived at Winchester railway station accompanied by her private secretary Sir Martin Charteris (formerly of the 60th Rifles, appropriately), where she was received by the Lord Lieutenant of Hampshire and the mayor of Winchester. In the meantime the scene was set at The Green Jackets Club cricket grounds at St Cross, where the rain ceased just ten minutes before Her Majesty arrived. The main parade was drawn up, comprising three guards formed by the 1st Battalion, the 2nd Battalion and the combined 3rd Battalion and the Rifle Depot. The black and silver of belts and swords, and the gold of the chevrons, lent that special air of sombre distinction unique to a regiment of riflemen. Yet Her Majesty was quick to note and approve the subtle and traditional battalion distinctions worn by officers and senior ranks – gorget cords on the collars of officers of the 1st Battalion, black and green whistle cords for officers and senior ranks of the 3rd Battalion, red rank backing for the officers and NCOs of the 2nd Battalion. The massed bands and buglers of the three battalions in Number One Dress were formed up in the rear of the inspection line. The 5,000 spectators were seated in specially constructed stands on three sides of a square, facing the parade and looking towards the Norman tower of St Cross Church and the green clump that crowns St Catherine's Hill. Her Majesty arrived on the parade ground along a route lined by recruits from the Rifle Depot, to be met by her three Colonels Commandant. As Her Majesty was received with the royal salute by The Royal Green Jackets, the regiment could but hope that Sir John Moore and many another veteran of the Peninsular War were stirring happily in their graves. Every principle and standard they had demanded had been carefully carried forward into the new regiment. Upon return to the saluting base, having inspected the guards, the Representative Colonel Commandant, Field Marshal Sir Francis Festing, made a short speech of welcome to which Her Majesty replied, both are worth reproducing for the record:

May it please Your Majesty
It is with warmth and a deep sense of privilege that Your Majesty's Royal Green Jackets welcome the first visit of their Colonel-in-Chief. Present here are also 2,000 Old Comrades of the former regiments, from which The Royal Green Jackets are proud to trace their origin. The Royal Green Jackets in this wider sense offer their loyal gratitude in that great privilege, extending over 200 years, of connection with the Crown through regimental title or royal colonels-in-chief and which is carried forward into the new regiment. Mindful of our old foundations but always eagerly searching for improvement, we pledge ourselves to try to be worthy of the great honour Your Majesty has done us and to serve the Crown in like manner as have those who have gone before.

Left: The Colonel-in-Chief inspects her new regiment for the first time, July 1967, St Cross, Winchester.

Below: Her Majesty the Queen, Colonel-in-Chief The Royal Green Jackets.

The Evolution of The Royal Green Jackets

Above: Her Majesty the Queen meets regimental personalities.

Right: Her Majesty The Queen's Regimental Brooch.

Bottom: Formal photograph before luncheon with the officers.

The Colonel-in-Chief replied:
Field Marshal Sir Francis Festing, officers, warrant officers, non-commissioned officers and riflemen of The Royal Green Jackets: When the new regiment was formed last year, I was delighted to become Colonel-in-Chief, and I am happy to review guards from the three regular battalions all of which have distinguished themselves in the last three years on active service in the Far East, and from the Rifle Depot which has successfully pioneered new training standards for the infantry. It is never easy for regiments of long tradition and strong individuality to accept change and re-organisation. You have done this admirably and I congratulate the famous regiments from which you were formed, and which are so well represented here today by their old comrades, on the spirit with which they entered into the new union of The Royal Green Jackets. I am confident that it will flourish.

'The brooch I am wearing today is your gift, and that of the Volunteers and Territorials and I thank you all very much indeed. The naval crown at its base reminds us that riflemen manned the rigging of Nelson's flagship at Copenhagen. Then, as now, they were always ready to put their hands to any new task – and do it well. Initiative and adaptability are the qualities upon which the reputation of riflemen as soldiers has been built and on which it will depend in the future.

One hundred and sixty-four years ago your predecessors were founder members of the Light Division. Next year The Royal Green Jackets will form part of this famous division once again, alongside other light infantry regiments. I am sure that wherever you are called upon to serve, at home or abroad, you will add lustre to its name.

I wish you all success and happiness.

The addresses were followed by a march past in the famous quick- and double-time of rifle regiments, followed by the 'advance in review order', the royal salute and loyal cheers. The regimental march and all the battalion marches were appropriately woven into the parade. For the first time 'The Road to the Isles' was used for the double and was subsequently recorded as the regiment's double march. Those who witnessed this element of the parade remarked upon the precise professionalism of the riflemen, relaxed and confident, symbolising the tradition and sense of purpose of the new regiment drawing strength from the roots of its past.

During a short interval the massed bands counter-marched, and the Old Comrades of the three former regiments and contingents of The Royal Green Jackets' volunteers, territorials and cadets were gathered together as the buglers sounded the 'Light Division Assembly' followed by the 'Advance', in a less formal parade. Two thousand Old Comrades paraded for the Colonel-in-Chief in almost equal numbers from each of the three former regiments. Her Majesty inspected the ranks, chatting happily to many an old rifleman; as well as the Chelsea Pensioners, resplendent in their scarlet uniforms, there were several on parade well over the age of eighty-five.

Near the chestnut tree that had for so many years been the rendezvous for Green Jacket cricketers, guests and regimental personalities were presented to Her Majesty The Queen, including all the battalion quartermasters and their wives. A mess for regimental warrant officers and sergeants had been located on the lawn by the Lower Pavilion, and there all Regimental Sergeant Majors (RSMs), bandmasters, the superintending clerk, and their wives, were presented to Her Majesty, over a glass of sherry. At this point the official visit ended and the Colonel-in-Chief left for the officers' mess at the Rifle Depot for a private luncheon given by the officers of the regiment.

Brigade) were convinced that in the modern army, subject as it was to continuous change, a single-battalion regiment, with its inherent lack of flexibility, made little sense. It was this factor that most influenced them in their decision. They also decided that it was preferable to make the changes then, on their own terms, rather than wait for what were considered to be the inevitable and perhaps less favourable conditions of a future order from the Ministry of Defence (formerly the War Office, abolished in 1964).

The announcement was made by HRH the Duke of Gloucester when he opened the rebuilt depot at Winchester on 28 May 1965. The new regiment would come into being on 1 January 1966. It was to be titled The Royal Green Jackets and, continuing the royal traditions of the former regiments, Her Majesty The Queen consented to be the first Colonel-in-Chief with HRH the Duke of Gloucester becoming deputy colonel-in chief. The battalions of the new regiment were styled:

- 1st Battalion, The Royal Green Jackets (43rd & 52nd)
- 2nd Battalion, The Royal Green Jackets (The King's Royal Rifle Corps)
- 3rd Battalion, The Royal Green Jackets The Rifle Brigade

Each battalion would have its own Colonel Commandant, one of whom would also act as the Representative Colonel Commandant. Officers would be commissioned, and riflemen enlisted, into The Royal Green Jackets. There would be conformity of dress, and cross-posting between battalions would continue to be a normal occurrence.

On 1 July 1968 the Light Division was formally reborn, linking The Royal Green Jackets with The Light Infantry, which had also chosen to follow the Army Board lead and form a 'large regiment'. Headquarters The Light Division, located at Winchester, became responsible for the central administration and career planning of officers, the commissioning of all ranks and the coordination of divisional and regimental affairs. It was also responsible for recruitment, the allocation of riflemen to battalions and the promotion of senior ranks – the last two roles in conjunction with the Infantry Manning and Records Office (South) in Exeter. Headquarters The Light Division gradually assumed responsibilities from The Light Infantry Regimental Headquarters at Shrewsbury and The Royal Green Jackets Regimental Headquarters at Winchester, with full control passing in January 1969. It was just over 150 years since the original élite Light Division had been formed during the Peninsular War under the redoubtable General 'Black Bob' Craufurd who, if perhaps pleased at the closer integration of his celebrated regiments, might have been disappointed that the new headquarters was an administrative command rather than a fighting command. Nevertheless, he would probably have been satisfied to know that it played a crucial part in the management of so many of the regiments he knew so well.

Yet it was still not time for the new organisation to settle down and consolidate. Just a year later, in 1968, a Defence White Paper on cuts in expenditure stated tersely, amongst an announcement on further infantry reductions: 'The Royal Green Jackets. The Third Battalion. The regiment will reorganise to form two battalions.'

Sir Arthur Bryant described this to readers of *The Illustrated London News* as a 'bewildering decision', and the question in everyone's mind was, how had it come about? All three battalions had returned from highly successful operational tours in the Far East, in the jungles of Malaysia and Borneo. The reputation of The

> I found myself much in agreement with a very wise letter in *The Daily Telegraph* the other day in which its writer, Lt Colonel C.B. Appleby, urged regiments threatened … with disbandment to accept amalgamation as the lesser of two evils. For even though a regiment suffers dilution through absorption in a larger regiment, the traditions of its component parts can still survive to be handed down to their descendants. 'The better the old regiment,' Colonel Appleby wrote, 'the more will it contribute to the big regiment and mould the latter.'
>
> – Sir Arthur Bryant, *Illustrated London News*, 10 August 1968

Royal Green Jackets was demonstrably high and much envied in the British Army as a whole, where it was generally referred to as 'The Black Mafia' because of its grip on the higher echelons of the army. The effectiveness of its battalions was also unquestioned. Although the regiment or former regiments had not previously lost a battalion in any reduction since The Green Jackets Brigade had been formed in 1958, it was still a blow and in many it left a sense of betrayal.

It is worth looking in some detail at the steps that led to that 'bewildering decision'. Firstly, the Chief of the General Staff (CGS) General Sir James Cassels wrote to the Colonels Commandant on 8 May 1967, stating: 'The infantry is undoubtedly going to be reduced in its number of battalions. Though at present I do not know what the scale of the reductions will be, I am afraid the loss could be considerable.' The letter went on to ask the Colonels Commandant what their plan would be if the regiment had to lose a battalion. The Colonels Commandant discussed it exhaustively, before deciding that if it became necessary they would 'create two new battalions, without subsidiary titles or other demonstrable connections with the former regiments' – but it was emphasised that it 'would be a surgical operation of exceptional severity – a grave step, and we cannot believe that the resulting loss of quality would be in the interests of the army'.

In a statement on 16 January 1968 the Secretary of State for Defence, Denis Healey, referred to the Services' plans made the previous July to reduce uniformed manpower by about 75,000 and civilian manpower by about 80,000 by the mid 1970s, saying that these cuts would now have to be achieved earlier 'though they will not be completed before 1972–3. The total reductions, when finally worked out, are likely to involve some increase in these figures – the rate at which [Army] units are amalgamated or disbanded and the Army is run down, will be increased.'

On 14 March 1968 the Colonels Commandant were asked for their plans if the regiment should lose either one or two battalions. The potential for a savage cut was obvious and caused a great degree of uncertainty. Throughout the previous year Regimental Headquarters had tried, with difficulty, to assess what chance the regiment had of escaping reduction in the next 'reorganisation'. Not only was the Ministry of Defence, quite rightly, wholly secretive about it, but also there was absolutely no indication of the criteria that would be used to decide which battalions were to be disbanded. How great were the overall reductions to be? What proportion of that would be infantry as distinct from the British Army's other arms and services? Were regiments to be judged on their past achievements or on their state of efficiency and fitness for war? Their ability to recruit both officers and soldiers, or by the prosaic touchstone of seniority? Could a three-battalion regiment actually be reduced any further? A cut of two battalions in The Royal Green Jackets – a possibility according to the letter of 14 March 1968 – would not only be devastating to the regiment but would make a complete mockery of the new divisional system then being introduced.

Regimental Headquarters was convinced that 'quality' would not be a deciding factor but only the number of battalions that would have to go overall. In the event, the decision was based not on any carefully calculated economic necessity, nor on the need to keep an army with arms and services properly balanced to meet potential tasks, but instead on equal misery for all, with those 'large regiments' that had not lost a battalion in recent years being arbitrarily subjected to a reduction. The pill was made no less bitter to swallow when The Royal Green Jackets battalion was named last of all to be disbanded in March 1972. The Under Secretary of State (Army) Sir Geoffrey Johnson-Smith revealed the method of selection when, during the debate on the Scottish Regiments, he conceded that 'there were fourteen infantry brigades and therefore the fairest method of effecting the reduction was to take a battalion from each'. This statement paid no attention to the differing sizes of those brigades – if it was simply one from each, The Royal Green Jackets was bound to lose a battalion. The Under Secretary of State was to say in a later debate that the cuts imposed on the infantry were solely related 'to the Government's preoccupation with the obligation they felt to establish an appearance of fairness'. And so another banal expression was introduced into parliamentary and military jargon – that of 'juniority'; the 'junior' battalion in each brigade or 'large regiment', regardless of its size, would go to the wall.

The Colonels Commandant decided that the plan to form two new battalions, without subsidiary titles or other demonstrable connections with the former regiments, was the only way in which the ethos, traditions and territorial associations of all three of the former regiments could be kept alive. Although it meant that the old regimental names were lost from the titles of the new battalions, the name of The Royal Green Jackets and the image of riflemen that it evoked would survive as a symbol and embodiment of all the singular virtues that had long been prized so highly and envied so much. Thus in May 1968, when it seemed more than likely that the regiment would lose a battalion, the Colonels Commandant agreed that the regular battalions should no longer carry the old names in brackets after their titles. This made it impossible for any one of the former regiments, from which the regular battalions were descended, to be identified as the one disbanded. The many connections and affiliations could be preserved in the two new battalions to be formed. Thus phase two of the Bower Report eventually came to be fulfilled.

When the Chief of the General Staff's letter arrived to give prior warning of the reduction, the Colonels Commandant, though unconvinced by the arguments, were certain that nothing would be gained in the long run by an undignified public outcry; it was not their way. Their formal reply concluded by stating that they 'could only assure you that we in The Royal Green Jackets will do our best to accept your decision with loyalty, in the hope that it is in the interests of the Army'. Letters of explanation were then sent by the Colonels Commandant to the three regimental committees, to the branches of the Old Comrades Associations, to all those in the counties who were connected with the regiment, and to certain Members of Parliament (MPs). Statements were given to the press. With the Ministry of Defence having decided that the junior battalions from each division of infantry were to go, the only effective argument to be employed in Parliament was that the infantry cuts were too severe and that they left the British Army with an inadequate balance of infantrymen for the likely tasks of the future – a prediction that was to become true as events developed rapidly in Northern Ireland.

A parliamentary motion deploring the loss of a battalion of The Royal Green Jackets was immediately tabled by a group of about twenty MPs. Initiated by Admiral Morgan Giles, the Member for Winchester, it was supported by all those who had served in any of the former regiments. On 25 July Sir Charles Mott-Radclyffe and James Ramsden spoke forcefully and with authority in the Defence Debate, the latter stating in the course of his speech:

the Army of the future will be the poorer for having only two Rifle regiments [sic] and I say that because of their contribution to the profession of arms, which has not only been distinguished but distinctive, with their own particular approach to soldiering and with the large number of officers they have been able to produce who have made their mark successfully in all quarters of the Army.

Based as it was on 'juniority', the cut was always certain to include a battalion of The Royal Green Jackets, and if a 'large regiment' had not been created it would have fallen with absolute precision on The Rifle Brigade. However, the sting had been drawn by the earlier decision to abolish the bracketed names of the predecessor regiments. Thus, although a former member could not find a wholly independent Rifle Brigade mess or battalion, this was equally true for veterans of the 43rd & 52nd or of the KRRC/60th. The same cap-badge had been worn by the battalions for the last ten years; what was to disappear in 1972 was one-third of the manpower strength of The Royal Green Jackets rather than one of the old regiments. That much was recognised by serving riflemen, and they were confident that they could forge a reputation in the future as brilliant and resolute as had their forebears in the Peninsular War and since. At the same time they were anxious to see that past members of all three regiments considered the reorganisation in the same light and that those serving would be assured of their support.

There is little doubt, however, that what hurt both the serving and the retired riflemen was that no account appeared to have been taken method chosen to achieve the economies – 'juniority' – was one that ignored the well-acknowledged professional excellence and reputation of the regiment. In *The Illustrated London News* Sir Arthur Bryant summed it up in an article on 10 August 1968 in which he

The Royal Green Jackets

From the Colonels Commandant, 12 July 1968

You will have seen with distress that in the second phase of the reductions in the Armed Forces, announced by HM Government in the July 1968 White Paper, The Royal Green Jackets are to lose a battalion by 1972. It is too early to foresee the exact way in which this will be effected, but as long ago as June 1967 the Colonels Commandant, faced with this possibility, had decided that if ever we were to lose a battalion, then two entirely new battalions should be created, without subsidiary titles and no demonstrable connections with any particular one of the three former regiments. Moreover, earlier this year, we agreed unanimously that the titles of the regular battalions should no longer bear the names of the former regiments in brackets and, as a result, the new and simplified titles of 1st, 2nd and 3rd Battalions The Royal Green Jackets have been in use since 15 June 1968. There were two main reasons for these decisions. First, it is now over ten years since 1st, 2nd and 3rd Green Jackets came into being and the names of the 43rd and 52nd, The King's Royal Rifle Corps and The Rifle Brigade, went into brackets. The majority of the serving officers and riflemen have learned to think of themselves as Green Jacket riflemen and feel the time has come for this to be recognised. Only the more senior ranks remain who ever wore one of the original cap-badges and today all the battalions are very much alike in outlook and experience, especially after their successive tours in Borneo. Already the links with the old regiments and individual battalions are becoming blurred with time and cross-postings, but each battalion unhesitatingly acknowledges its indebtedness to all three of the former regiments from which it derives its traditions, its proud historical record of valour and its high professional reputation. Secondly, parting with the bracketed titles made it impossible for the Ministry of Defence to indicate the original regiment from which any battalion eventually to be nominated for reduction, had stemmed. Thus it is possible for us to preserve the many connections and territorial associations which in the past have given the old regiments so much help and pleasure and which will remain invaluable to The Royal Green Jackets in the years to come.

You will know that decisions such as these are only reached after exhaustive discussion by the Colonels Commandant. Our course of action was agreed unanimously, though not without feelings of great sadness, as the only practicable one in the present climate of stringent defence economies. None of us must regard this as a break in our ties with The Rifle Brigade, whose essential spirit lives on with that of the other two former regiments in The Royal Green Jackets. We must regard it rather as a cut of one third in the strength of The Royal Green Jackets. What we are now trying to forge are even stronger links between the old regiments and The Royal Green Jackets as a regiment embracing the Regular, Volunteer and Territorial Battalions, the Cadets, the clubs and the associations. For this task we, and all serving riflemen, ask for your active and loyal support.

Francis Festing (Field Marshal)
Representative Colonel Commandant and
Colonel Commandant 3rd Battalion

John Mogg (Lieutenant General)
Colonel Commandant 1st Battalion

Alick Williams (Major General)
Colonel Commandant 2nd Battalion

3rd Battalion The Royal Green Jackets double-past Reorganistion Parade, June, 1971.

reflected the residual association of the then battalions to the former regiments, by referring to 'The Rifle Brigade – that shining exemplar of all the fighting soldier's values'. He ended:

For even though a regiment suffers dilution through absorption in a large regiment, the traditions of their component parts can still survive to be handed down to their descendants. The better the old regiment the more it will contribute to the big regiment and mould the latter. To destroy a regiment is to destroy a perpetual and self-renewing fount of human selflessness and devotion: rather than allow it to perish, its brave heart should be transplanted and given to another.

In the particular case of The Royal Green Jackets it was not a question of transplantation, because all the former regiments were going to contribute equally to the new. Most people accepted that events had proved the wisdom of the decisions to form a Green Jacket Brigade and later a 'large regiment', and, perhaps most difficult of all, to create two new battalions. What hurt most was the realisation, despite the lack of any firm assurances that 'large regiments' would be spared, that by having gone early and enthusiastically down that road – in the interests of a more flexible infantry system and in accordance with the stated intentions of the Army Board – the regiment had in effect been betrayed. Less political flak was generated if difficult decisions were avoided, such as those that would have led to the loss of a cap-badge. This meant the easy solution, politically, was to target those regiments with more than one battalion, which could therefore lose one without it meaning the loss of a cap-badge. The single-battalion regiments, which had steadfastly resisted change, found that their interests coincided with those of the politicians. It is worth reproducing the letter sent from Regimental Headquarters on 12 July 1968 by the Colonels Commandant to all the regimental organisations and representatives (see above).

Sure enough, developments were soon overtaken by events. In 1969 troops were first deployed on the streets of Northern Ireland, where they were to remain in support of the police for some thirty-eight years, the formal end to the operation being declared in July 2007. At the very moment reductions in the infantry were being planned, infantry commitments were beginning to rise. By 1972 there were 26,000 troops deployed in Northern Ireland to assist the police in the fight against terrorism. Reversals in the planned reductions in the infantry were soon to materialise. These started with a letter, dated 6 August 1970, from the Ministry of Defence that outlined amendments to the White Paper of 1968. It offered those infantry battalions that had been selected for disbandment the opportunity to remain in being, but at company size. The Colonels Commandant accepted this for the 3rd Battalion The Royal Green Jackets. To be formed on 1 August 1971, the new company was to be known as 3rd Battalion, The Royal Green Jackets, R Company (the R standing for Representative). With the running down of the 3rd Battalion to a single company, the Colonels Commandant decided to transfer to the 2nd Battalion the title of I Company, thus preserving a tradition that had existed for more than 120 years in the 1st Battalion, The Rifle Brigade and subsequently in the 3rd Battalion, The Royal Green Jackets.

Reorganisation Day, 29 June 1971, was marked by a final parade at Lucknow Barracks in Tidworth, taken by the Representative Colonel Commandant (General Sir John Mogg) and the Colonel Commandant of the 3rd Battalion (Lieutenant General Sir Dick Fyffe). The parade was a moving occasion, particularly for all those serving in the battalion, and for all those who had been connected with it in any way. Nevertheless, great pains were taken to emphasise that this was not a wake, and both of the Colonels Commandant stressed in their addresses that true riflemen did not hark back to the past but looked ahead and adapted to meet changing situations. Members of the battalion were posted to new homes throughout the regiment and the Light Division. Meticulous care was taken to ensure, as far as was possible, that each individual rifleman was posted to the battalion of his choice, whether it was The Royal Green Jackets or The Light Infantry.

As the then Regimental Sergeant Major (RSM), later Major, Ron Cassidy recalled:

The commanding officer Lieutenant Colonel (later General) Jimmy Glover and the Adjutant David Roberts had persuaded the Infantry Manning and Records Office to agree that all the Warrant Officers and members of the sergeants' mess, every junior NCO and rifleman, could choose where he wanted to go when the battalion was reorganised. During the months on the preceding UN tour in Cyprus these two, assisted by the company commanders and the RSM, carried out this prodigious task. This resulted in a few unhappy individuals, and some of these were to receive promotion in their new home, which, for obvious reasons, could not be disclosed prior to posting. Perhaps the best example of the success of this approach was to see how the newly formed R Company was perceived by one and all. In the short time it was the Representative Company its reputation was second to none, and during its Northern Ireland tour in the hotly contested Lower Falls area of Belfast it earned more honours than any single company during the Northern Ireland emergency. The battalion was reorganised and it was sad to see it go, but it went out in a blaze of celebrations for what had been achieved over the many years and there are many who will long remember the friendships, the farewell parties and perhaps the best of them – the all-ranks party where Colonel Vic Turner VC had a group of riflemen round him all night. There were penalties to be faced, some few months later. When the 3rd Battalion was reformed, many of those who had chosen where they wanted to go on reorganisation decided not to go back. This was purely because, though their time with the 3rd Battalion had, in their minds, been unsurpassable, it had also been one of constant moves and change in roles, and their present home, which they had chosen, had given a sense of stability – in lots of cases promotion. Moreover, for the married soldiers the thought of another move six months after the last didn't bear thinking about – the stability of their children's education being a critical issue.

Although everyone understood the reasons for reorganisation, almost all – whether rifleman, NCO, warrant officer or officer – thought it absurd that a battalion with such a reputation should have gone to the wall. This feeling was prompted not by conceit or mere regard for the battalion in which they served but by an awareness of the well-acknowledged effectiveness of the regiment and the respect in which it was held.

By 2 July 1971, one month before internment was introduced in Northern Ireland in an effort to combat rapidly growing IRA terrorism (a development that proved to be the catalyst for an outbreak of violence on an even larger scale), the battalion departed on leave, prior to individuals taking up their new postings. As it turned out, the 3rd Battalion, in the form of R Company, existed only from August to December 1971, but in its short life its operational record was second to none (for their exploits, see pages 116–7).

By October 1971 the news was already out that the 3rd Battalion would be reformed in January 1972. Looking back, one is struck by how easy it had been to squander a good battalion. It is a long, painstaking process to put one together; there is no instant formula for the creation of spirit and cohesion that gets built up over many years. The process began again on 15 January 1972, but those returning in the hope of seeing R Company expand into a replica of the old 3rd Battalion were to be disappointed. It was a mixture of new and old faces that formed up in the barracks at Shoeburyness, Essex, to begin the exciting but challenging task of rebuilding and re-establishing the reputation of the battalion, but it was not an easy job. The strength of the sergeants' mess in particular had been dissipated after years of planning and nurturing. After several tours in Northern Ireland, which provided an operational focus that helped the battalion re-form, the battalion was posted to Berlin, 100 miles (160km) behind the Iron Curtain. This had the superficial gloss of an operational tour, but the real focus was on ceremonial and seemingly pointless duties. It was to be an unhappy and unrewarding tour.

When the Berlin Wall came down and then the Cold War ended, the removal of the threat posed by the Soviet Union and the Warsaw Pact was the catalyst for demands for a 'peace dividend', in other words for further cuts in defence spending. On 25 July 1990 the then Secretary of State for Defence, Tom King, announced Options for Change in the House of Commons, informing MPs that the British Army would be reduced in size by some 25 per cent. He said nothing about individual regiments. The Chief of the General Staff, General Sir John Chapple, subsequently added that no announcement on this reorganisation could be expected before early 1991; he then went on to say that once the size of the infantry had been decided, the Director of Infantry would be required to consult with the Colonels Commandant of infantry divisions on the future regimental structure. The Executive Committee of the Army Board (ECAB) would then take the necessary decisions. It was clear that more change was on the way.

Once again events conspired to complicate matters. On 2 August 1990 Saddam Hussein invaded Kuwait. Although this certainly affected work on Options for Change, it did not stop it. As far as the British Army was concerned, it was akin to attempting to mesh together two contra-rotating cogwheels: Options for Change demanded reductions; impending war in the Middle East required reinforcements. The British Army's working group, chaired by the Assistant Chief of the General Staff, would gather at seven o'clock in the morning to deliberate reductions and reorganisation, then from nine o'clock would concentrate on the more pressing demands of going to war.

The Executive Committee of the Army Board (ECAB) met in January 1991 to discuss whether Arms Directors, including the Director of Infantry, should be invited to work out how they would reduce their arm of service to the order of battle that was then being considered. The timetable took no account of the Gulf War, but ECAB decided that it would be quite wrong to make any announcements concerning reorganisations, disbandments or amalgamations before the war was over – it was unthinkable that a regiment should be ordered to cross the start line not knowing whether or not it would still be in existence when it reached the objective. Options for Change was therefore put on hold temporarily, and the decision was reinforced by Prime Minister John Major when he visited the Gulf in March 1991 immediately after the war had ended.

This short-lived 'hold' was lifted on 4 June 1991, leaving very little time for consultation if the Secretary of State for Defence's undertaking to the House of Commons was to be honoured. He had assured the House that he would make an announcement on the future size and shape of the Army, including the naming of the regiments affected, before the summer recess; in effect, this meant by 18 July. Tom King had demonstrated time and time again during the Gulf War his reluctance to amend anything he had said in the House, particularly where troop numbers were concerned. He was not likely to seek further time for the proper reorganisation of the Army. The Chief of the General Staff had also given an undertaking to Arms Directors that they would have at least a month in which to consult Colonels Commandant. This left ECAB only fourteen days in which to hear the considerations of the directors, prepare its own case and discuss it with ministers. This period also included a meeting between the Chief of the General Staff and the Prime Minister to discuss the outcome of the Options for Change process.

The Secretary of State duly announced, on time, that the cuts were to occur in phases, timed around reductions in the British Army of the Rhine (BAOR) and withdrawals from Berlin and Hong Kong. The resizing of individual units was to be coordinated with those events. The infantry, the workhorse of the Army, was to suffer a draconian 35 per cent reduction, from a total of fifty-five battalions to thirty-eight by 1 April 1995, and then to thirty-six within a further three years. Following the announcement, ECAB laid down certain fundamental principles, which the Director of Infantry was to follow to determine how it all should be enacted. It is worth recalling some of them.

The infantry was to continue to be organised on a regimental basis rather than as a homogeneous corps of infantry. Previous amalgamations undergone by some regiments were to be borne in mind when formulating the 'Infantry Enabling Plan'. The scale of reduction envisaged in Options for Change meant that some cap-badges would inevitably be lost, but the guiding principle to be applied was that all officers and soldiers must be provided with a 'regimental focus' for their loyalty. The criteria to be used as determinants in the selection of battalions were to be manpower and manning – and if manning was to be used as an indication of the health of a regiment it should be studied over several years and projected into the future, to take account of economic and demographic trends. The Director of Infantry was to take into account current and potential undermanning, but, above all, had to ensure that the future structure of the infantry allowed maximum flexibility to enable commitments to be met. Seniority was not to be the deciding factor in determining who should go to the wall. In principle, those regiments that had escaped amalgamation until now were to be considered ahead of those that had not – in the event, and without explanation, this principle was completely ignored; the one applied was that the effects of change should be shared as broadly as practicable across the entire Army, but only in as far as this complied with the requirement to create an Army that was robust to further organisational changes. The groupings should allow the maximum flexibility for employment and deployment in peace and expansion in war. Larger groupings should be encouraged but might be achieved in different ways, either by forming 'large regiments' or by closer associations between single-battalion small regiments.

Based on these principles, the Colonels Commandant made it abundantly clear to the Colonel Commandant of the Light Division that they wished him to represent certain key points in the discussions with the Director of Infantry. Their instincts and all their experience told them that the proposals for the infantry had gone too far. They felt strongly that the outcome would leave the infantry in a position where it would be hard put to fulfil its commitments, and would retain no flexibility with which to meet the unexpected. They did not believe it would be prudent.

Lieutenant General Sir Garry Johnson, Colonel Commandant the Light Division, 1991.

The Evolution of The Royal Green Jackets

3rd Battalion The Royal Green Jackets double past for the last time, Fort Burgoyne, Dover, 24 July 1992.

The Colonels Commandant had no difficulty with the recommendation that once decisions had been taken, the management of reductions should be left to the existing divisional organisation. They also believed the Army Council's decision in 1957–62 that the infantry should be organised into regiments 'which at no time should contain less than three battalions each' should now be insisted upon by the Army Board. Some regiments had been allowed to renege and the result was a mismatch of large and small regiments, making it impossible to implement the demands of Options for Change without the 'endless pain' that Field Marshal Festing had been determined to avoid when agreeing to the formation of The Royal Green Jackets. The Colonels Commandant were concerned that those 'large regiments' that had conformed appeared to be much easier to reduce further, without the military and political emotion involved in the loss of a cap-badge, than were the remaining small, single-battalion regiments, and that it would be totally wrong – and impossible to explain – if the former were disadvantaged in any way. The infantry should grasp the opportunity to adopt a forward-looking structure, which would end, once and for all, the anomaly in its make-up.

The case for The Royal Green Jackets was represented strongly by the Colonel Commandant, the Light Division, General Sir Garry Johnson and the Colonels Commandant of the other 'large regiments'. Subsequently the Colonels Commandant told the Chief of the General Staff (CGS) that they could live with the Director of Infantry's conclusions; given that the CGS had used his casting vote in favour of the small regiments rather than favouring the flexibility offered by the 'large regiments'. The outcome was a predictable repeat of the previous occasion when the 3rd Battalion had been selected for disbandment. Reluctantly, the Colonels Commandant agreed that on account of the size of the required reductions, and on a pro rata basis across the infantry divisions, the regiment would be reduced by one regular battalion; but in doing so they made the point that they believed that yet again an opportunity had been missed to produce a rational structure for the infantry that would be robust and flexible enough to take it into the next century without further debilitating acrimony. So it was that the Representative Colonel Commandant, General Sir David Ramsbotham, wrote to the Chief of the General Staff on 15 August 1991 saying that 'he could not pretend that the regiment is happy with the decision that we should lose a battalion, but we would not be human if we were. The Royal Green Jackets has made a significant contribution to the Army in its twenty-five-year history, and it was in that spirit that we look forward to making a similar contribution in the years ahead.'

The Colonels Commandant had taken commanding officers into their confidence throughout, and also co-opted the honorary colonels of the 4th and 5th Battalions (both from the Territorial Army) to all the meetings to discuss and confirm the regimental line. Once the decision had been taken that the regiment was to lose a battalion, there was to be no looking back and agonising. Early compliance with the Options for Change directive was to take advantage of the redistributed manpower that would become available from the lost battalion. The Colonels Commandant then took the decision to renumber the regular battalions, because with only two remaining there could no longer be any readily identifiable link with one of the former regiments. As always intended, it was to be the regiment as a whole that was the inheritor of the proud heritage of the antecedent regiments.

The 1st Battalion, when it returned from Cyprus, was merged into the 2nd and 3rd Battalions. The 2nd Battalion was at that time in Omagh, Northern Ireland, and the 3rd Battalion in Dover, as part of the Allied Powers Central Europe (ACE) Mobile Force. The Regiment reformed as the 'new' 1st and 2nd Battalions. The merger took place on 25 July 1992, the regimental birthday, and was marked by a battalion parade and Sounding Retreat at Dover Castle.

The Colonels Commandant also decreed what traditions should be maintained, eliminating in the process a number of links with the antecedent regiments that had crept back into battalion custom since 1966. Thus the 1st and 2nd Battalions of The Royal Green Jackets enjoyed a proud and direct link not only with all that had been established since The Royal Green Jackets had been formed but also with the three historic regiments that had come together. And so it remained until 2007 when the Green Jackets voluntarily took another bold step to merge its unique identity into a new regiment, The Rifles, the successor black-button rifle regiment. This story is recounted in Chapter 12, and it brings to an end the story of continual evolutionary change that defined the forty-year life of The Royal Green Jackets.

Left: Major General Sir John Foley, Colonel Commandant 1st Battalion The Royal Green Jackets, 1991.

Centre: Lieutenant General Sir David Ramsbotham, Representative Colonel Commandant and Colonel Commandant 2nd Battalion The Royal Green Jackets, 1991.

Right: Lieutenant General Sir Edward Jones, Colonel Commandant 3rd Battalion The Royal Green Jackets, 1991.

The Green Jacket Approach to Leadership

In 1966 the commanding officer of the 2nd Battalion, The Royal Green Jackets, Lieutenant Colonel Edwin ('Dwin') Bramall (later Field Marshal) wrote a short booklet entitled *Leadership the Green Jacket Way*. In it he set out the essentials of doing business that had been inherited from the antecedent regiments. The booklet was issued to junior NCOs and new officers until it was replaced in 1998 with an updated version, *The Green Jacket Way*, which drew heavily on its predecessor but took account of various social changes in the thirty years since. The following is quoted directly from it.

Bottom left: New Recruits, 1968.

Below: Field Marshal the Lord Bramall of Bushfield.

What marks riflemen as different is, perhaps, the way they conduct themselves: with a light touch and a sense of humour, with a sense of style and a spirit of adventure; but all without pomposity – no fuss, nor any form of rigid formality. It is a way based on mutual confidence, mutual respect, mutual affection and a love of soldiering. Riflemen are expected to think and are therefore expected to have a view, which they are encouraged to express. Many a senior inspecting officer from outside the regiment has been surprised, and not a little anxious, to find individual riflemen willing and able to stand their ground in discussion, rather than taking the easier and more usual route of simply agreeing with their superior officer. Riflemen have never been backward in coming forward and can be expected to enter into an animated discussion, conducted with the passion of their convictions. Those more comfortable with a greater

The Green Jacket Approach to Leadership

Top: 'Needing a light touch and a tight grip.'

Above: The first and last versions of The Green Jacket Way, issued to all Green Jacket officers on joining the Regiment.

degree of deference, brought up in a 'Yes Sir, No Sir' culture can find this – to the glee of the riflemen and, it must be said, their officers – disconcerting.

The Green Jacket way, then, requires leadership that is a complex blend of light touch and tight grip. This is not an easy combination to pull off, but it is a style of leadership that the regiment believes works best, because all ranks feel empowered and motivated as personal contributors. The Royal Green Jackets would be the first to acknowledge, indeed celebrate, the fact that the gap between their way of doing things and the conduct of the rest of the British Army has narrowed enormously over the last 200 years. But if there is a difference today it is probably one of degree and lightness of touch. The regiment also acknowledges that the system has shortcomings. It is often said that there are no bad battalions, only bad officers – and it is the responsibility of Royal Green Jacket officers, and the commanding officer in particular, to ensure that the system works in the way it did for their forebears. Individual initiative, unless it is directed and channelled through the chain of command firmly and thoughtfully by a strong officer, can result in a lack of cohesion and a break down in discipline.

Perhaps it was these concerns about light troops in the late eighteenth century that led Major General Dundas, or 'Old Pivot' as he was known because of his strict adherence to Prussian principles (see Chapter 1), to complain of light troops in the manual he wrote in an attempt to standardise tactical drills: 'By their present open order and independent ideas, they are under very little control of their officers; and their practice seems founded on a supposition of the spirit and exertion of each individual, more than on the real feelings by which the multitude are actuated.'

All infantry battalions in the British Army have developed their own particular way of working, evolved over centuries as a by-product of the regimental system. It is perhaps for this reason that the British infantry is sometimes described, mischievously, as more akin to 'a loose collection of warring tribes'. Some battalions are heavily reliant on the sergeants' mess, others rely more on the officers' mess. In The Royal Green Jackets it is a source of much discussion where the dominant influence in the battalions really lies. Of course, sergeants believe, and in some ways are encouraged to believe, that they constitute the powerhouse of the battalion – every visiting senior officer always tells them so, because in most regiments the sergeants' mess is just that. Vital as a strong sergeants' mess is in a Green Jacket battalion, true to the traditions of Sir John Moore it is still the officers' mess that is, and should be, the driving force. Consider the qualities that a Green Jacket officer is expected to have: he should be deeply interested in his profession, thoroughly competent, have real empathy with his riflemen, be full of ideas from the beginning and be able to lead by example from the front without

33

The Royal Green Jackets

standing on ceremony. These sort of officers would expect the battalion to be driven from nowhere else but the officers' mess. And the riflemen, in turn, look to them to do so.

When a newly joined young officer first takes command of his platoon he is taught that after caring for his riflemen his primary purpose is to make his platoon as effective as he can in every way. The standard of his platoon is the standard by which he will be judged. From the rifleman's perspective, one of the strengths of very junior, confident but still inexperienced, Green Jacket officers is their ability to listen to their platoon sergeant and to their section commanders, seeking practical advice with confidence and without fear of losing the respect of their subordinates. The junior officer who does not listen, or appears not to listen, to his platoon sergeant or section commanders rarely finds it easy to win early respect from his riflemen.

A young platoon commander from 3rd Green Jackets, Johnnie Stephens, wrote: 'I can say that commanding a Rifle Platoon is about as good as it gets. The Green Jacket way is difficult to define but it involves young officers learning from riflemen and NCO's just as much as the other way round. I was blessed with many outstanding examples of both. Tony Martin, sadly to die in Borneo, commanded one of my sections when I took command of 1 Platoon on the streets of Nicosia fresh out of RMA Sandhurst. To say that I had a lot to learn was an understatement. Martin who was an exceptionally talented soldier was responsible for a big chunk of my education. The riflemen can smell incompetence or weakness at about a hundred yards. If as a young officer you are not up to it they will find you out. There is indeed a lot of truth in the saying 'there is no such thing as a bad rifleman, only bad officers.'

High morale has always been recognised as an essential requirement for military success. It is not an especially complicated notion and is usually based on a mixture of discipline and self-respect, knowledge of what is going on and the part each individual is supposed to play, confidence in one's commander and in one's equipment, good administration and properly conceived training. During operations, discipline means continuing to fight when one's every instinct calls for self-preservation. For Field Marshal Earl Wavell, discipline was: 'teaching which makes a man do something which he would not, unless he had learnt that it was the right, the proper and the expedient thing to do. At its best, it is instilled and maintained by pride in oneself, in one's unit, in one's profession; only at its worst by fear of punishment.'

From the beginning The Royal Green Jackets and its antecedents emphasised the notion of self-discipline, the first part of Lord Wavell's definition, as opposed to imposed discipline. But there is a balance to be struck. On the one hand the regiment seeks, by good leadership, by force of example, by explaining what it is doing and by generally treating those for whom it is responsible with common sense and respect, to evoke a loyal response and a sense of mutual responsibility, one man to another; riflemen who understand why an order or routine is necessary will tend to carry it out willingly, but they are even more likely to do so if they see that those who are administering the order are competent and disciplined. On the other hand, the regiment stresses the need to have the moral courage to take the necessary action when people step out of line.

The Green Jacket commander – be he the commanding officer, company commander, platoon commander or section commander –

Far left: Officers' Mess 1RGJ, Aldergrove, Northern Ireland, 1982.

Above: Sergeants' Mess 2RGJ, Palace Barracks, Belfast, 2000.

Below: 'Self respect – the basis of high morale.'

The Green Jacket Approach to Leadership

is expected, each in his own way, to hold himself responsible for the actions of his riflemen both on and off duty, because reputation impacts on the morale and efficiency of the regiment. In stark contrast to civilian life, the philosophy of turning a blind eye to what people do in their own time, in the belief that it is their own affair and has nothing to do with anyone else, is regarded in the regiment as abrogation of a leader's responsibility. Such firmness calls for fine judgement, particularly in today's social climate. It is the officer's responsibility to set a consistent standard and make sure that it is maintained by the NCOs. Riflemen take their lead from the example set to them, and that is why officers are reminded that their own moral standards need to be beyond reproach. It is impossible to adopt a 'relaxed' leadership style until certain minimum standards have been firmly understood and riflemen of all ranks know exactly where they stand. It is this element of Green Jacket discipline that can, occasionally, be misunderstood. The Green Jacket way is different – it is more relaxed and less rigid than usually found elsewhere in the British Army, and it is more difficult precisely because it is less rigid.

In a Green Jacket officer's relationship with his riflemen there is a fine line between informality, underpinned by mutual esteem and affection, and a lack of respect stemming from excessive familiarity. Amongst the officers, all are on first name terms at all times except for the commanding officer who is referred to simply as 'colonel' – or with the addition of his first name, such as 'Colonel David'. To the consternation and confusion of unwitting visitors, officers do not wear rank insignia on their mess dress, and their easy relaxed behaviour with each other does little to help visitors differentiate among them.

The regiment has always stressed the importance of self-respect as the basis of high morale, believing it links directly to self-discipline. Riflemen are encouraged to respect and take pride in themselves and each other. Self-respect implies the maintenance of proper personal and collective standards of behaviour. A rifleman who respects his comrades and himself will hesitate before allowing his standards to slip. And if the chain of command sets high standards, good discipline tends to follow naturally. Equally, efficiency is inseparable from self-respect. Riflemen need to have pride in what they are and what they do, and so the conditions in which they live, including their barrack rooms and amenities, should be of the highest standard possible. Regimental officers need to take, and to be seen to take, an interest in these conditions and to insist that the best possible ones are provided. Well-run officers', sergeants' and corporals' messes provide an important element in fostering self-respect and in maintaining that slight, but significant, psychological separation between ranks without which the implementation of even the most humane and intelligent military discipline becomes problematic.

Much emphasis is placed on the development of mutual trust between all ranks. Officers and NCOs are expected to know their subordinates' strengths and weaknesses and how to get the best from each of their rifleman. Once they know this they are able to work out for themselves how much freedom of action they can give to each individual. This is not new to the regiment – riflemen have never been mere automata; as long ago as 1808 Regimental Orders recorded these formal instructions:

It is the duty of every officer carefully to provide for the wants of his men. This he may be assured will give him their confidence and esteem ... The officers should endeavour to learn the capacities and characters of their men, that they may employ them to the best advantage; this may be easily done by conversing with them, and hearing their opinions and sentiments on different subjects.

These were Major Davy of the 5th Battalion 60th Rifles' orders whilst on board the *Malabar* in Cork

Right: Major William Davy, 5th Battalion 60th, 1808.

Bottom right: A focus on explaining the reason why; Brigadier Ed Butler, late RGJ, briefs Gurkha riflemen in Afghanistan, 2006.

The Royal Green Jackets

Harbour, embarking for Portugal; a completely different approach from the army at large.

Knowledge is regarded as the next element of high morale: knowledge of what is going on and what is required. It goes without saying that the officers are expected to be thoroughly professional and competent. Lieutenant John Cooke, 43rd Light Infantry, described his initial training on joining the 2nd Battalion of his regiment as an ensign in March 1809:

> When an officer entered this corps it was the custom to send him to drill with a squad composed of peasants from the plough tail and other raw recruits, to learn the facings, marchings, and companies' evolutions. That being completed, he put on cross belts and pouch and learned the firelock exercise, again marching with the same. When it was considered that the whole were perfect, with and without arms, they began to skirmish in extended files. Last of all they learned the duties of a sentry, and to fire ball cartridge at a target. The officer was not considered clear of the adjutant until he could put a company through the evolutions by word of command, which he had practised in the ranks. It generally took him six months in summer at four times a day, an hour at each period, to perfect all he had to learn. The drill was never kept more than an hour under arms when, to a minute, the time beater rolled his drum, the only one in the corps (the light infantry regiments using bugles), and the recruits were instantly dismissed … The officers never quitted their company to lounge about so long as the soldiers continued under arms.

This description tells us much about the standards of professionalism demanded of the officers of the then newly forming Light Brigade – the way the officers built a rapport with their soldiers, the close interaction between officers and men, the requirement to be able and willing to do anything asked of their men, and the recognition that officers were expected to set the standards by personal example. Such an ethos continues to be handed down through the regimental family to each generation in turn. 'Handed down' is an accurate description, because in the British Army's regimental system there is a direct line of succession running through each regiment back to its original formation.

Green Jackets have always stressed the importance of 'the reason why', therefore great effort is made to ensure that everyone in the battalion is kept informed about battalion policy, the reasons behind it and the role that each individual is expected to play. Although clearly having something to do with discipline and leadership, this explanation is also partly to do with building confidence and self-respect because it invokes understanding and appreciation, which produces the most willing form of cooperation. The commanding officer will lay down policy, but it is the duty of the officers and NCOs to pass it on, to explain it and make it happen. The importance of understanding the intention of the commander, both generally and specifically, is stressed – it is one's responsibility to fulfil that intention based on a clear understanding of common doctrine, mutual trust between commanders, obedience to orders, and the initiative to act within any freedom of action given (or purposefully in the absence of further orders). In other words, the philosophy reflects that of the 'fighting, thinking rifleman', a credo that the regiment's antecedents did so much to foster and develop; it is the mind-set that underpinned the legendary successes of the Light Brigade, and subsequently the Light Division, during the Peninsular War; and it is the philosophy that has now been embraced by the British Army at large and enshrined formally into British military doctrine.

Left: Ben Casey and Cpl Leslie controlling the battlegroup.

Below: 'Relevant and challenging training.' Rfn Lightonlers leads the way across the Rio Grande, Jamaica, 2003.

Left: A company commander, Patrick Sanders, briefs the Colonel Commandant.

Right: Defence of Calais, 1940.

It is particularly important that the modern British soldier has an understanding of the complex world about him, and the British Army's place within it. War can occur where it is least expected and may assume at least a partly unforeseen form. The military is now committed routinely to the most complex of situations under tight political control with demanding rules of engagement and complicated legal implications. As unabashed professionals, Royal Green Jacket officers are encouraged to keep themselves informed and educated by reading widely, and to explain to, or discuss events with, their riflemen.

Confidence builds high morale and it is generated through success – obviously so on operations, but prior to that, in preparation for active service, it will come from knowledge, effective training and sound administration.

Riflemen must not only be taught their own trade, but they must also have complete confidence in the skills of their fellow riflemen. This is usually achieved by ensuring the training is relevant and challenging, interesting and realistic. Green Jackets take particular pride in training as hard and as realistically as possible. The best training sets an aim and objectives that appear to be unattainable, but that the commander judges is just within the capabilities of his men. When the end is achieved there is a feeling amongst the men of immense satisfaction and confidence, with a corresponding boost to morale. Military training is invariably demanding and often dangerous, and one of the difficulties in peacetime, particularly in an increasingly litigious world, is to strike the balance between risk and safety. It is essential to prepare soundly, in terms of planning, briefing and anticipation. The chain of command encourages people to use their own initiative and to take sensible risks without fussing about it. Mistakes are expected to occur, but commanders are encouraged to stand back, give people their head and underwrite the honest mistakes of subordinates. Only by doing so are the subordinates able to develop their initiative and experience. The ability to deliver constructive criticism, rather than walking away, and the ability to receive criticism, and handle it without sulking, are part and parcel of learning from mistakes.

What has come to be known in the British Army as 'adventurous training' has long been a priority in The Royal Green Jackets. Henry Bouquet, founding father of the 62nd (Royal American) Regiment, insisted on such work not only as a form of self-development but also so that the officers and men would grow to know and respect each other. The Royal Green Jackets continued this tradition by mounting expeditions around the world on a regular basis (see Chapter 11).

Sound administration – an aspect of Coote Manningham's original regulations – remains an important part of building confidence because every rifleman needs to feel he belongs to an efficient organisation. He needs to have faith in his weapons, equipment and vehicles, and he expects to see that the officers and NCOs are genuinely interested in his welfare. Platoon commanders are taught to be wary of treading on the administrative toes of their platoon sergeant. But whilst the sergeant handles most of the administration within the platoon, and acts as the more experienced adviser and confidant for his commander until the latter has had the chance to learn his trade, platoon commanders are reminded that ultimate responsibility and accountability for their platoon is vested in them alone.

So what really motivates a rifleman? What it takes to get people to fight is known in modern army doctrine as 'the moral component'. Riflemen who are well motivated and well led will work naturally as an effective team. Teamwork in turn generates comradeship, and there are few closer bonds in human relationships than that of comradeship-in-arms, born out of adversity and shared dangers, which leads to the sort of pride in belonging that is often described as 'esprit de corps'. To illustrate this one need turn no further than the reply given by Captain Tom Acton, adjutant of the 1st Battalion, The Rifle Brigade, at Calais in 1940. When asked, by a lecturer who was researching a talk on 'determination in battle', why they had fought so well, Acton replied: 'The regiment had always fought well, and we were with our friends.' In *The Flames of Calais* Airey Neave put it another way: 'It may be fashionable today to sneer at regimental loyalty; Calais could not have been held so long without it.' Exactly the same sentiments have been echoed by Patrick Sanders, commanding 4th Battalion The Rifles in Basra, Iraq, in 2007.

The Royal Green Jackets and its antecedent regiments shared a strong family tradition. Successive generations joined the regiment – father to son, uncle to nephew, cousins, in-laws; many members of the regiment served because their fathers, relatives or friends also served. 'Once a rifleman always a rifleman' holds as true today as it did in the past.

The Royal Green Jackets

Strong motivation also requires a powerful sense of purpose. The starting point for this at platoon level is to build teamwork. This comes more easily from having a stable organisation, keeping teams together for as long as possible. It can be difficult to achieve, but, exactly as laid down in Coote Manningham's original regulations, the aim is to keep sections and half-sections together so that the riflemen get to know each other, relationships develop and the men trust each other simply because they have become friends. Regulations for The Rifle Corps stated:

> *This attention to retaining the same men and officers together, is on account of riflemen being liable to act very independently of each other, and in numerous small detachments in the field, when they will feel the comfort and utility of having their own officer, non-commissioned officer, and comrades with them; the service will be benefited by the tie of friendship, which will more naturally subsist between them.*

And in the end it is this trust and comradeship that lie at the heart of what it is that makes soldiers fight, when every natural instinct is for self-preservation. Riflemen fight for each other and have an overwhelming desire not to let each other down. This was realised by Coote Manningham who went so far as to lay down in his regulations the 'arrangement of comrades' a pairing of riflemen that was 'never to be changed without the permission of his captain' – comrades were kept together both in barracks and in the field, performing all operational and administrative duties together.

The Royal Green Jackets has always taken pride in a 'work hard, play hard' culture. Organised sport is one way to develop teamwork and has an important role to play in generating morale and success. An individual sport such as boxing helps to foster *controlled* and *disciplined* aggression – valuable attributes for the infantryman whose ultimate purpose is to close with the enemy and kill him. The requirement for toughness and aggression can sometimes confuse a young, new rifleman, eager to make his mark, when it is stressed to him that ill-disciplined fighting, physical or verbal bullying, or using excessive violence within a team situation is not the Green Jacket way. Many a recruit has had to have it explained to him that the regiment would be happy to see a display of courage and fighting skills in the boxing ring, but not in the local pub.

Morale, motivation and what it takes to get people to fight, all rely on leadership – the projection of personality and character in order to inspire people to get things done. Officers and NCOs would not be in the chain of command if they did not have initiative, courage, willpower and judgement, to name but a few of the qualities required. But upon arriving for the first time in a battalion it is accepted that young officers will probably be uncertain as to how leadership should be exercised for real in what is a strange and new environment. Leadership is essentially a personal quality, and the Green Jacket way readily accepts that an approach that will work for one leader may not necessarily work for another. But what is clear is that no approach will work unless officers and NCOs really *know* those they are privileged to command.

Second Lieutenant Vic Turner was given the following advice when he joined The Rifle Brigade: 'The characteristics of each rifleman in that platoon, his good qualities and his weaknesses, should be known to you. His training, his games, and his interests should be your continued care. The welfare of your men must be your aim and object. If you follow these principles, your men will love and respect you and stand by you in battle.'

Above: Running the battle at Brigade level.

Below: Lieutenant Colonel Vic Turner VC, Commanding Officer 2RB, Battle of Alamein, 1942.

And indeed they did, to perfection, during the heroic defence of Kidney Ridge by the 2nd Battalion, The Rifle Brigade, commanded by the then Lieutenant Colonel Vic Turner, at the Battle of Alamein: '[The Snipe action] showed the British soldier in one of his finest hours, not only was it unexpectedly to deal one of the most telling blows against the German counter-attack that matured next afternoon, but also it was to illustrate in the most vivid fashion how the mischances, misunderstandings and dark uncertainties that beset soldiers in a vague and confused situation can be overcome by his own self-reliance and battle discipline.'

For this action Lieutenant Colonel Vic Turner received the Victoria Cross, one of fifty-nine awarded to members of the antecedent regiments of The Royal Green Jackets.

When speaking about leading riflemen, the word most emphasised in the regiment is *care*, for there is nothing more laudable than to be thought of as a leader who really *cares* for his men, and this includes their families. Green Jacket officers should know and take an interest in the domestic background of their soldiers, remember their wife's name and what her interests are, how many children they have, their names and ages. Officers and NCOs are reminded that riflemen will all differ; some will be stronger than others, some will be better at this, others at that. The trick, and it comes from knowing and caring for them as individuals, is to be able to get the best out of each one. In this way they can all contribute in their individual way towards achieving the overall objective.

In practical terms officers are reminded that it is a question of *showing* that they care and that they can do this by always being approachable and by really getting to know their riflemen. They will know when they have succeeded because their men will feel able to speak freely and easily with them, and indulge in 'riflemen's banter'. They will offer opinions, seek their officer's opinions and feel able to speak their mind. All this lies at the heart of the Green Jacket way, where every member of the team has always been valued in his own right as an individual.

It has been this way since the earliest days when open-order tactics had demanded a completely different approach. Officers were taught that if they were honest with their riflemen, they would be trusted in return. If they promised to sort out a rifleman's affairs, then they had to ensure they delivered. Officers should visit their riflemen when they are on guard; go to the mess hall, whether on or off duty, and seek their views, not only about the quality of the food but to discuss matters in general; and to visit them if they are in detention. In this way the rifleman realises that 'his officer' really takes a personal interest in him and cares about him.

This philosophy is the essence of the Green Jacket ethos, and it informs the Green Jacket way of doing things. Field Marshal the Lord Bramall, when a Lieutenant Colonel commanding the 2nd Battalion in 1966, summarised it as: 'pride in fighting qualities and professional skill, intelligent and humane discipline, sympathy and understanding between all ranks and concern for the individual, for his welfare and for that of his dependants.'

The Royal Green Jackets strived to emulate the standards handed down by their antecedents, of whom Sir John Moore wrote when he inspected his regiment, 52nd Light Infantry, in Sicily in 1806: 'I have the pleasure to observe that this regiment possesses an excellent spirit and that both officers and men take a pride in doing their duty. Their movement in the field is perfect; it is evident that not only the officers, but that each individual soldier knows perfectly what he has to do; the discipline is carried on without severity: the officers are attached to the men, the men to the officers.'

There could hardly be a better summary of the ideals and ethos of The Royal Green Jackets and what lies behind doing business the Green Jacket way.

Below: The Snipe action at Kidney Ridge – 2 RB at the Battle of Alamein, 27 September 1942.

Right: Bronze bust of Field Marshal the Lord Bramall that sits in the Ante Room of the Officers' Mess, 56 Davies Street.

Inside the Regiment

This chapter records some of what, for 40 years, was going on behind the scenes in support of the Regiment in its widest sense, orchestrated in the main from Regimental Headquarters situated at Peninsula Barracks, Winchester. In doing so it also provides an insight into the workings of the regimental system, as practised in the British Army. Much of the structure, organisation and workings of The Royal Green Jackets will be carried forward from 2007 into The Rifles.

The Royal Green Jackets Regimental Structure within the British Army

The regimental hierarchy above the level of the commanding officers of the battalions does not appear in the British Army's order of battle, but it is nonetheless important in maintaining the ethos, standards and traditions of the regiment – crucial, in fact, to maintaining all that is special about the British Army's regimental system. The commanding officers of the battalions are responsible on a daily basis to their operational chain of command. And that is where it stops for most armies. In the British Army each regiment has a particular regimental organisation.

Her Majesty the Queen, as Colonel-in-Chief of The Royal Green Jackets, took a close interest in the workings and activities of her Regiment, and on her behalf the Colonel Commandant of each battalion wielded power and influence. They would meet regularly with commanding officers to decide regimental policy on purely regimental matters – for instance, officer and soldier recruiting; dress issues; funds and expenditure priorities for regimental funds; 'affiliations' and 'bonds of friendship'; and the museum, club and association issues – as well as no less important issues concerning the regiment's position on important military issues of the day.

Each regular battalion had a Colonel Commandant, one of them representing the regiment as Regimental Colonel Commandant whenever required. Overall responsibility for the general wellbeing of the regiment in its widest sense would lie with him. In addition, he would chose from those qualified his nomination for the coveted appointments of commanding officer of each battalion, indicating to the Military Secretary his nomination for formal approval. In the

Above left: The Colonel-in-Chief visits the Regiment, Celle, Germany, May 1984.

Above: The Colonel-in-Chief visits the Regiment, Dover, October 1994.

Inside the Regiment

Above: Charles II's palace at Winchester, designed by Sir Christopher Wren, later to become the Rifle Depot.

Far right: Royal Green Jackets window at the Light Division Chapel, Sir John Moore Barracks Winchester; home of the Light Division.

Right: The Light Division Chapel, serving The Light Infantry and The Royal Green Jackets.

Bottom: Upper Barracks Winchester as it was when the 43rd Light Infantry were stationed there in 1784.

case of the RGJ, a Green Jacket senior officer could also hold the appointment of Colonel Commandant the Light Division, responsible for representing the interests of the two regiments that then comprised the Light Division – The Royal Green Jackets and The Light Infantry. Additionally, a former Green Jacket Territorial Army (TA) officer could hold the appointment of Deputy Colonel Commandant (TA and Cadets), responsible to the Regimental Colonel Commandant for matters concerning the Regiment's territorial and cadet forces.

Regimental Headquarters (RHQ)

Prior to The Royal Green Jackets merging into The Rifles, the Colonels Commandant were advised and supported by the Regimental Secretary and the three Assistant Regimental Secretaries based at Regimental Headquarters (RHQ), located together with the regimental museum on the site of the old Rifle Depot at Peninsula Barracks in Winchester. In addition to the Regimental Secretary and the Assistant Regimental Secretaries, Regimental Headquarters (RHQ) was staffed by a Regimental Adjutant, a small museum staff, clerical support and some volunteer archivists. Situated in offices in Short Block at Peninsula Barracks, RHQ The Royal Green Jackets shared the location with RHQ The Light Infantry where today both have merged into a single RHQ for The Rifles on the same site.

For 150 years Winchester was the home of The Royal Green Jackets and its antecedent regiments, and is still regarded by Riflemen as their regimental and spiritual home. RHQ The Rifles will carry on this tradition and the strong regimental affiliation with the City of Winchester. At Flowerdown, just outside the city, is Sir John Moore Barracks, the home of the Light Division (and formerly the Light Division Depot), with the Light Division Chapel and the specially commissioned statue of Sir John Moore. Not far from Peninsula Barracks is the regimental cricket ground, at St Cross, and twenty-one regiment-owned homes for deserving retired riflemen and their families at Green Jacket Close.

Regimental Headquarters The Royal Green Jackets disbanded in 2007, and RHQ The Rifles will, over the next two years, assume full responsibility for other RGJ assets transferred across to the new regiment, including Regimental funds, property, the Green Jacket Club, Riflemen's Aid Society and, in time, the Museum.

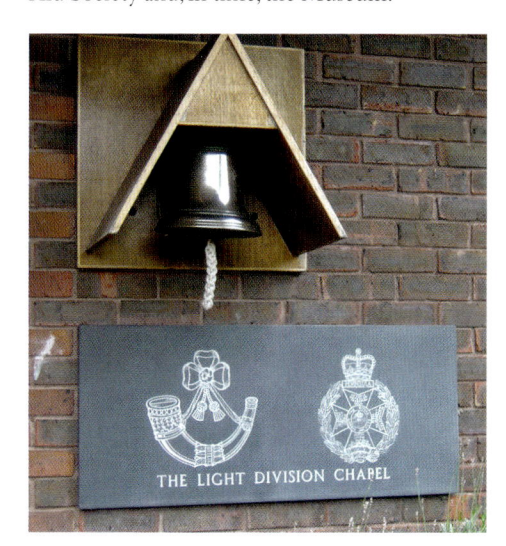

The Royal Green Jackets

Royal Green Jackets Regimental Trustees

Regimental trustees have always played an important role in the life of the Regiment and hardly a section of the chapter fails to include mention of them. Most British regiments have amassed considerable assets during the course of their existence, owning outright valuable pictures, silver and furniture, and some also have property. None of these possessions belong to the Ministry of Defence or the British Army; they belong to the regiments. All regiments run regimental charities, and it falls to their trustees to administer all these interests and charities in support of the regiment.

The trustees were first elected in 1966, on the formation of The Royal Green Jackets, to manage the amalgamated benevolent funds of the three antecedent regiments, which included the Officer's Funds, the Central Trust Funds, and the Riflemen's Aid Society; they also incorporated the twenty-one houses in Green Jacket Close. *Ex officio* members of the Trustee Board comprised the Regimental Colonel Commandant, the battalion Colonels Commandant, and eight volunteer trustees drawn among the body of retired officers of the former regiments.

Broadly, the charitable objectives of the funds were to improve the welfare of serving members of The Royal Green Jackets and benevolence for past members of the antecedent regiments. The trustees were responsible for the distribution of grants of such income as was available from the funds. Over time this process has kept pace with developments in charitable practice and the number of trustees has been increased. The trustees now number fourteen, including the four retired officers at RHQ who together form a quorum for routine decisions outside the committee.

Whereas the Regimental Colonel Commandant chaired all meetings up to 1981, it became the routine practice for an elected member of the Trustee Board to chair meetings. This task fell initially to Colonel Tod Sweeney, then from 1989 to 1994 it was the turn of Brigadier John Cornell, and from 1995 onwards it was the task of Colonel Mike Robertson, all retired officers of the regiment.

The Trustee Act 2000 highlighted the duty of care and personal accountability expected of trustees. Some millions of pounds are professionally managed on behalf of the regiment, and it is overseen by a small investment committee that reports to the main board. A system of block grants to the battalions has given commanding officers greater flexibility in the disbursement of funds, while at the same time ensuring accountability. The majority of trustees are now retired Royal Green Jackets officers, but the well-being and benevolent care of past members of the antecedent regiments remains a key part of their work.

The Riflemen's Aid Society, Green Jacket Close

The aim of the Riflemen's Aid Society is to assist, either financially, in kind or in any other appropriate manner, those serving or ex-serving riflemen, their wives, widows or other dependants, who may find themselves in need of assistance. The Riflemen's Aid Society was first established as a registered charity in 1886. It derives about one-third of its income from the One Day's Pay Scheme, whereby all ranks voluntarily contribute a day's pay to the society, and two-thirds from dividends earned by the society's investments, the legacy of the antecedent regiments. Additional donations are received from collections and individual gifts, often resulting from legacies.

In a typical year some hundreds of cases are handled resulting in grants that could total over £120,000. Assistance is also given with annuities and top-up fees for nursing homes, and further grants of some tens of thousands of pounds are made to those charities that directly support former riflemen. These charities include the Army Benevolent Fund, St Dunstans, BLESMA, the Royal Star & Garter Home, the Not Forgotten Association, Combat Stress, the British Commonwealth Ex-Service League, the Ex-Service Fellowship Centres and the Royal Patriotic Fund.

Green Jacket Close was originally opened in 1904 as a memorial to the 44 officers and 550 riflemen of the Kings Royal Rifle Corps and the Rifle Brigade killed during the Boer War, by Field Marshal HRH The Duke of Connaught, Colonel-in-Chief of the Rifle Brigade and HRH The Prince Christian of Schleswig Holstein, whose son, Prince Christian Victor, had died in 1900 in South Africa whilst serving with The King's Royal Rifle Corps. The cost of the homes, some £6000, was raised by the Riflemen's Aid Society, much of it by subscription from serving and former officers, NCOs and riflemen of the regiments, together with a number of individual donations. The Close, situated at St Cross, Winchester, now consists of twenty-one properties. A mix of

Top: Colonel Commandants' Meeting with Commanding Officers and Trustees.

Above: KRRC Memorial Cottages opened in 1904 in memory of the Riflemen who died in the South African War. Eight such cottages were built and funded, four each by the KRRC and The Rifle Brigade. The cottages later expanded into Green Jacket Close. The cottages were administered by the Riflemen's Aid Association established in 1883/4.

Inside the Regiment

Above: Annual Regimental Dinner, Davies Street.

Bottom right: London and Essex Branch of the KRRC Association gather for lunch at Davies Street, 2007.

semidetached houses, maisonettes and flats, these homes are allocated to former riflemen or their widows. When selecting residents, consideration is given to length of service, character, financial situation and any other special circumstances, such as war wounds or other physical disability. Residents usually move in after they have reached the age of sixty. They are expected to pay their own council tax and water rates and a small weekly accommodation charge. There are 27 residents from the three former regiments, and The Royal Green Jackets, with a combined age in January 2007 of 1,971 years.

The Royal Green Jackets Ladies Guild

The Royal Green Jackets Ladies Guild is a charitable trust administered by the trustees of the Riflemen's Aid Society and it looks after the interests of needy widows of former riflemen. There are currently sixty-two widows on the books. In addition to the support given to the widows, all children of riflemen who have died whilst serving with the regiment receive a cheque at Christmas until they reach the age of eighteen. There are currently over twenty such children. Further assistance is arranged for widows and children on a continuous basis as deserving cases come to notice. The Ladies Guild will continue after the formation of The Rifles in 2007. The intention is to start The Rifles Ladies Guild with which, in time, The Royal Green Jackets Ladies Guild may merge. With the demands of continuing operations in Iraq and Afghanistan the continuing need for the Ladies Guild will likely be reinforced.

The Officers' Club and the Regimental Association

Formerly, RHQ RGJ also had responsibility for the Green Jackets Officers' Club and The Royal Green Jackets Association, as well as for the officers' clubs and associations of the three antecedent regiments – namely the 43rd and 52nd Officers' Club and the 43rd and 52nd Old Comrades Association; the Celer et Audax Club and The King's Royal Rifle Corps Association; the Rifle Brigade Club and the Rifle Brigade Association. As we have seen, subsequent to the merger with The Rifles, the Club and the Association have taken over outreach and support to former serving members of RGJ and antecedent regiments.

The Green Jackets Officers' Club will continue to hold the annual regimental dinner at Davies Street in London, and The Royal Green Jackets Association will continue to hold its annual reunion each July at Sir John Moore Barracks outside Winchester, when several hundred retired riflemen of all ranks gather for the day to renew old friendships

The Royal Green Jackets

Left: Regimental Dinner, Major Roy Stangar keeps his table entertained.

Below left: Durbar.

Below centre: 'Last Out, First In' battlefield tour.

Below right: The Rear Guard, the RGJ Association Australasian Branch Newsletter.

and catch up on the gossip. Association day also includes a Sounding Retreat, which remains as popular as ever. Since 2001 an annual Durbar – from the Indian term describing the assembling of people for a commemoration – is also held for the Green Jacket family of regiments at a holiday camp on the south coast. A week is set aside for Green Jackets and their families to gather for as much or as little time as they wish – many come for a day, others a three-day short break, and some for the full week. Durbar comes into its own in the evening when families have returned from their day's activities and everyone gathers as fellow riflemen to eat, drink and remember, and to dip into and out of the varied nightly entertainments and star cabaret.

In recent years General Bob Pascoe has organised regimental battlefield tours, under the banner 'Last Out, First In', for members of the associations. These tours concentrated primarily on Calais and the Normandy battlefields.

There are branches of The Royal Green Jackets Association across Britain, and overseas branches are thriving in Australia, Canada, Germany and the USA. For example, the Australasian Branch, chaired by Chris McDonald, a former corporal of 3rd Battalion Royal Green Jackets (3RGJ) and later a police sergeant in Perth, has grown under his enthusiastic leadership to a membership nearing a hundred former riflemen of all ranks. The Australasian Branch also published a monthly internet magazine 'Rifles', which to avoid confusion with the arrival of the new regiment as The Rifles, has now been suitably recast as 'The Rear Guard'. The Association also participates in the annual Remembrance Sunday and ANZAC Day parades and has a thriving social programme. In 2007, to much acclaim, the Branch marched at a brisk 140 paces to the minute through the streets of Perth behind the Band of The Rifles at the ANZAC Day parade. The Band of The Rifles was on an official tour of Australia, providing a perfect opportunity for the old regiment to support the new, and for new linkages and friendships to be made.

Below: Anzac Day in Perth, 2007.

Below left: John Parker after the Anzac Day parade, 2007.

Bottom: London Branch RGJ Association before Remembrance Sunday parade at the Cenotaph, Whitehall.

Above: Chris MacDonald (centre), Chairman Australasian Branch, Royal Green Jackets Association, with (l to r) Jeff Robinson, Bugle Major of The Rifles Band and Bugles, Dave Sunley and Les Birrell, Perth, 2007.

Inside the Regiment

RGJ Association Branches

Aylesbury	West Midlands	Yorkshire	Australasia
Milton Keynes	North East	Wiltshire	Canada
Colchester	North West	Winchester & District	Germany
Harlow	Oxfordshire	Scotland	USA
Kent	Shrewsbury	Oxfordshire and Buckinghamshire	
London	Telford	Light Infantry Branch	
Midlands	Suffolk		

The original RGJ website www.royalgreenjackets.co.uk established itself as an invaluable asset for passing news around the Association and for anyone seeking information about the regiment. Today it is a portal for information about the RGJ Association and the Green Jacket Club, and a vital hub for keeping in touch.

The Royal Green Jackets Association will continue to maintain the spirit, history and traditions of the RGJ, conserve its archives, and keep in touch with the many RGJ associations all over the world, while supporting The Rifles as the RGJ's natural successor.

Right: Green Jackets Club Cricket Ground, St Cross, Winchester.

Below: Matthew Fleming celebrates taking a wicket for Kent.

Cricket and St Cross – Green Jacket Cricket Club

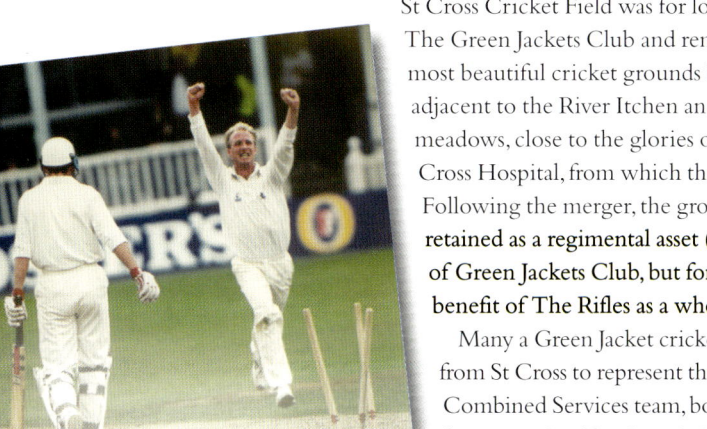

St Cross Cricket Field was for long the home of The Green Jackets Club and remains one of the most beautiful cricket grounds in England. It lies adjacent to the River Itchen and its famous water meadows, close to the glories of the medieval St Cross Hospital, from which the ground is leased. Following the merger, the ground **will be retained as a regimental asset (probably in name of Green Jackets Club, but for the ultimate benefit of The Rifles as a whole)**.

Many a Green Jacket cricketer has gone on from St Cross to represent the British Army or Combined Services team, both of which have been captained by Captain James Fulton from the 2nd Battalion, while Matthew Fleming progressed to captain Kent and play for England. Annually the Green Jacket Club's cricket team played some eighteen fixtures a year, most at St Cross. Opponents have included Eton, Stragglers of Asia, The Royal Armoured Corps, Infantry, The Guards, The Royal Military Academy Sandhurst, Winchester College, Eton Ramblers, Free Foresters, I Zingari, Gemini, The Light Infantry and Lord Carnarvon's XI.

The highlight of the season was traditionally Green Jacket Week in early July, during which up to five matches were played. From 2007 Green Jacket Week takes place under the banner of The Rifles. Green Jacket cricket will continue to be played at St Cross and elsewhere. Few regiments can ever have boasted such a well-established, well-supported and successful cricket club, with the 2nd Battalion becoming the British Army's cricket champions once again in the 2000 and 2002 seasons. This cricket pedigree is certain to be continued under The

The Royal Green Jackets

Rifles. Finally, no summary of the RGJ cricketing heritage could fail to mention the key contributions of Roy Clarke, an excellent groundsman and creator of one of the finest wickets in Hampshire, who has worked for the club since 1974, finally retiring in 2007.

Golf – Green Jackets Golfing Society

At a time of frequent change it is worth reflecting on the longevity of the rich vein of golf played by Green Jackets Club members, which has lasted in several instances for well over fifty years. Fifty-two years ago, as recorded in the 1955 Rifle Brigade *Chronicle*, Green Jackets golf matches were already being played against the Bar, the Wine Trade, and the Army Golf Society. The regular visit to Littlestone took place for the Annual Meeting. All of these continue today, together with matches against Liphook, Sunningdale, The Berkshire, Huntercombe, St Enodoc, Rye and Boodles Golf Clubs. Other opponents include Eton Boys, Old Etonians, The Woodpeckers, Old Wykehamists, The Guards, and The Light Infantry. From 2007 and the formation of The Rifles, Green Jacket golf will be able to call upon a larger pool of players, and the Society looks forward to integrating new players.

Green Jackets Sailing Club

The Green Jackets Sailing Club has an affiliation with the Household Division Yacht Club, keenly competing for the Green Jackets Cup presented to HDYC some thirty years ago. The Light Division Regatta is held at Seaview in June each year, attracting well over fifty competitors annually.

The Royal Green Jackets Museum and Regimental Archives

The regimental museum is of special importance, with its exhibits and displays serving to remind the present generations of the remarkable courage and stirring deeds of their predecessors. Now, of course, that importance holds even greater weight. The Royal Green Jackets Museum records the history and traditions of the regiment, and those qualities that have distinguished Green Jackets from other soldiers, thereby engendering a sense of pride and belonging. Situated in the former headquarters building of the Rifle Depot at Peninsula Barracks, Winchester, the museum receives over 12,000 visitors a year.

Prior to the formation of The Royal Green Jackets, each of the antecedent regiments had their own collections. In 1964 these were brought together on the top floor of the modernised Rifle Depot, though each collection was separately managed by its own set of museum trustees. The 43rd & 52nd trustees retained a substantial element of their collection, which is on display in the Oxfordshire & Buckinghamshire Light Infantry Museum, at Slade Park Camp, near Cowley, Oxford.

Initially, the formation of The Royal Green Jackets had little impact on the operation of the museum trusts of the antecedent regiments, albeit their collections (less elements of the 43rd & 52nd) were displayed under one roof and under the title of the regimental museum. It was not long, though, before thoughts turned to beginning the process of collecting artefacts and material for future display. In 1969 a separate exhibition area was created and a single museum shop opened. In 1977 Major General Giles Mills became the first chairman of the newly created RGJ Museum Trust, and the trustees met for the first time in 1978. In 1985, prompted by concern that the museum collections might be homeless once the Light Division depot at Peninsula Barracks closed in 1986, the Army Board agreed to the MOD's retention of the headquarters block for use by the museums of The Royal Green Jackets and The Light Infantry. The trustees then agreed collectively to engage Richards Daynes, a well-known design consultant, to produce a completely new layout for the museum. An appeal was launched, and just over £600,000 was raised in donations from members of the regiment and others, and in grants from public authorities and charitable trusts,

Left: Roy Clarke, groundsman, Green Jackets Club Cricket Ground, St Cross, 1974–2007.

Below: Mitary General Service Medal 1793–1814 with nince Peninsular War clasps each for a separate battle.

Bottom left: Green Jackets Club Golf AGM, Littlestone, 2005.

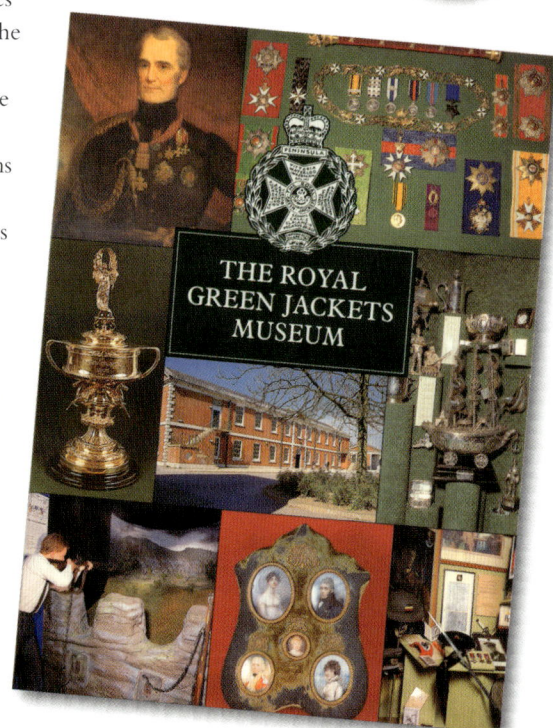

Inside the Regiment

Right: The Rifle Corps, early days.

Below: Victoria Cross, one of 59 awarded to the antecedent regiments of The Royal Green Jackets.

including £90,000 from regimental funds. At the end of 1987 the museum was closed for refurbishment and fitting out.

On 1 December 1989 the Colonel-in-Chief declared the new museum open. In 1990 the Rifle Brigade Museum trustees handed their collection over to the RGJ Museum trustees. In 1994 The King's Royal Rifle Corps (KRRC) regimental trustees did the same. Only the 43rd & 52nd trustees continue to retain ownership of their collection, much of which is on loan to the RGJ Museum Trust. The principal feature of the new museum was, and still is, the integration of the collections of the antecedent regiments into a series of displays allowing visitors to follow in chronological order their various actions and campaigns.

The museum's trustees have sought ever since to maintain its quality and excellence by pursuing a programme of continuous improvement. In 1991 a second appeal was successful in creating a £60,000 endowment fund to enable the trustees to acquire important artefacts and material offered for public sale. More recently, more than £80,000 was spent on enhancing the facilities to provide new displays and better presentation. In 2003 'The Friends of the RGJ Museum' scheme was launched to encourage past and present members of the regiment and the general public to show their appreciation for the museum and to contribute to its continuous improvement by subscribing as a Friend.

Among the most impressive and popular attractions is the Waterloo diorama, acquired in 1985. Measuring 22 by 11 feet (6.7 by 3.35 m), with 22,000 models and horses, the diorama includes an accompanying sound and light commentary highlighting the critical part played in the battle by the 52nd Light Infantry and the 95th Rifles.

By 1989 the museum housed more than 7,000 medals, many of great interest to collectors, including a large number from the Peninsular War and Waterloo. Many more medals have since been acquired, and space is now at a premium in the splendid Medal Room. The museum is also fortunate either to own or to have on permanent loan thirty-four out of the fifty-nine Victoria Crosses awarded to members of the antecedent regiments of The Royal Green Jackets. No other Infantry regiment in the British Army prior to the current round of mergers and amalgamations has been able to lay claim to a greater number. A new display for the Victoria Crosses was created in 2002, with touch-screen access to a significant database of additional information about the award itself and each of the Regiment's recipients.

It remains an objective to record, collect and display information about the history of The Royal Green Jackets, which in 2001 resulted in the completion of a substantial new section with displays covering, amongst other things, the Regiment's participation in Northern Ireland, the Gulf War and the Balkans. The important role within the Regiment of the Territorials and cadets is also highlighted.

Above: Lieutenant General Sir Christopher Wallace, Chairman Royal Green Jackets Museum Trust.

Right: Waterloo Diorama, RGJ Museum, Winchester.

47

Peninsula Barracks: The Past, Present and Future

Major R.D. Cassidy

A brief history of the Winchester Depot, and how it became the home of The Royal Green Jackets.

The site of what was to become the Peninsula Barracks has a colourful history, beginning with the second Roman invasion of Britain in AD43. The area now occupied by Lower Barracks was within the Roman city boundaries, the line of the Roman wall being on the line of the embankment that divides the upper and lower sites. When Alfred the Great restored Winchester to its original state in the late ninth century, the future Depot site became a royal residence. It was from this residence that in 1034 the great Viking king Canute set off to the beach at Southampton to show his courtiers the limits of kingly power – even a king could not turn back the tide.

In 1069 William the Conqueror began to build a castle, the foundations of which still survive beneath the Square of the barracks. Most castles in the south of England stand in the centre of town: William, however, erected his castle on the highest point, which was immediately outside the city boundary. William's castle was 850 feet (260 m) in length from north to south and 250 feet (76 m) wide, and occupied the area on which the Peninsula Barracks complex stands. The castle green was where the railway cutting now is, and this was the training ground for archers and men-at-arms, and the scene of many bloody state executions, which took place after trials in the Great Hall – now all that remains of the castle and a major tourist attraction.

The castle was much developed during the twelfth century and saw the coronation of Richard Coeur de Lion in 1124. Henry II was born in the castle, while Henry V – who was educated at Winchester College – was to gather his Hampshire bowmen and men-at-arms at the castle before embarking at Southampton for victories at Crécy, Poitiers and Agincourt. After the death of Richard II, the last of the House of York, the triumphant Henry Tudor brought his wife Elizabeth of York to the castle so that his first child should be born in the ancient capital of England. This child was christened Arthur, claiming descent from that great king, and perhaps the event was responsible for the revival of the legends of the Round Table: a fanciful version of the Table hangs in the Great Hall today.

Forward to 1645, when Cromwell appeared on the scene to reduce the city and its castle to the authority of Parliament. The main attack, which lasted two days, was on the castle itself, Cromwell concentrating his cannon at one spot near the Black Tower until a breach was opened. The foundations of this tower were uncovered in 1962. Cromwell reported that he had lost twelve men in the attack. Although Parliament ordered that the castle be destroyed, it remained intact for some years, and Charles I, who was the last sovereign to stay within its walls, lodged there in December 1648 on his way to trial and execution in London.

In 1682 Charles II decided to make Winchester his ordinary residence, and planned a palace on the spot where the former castle had stood. Interestingly, the City and other parties sold to Charles and his heirs, for the nominal sum of approximately £2,622, the ruined castle, the castle green and ditch comprising by estimation 8 acres. Sir Christopher Wren was appointed architect and Charles himself laid the foundation stone in 1683. Unfortunately, only two years after the work had begun, Charles died and the work stopped.

During the reigns of James II and William II and Mary II no work took place. On her accession in 1702 Queen Anne had an estimate prepared for completion but the expense of the Great Continental War prevented it.

At about this time much of the land was purchased for development: one of the areas developed was Serles House, constructed about 1730 and later the Regimental Headquarters of the Royal Hampshire Regiment. (It is interesting to note here that for a period of time it was the Regimental Headquarters of The Green Jackets.) Serles House is now occupied by The Royal Hampshire Regiment Museum.

During the Seven Years' War (1756–63) a great number of French prisoners were taken, and the Government decided to confine them in the King's House (later, after this building had been destroyed by fire, its replacements were to become known to so many riflemen as the Long and Short Blocks). Under George III, during the American War of Independence in 1775, it was successively occupied by French, Spanish and Dutch prisoners. Then in 1779 prisoners from a captured French hospital ship brought a pestilence that killed off the jailers and their prisoners in great numbers. They were buried in the ancient castle ditches and apparently contributed greatly to reduce the depth thereof!

It was in 1796 that the building was first used as a purely military establishment (it had formerly been used by the local militia) and converted to accommodate regular British troops. In 1839 the main line of the South Western Railway was opened to Southampton, and the cutting alongside the barracks was one of the deepest on the line. During excavation skeletons and skulls of the 1797 plague victims were found.

From 1798 various regiments were housed within the palace and its grounds, and it was in 1855 that the arrival of the Rifle Brigade heralded a long association with the barracks and of course with Winchester itself. Three years later the Rifle Brigade was joined by The King's Royal Rifle Corps, and the barracks became the Rifle Depot, the training centre for both regiments.

It is also interesting to note that in 1740–1 the 43rd, who were raised as he 54th Regiment of Foot, were located around Leighton Buzzard with headquarters at Winchester and indeed were stationed in the barracks in 1784. Certainly it is true to say that the three former

Major Ron Cassidy and Major Ken Gray, past and present RGJ Museum Curators.

Inside the Regiment

Winchester Barracks on fire, 1894.

regiments, the 43rd & 52nd, The King's Royal Rifle Corps and The Rifle Brigade, had a very, very long historical connection with Winchester and Peninsula Barracks.

In December 1894 fire broke out in the King's House, and the buildings designed and built by Wren in 1685 were destroyed. The Rifle Depot, as it was called, moved to Gosport while the barracks were rebuilt. It took ten years to replace the original King's House with two new buildings, which came to be known as the Long and Short Blocks, and once more became the Rifle Depot in 1904.

In 1958, following the decision to reorganise the British Army on a brigade basis, the 43rd & 52nd, the KRRC and the RB formed the new Green Jackets Brigade and the barracks became the Brigade Depot. A masterplan was drawn up under the personal instruction of General Sir George Erskine, Colonel Commandant of the KRRC, for modernisation of the barracks to equip it for its new role. Work started in January 1962, the Depot having moved to temporary quarters in the hutted camp at Bushfield. On the brigade's return to Winchester in 1964 from Bushfield, the Upper Barracks (as it was named) was renamed Peninsula Barracks, chosen because all three antecedent regiments had earned great fame in the Pensinsular War in Spain against Napoleon.

The year 1985 saw the Regiment move out of Peninsula Barracks into Sir John Moore Barracks, just under two miles away on the north side of Winchester. This move into a purpose-built barracks – the most modern in Britain – was brought about because of lack of space and facilities in the Peninsula Barracks: thus The Royal Green Jackets were the last regimental depot in the country to make a Divisional Depot (by combining with The Light Infantry).

After 1985 Short Block housed the Regimental Headquarters of The Royal Green Jackets and The Light Infantry, the museums of The King's Royal Hussars and Gurkhas and also Home Headquarters (South) King's Royal Hussars. The former 'T' Block became our own museum, which occupies the whole of the top floor and half of the ground floor, and also The Light Infantry Museum, which occupies the other half of the ground floor.

Today, in 2007, we see the culmination of a process of redevelopment by Arundel Estates, whereby the former Parade Square has been replaced by formal gardens and a water feature, and where Lower Barracks has now become private housing.

This development has thus firmly integrated a site of historic importance into the City of Winchester, while at the same time providing a museum complex that advertises the story of a 200-year association between historic regiments and the city itself.

The excellence of the museum today is the product of much hard work by a relatively small number of highly committed people. Principal among them has been Giles Mills, assisted (especially during 1987–9) by the fund-raising efforts of Field Marshal Edwin Bramall and Major Gerald Carter and by the dedication and knowledge of experts such as Colonel John Baker and Colonel John Tillett. Regimental officers have continued to commit themselves to the museum after retirement. In 1991 Brigadier Clinton Henshaw succeeded Giles Mills as chairman of the museum trustees, followed in 1999 by Lieutenant General Sir Christopher Wallace. The museum has also benefited from similar continuity at curatorial level, with Major Ron Cassidy, who became curator of the new museum in 1989, being followed by Major Ken Gray in 1999.

The creation of the new museum at the end of 1989 and the handover of the KRRC and The Rifle Brigade (RB) collections to the RGJ Museum trustees provided the catalyst for amalgamating the KRRC, RB and Royal Green Jackets material into what is now known as the Regimental Archives. Permanent space was found for them in 1992 at RHQ, where they form part of the museum collection in the custody and care of the RGJ Museum trustees.

The Regimental Archives contains a comprehensive library of regimental histories and many books, not readily found elsewhere, that detail the countless battles and campaigns in which the antecedent regiments participated. There are also copies of all the regimental chronicles since their first publication in 1890, together with the 1914–18 war diaries of The King's Royal Rifle Corps and The Rifle Brigade, and the microfiche records of all other ranks who were pensioned between 1780 and 1850. Other material includes 8,000 photographs, the earliest taken in 1854 in the Crimea, and more than 3,000 documents varying from campaign rolls and medal lists to individual diaries, letters and hand-drawn maps.

The Training and Recruiting of Riflemen

It was in 1855, with the arrival of The Rifle Brigade, that the long association with Winchester began, at what was then Upper Barracks, later to become Peninsula Barracks. Three years later The Rifle Brigade was joined by The King's Royal Rifle Corps, and Upper Barracks became the Rifle Depot, the training centre for both regiments. Interestingly, the 43rd had been stationed in the barracks as early as 1784 – the antecedent regiments of The Royal Green Jackets therefore have a long historical connection with Winchester.

The site remained known as the Rifle Depot up until 1963, apart from a ten-year period of rebuilding following a fire in 1894 which destroyed the original buildings – designed and built by Sir Christopher Wren in 1685 as a royal palace for Charles II. With the formation of The Green Jackets Brigade in 1958 and the requirement to expand and modernise the training centre, the depot was moved to Bushfield Camp just outside the city, where it had been located temporarily during the Second World War when American troops had been billeted in the Rifle Depot. Bushfield Camp holds fond memories for many of the generation who were trained in this unremarkable collection of huts – not least Field Marshal Bramall, who has taken the title Lord Bramall of Bushfield. Work started on expanding the barracks in January 1962, and upon the return to Winchester in 1964 the Upper Barracks was restyled Peninsula Barracks – named to reflect a significant battle honour common to all four of the antecedent regiments of The Royal Green Jackets. In 1983 the Rifle Depot became the Light Division

The Royal Green Jackets

Depot (Winchester), and in January 1986 the new depot for the Light Division opened, with the arrival of 105 adult recruits, at Sir John Moore Barracks, less than two miles away on the northern side of Winchester, bringing the training of riflemen and light infantrymen together once more in the same place.

Peninsula Barracks holds a special place in the hearts of Royal Green Jackets' riflemen who were trained there prior to 1986. Thousands have 'Long Block' and the square in front of it etched into their memories. This was where the Green Jacket ethos was implanted over generations. The aim was always to develop in the recruit a degree of trust in the training system, more than just blind obedience. It was a strategy not without associated difficulties and challenges, but it usually worked, and in doing so, the Rifle Depot turned out trained riflemen, each one mentally and physically equipped to serve in one of the battalions.

Whilst there was never any great emphasis in The Royal Green Jackets on drill, Passing Out Parades were nevertheless the climax of the months spent in training. Whatever the Army context, drill does, if not taken to excess, have an important part to play in basic training by teaching recruits to react to orders instantly, and how to move smartly as a formed body in uniformity. It makes for quick reaction, and such reactions on the battlefield save lives.

In the case of the RGJ, with orders being given on the bugle, the best recruit being awarded special recognition, and likewise for the best shot and section, the Passing Out Parade would have been very familiar to the old Light Brigade. Indeed it could almost have been drawn from Coote Manningham's 'Regulations for the Rifle Corps' (see pages 12 and 37). The parade was a rite of passage and an opportunity to celebrate with friends and family. The Green Jackets traditionally recruited from many different regions, inluding the Commonwealth, so parents, family and friends came from far and wide to see the event, which everyone would strive to ensure was a very special day. For spectators without Green Jacket connections this was often the first time they had seen a parade with the band and bugles playing at the traditional quick rifle pace. They would have recognised that their sons were joining something rather different.

With the formation of the Green Jacket Brigade in 1958, the end of National Service and the introduction of the three-year regular rifleman, the regiment adopted an innovative approach to recruiting, both at adult and junior level. Recruiting sergeants were in the main taken from among the younger element of the sergeants' mess, in order to be able to relate better to the young recruit. Then in the 1960s a seasoned soldier, Warrant Officer, Second Class (WO2) Byrne MM (Military Medal), proved the reverse of this policy and recruited many riflemen both adult and junior. He would make a point of taking potential recruits on visits to the depot, especially at parade times – where they could see the particular RGJ *esprit* to fullest advantage. The recruiting sergeants were instructed to accept only those at the top end of the 'pass mark' of the statutory British Army entrance exam for

Below far left: The Westgate, 50 yards from the front gate of Penisula Barracks, well known to generations of Riflemen trained at the Rifle Depot.

Below left: Colour Sergeant Pashby, the 'Shepherd of the North', responsible for the support and guidance of new recruits at the Infantry Training Centre, Catterick.

Left: Sir John Moore, at the home of the Light Division, Sir John Moore Barracks, Flowerdown, Winchester.

infantrymen, then administered at recruiting offices throughout the country, thereby ensuring quality was always maintained.

Green Jacket recruiting had its ups and downs. The widely spread recruiting base always demanded considerable resources, while the degree of official British Army support varied over the years. The British Army must be one of the few where infantry regiments largely recruit their own soldiers, yet this effort has been generally inadequately resourced from central MOD funds. Many infantry regiments – recognising the importance of full recruitment to survival – have had to dig deep into private regimental funds to support their own efforts. Throughout the life of the regiment, Royal Green Jackets' Colonels Commandants consistently made recruiting a top priority and the regiment's administrative trustees supported this financially. Captain Mark Robson, formerly head of the regimental recruiting effort, gives a flavour:

> With the trustees' support we chose to spend on items urgently required to promote the image that best reflected The Royal Green Jackets. To this end we purchased two marquees in regimental colours, television video combinations, deactivated weapons and other items. Almost at the same time the Army Recruiting Group issued us with two 4x4 Ranger vehicles and trailers. This enabled us to split the recruiting team and cover two areas at once. I was also able to create recruiting cells within the battalions headed by a SNCO [Senior NCO], where possible one with recruiting experience. Annually those involved in recruiting met to discuss the past year's activities and achievements and to plan the way ahead. Here we decided how best to recruit in our allocated areas and where to send small skirmishing teams on overt mini recruiting drives. These took place for some forty weeks of the year and were perhaps the mainstay of our proactive approach.

From all this it will be clear that, rather surprisingly, the British infantry still depends on a recruiting methodology, including the use of private funds, that would have been recognisable to Marlborough or Wellington.

For forty years The Royal Green Jackets recruited from the same traditional and historical recruiting grounds as their antecedent regiments: Oxfordshire and Buckinghamshire and the traditional recruiting grounds of The King's Royal Rifle Corps and The Rifle Brigade. The regiment was fortunate in that it recruited widely, and mainly from the larger cities. Riflemen tend to be 'city boys' rather than 'country boys' and therefore to be especially streetwise. A Royal Green Jackets' recruiting sergeant, each one specially selected by his battalion, was to be found in each of the recruiting offices in the regiment's official recruiting areas: Blackheath, Croydon, Ilford and Wembley in the London area, and Mansfield, Birmingham, Liverpool, Oxford and Milton Keynes in the regions. The best recruiter was determined to be

Above: Freedom Parade.

Below right: Captain Mark Robson, Regimental Recruiting Officer.

Bottom right: RGJ Recruiting stand.

The Royal Green Jackets

the 'satisfied rifleman', and over the years commanding officers selected with care those Senior NCOs (SNCO) and riflemen who would be good at 'selling the regiment' and be prepared to chaperone a would-be rifleman from initial meeting through to enlistment. A potential recruit could, of course, have joined the regiment from outside those areas specifically allocated, but at all times recruiting sergeants were briefed to select 'stayers' rather than 'goers'. A poor-quality man enlisted and then failing training represented an allocated vacancy wasted. The regiment sought quality in sufficient quantity, in that order.

The battalions played a significant role in the recruiting effort, mounting their own recruiting tours known as 'Keeping The Army in the Public Eye'. These deployments typically involved up to 100 riflemen and in a typical year might be mounted in Birmingham, Liverpool, London, Oxfordshire and Buckinghamshire. The Regiment also held regular mini recruiting drives in places such as main shopping areas, youth centres, leisure centres and job centres. Stands were erected in those schools prepared to have them (extraordinarily, not all schools are prepared to lend support to a military career), and supportive schools offered presentations with, if possible, 'I was there' stories from riflemen who were former pupils of that school. Support was also given to Army Cadet Force (ACF) training evenings and to the Territorial Army (TA) on drill nights. About ten weekend 'Look at Life' sessions were arranged for ACF and Combined Cadet Force (CCF) detachments each year, which became so popular that they were generally fully booked well in advance.

Over the years there were many 'carrots' to encourage potential recruits to enlist – one of them was the opportunity to learn to drive, but in latter years there were fewer eighteen-year olds who could not drive, which meant a more original approach had to be taken. Captain Robson amplifies this effort further:

Another way of diversifying our sales pitch was to offer day trips to either the Army Training Regiment at Winchester, or to one of the battalions. These were called 'Look at Life' or 'Personal Development Activities'. We even ran five-day Look at Life sessions in the battalions, which we called 'Sharpe's Encounter' or 'Sharpe's Revenge' after the colourful character in the 'Sharpe' series of films that so accurately captured the Green Jacket ethos.

The effort, then, that went into recruiting the Regiment's riflemen and that will continue with The Rifles, was and is enormous. Happily the British Army has now returned to recruiting junior soldiers, having previously abolished that entry level in a wave of earlier cost-cuttings, and learned a detrimental lesson for infantry recruiting the hard way. The junior entry was always a fruitful supplier of aspirant infantrymen. According to their academic ability, junior soldiers are now allocated either to the Army Foundation College at Harrogate, emulating the old 'Junior Leaders' course where so many an SNCO began his career, or to the Army Development Course – the Combat Infantryman Course (Junior) – at Bassingbourn, emulating the old 'Junior Soldiers' entry. After completing their respective training courses, followed by a shorter specialist infantry training course at Catterick, the two groups are divided equally amongst the battalions.

Once enlisted, the potential adult recruit could face a lengthy period of time between his first 'touch of green' and the day he entered basic training. It could take three to five months to get a recruit through the recruiting office, to sit the Basic Army Recruit Test and to attend a Recruit Selection Centre for final interviews and attestation. Infantry recruits now attend the Combat Infantryman's Course, recently extended from twenty-four to twenty-six weeks, at the Infantry Training Centre at Catterick. Every effort is made to pass out as many suitable recruits as possible, but standards are not lowered and wastage has been as high as 35 per cent. With the introduction of a Light Division Company at the Infantry Training Centre, a return to previous practice for which The Royal Green Jackets and The Light Infantry had long been pressing, wastage was reduced to as low as 14 per cent. With the lower wastage in training, directly attributable to the ability to train would-be riflemen as riflemen, using Light Division instructors to inculcate that special ethos from the start, the regiment led all others in the number of trained soldiers it passed out from Catterick. Similar results continue to this day. Having completed the Combat Infantryman's Course, the successful recruit takes his place in an operational rifle platoon in one of the battalions, possibly finding himself on operations round the world in a matter of days thereafter.

Above: Sean Bean playing Richard Sharpe, 95th Rifles as depicted by Bernard Cornwell.

Left: Rifleman, 5/60th Rifles, Peninsular War.

Inside the Regiment

Major Spencer Bull commanded the Light Division Company, now The Rifles Company, at the Infantry Training Centre, Catterick:

It is no mean feat to prepare our riflemen and all credit must go to the instructors that train them, in particular to the JNCOs. A thoroughly demanding and intensive job, it is significant to note that we do not consider our instructors to be Directing Staff. Rather, they are platoon commanders, platoon sergeants, and section commanders – leaders of riflemen. Role models for the future, they not only take great pride in what they do at the Infantry Training Centre, but they also really believe in it, realising that the future lies with the riflemen we train today. We foster and nurture our ethos from day one and prepare our riflemen to deploy directly on operations as part of the team. The onus on the regiment only to send quality instructors to train our riflemen remains the highest priority.

The Selection of Officers

The Green Jacket system was always noted for its selection of potential officers for entry into the Royal Military Academy (RMA) Sandhurst, which relied to a great extent on members of the regiment, serving and retired, regular or territorial, nominating suitable young candidates to RHQ for interview. The presence of a Green Jacket officer, supported by Green Jacket Senior NCO instructors, on the staff at Sandhurst was also important in the officer selection system, for it is here that those with potential who had not already come to the notice of the regiment could be talent-spotted. Many aspirant officers were picked whilst at school or university, where the regiment cherished its links with ex-Green Jacket academics, or friends of the regiment, and the staff at the university's Officer Training Corps (OTC).

The success of Green Jacket officer recruiting owed much to the highly effective system run originally from RHQ and subsequently from Headquarters The Light Division. Tony Palmer and John Tillett, both former regimental officers, got The Royal Green Jackets

Right: A Rifleman on exchange training at home in Jamaica.

Below left: Captain Jamie Gordon, Adjutant 3RGJ, Battle Group training BATUS (Canada), 1986.

Below right: Captain Willy (Bill) Shipton, Reconnaissance Platoon commander, 3RGJ, Battle Group training BATUS (Canada), 1986.

Right: The last Royal Green Jackets instructors at the Infantry Training Centre, Catterick, before the formation of The Rifles on 1 February 2007.

Above: The Regimental Colonel Commandant, Major General Nick Cottam, presents the Baker Rifle to the 'Best Rifleman', the Light Division Company, Infantry Training Centre, Catterick, September 2006.

53

off to a good start in the early days by establishing close personal relationships with potential candidates' parents, as well as headmasters and other key staff at schools throughout the country. There was nothing particularly subtle or clever about the system they adopted. It depended on having the right retired regimental officer in place – one prepared, and indeed financially able (given the retired officer's derisory pay), to devote his energies to the regiment. It demanded continuity over a long period of time, the right contacts, and the personality, energy and charm to cajole and persuade the right sort of young men to muster the courage to risk failing to get into the one of the most sought-after regiments in the British Army rather than perhaps taking an easier option.

Tim Hartley followed John Tillett. A retired Royal Green Jackets officer with a 43rd & 52nd pedigree, Tim was responsible for officer recruitment for the regiment for twenty years, from 1980 to 2000, building on an already flourishing system. Its strength was that it was based on common sense, on networking and on a series of personal friendships. It was often said that Tim's system really relied on 'chatting up the mothers'. The bedrock was the high regard in which the Green Jackets was generally held both within and outside the British Army. To use commercial terminology, The Royal Green Jackets, through its antecedent regiments, had established an enormously strong 'brand'. The 'product' was a glamorous one – the Green Jackets was a fighting regiment with a glorious history. It was a history very different to the heavy infantry regiments and the footguards – and all three of the former regiments brought something special to the party. The Green Jackets was an attractive target for young men who wanted to serve in a regiment that would treat them both as serious soldiers and part of the tight 'family of riflemen' from the moment they joined. Whilst it might have been a product with some social cachet, much more importantly it was well known that The Royal Green Jackets was a professional organisation that demanded particularly high standards from its officers. 'Cocktail party soldiers' were not encouraged to join; to become a rifleman required a real interest in soldiering and the character and personality that could readily relate to the riflemen whom it would be their privilege to command.

Once introduced to Regimental Headquarters, a potential officer was invited to Winchester for an initial interview. If this was successful he was encouraged to visit one of the battalions. He was also strongly encouraged to visit other regiments to get a first-hand feel for the differences. Each regiment has its own character, and it is important that people feel completely at home in the one they seek to join. These visits played a vital part in the selection of future Green Jacket officers – the aim was to expose the aspirant officer to the workings of the battalion, to meet as many riflemen as possible, to mix with the SNCOs in the sergeants' mess and to mingle with the officers. The best form of visit was one that combined field manoeuvres and some time in barracks, over the course of three or four days. In this way it became very obvious whether or not the potential officer was 'good Green Jacket material'.

There were really three 'tests' that had to be passed. Firstly, the aspirant had to show himself able to communicate easily and naturally with the riflemen; he had to show an obvious interest in them as individuals and be able quickly to earn their respect. Riflemen have never had much time for a haughty or arrogant leader. Secondly, he had to be judged by the members of the sergeants' mess, where there is always an abundance of experience, to be the sort of young man who would be able to lead riflemen. And only lastly, he had to be judged by the officers to be the sort that could add something to the officers' mess and get on easily with his fellows.

Once such a visit was completed RHQ received a report, initiated by the hosting platoon commander, amplified by the company commander and completed by the commanding officer. It recorded how the potential officer came across to those he met. It concluded with a definitive recommendation either that he should be invited to join the regiment, or be encouraged and assisted to go elsewhere. Ideally these visits were completed before entry to Sandhurst, but they were in any case arranged for all potential

Below: Green Jackets officer selection; 'Initial Interviews' by Bryn Parry, late RGJ.

officers whilst at Sandhurst. The final hurdle was an interview with the Regimental Colonel Commandant. This usually took place first over dinner at the former Royal Green Jackets London Club in Davies Street, London, and subsequently at Sandhurst. By the time the individual met the Regimental Colonel Commandant the regiment was pretty clear whether it wanted him or not. The Regimental Colonel Commandant would of course have been briefed as to how the aspirant had performed to date, both in contacts with the regiment and at Sandhurst. Final acceptance lay with him.

In 2004 Major David Day, who was then responsible for officer recruitment after taking over from his stepfather Tim Hartley, wrote:

> I am interviewing about 225 potential officers each year, and I have files on over 1,800. Currently forty-nine of the 750 or so officer cadets at Sandhurst have been interviewed by me and I have sent twenty-seven of them to visit a battalion. From these twenty-seven we are aiming to select about ten, which is roughly what we need per year. I try and make a point of helping and advising those that don't or won't make it into the regiment in selecting alternative regiments or corps so that they are not lost to the Army as a whole. Whilst we would like to think of ourselves very much as a true meritocracy, and family ties are no guarantee of acceptance, family ties still play an important part in stimulating an interest in the regiment. At the moment we have some fifteen sons of serving or former members of the regiment on the books. In addition to that there are also numerous grandsons, nephews, godchildren and the like.

Over many years, young men who were subsequently commissioned into regiments throughout the British Army remember their introduction to the British Army as riflemen. The Green Jackets always encouraged potential officers to serve for at least a few weeks as what used to be called 'O Type' riflemen before attending the Regular Commissions Board (RCB), but it was never a prerequisite if it did not suit an individual's timetable. What made Green Jacket 'O Type' training different was that recruit training was not altered in any way to accommodate potential officers. They were mixed together with recruits in the normal way, not separated as a squad labelled 'potential officer'. In this way they developed quickly whilst gaining a real understanding of what motivates a rifleman – knowledge that would stand them in good stead in whatever regiment they were eventually commissioned.

Above: 'Tim's Last Batch.' Tim Hartley with his last batch of Sandhurst Cadets on commissioning in The Royal Green Jackets, 11 August 2000. L–R: OCdt R. Brine, OCdt A.S. Hodson, Major D.C. Day, RGJ, OCdt I. Posgate, Major T.H. Emck, MBE RGJ, Major General A.R.D. Pringle, CB CBE, Major (retd) T.M. Hartley, MBE, Liz Vyvyan, Major General C.G.C. Vyvyan, CBE, Colour Sergeant C. Gibson, RGJ, OCdt E.C. Corry, OCdt J.C. Higgs, OCdt A.B. Horrocks.

Right: Keeping it in the family. Major David Day succeeded his step-father Major Tim Hartley in responsibility for officer recruitment.

Far right: 'No more parades today.'

Ceremonial, Band and Bugles

On formation of the regiment in 1966, each of the three regular battalions retained its own band. On operations the bandsmen had an operational role as stretcher-bearers or medics, and operated as such during the first Gulf War. In 1984 the three bands were reduced to two, the Normandy and Peninsula bands. In 1994 these two were disbanded and the Band of the Light Division was created in their place to serve both The Light Infantry and The Royal Green Jackets. In the same year the Waterloo Band of the 5th (Volunteer) Battalion, which had existed unofficially since 1988, and supported by regimental funds, was formally established as a Territorial Army (TA) band. From 1994 it was the only cap-badged Royal Green Jacket Band. Bandsmen are no longer cap-badged into the regiment, all regular bandsmen now being members of The Royal Corps of Music. The provision and training of buglers, each a fully trained combatant rifleman, remains the responsibility of the battalions. Buglers are provided on rotation to provide support to The Band of the Light Division.

Green Jacket Music and The Rifles Tradition

Green Jacket music was traditionally played at a quick tempo to conform to the pace of rifle regiments. At its core is to be found the silver bugle, which has a distinctive, much sharper tone than the brass bugle. The bugle holds a special place in Green Jacket tradition for historical reasons, and on parade the band was always led by the Bugle Major and the buglers. As a Rifle Brigade document published in 1882 stated:

Public Duties: Buckingham Palace

1st Battalion • 2nd Battalion • 3rd Battalion • Normandy Band
Peninsula Band • Waterloo Band • Light Division Band

Royal Green Jackets battalions periodically took their turn on London duties, mounting guard at the royal palaces and the Tower of London. The differing pace, words of command and drill movements always made for an interesting ceremony when combined, not without difficulty, with the slower and more deliberate ceremonial of the Guards Division. The honour of commanding the first-ever Royal Green Jackets Buckingham Palace guard fell to Major Gray Gilbert and the 1st Battalion in 1976. The occasion made a marked impression on him, as he recalls:

I suppose the only claim I have to uniqueness is that I was the first Royal Green Jacket officer to command a formed body of riflemen in the forecourt at Buckingham Palace, when A Company 1RGJ took up public duties in February 1976. This distinction in no way reflected on my personal standards of drill – always somewhat idiosyncratic – it was more the commanding officer, Edward Jones, recognising that A came before B in the alphabet.

Although affecting an air of sang froid, I have to confess that this was a fairly nerve-racking experience, not dissimilar to one's first parachute jump. For weeks we had been rehearsing on the wintry square at Dover under the watchful eye of Sergeant Major Wragg and Drill Sergeant Duggan of the Coldstream Guards. Expectations on the day were running high and the forecourt was jammed with Green Jacket glitterati who had come specially to witness this historic event. My fellow company commanders were also there in support, but no doubt privately relishing the prospect of imminent disaster. Rumour had it that lace curtains were seen twitching on the first floor. Japanese tourists were packed against the railings. It was quite obvious to me there was absolutely no room for error, notwithstanding Sergeant Major Wragg's helpful responses to my constant questions, 'Whatever is the regimental custom, Sir!'

My nerves had not been settled by the fact that the previous night I had the most appalling dream in which, having led A Company through the gates, I totally failed to give the words of command which would turn us left and bring us gracefully to a halt facing the dismounting guard. Instead we piled into the palace adjacent to the Keeper of the Privy Purse's office.

Come the day, we were required to change into our gladrags in cramped portakabins in Wellington Barracks. During the process the Coldstream sergeant major came to wish me luck, telling me 'The officer commanding the dismounting guard' – who happened to be Peter Mills, a friend from childhood days – 'has been away with The Guards' Independent Parachute Squadron for two years and knows nothing about proper soldiering, so you'll be just fine, sir!'.

After the changing of the guard was complete I led the St James's Palace contingent off down the Mall. This is a fair distance at rifle pace, especially if you are long in the leg like me. I rather wished I had invoked the 'whatever is the regimental custom, Sir!' and doubled the guard off to St James's. Doubling at 180 paces to the minute is somehow easier than marching at 140 paces to the minute for those over six-feet tall. As it was I was completely knackered when I eventually arrived in the Guard Room Officers' Mess to find all those Green Jacket generals tucking into the gin at my expense.

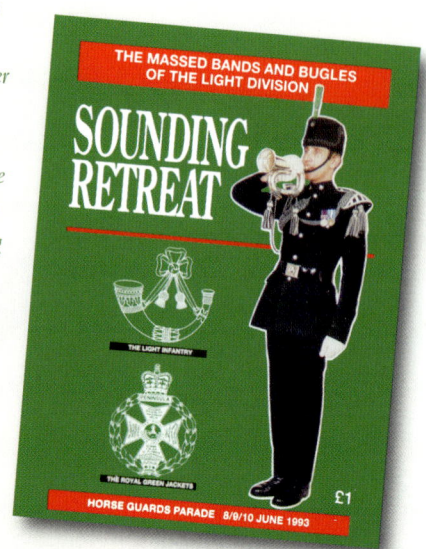

Major Kit Owen, commanding C Company, 1RGJ, 'Pacing the time', Buckingham Palace, February 1976.

It is the pride of the buglers of the regiment to sound their calls quicker than other regiments and when this speed is accompanied by accuracy the result is very good. But this speed must not be pushed too far. There is no surer way of spoiling the bugling of a battalion than to hustle buglers beyond their pace. A regiment whose badge is a bugle should be the master in the use of it.

And so it is to this day under The Rifles banner when an emphasis is still placed on learning the different calls, and the buglers, quite apart from their operational duties, play a significant role on every occasion the battalion is on parade or on show.

The Royal Green Jackets and The Light Infantry, as sister regiments of the Light Division, shared a common form of drill very different to that practised by the rest of the British Army. There was no slow march; in The Rifles tradition the quick march was 140 paces to the minute rather than the standard 110–120 paces, and the double march was 180 paces to the minute. The drill also required far fewer words of command, the historical origin of which was the need to move riflemen and light troops quickly around the battlefield. It also reflected the rifleman's role as a sharpshooter operating on the fringes of the battlefield and needing to change position often, moving from place to place with the least fuss and the utmost rapidity.

Whilst heavy infantry require three commands to move together to the right from the 'at ease' position, a rifleman requires only one. Moreover, a rifleman can do this to the order of the bugle,

Inside the Regiment

Right: 3RGJ, Allied Forces Day Parade, Berlin, 1975.

Below: Massed Bands and Bugles of the Light Division.

Below right: Bandmaster, WOI McTomney and Bugle Major Smith, 1RGJ, Celle, Germany, 1972.

accompanied by the beat of the bass drum in the band, and step off at quick or double pace, adopting the 'trail arms' position with his rifle as he does so. Green Jackets therefore have never failed to cause a stir amongst spectators at ceremonial occasions partly because spectators are more used to the traditional form of ceremonial epitomised and performed with such precision every year in London at the Queen's Birthday Parade, but also because of the quick pace, excitement and differences, accompanied by the very particular tone of silver bugles.

Riflemen and light infantrymen are used to moving to bugle-sounded orders. Every year the battalions held an annual Commanding Officer's Bugle Competition in which the buglers competed for the distinction that accompanied selection as the commanding officer's, adjutant's or regimental sergeant major's bugler. Buglers were always at the forefront of the action; the regiment's first operational fatality in Northern Ireland was the commanding officer's bugler, Corporal Bankier. The bugle remains an important symbol, and when regimental association members 'March Past' at the annual reunion true to tradition the only word of command given is 'Bugle Major Sound the Advance'. The rest is done on the bugle. It is said that the members wouldn't have it any other way.

57

The Royal Green Jackets

Ceremonial

Every regiment in the British Army has its own ceremonial forms and traditions, and The Royal Green Jackets was no exception. Recalling 3RGJs tour in Berlin in the early 1970s, Andrew Pringle:

The language of Green Jacket ceremonial is different – with many of the words of command unique to the Light Division. Bayonets are referred to as 'swords', rifle slings are 'fixed loose' so that they can be wrapped round the arm for a steady shot, and 'quick easy' drill movements are made with the minimum of shouting and foot-stamping. Beating Retreat, a popular ceremony deriving from the evening recall for those outside the camp to retire to quarters, is known as Sounding Retreat.

Green Jackets on parade with other regiments therefore become a drill sergeant's nightmare. Different pace, different words of command, always finishing in the 'at ease' position, no colours, no mascots … nothing conforms. The opportunities for such parades are rare, but tours in Berlin, where ceremonial played a large part of life for the Berlin Brigade, allowed Green Jacket battalions to demonstrate their distinctiveness and differences to the other battalions in the brigade. Both the 1st Battalion and the 3rd Battalion served in Berlin during the Cold War. Each year the Queen's Birthday Parade was held on the Maifeld in front of the Berlin Olympic Stadium. There were usually three infantry battalions from different regiments on parade. These parades effectively had to become two parades in one, because of the differences in drill and pace. As is normal the heavy infantry battalions would march past with colours flying and bayonets fixed, first in slow-time and then in quick-time. The riflemen would stand fast until their turn came. Once the heavy infantry had resumed their place, from the extreme left of the line, their traditional position, a simple alerting command 'Royal Green Jackets' would be given by the commanding officer, followed by 'Bugle Major Sound the Advance'. Then without more ado, without colours and with swords in scabbards, reacting solely to the bugle and the bass drum, the battalion would 'move to the right at the trail, quick march', marching past first by companies and then reforming as a single block doubling past en masse. Orders such as 'eyes right' and 'eyes front' would be sounded on the bugle. The battalion would halt, shoulder arms and face to the front, all on the double-beat of the bass drum. The citizens of Berlin had never seen anything like it and invariably rose to their feet and cheered. No rifleman, despite a traditional aversion to drill, could say he did not enjoy displaying his different ceremonial, nor even the hard work that had very necessarily preceded it.

Marksmanship

Speaking in 1979 at the Army Central Rifle Meeting, General Sir Edwin Bramall, then Chief of the General Staff, addressed his audience thus: 'Churchill once commented that, "nothing in life is so exhilarating as to be shot at without result". The terrorists in Northern Ireland must at times be a pretty exhilarated bunch, because, quite simply, the general standard of marksmanship in the army is not good enough. There are many reasons for this but I believe that one of the most important ones is that comparatively few officers take a real interest in this important part of the soldiers' training.'

There are several ways in which Green Jackets differentiated themselves over time. From the earliest days the regiment had always placed particular emphasis on marksmanship – it

Above left: 3RGJ Shooting Team, 1983.

Left: Rifleman Navickas, winner of the Baker Rifle and Tom Plunkett Trophy (Best Shot), 2RGJ, 2003.

Far left: Queen's Birthday Parade, Berlin, 1976, 3RGJ double-past.

Above: 2RGJ. Inter Company shooting competition, 2003.

Above right: The winning Methuen team, Bisley 1976, led by Major Greville Goodwyn.

was, after all, in the blood. The Queen's Medal for the best rifle shot in the British Army was first won by a rifleman, Sergeant T. Armstrong, DCM, 2nd Battalion, The Rifle Brigade, in 1878. Sergeant Armstrong had impeccable Royal Green Jacket credentials, having first enlisted in the 52nd Light Infantry before transferring to The Rifle Brigade in 1864. He won his DCM (Distinguished Conduct Medal) in the Ashanti Campaign (1873–4) when a small party he was commanding was ambushed and he killed two of the enemy with his rifle and one with his sword. A few years later Sergeant Instructor J.A. Wallingford of the School of Musketry, but lately The Rifle Brigade, was British Army champion six times, and, had not the medal been in abeyance, could have won it several times more. In the years up to and after the Second World War the Queen's Medal was won with astonishing regularity by individual riflemen (or, in four instances, lately riflemen – it does not seem wrong to include them). The 60th and The Rifle Brigade dominated the Major Unit Championship, known as The King's Royal Rifle Corps (KRRC) Cup. The cup was presented by the 60th Rifles in 1935 and on the twenty-two occasions it was competed for between 1935 and 1964 it was won by a battalion of the 60th or The Rifle Brigade – and once by the Rifle Depot – in all but five of those years.

In the time covered by this account, Corporal Alan Notley (3rd Battalion), Sergeant Roy Smith (2nd Battalion), Sergeant Vic Brooks (3rd Battalion) and Sergeant Mick Dorey (1st and 3rd Battalion) were all winners of the Queen's Medal – and with it the Army Rifle Association's Gold Jewel. Alan Notley was also runner-up (Silver Jewel) once, and recipient of the Bronze Jewel three times. He went on to join the British Biathlon Team and represented Britain in three Olympic Games, having also coached and captained the team. He was also British Ski Cross-Country Champion three times and British Biathlon Champion twice. Warrant Officer Second Class (WO2) Roy Smith went on to captain the 2nd Battalion's team and coached other British Army teams at international level. Sixteen years after his first success, and whilst serving as a WO2 with the 7th Battalion Light Infantry (TA), Vic Brooks won it a second time in the TA competition. Mick Dorey, by now a WO1, after many other shooting successes, once commented that all he had achieved in rifle competition was due to the coaching he had been given by Alan Notley, Vic Brooks and WO2 Phil Young (3rd Battalion), one of the best shots in the British Army.

Some officers were nearly as competent, but perhaps not quite as 'lucky'. Major, later Major General, Peter Welsh (runner-up for the Queen's Medal in 1962, third in 1963 and a six-time member of the Army VIII), was certainly the most outstanding of the officers and amongst the top four shots in the British Army. The fourth-best shot was Rifleman Burke, who was categorised as a 'Class B' shot, that is one with fewer than four years' service. Captain Hugh Babington-Smith had exceptional ability and was twice captain of a winning Light Division Methuen Team. Lieutenant Les Airey, then serving with the Regiment's 4th Battalion (TA) won the TA Queen's Medal in 1970 and had also been a very well-known shot during his regular service.

The Regiment performed very well in the Non-Central matches and other prizes several times, but conditions for the matches were changed in the 1970s when the competition was linked to the Annual Personal Weapons Test. After that the Regiment returned more modest results, albeit sometimes still very presentable ones. For three consecutive years, from 1996 to 1998, the 2nd Battalion won the King George Cup, now an infantry rifle team match; and in 1998 it also won the Sniper Cup.

During the decade 1994–2004 there were several notable successes in target rifle shooting. Major Charlie Sykes represented the Army in inter-services target rifle team matches eighteen times since first winning the Army Target Rifle Championships in 1990. He represented the Combined Services on three occasions and in 1995 was selected for a National Rifle Association team that toured the continent, beating both the French national team and a representative Europe team. Later, Major Sykes was joined by three other members of 2RGJ, including the commanding officer, Lieutenant Colonel Harry Emck, all subsequently vying for places in the Army Target Rifle Team.

Such results over the decades were reward for the encouragement and cultivation of marksmanship, but despite some very good performances Green Jacket domination in Army competition

The Royal Green Jackets

A Selection of Regimental Shooting Trophies

Winners of the Queen's Medal and ARA Gold Jewel 1963
Corporal A. Notley 3rd Green Jackets RB
1964 Sergeant R. Smith 2nd Green Jackets KRRC
1966 Corporal V.C. Brook 3RGJ
1976 Sergeant M. Dorey 3RGJ

Silver Jewel
1962 Major P.M. Welsh 2nd Green Jackets KRRC
1971 Warrant Officer Second Class (WO2) P.G. Young 3RGJ
1972 Sergeant A. Notley 2RGJ
1974 Corporal M. Frape 1RGJ

Bronze Jewel
1961 Corporal A. Notley 3rd Green Jackets RB
1962 Sergeant D. York 2nd Green Jackets KRRC
1963 Major P.M. Welsh 2nd Green Jackets KRRC
1966 Captain N.J.R. Sale 1RGJ
1973 Sergeant A. Notley 2RGJ
1974 Sergeant A. Notley 2RGJ
1985 Corporal G. Brewer 1RGJ
1987 Corporal D.G. McKenzie 2RGJ
1988 Corporal M. Frape 1RGJ

HM Queen's Medal (TA)
1970 Lieutenant L.E. Airey 4(v)RGJ
1971 Warrant Officer Second Class (WO2) V.C. Brooks (then 7LI)

Minor Units (RASC Cup)
1961–1965 Green Jackets Brigade Depot
1966 Rifle Depot
1969 Rifle Depot
1970 Rifle Depot
1977 Rifle Depot
1978 Rifle Depot
1987 Light Division Depot

Army Target Rifle Champion and Winner of the ARA Gold Jewel
1990 Second Lieutenant F.C. Sykes RGJ (Oxford University OTC)
1992 Lieutenant F.C. Sykes 3RGJ
1993 Lieutenant F.C. Sykes 2RGJ

Sergeant Mick Dorey, winner of the Queen's Medal, Bisley, 1976.

shooting declined in the 1970s. In the 1960s The Royal Green Jackets produced three Queen's Medal winners and the 2nd Battalion won the KRRC Cup three times, in 1961, 1963 and 1964; in the 1970s, there was one medallist, with none since, while the regiment failed to match its previous successes in the KRRC Cup. No regiment can expect to maintain high shooting standards without deeply committing itself to it, which the Green Jackets had traditionally done – but priorities and demands change over time. Perhaps because there was so much more to be done by the regular battalions, and the pace of life had become so relentless, whilst individual marksmanship remained key, the regiment came to place less emphasis on competition shooting as a team. There was no longer enough time available to set aside a sizeable squad to achieve the standard required. This became a source of some anxiety to the 'old and bold', brought up in another era and with different priorities and different pressures. Notwithstanding this, in the late 1980s the Bugle Platoon of 3RGJ won the coveted General Purpose Machine Gun (Sustained Fire) – GPMG (SF) – Match 83 competition four years running, the Territorial Army 4(v)RGJ regularly wiped the board at the London District Skill At Arms Meeting throughout the 1990s and 2RGJ won the Warrior Sword Competition for Warrior armoured fighting vehicle gunnery twice during their tour as an armoured infantry battalion in Germany in the late 1990s. More recently, in 2003 the snipers from 2RGJ represented the British Army in the United States where they beat all the US teams and those from five other nations. Bringing these reflections up to date, it is heartening therefore to record 2RGJ's successes with their Combat Shooting Team in 2006, their last year as Green Jackets. In the third season since their return to 'serious' competition shooting the team won four of the five competitions in the Brigade Skill at Arms Competition and won the Best Major Unit Cup. Going on to qualify in second place, out of thirty five teams, in the Division Skill at Arms Meeting, the team managed to exceed all expectations in the Army Central Skill at Arms Meeting at Bisley with six out of eight members of the team in the coveted top 100, finishing seventh out of twenty-nine teams in the Unit Skill at Arms Championship. The Sniper teams excelled themselves, taking 1st and 2nd places in the Short Range Cup, and the first three places in the Sniper Team Cup, classifying them as the best Sniper Platoon in the British Army. Their expertise would stand them in good stead when the Battalion deployed to Iraq the following year.

Expeditions and Adventurous Training

Green Jackets were always known for taking a healthy interest in the mounting of expeditions round the world, usually led by young officers, supported financially by the regimental trustees, and invariably involving all ranks. The annual regimental chronicles record a variety of such expeditions, such as Major Carol Gurney's ascent of Mount Kinabalu in Sabah with ten riflemen from 2RGJ in 1966, Captain Winwood's exploration of the Gibson Desert in Central Australia and Richard Willan and Peter Blaker's return from Penang to the UK overland in 1967, and the regiment's team entry in the London to Sydney Marathon in 1968. These are merely a few of the expeditions of one sort or another; there have been too many for all of them to be mentioned. However, four in particular deserved to be recalled in detail, beginning with the expedition marking the 175th anniversary of a legendary Light Brigade action.

The Royal Green Jackets enter a car in the London to Sydney Marathon, 1968, driven by Lieutenant George Yannaghas, 4(v)RGJ and Lieutenant Jack Dill, 1RGJ – replacing Jeremy Palmer Tomkinson after the latter had to fall out to play the skiing scenes in the James Bond film On Her Majesty's Secret Service.

Inside the Regiment

Far right: L–R: Rifleman West (2RGJ), Captain Blackmore (3RGJ), Captain Bowden (3RGJ), Bandsman Selley (1RGJ), departing Wadi Rumm for El Mudawwarah in the footsteps of T.E. Lawrence, 1985.

Below: Beside the tomb of Sir John Moore in Corunna, January 1984. Captain Blackmore (1RGJ) led an expedition comprising Lieutenant Bowden (3RGJ), Lance Corporal O'Meira (1RGJ), Rifleman Lee (3RGJ), Rifleman McNish (3RGJ), Rifleman Pearce (1RGJ), and Rifleman Hayward (3RGJ), retracing the exact route of the retreat, 1808–9.

On Christmas Eve 1808 elements of the rearguard of Sir John Moore's army were at a ruined monastery outside Sahagún in northwestern Spain. A French army of 200,000 men, led by Marshal Soult, was gradually encircling a depleted British force of 20,000, and threatening to cut it off from the Royal Navy and all lines of supply and communication. In deep snow with little rations, and many of the men barefooted, the rearguard from Sir John Moore's Light Brigade prepared to cover the army's withdrawal. One hundred and seventy-five years later, Christmas Day was again dawning as eight men in the uniforms of the 95th Rifles marched out of that same monastery's courtyard and down a frozen, muddied track to cover the 26 miles (42 km) to Mayorga. The leader of this meticulously researched and planned expedition was Captain Charles Blackmore of 3RGJ. It was to be the first leg of the re-enactment of the regiment's famous rearguard role in the 'Retreat to Corunna'. The expedition members from the 1st and 3rd Battalions of The Royal Green Jackets retraced the 310 mile (500 km) route marched by the rearguard (comprising battalions of the 43rd, 52nd and 95th) from Sahagún, northwest over the Galician Mountains to Corunna (La Coruña), following the same daily timings and distances of 175 years earlier. The modern-day party also endured similar inclement weather, tender feet, aching shoulders and food poisoning, as well as a crashed support vehicle – all of which lent suitably realistic friction. Upon their arrival in Corunna 'Los Reales Chaquetas Verdes', as the party was called by the Spanish press, placed a wreath on the grave of Sir John Moore, who had fallen in the closing stages of the final battle.

In February 1985 Captain Charles Blackmore was again planning, this time with Captain Jamie Bowden, Rifleman West and Bandsman Selley. The four were to take part in an expedition to Jordan to commemorate the fiftieth anniversary of the death of T.E. Lawrence (Lawrence of Arabia) by riding 1,000 miles (1,600 km) across the Jordanian desert on camels. The selected route retraced some of Lawrence's own journeys during the Arab Revolt, which he mapped and described in *Seven Pillars of Wisdom*. The expedition was the first of its kind to retrace Lawrence's travels using the same means and, as near as possible, under the same conditions, which of course injected the element of hardship into it. Camels went lame, contracted dysentery and grew stubborn, whilst people suffered from thirst, hunger and bitter temperatures and winds. After starting out in Wadi Rumm on 14 February 1985, the camel-borne expedition successfully reached Petra on 10 March, all the richer for the experience of having lived alongside the desert tribesmen who had accompanied them on the tough and fascinating journey. Less than a decade later, in 1993, Charles Blackmore, having left the British Army for the City of London, led the first crossing of the Taklamakan Desert in Chinese Central Asia. John Blashford-Snell, one of Britain's great explorers of the late twentieth century, described the accomplishment as 'one of the epic feats of exploration in the last fifty years'.

Also in 1985, but this time at the frozen south of the globe, there was another historic re-enactment with Captain Roger Morgan-Grenville successfully leading members of 1RGJ across South Georgia to retrace the epic journey conducted by Ernest Shackleton and his party in May 1916. In 2008 Lieutenant Colonel Henry

Right: Adventure Training.

61

Worsley will lead a centenary expedition comprising a small team of direct descendents to retrace and hopefully complete Shackleton's unsuccessful Nimrod Expedition, which got to within 97 miles (157 km) of the South Pole in 1908.

In 1988 regimental history again provided the inspiration for an expedition. On 14 January 1897 the Royal Indian Marine Ship *Warren Hastings* was transporting nearly a thousand officers and riflemen of the 1st Battalion The King's Royal Rifle Corps to India. At 2.20am the ship struck rocks off Réunion Island, a French colony lying 120 miles (190 km) southwest of Mauritius and 500 miles (800 km) east of Madagascar. The *Warren Hastings* was smashed to pieces and sank; there was little loss of life, but nearly all the battalion's silver went down. Ninety-one years later Captain Murray Whiteside, Lieutenant Charlie Drax and nine other Junior NCOs and riflemen drawn from across all three regular battalions planned a return to Réunion in order to end speculation as to the whereabouts of the wreck and the missing silver. Using the captain's report, archived at the India Office Library, a description of latitude and longitude and photographs taken by the salvage party in 1897, the expedition members began the painstaking preliminary work of pinpointing the wreck's location. After arriving on Réunion, local fishermen, some of the parents of whom had taken part in the original rescue, helped to find the wreck. Alas, despite newspaper headlines there was no sign of the silver, although eighty-six prized items were recovered, including a complete brass porthole with both the deadlight and glass intact. Most of these items are now visible in the *Warren Hastings* display at the regimental museum in Winchester.

There have been many other instances of adventurous young officers leading riflemen to all corners of the globe, climbing, trekking and diving. Captain Henry Worsley took five members of 3RGJ to the Annapurna base camp in the Himalayas, followed by the team's appearance representing Great Britain in the World Elephant Polo Championships in Nepal. Major Bob Churcher was a frequent visitor to the Himalayas, and Major Charlie Sykes was a member of the British Army's Millennium Climbing Expedition to ascend fourteen peaks in Nepal. Lieutenant Alastair Maxwell led a party of nine to Machu Picchu. A hallmark of the regiment, then, was not only to use expeditions to encourage leadership and to broaden the riflemen's awareness of the world, but also to bring parts of the regiment's colourful history to life.

Captain Murray Whiteside leads a diving expedition in 1988 to the wreck of RIMS Warren Hastings, Reunion Island. The other expedition members were Rifleman Millar, Lance Corporal Johnstone, Rifleman Burden, Lance Corporal Creek, Rifleman Verity, Sergeant Flooks, Lieutenant Drax, Sergeant Theobald, Rifleman Penfound and Rifleman Allen.

Far left: 3RGJ Elephant Polo Team, World Elephant Polo Championships, Tiger Tops, Nepal, 1986. L–R: Rfn Wilson, Rfn Rising, Lance Cpl Barnett, Capt Worsley and WO2 McWilliams.

Inside the Regiment

The regiment encouraged parachuting and for many years it sponsored its own successful free-fall team, which in 1970 set the European record for star jumping.

Members of the Free Fall Parachute Display Team, 1968, Rifleman Friel, Rifleman Beard, Lieutenant Freeman, Corporal Crawley, Rifleman Harrison and Corporal Waterman.

Opposite top: RGJ Free Fall Display Team, eight man star, European Record, October 1970.

following year, the 1st Battalion came fourth in the combined Army results. Rifleman Richard Wiecik was picked for the Army team. Rifleman 'Scotty' Barber, practically a novice at the start of the season, promised great things, with much of the credit going to the team trainer, Ingie Christopherson, a former member of the British Ladies' team.

By the start of its third season in 1976 the team, now incorporated into 3RGJ, had a realistic prospect of winning the Army Alpine Championships. As it turned out, a couple of mistakes in the team slalom pushed the team into second place overall, behind 94 Locating Regiment, Royal Artillery. The team none the less took as many cups as the champions, with 3RGJ worthy winners in the giant slalom and downhill events, Richard Wiecek becoming Army Downhill Champion. Lance Corporal Jones, Riflemen Wiecek and Barber were all picked for the British Army squad and at the following Inter-Services Meeting Rifleman Wiecek once again won the downhill, by the astounding margin of four seconds.

Wiecek went on to become overall Inter-Services Champion, with Lance Corporal Jones the runner-up. More excellent results were produced in 1977, including a decisive win in the team downhill event, but again the championship eluded The Royal Green Jackets. The next year, 1978, was to be the one in which the *Daily Telegraph* headline declared, 'Green Jackets Reign Supreme'. Having won the UK Land Forces Championships, the team moved on to the Army Championships at Ischgl in Austria. The individual giant slalom was won by Rifleman Barber, who beat nearly a

Alpine and Nordic Skiing

The regiment was fortunate to have its own adventure training centre in Bavaria, where many riflemen were introduced to activities ranging from hang gliding to abseiling, canoeing to white-water rafting, and sailing to rock climbing. The existence of this centre enabled the regiment to put considerable emphasis on winter sports.

Green Jackets have excelled over the years at skiing, not least thanks to opportunities offered by tours in Cold War Germany. Alpine sporting successes were given particular impetus by two commanding officers, Lieutenant Colonel (later General) Bob Pascoe (1RGJ) and Lieutenant Colonel (later Brigadier) Christopher Dunphie (3RGJ). Both provided great support to the regimental ski hut at Steibis, Bavaria, and to Alpine racing.

Racing first got under way when the 1st Battalion team was formed in 1974. Most of the team members learned to ski at Steibis (see below), went on to become ski instructors there and passed on their skills – and a taste for racing – to large numbers of riflemen over the years. The British Army ski meeting in 1974 produced a credible fifth for the regiment in the downhill team event. The

Right: The Army Champion, Rifleman Barber in the Team Slalom, 1978.

63

The Royal Green Jackets

3RGJ Racing Team, 1975. L–R: Major Williamson, Rifleman Wiecek, Lance Corporal Monan, Captain Dixon, Rifleman Barber and Second Lieutenant Russell-Scarr.

hundred other competitors; Lance Corporal Jones was fourth, and Lance Corporals Butler and Ibbotson skiied well. In the team giant slalom the Green Jackets' team emerged as clear winners by seven seconds over 94 Locating Regiment, Royal Artillery. In the individual slalom, the team held the first four positions after the first run. After the second run the final results were Barber first, Jones third, Butler sixth and Ibbotson ninth.

The downhill was to be a difficult race. Just one run over the course 1½ miles (2.5 km) would decide both the team and individual results. Rifleman Barber, having already won two of the three individual titles, knew that a good result would make him overall Army Individual Champion. He decided, however, that the team result was more important and contented himself with skiing safely into sixth place. With Jones fifth and Butler tenth, the Green Jackets emerged as team winners by nearly eight seconds. With the race run in almost white-out conditions, courage and determination were essential. That evening it was announced that Barber's result had been sufficient for him to become the Army Individual Champion, the first rifleman since Jeremy Palmer-Tomkinson to achieve this honour. Only one first prize of the eight had eluded the team – the individual downhill. All four team members ended the meeting in the top ten places in the Alpine combination, with Barber first and Jones third. At the Inter-Services Meeting, Barber, Jones and Butler went on to win their British Army colours and once again Barber won the slalom, while Jones was individual runner-up.

With the 3rd Battalion posted to Celle, Germany, in the 1980s there were ample opportunities for skiing. One member of the 1976 team, Ibbotson, who was now a sergeant, was still in the battalion. He was joined by Rifleman Dobson, recently recruited into the regiment from the British Alpine Squad. Drawing on this depth of experience, the team, which included Captain Henry Worsley and Corporal Tandy, went on to win the 1st Armoured Division Championships, and subsequently became the Army's slalom champions. Rifleman Dobson represented the Army and Combined Services, and no one came close to beating him.

The Steibis ski-hut in Bavaria, first discovered by the 2nd Battalion in 1968, is actually located at Alpe Eibele. It took its name from the village of Steibis-Im-Allgau 3 miles (5 km) away, from which it was gloriously isolated along a narrow, snow-covered track. The hut lacked central heating, mains electricity and a reliable water supply, but it was the envy of the rest of the British Army. With a staff of fifteen, including seven ski instructors, the regiment could host 'Exercise Snow Queen' courses for up to fifty-five riflemen at a time. The sight of these skiing novices hurling themselves fearlessly down the slopes, immediately after being issued with ill-fitting

3RGJ Nordic Ski Team, 1988, led by Patrick Sanders, at the start of the Patrol Race.

clothing and somewhat battered equipment, was the cause of some amazement to the locals. But by the end of the first day champions-in-the-making were emerging. By 1974, with the support of the Berlin Brigade with which the regiment had formed a partnership for the manning and support of the ski-hut, the hut had changed forever, with central heating, a sports shop, fresh food in abundance, and a bar. Right behind the hut was the gondolbahn to lift the riflemen to the summit of the Hochgrat 6,000 feet (1,800 m), which during the week they had virtually to themselves.

The ski instructors spent considerable time at Steibis, teaching both Alpine and Nordic cross-country skiing (combined with snowcraft) in the winter, and adventurous training pursuits such as rock climbing, mountain trekking, abseiling, canoeing and sailing in the summer. Some eventually left the British Army, married local girls and settled in the village. Scotty Barber can be found there to this day. No record of Steibis is complete without mention of Georg, who drove the snowplough and cleared the snow from the track to keep the link with the village open. A great local character and heavy drinker, he habitually slept things off in his snowplough wearing only a shirt and trousers during some of the coldest nights, all without suffering any ill effects.

In the 1980s the regiment placed more emphasis on Nordic skiing, competing regularly in both the infantry and the divisional Nordic skiing championships. In the early 1990s 2RGJ dominated the infantry cross-country skiing championships, including biathlon, inspired by Captain Tony Abell on his return from two years as the manager of the Great Britain Biathlon Team. Tony Abell, Patrick Sanders and Tim Adams led a succession of successful teams, which collected numerous trophies along the way. Particular emphasis was placed, naturally, on the annual Infantry Patrol Race, for which team training usually took place in Norway at the beginning each season.

Far right: Commanding Officer 3RGJ shows how it's done!

Below: RGJ Cresta Team 1988 and the associated 'Swift and Bold' Handicap, Royal Green Jackets Regimental Race timesheet.

The Cresta Run

In 1980 William Shipton joined the 3rd Battalion as a young officer. An experienced rider of the famous Cresta Run in St Moritz, over the following six years William Shipton introduced the regiment to the St Moritz Tobogganing Club and the thrills, spills and all-round adrenaline rush of the Cresta. He captained the victorious British Army team throughout the 1980s (Captain Henry Worsley was a fellow team member), and at one time he held the record as the fastest British rider on the run. Participation remained at a healthy level, with riflemen of all ranks riding the run most years, assisted to do so each winter through the generosity of the regimental trustees. In 2002 and 2003 corporals Reeve, Bowerman and Armon-Jones represented the regiment, with Captain Will Scrase-Dickins gaining a place in the British Army team and Corporal Reeve a place in the British Army squad. In 2004 the regiment won the Inter-Regimental Cup; Captain Will Scrase-Dickins, on leave from Iraq, and Corporal Armon-Jones gained places in the victorious British Army team and won the Prince Philip Trophy, the inter-services Cresta Run competition held annually between the three Services. Corporal Armon-Jones is believed to be the first non-commissioned rider ever to represent the British Army in this event, which is a fitting tribute to the support given by the trustees. The Regiment has sent parties of riders to the Cresta Run in successive years, supplying a number of members of the Army Team and building a solid foundation for the regimental team which has now won the coveted Inter-Regimental Championships and the 17th/21st Lancers Cup four times in the last five years. In their final season as Green Jackets the regimental team was determined to win the cup back from the Irish Guards, to whom they had inadvertently lost it in 2006, and return it to its traditional position in the Officers' Mess of the 2nd Battalion Royal Green Jackets. This they duly did. In 2008 the Regiment will return to the Cresta Run as The Rifles, and the new Regiment will continue to provide the opportunity to any who care to experience the thrills and spills of that exciting sport.

The Royal Green Jackets

Boxing

Boxing was encouraged at all levels and played an important part in battalion life. Novices' boxing competitions were held annually and the inter-company bouts were invariably displays of guts mixed with differing degrees of skill. Seen as the route into selection for the battalion boxing squad, novices' boxing was where the talent was first discovered and then nurtured. Boxing will have occupied the mind of every rifleman at one time or another, and many recruits will remember going through their two minutes in the ring, designed to test their character, stamina and the will to succeed. Very few failed to give of their best.

For periods in the 1960s and 1970s the regiment excelled in the ring. Whilst the officers encouraged and took part in boxing at various levels, only occasionally were they selected for a battalion team. In Green Jacket Brigade days, the 3rd Battalion had three officers – Gerald Carter, Paul Greenwood and Mike Carleton-Smith – who were very good boxers, and they were to be followed later in The Royal Green Jackets by Graham McKinley, Tim Corry and Crispin Beattie, amongst others. In 1958 Gerald Carter recruited several National Servicemen who were first-class amateur boxers from London boxing clubs. These formed the nucleus of the regiment's early boxing teams and they helped to promote the name of the regiment in its traditional recruiting areas in a way that appealed to potential recruits. During that era the regiment was fortunate to have a number of outstanding sportsmen in its ranks.

In the 1968–9 season the 3rd Battalion won the British Army's inter-unit team championships, having been losing finalists on several occasions in previous years. The battalion had to fight its way through the divisional and BAOR (British Army of the Rhine) finals before taking on the winners of the United Kingdom competition in the grand final. At each stage the 3rd Battalion managed to beat the previous year's winners, before they finally faced the reigning champions, The King's Regiment, in the Army Finals and emerged victorious. The King's Regiment was a great boxing regiment – sadly, it lost a number of that team a few years later to an IRA ambush in West Belfast.

The architect of this Green Jacket boxing success, and an inspiration for many years to come, was CSMI McCabe of the Army Physical Training Corps. Amongst the names that went down in Green Jacket boxing history from those halcyon days are riflemen Case, Ewin (later to become ABA Light Welterweight runner-up), Jackson, Donnison, Williams, Cheetham, Netzler and Short, and corporals Brennan, Crombie, D'Cruze, Hawkins, Matthews (who narrowly avoided being shot in Belfast and went on to become an England boxer), Corporal Tracey and many others.

Both the 1st and 2nd battalions also excelled in the ring. In the 1972 season the 1st Battalion team won the BAOR finals in a magnificent six bouts-to-five result against the hugely strong 10 Regiment Royal Corps of Transport, before going on to lose in the finals at Aldershot in a seven-to-four, but closely fought, contest against the regiment's old rivals, The King's Regiment. This time the IRA had cost the 1st Battalion its heavyweight, Lance Corporal Munro, who had sustained a badly cut arm in a bombing at Aldershot. As if to prove that 1969 had not been a one-off, the 1st Battalion won the Army Championship again for the regiment in 1976, beating 10 Regiment Royal Corps of Transport by seven bouts to four.

Top left: 3RGJ, Army Boxing Champions, 1972.

Top: 2RGJ Novices Boxing Competition, 2003.

Above left: 3RGJ Boxing Team 1968, trained by CSMI McCabe, Army Physical Training Corps.

Above: Sergeant Brian Ewin winning the BAOR light welterweight title, 1976.

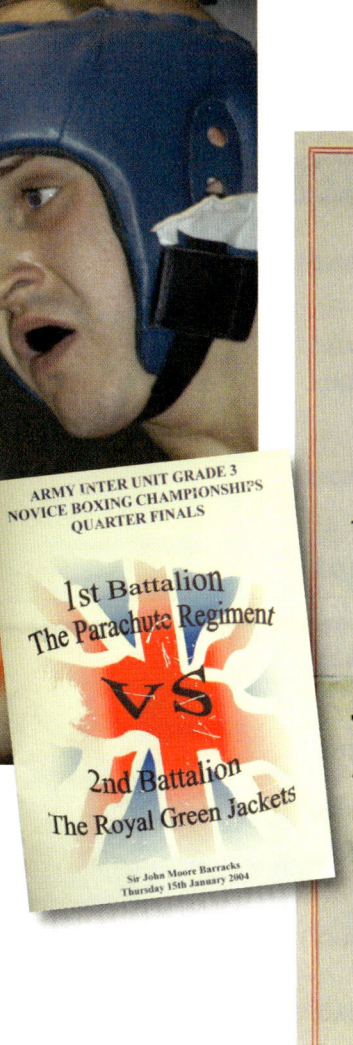

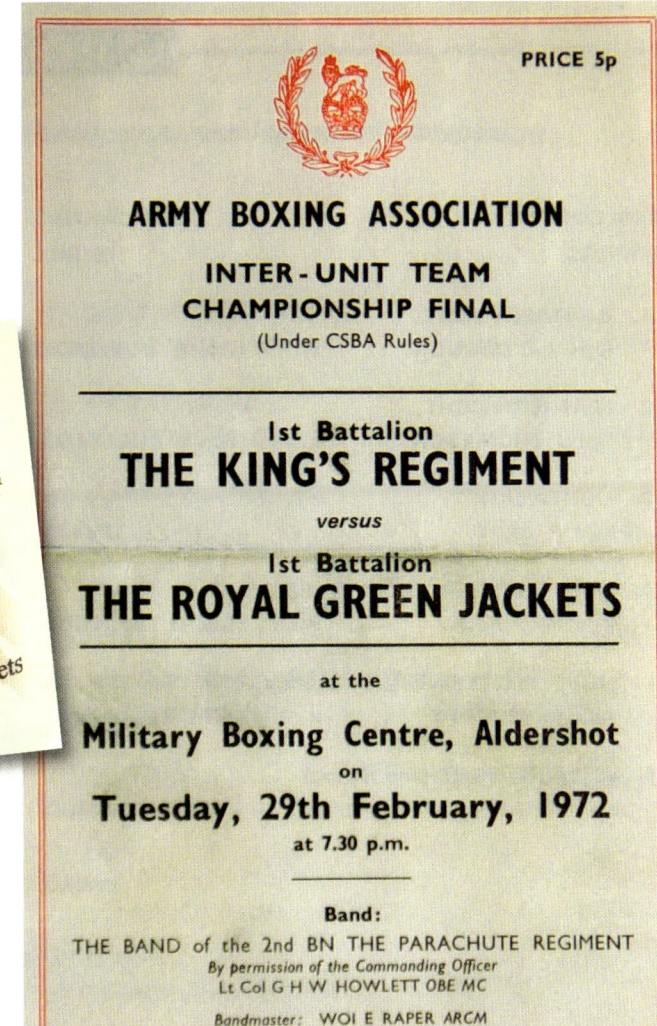

Inside the Regiment

All these successes owed much to the contribution and participation of all the squad members over many years; whether or not they finally wore the regimental strip in the ring on the night, they had supported Royal Green Jackets' boxing. With the 3rd Battalion and then the 1st Battalion stationed in Celle, near Hanover, the town effectively became The Royal Green Jackets' home in Germany. Members of the regimental boxing squad fought regularly for the civilian Celle Boxing Club, and the Regiment became well known on the German boxing circuit.

Such was the strength of the battalion teams in the 1960s and 1970s that many Green Jacket boxers were called up to the British Army squad. In the 1972–3 season Riflemen Williams and Cheetham, Lance Corporal Donnison and Corporal Mathews all fought in the Army Championships, the latter going on to win the Combined Services Boxing Association Light Heavyweight title and continuing as far as the quarter-finals of the ABA Championships. Rifleman Cheetham was awarded his Army Colours, and Corporal Mathews was selected to box for England against France. In recent years perhaps the most successful Green Jacket boxer has been Lance Corporal Tony Velinor, who represented both the Army and the Combined Services and made various international appearances for England, including selection for the Commonwealth Games and the British Olympic squad.

In 1999 the 1st Battalion, based at Belfast's Palace Barracks, were finalists in the Northern Ireland Boxing Competition. Being successful in any team sport requires a certain stability and continuity of manpower. Back-to-back six-month tours in the Balkans, as the 2nd Battalion experienced over the three years from 1996 to 1998, or the demands of operations in a volatile Northern Ireland, as experienced by the 1st Battalion, made building a team that could excel in the boxing ring a difficult thing. With the transfer of the 2nd Battalion to Warminster came the chance once again to focus on boxing. In their first year back in the competition for some time, the battalion reached the 2003 finals of the Major Units Novices Boxing Competition, with two members of the squad going on to reach the finals of the Army Individual Boxing Competition, and Corporal Summers, a skilful middleweight, being selected for the Army Boxing Team.

In the 2004 season the 2nd Battalion fought through successive rounds in the Army Major Units Novices Boxing Competition to reach the final, beating 2 Signal Regiment, 1st Battalion The Parachute Regiment, and The Green Howards, the reigning champions, on the way. In the final they defeated 3rd Battalion The Parachute Regiment to become the champions.

The Royal Green Jackets London Club

The original Territorial Army drill hall in Davies Street was let to the Queen Victoria Rifles by the present Duke of Westminster's grandfather more than a century ago for a peppercorn rent. The Royal Green Jackets enjoyed a close relationship with the present Duke of Westminster, who is a dedicated TA soldier himself. Davies Street became the headquarters of the 4th Battalion The Royal Green Jackets and and the site of the drill hall and the Officers' Mess. The Officers' Mess hosted The Royal Green Jackets London Club. Following reductions in the Territorial Army, Davies Street continued as the home of F (The Royal Green Jackets) Company of The London Regiment and of the NW Middlesex Cadet Contingent.

However, if any further evidence is needed that Royal Green Jackets regimental life was always extraordinarily well blessed with unusual facilities and assets, The Royal Green Jackets London Club

Below: The Royal Green Jackets London Club. Sergeant Fawbert and Rifleman Brooker.

67

Senior Riflemen's Dinner, October 1992, Winchester (with a combined 942 years service in the Regiment). Each year a dinner is held for the 'Senior Riflemen' who entered service as Riflemen and were subsequently commissioned.

provided it. Situated at 56 Davies Street, close to Bond Street tube station, the club developed into more than the luncheon club it started out as. It was very much The Royal Green Jackets 'home' in London. Although an officers' club, the premises continue to be used regularly by associations of the regiment, past and present. An affiliation with the Lansdowne Club permits members to stay overnight at the Lansdowne, and its affiliation with Buck's Club allows members the privilege of evening dining there all year round – and that of lunching there when Davies Street is closed. Add to this the 'business breakfasts' at Davies Street, racing at Goodwood at the Celer Et Audax Stakes, clay pigeon shoots, band concerts, lectures, daily lunches at Davies Street, and the use of the club for private and corporate occasions, and it is clear that the regiment is fortunate to have had such an asset, whose traditions will continue under The Rifles.

Affiliated and Allied Regiments and Ships

Since the siege of Delhi in 1857, when The Sirmoor Battalion of the Goorkhas fought alongside the 60th Rifles, the regiment has maintained a friendship with 2nd King Edward VII's Own Goorkha Rifles (The Sirmoor Rifles). This friendship has been perpetuated in many different ways. Following the partition of India in 1947 when 2nd Goorkha Rifles became a regiment of the British Army an affiliation with the Kings Royal Rifle Corps was approved. The Rifle Brigade maintained an affiliation with 6th Queen Elizabeth's Own Gurkha Rifles. Both these affiliations were subsumed within the affiliations of The Royal Green Jackets, and continued on the formation of The Royal Gurkha Rifles.

As a Rifle Regiment the Gurkhas had many similar traditions to The Royal Green Jackets, in particular the same rifle drill, similar uniforms and an emphasis on rapid movement to orders on the bugle. Whenever Green Jacket and Gurkha battalions or bands have been able to combine on the parade ground, the result has always been striking and different, as recently displayed at a joint Green Jacket/Gurkha celebration of the 150th Anniversary of Delhi Day held at the Royal Military Academy Sandhurst, where the massed bands and bugles of the Gurkha Rifles and The Rifles sounded retreat.

The regiment also maintained historical alliances with regiments in Australia, Canada, New Zealand, Pakistan and South Africa. An officer exchange programme between the regiment and Princess Patricia's Canadian Light Infantry continued successfully for many years. Several officers from the Sydney University Regiment served in 4(v)RGJ whilst working in London.

Bottom far left: 150th anniversary of Delhi Day, 2007 flyer.

Bottom left: Menu card from the Centenary Regimental Dinner of the Sydney University Regiment.

Alliances

Australia
Western Australia University Regiment
Sydney University Regiment
Melbourne University Regiment

Canada
The British Columbia Regiment (Duke of Connaught's Own)
Princess Patricia's Canadian Light Infantry
The Queen's Own Rifles of Canada
The Brockville Rifles
The Royal Winnipeg Rifles
The Royal Regina Rifles

New Zealand
1st Battalion, Royal New Zealand Infantry Regiment
6th Battalion (Hauraki), Royal New Zealand Infantry Regiment

Pakistan
2nd Battalion The Frontier Force Regiment (Guides)

South Africa
The Durban Light Infantry
The Buffalo Volunteer Rifles

CIVIC PRIVILEGES

The regiment is honoured to have been granted the freedom of a number of cities with which it has close connections.

Aylesbury
Banbury
Bicester
High Wycombe
Milton Keynes
City of Oxford
City of Westminster
City of Winchester

Top far right: HMS Somerset, *Ceremonial Sunset, Belfast, June 2000.*

Top right: HMS Somerset, *commanded by Commander Keith Blount, 2002.*

Right: Sharpshooters from the Corps of Riflemen, at Copenhagen, 2 April 1801.

Bottom: Detail from Royal Green Jackets cap-badge displayed the battle honour 'Copenhagen, 2nd April, 1801', the start of a long association with the Royal Navy, continued to this day.

Bonds of Friendship: The Chestnut Troop

Ever since the 43rd Light Infantry, 52nd Light Infantry and the 95th Rifles fought together in Sir John Moore's Light Brigade during the Peninsular War, a special relationship was maintained between these regiments and with their supporting horse artillery battery, The Chestnut Troop, Royal Horse Artillery. This bond of friendship was subsumed by The Royal Green Jackets. A Chestnut Troop officer would invariably be asked to The Royal Green Jackets regimental dinner, and the Chestnut Troop would ask a Royal Green Jacket officer to the 1st Royal Horse Artillery dinner. Occasionally a Green Jacket battalion might be lucky to find itself supported by the Chestnut Troop as their battle group direct support battery. The 3rd Battalion The Royal Green Jackets was fortunate to find itself in this position whilst serving in Celle 1982–7 when every opportunity was taken to rekindle old friendships. With 2RGJ, now 4 RIFLES, in the same brigade as the Chestnut Troop, this enduring friendship is set to continue.

Royal Navy: HMS *Somerset*

The regiment has treasured a link with the Royal Navy that dates back to 1801, when The Rifle Corps acted as Nelson's sharpshooters at Copenhagen and both the 43rd and the 52nd were part of the landing assault force. The battle honour 'Copenhagen' on the cap-badge, together with the Naval Crown, commemorates the event. Therefore it is natural that a special 'bond of friendship' was maintained with a Royal Navy ship. For several years, from when it was commissioned in 1977 until decommissioned in 1994, the regiment enjoyed a bond with HMS *Alacrity*, a Type 21 Frigate. It was HMS *Alacrity* that 'proved' the Falkland Sound in May 1982 during the Falklands War by running the gauntlet. News of this captured the imagination of the riflemen at Fulham House, home of B Company 4(v)RGJ, many of whom had spent time with the ship's company. A whip-round was quickly arranged and a generous cheque was sent from the company, together with the message, 'give them one from us and return safely'. This they duly did.

That 'bond of friendship' passed in 1996 to HMS *Somerset*, a Type 23 Frigate. Members of the ship's company spent time with the battalions or at the Rifle Depot, exchanges were arranged and the regiment attached officers, riflemen and buglers to HMS *Somerset* on numerous occasions, including on active operations in the Adriatic during the Kosovo campaign in 1999 when, at action-stations, two riflemen could be found manning the machine guns either side of the bridge. HMS *Somerset* entered her first Refit Period in 2006 after ten years of operational service and will rejoin the Fleet in July 2007 to commence a new operational programme.

Conclusion

No fighting regiment can operate without a 'backbone'. This chapter has attempted to describe what constituted that 'backbone' for The Royal Green Jackets. Regiments are nothing less than extended families: each has a character and a way of doing things that has evolved over the years, and often over hundreds of years. The Royal Green Jackets had its own way of doing things – it had taken the best from its antecedent regiments into a family of riflemen with a forward-looking ethos and a flexible organisation that was ideally suited for the challenges which face the British Army of the late twentieth and early twenty-first centuries.

The Green Jackets' Contribution to the Wider Army

The ethos of The Royal Green Jackets provided an alternative way of thinking – one could almost say an antidote to convention, which may, in part, have been why the regiment attracted such a large number of capable officers. When it came to obtaining command of a regular battalion there were frequently insufficient vacancies within the regiment for all those whom the selection board wished to appoint, and therefore many Green Jacket officers have been privileged to command other regiments. But it was at the more senior levels of command that the contribution of Green Jackets to the wider British Army was most significant. In 1984 the following senior Green Jackets were all serving officers at the rank of major general or above (pictured below at John Tillett's retirement lunch):

Field Marshal Sir Roland Gibbs, GCB, CBE, DSO, MC

Field Marshal Sir Edwin Bramall, GCB, OBE, MC –
Chief of the Defence Staff

General Sir Frank Kitson, CBE, KCB, MC, ADC Gen –
C-in-C UKLF

General Sir Roland Guy, KCB, CBE, DSO, ADC Gen –
Adjutant General

Lieutenant General Sir James Glover, KCB, MBE –
C-in-C UKLF (designate)

Lieutenant General Sir David Mostyn, KCB, CBE –
Military Secretary

Major General R.A. Pascoe, MBE –
Chief of Staff HQ UKLF

Major General M.E. Carleton-Smith, CBE –
Defence Adviser, Australia

Major General P.M. Welsh, OBE, MC –
President Regular Commissions Board

Major General D.J. Ramsbotham, CBE, MA –
Commander 3rd Armoured Division

Major General C.E.W. Jones –
Director General Territorial Army

Major General G.D. Johnson, OBE, MC –
Assistant Chief of the Defence Staff (NATO and UK)

This snapshot in time comprises thirty-six stars. It does not include the three brigadiers then serving, making a total of thirty-nine stars serving at the same time in one regiment.

Of those listed, both the lieutenant generals and four of the major generals went on to become full generals – a generation unique in the history of The Royal Green Jackets. A list of Green Jackets holding senior appointments in the army since 1966 together with a list of those officers appointed to command divisions and brigades is included on page 72, the most sought-after appointments in the British Army. This represents an extraordinary achievement for one regiment and it goes some way to explaining why it was said that 'the Green Jackets run the Army', and why the regiment, with its distinctive uniform and black buttons, was widely known as 'The Black Mafia'.

The Green Jackets' Contribution to the Wider Army

Right: Green Jackets at PJHQ. Major Mark Mangham, Lieutenant Colonel Jamie Gordon, Major General Andrew Pringle, Lieutenant Colonel Johnny Schute, Lieutenant Colonel Neil Baverstock and Major Tom Copinger-Symes.

In the early 1990s, when the British Army was reduced in size and The Royal Green Jackets was stripped of a battalion (from three to two), such a degree of regimental domination became far more difficult to sustain. Yet, in 2007 when merged into the newly formed regiment The Rifles, there was still a considerable pool of talent in The Royal Green Jackets in contention for places at the highest levels of the Army.

At the end of the twentieth century the regiment was a significant contributor to the forward-thinking Permanent Joint Headquarters (PJHQ). Created in 1996 to improve the UK's ability to conduct joint military operations in the uncertain environment of the post-Cold War world, PJHQ has since cut its teeth directing operations all round the world. Its architect and first commander was Lieutenant General Sir Christopher Wallace, and since its inception

Lunch at 56 Davies Street, 5 June 1996 (from far right, anti-clockwise): Field Marshal Sir Roland Gibbs, Field Marshal the Lord Bramall of Bushfield, General Sir Thomas Pearson, General Sir Frank Kitson, General Sir James Glover, General Sir David Ramsbotham, General Sir Garry Johnson, General Sir Edward Jones, General Sir Robert Pascoe, General Sir David Mostyn, General Sir Roland Guy, General Sir Richard Worsley, General Sir Antony Read and General Sir John Mogg.

71

The Royal Green Jackets

Field Marshals and General Officers of The Royal Green Jackets 1966–2007
SHOWING YEAR OF FIRST APPOINTMENT AND HIGHEST RANK ACHIEVED

1966	Field Marshal Sir Francis Festing
	General Sir Gerald Lathbury
	General Sir John Mogg
	General Sir Anthony Read
	Major General PGF Young
	Major General TH Acton
	General Sir Thomas Pearson
	Lieutenant General Sir Richard Fyffe
	Major General DL Darling
	Major General EAW Williams
1969	Field Marshal Sir Roland Gibbs
1970	Lieutenant General Sir James Wilson
1971	Lieutenant General Sir David House
	Field Marshal Sir Edwin Bramall
1972	Major General HDG Butler
	General Sir Richard Worsley
1973	Lieutenant General Sir Peter Hudson
1974	Major General GH Mills
1975	Major General DB Alexander-Sinclair
1976	General Sir Frank Kitson
1977	General Sir David Mostyn
1978	General Sir Roland Guy
1979	General Sir James Glover
1982	General Sir Robert Pascoe
	Major General ME Carleton-Smith
1983	Major General PM Welsh
1984	General Sir David Ramsbotham
	General Sir Edward Jones
	General Sir Garry Johnson
1989	Lieutenant General Sir John Foley
1990	Lieutenant General Sir Christopher Wallace
1993	Major General CGC Vyvyan
1997	Major General ARD Pringle
2000	Lieutenant General AMD Palmer
2001	Lieutenant General NR Parker
2002	Major General NJ Cottam
2005	Major General JMJ Balfour

Brigade and Divisional Commanders

1966	Brigadier DG House	51 Gurkha Infantry Brigade
	Major General TH Acton	43 (Wessex) Division
	Brigadier JHP Curtis	8 Infantry Brigade
	Major General DL Darling	53 (Welsh) Division
	Brigadier AJ Wilson	147 Infantry Brigade
	Brigadier HDG Butler	24 Infantry Brigade
	Brigadier RE Worsley	7 Armoured Brigade
	Brigadier HMG Bond	12 Infantry Brigade
1967	Brigadier GH Mills	8 Infantry Brigade
	Brigadier ENW Bramall	5 Infantry Brigade
1968	Brigadier P Hudson	39 Infantry Brigade
1969	Brigadier JAC Cowan	8 Infantry Brigade
	Brigadier OG Pratt	5 Airportable Brigade
1970	Brigadier FE Kitson	39 Infantry Brigade
1971	Major General ENW Bramall	1 Armoured Division
	Major General RE Worsley	3 Armoured Division
	Brigadier DB Alexander-Sinclair	6 Armoured Brigade
1972	Brigadier RK Guy	24 Airportable Brigade
	Brigadier JDF Mostyn	8 Infantry Brigade
1973	Brigadier JM Glover	19 Airportable Brigade
1974	Brigadier PM Welsh	5 Infantry Brigade
1975	Major General DB Alexander-Sinclair	1 Armoured Division
	Major General FE Kitson	2 Armoured Division
1976	Brigadier RA Pascoe	5 Field Force
1977	Brigadier ME Carleton-Smith	Gurkha Field Force
	Brigadier DJ Ramsbotham	39 Infantry Brigade
1981	Brigadier CEW Jones	6 Armoured Brigade
	Brigadier GD Johnson	11 Armoured Brigade
1984	Major General DJ Ramsbotham	3 Armoured Division
1986	Brigadier CBQ Wallace	7 Armoured Brigade
1987	Major General CEW Jones	3 Armoured Division
	Brigadier CGC Vyvyan	3 Infantry Brigade
1989	Brigadier CJMcC Harrisson	107 (Ulster) Brigade
1990	Major General CBQ Wallace	3 Armoured Division
1992	Brigadier GdeVW Hayes	2 Infantry Brigade
	Brigadier AMD Palmer	8 Infantry Brigade
1994	Brigadier ARD Pringle	20 Armoured Brigade
	Brigadier NJ Cottam	8 Infantry Brigade
1995	Brigadier JMJ Balfour	3 Infantry Brigade
	Brigadier DH Godsal	2 Infantry Brigade
1997	Brigadier NR Parker	20 Armoured Brigade
	Major General ARD Pringle	Multi-National Division (SW)
	Brigadier JH Gordon	CBF Falkland Islands
	Major General NR Parker	2 Division
2004	Brigadier NP Carter	20 Armoured Brigade
	Major General NJ Cottam	5 Division
2005	Brigadier JIS Plastow	2 Infantry Brigade
2006	Brigadier JP Jackson	43 (Wessex) Brigade

Right: Capt Murray Whiteside, later to transfer into the Army Air Corps.

Green Jackets have served in the headquarters in many different capacities. From 1998 to 2001 Major General Andrew Pringle was Chief of Staff and Director of Operations, with Lieutenant Colonel Neil Baverstock, Lieutenant Colonel Jamie Gordon, Lieutenant Colonel Johnny Schute, Major Tom Copinger-Symes and Major Mark Mangham all serving on the staff. As Andrew Pringle noted in an article for the annual Green Jacket *Chronicle*, 'As a staff job, this is the place for riflemen to be; at the heart of operations'.

In the days when both The Parachute Regiment and the Army Air Corps relied to a large extent on seconded officers, Green Jackets were never slow to step forward. Mike Tarleton perhaps typifies this breed of Green Jacket, having served with The Parachute Brigade in 1961 as a young officer, then with 38 Group RAF as a staff officer, then towards the end of the 1970s as brigade major of The Parachute Brigade. He subsequently commanded 3RGJ. Numerous Green Jackets have served with the Army Air Corps, including Colin Harrisson, Peter Blaker, Anthony Stansfield who commanded 657 Sqn and then went on to command the AAC TA Sqn and as a civilian took the Chair of Brittain Norman Islander, Mike Leeming, Tom de la Rue and Mike Robertson. Murray Whiteside who commanded 4 Regt AAC, Anthony Slessor who commanded 7 Regt

Deputy Constable Dover Castle

Above: The keys to Dover Castle passsing from the 205th to the 206th Deputy Constable, 1996.

Right: Constables Tower Dover castle home to the Deputy Constable.

Most of those who read this book, especially if they were in The Royal Green Jackets, will have travelled to and from the continent via Dover or perhaps have been stationed there. You may only have been crossing the channel on a 'booze cruise or for a holiday but whatever the reason you will undoubtedly have glanced at the imposing sight of Dover Castle dominating the town and the surrounding countryside from the heights above the port. What you may not have appreciated is that the castle provides the married quarter for the senior serving army officer in south east England, at the time of writing the Commander of 2 Infantry Brigade. The 'quarter' is Constables Tower, built originally in the twelfth century, rebuilt as the main entrance to Dover Castle in the thirteenth century and extensively 'modernised' in 1881.

As the senior serving soldier in the area the Brigadier is also an important civic figure within the Confederation of the Cinque Ports. He is Deputy Constable of Dover Castle, an appointment that has an unbroken history since Saxon times, and is responsible to The Lord Warden of the Cinque Ports and Constable of Dover Castle for the safe keeping of the castle – note that you pronounce Cinque in the old English way – 'sink' not 'sank' with no concession to a French accent. He is also Resident Governor of Dover Castle, Member of the Grand Court of Shepway, Fellow of Brotherhood and Guestling and a Residual Baron of the Cinque Ports. Royal Green Jacket officers have been appointed to this unique post on three occasions:

205th Deputy Constable Brigadier Vere Hayes – 1992

206th Deputy Constable Brigadier David Godsal – 1995
the first time two Green Jackets in succession had been appointed since Brigadier Sir Hereward Wake (1929) and Brigadier Howard (1932).

209th Deputy Constable Brigadier James Plastow – 2005

The Royal Green Jackets

BRAVO TWO ZERO

For the general public, and probably serving RGJ soldiers as well, the most widely known former member of the SAS is Andy McNab, author of the best selling book *Bravo Two Zero*. A Royal Green Jacket who joined the SAS in the mid 1980s Andy McNab was awarded the Distinguished Conduct Medal following the Gulf War of 1991. His account of the patrol that he led behind Iraqi lines in that war provides the title for his book that was controversial at the time and remains so.

In March 2007 he visited 2Rifles (nearing the end of an operational tour in Basra that they had started as 1RGJ). He wrote on return: 'What I witnessed here was the most professional, motivated and well armed generation of soldiers our country might ever have seen.'

Left: Memorabilia from the Gulf War, including the PW jacket worn by Andy McNab, housed in the RGJ Museum.

Far left: Andy McNab with 2Rifles on operations in Basra, March 2007.

RGJ COMMANDING OFFICERS AND THEIR EXTERNAL COMMANDS

1967
Lieutenant Colonel J.R. Baker MC
1st battalion The Cheshire Regiment

1969
Lieutenant Colonel I.W. Lynch
Infantry Junior Leaders Battalion Oswestry

1971
Lieutenant Colonel R.M. Koe
Junior Infantry Battalion Shorncliffe

1973
Lieutenant Colonel P.N. Trustram-Eve
Oxford University OTC (UOTC)

1975
Lieutenant Colonel I.H. McCausland
3rd Battalion The Ulster Defence Regiment

1979
Lieutenant Colonel C.J. McC Harrison
1st Battalion The Ulster Defence Regiment
Lieutenant Colonel G.P. Blaker
Cambridge University OTC

1983
Lieutenant Colonel D.A.B. Williams
Infantry Junior Leaders Battalion Shorncliffe
Lieutenant Colonel G.F. Smythe MBE
Commandant NCO Tactics Wing Brecon

1984
Lieutenant Colonel N.H.H. Adams
Cambridge University OTC

1987
Lieutenant Colonel J.S. Carter
8th Battalion The Ulster Defence Regiment
Lieutenant Colonel S.C. Hearn
1st/9th Battalion The Ulster Defence Regiment UDR

1988
Lieutenant Colonel R.N.R. Jenkins
5th Battalion The Light Infantry

1989
Lieutenant Colonel M.J. Mangnall MBE
8th Battalion The Ulster Defence Regiment
Lieutenant Colonel M. Smith MC
4th Battalion The Ulster Defence Regiment UDR
Lieutenant Colonel T.R. Hamilton-Baillie
Comdt Infantry Trials and Development Unit

1990
Lieutenant Colonel R.J. Rimmer
HQ Regiment 1(BR) Corps

1991
Lieutenant Colonel A.J.R. Jackson
1st/9th Battalion The Ulster Defence Regiment

1995
Lieutenant Colonel P.J. Mostyn
1st Battalion The Royal Regiment of Fusiliers

1996
Lieutenant Colonel P.J. Pentreath
6th Battalion The Light Infantry

1997
Lieutenant Colonel C.E.I. Beattie
Exeter University OTC
Lieutenant Colonel NAC Baverstock MBE
9th Battalion The Royal Irish Regiment

1998
Lieutenant Colonel R.J. Carrow
Aberdeen University OTC

2000
Lieutenant Colonel D.M. Tobey
University of Wales OTC
Lieutenant Colonel D.W. Brown
1st Battalion Infantry Training Centre Catterick
Lieutenant Colonel E.A. Butler MBE
22 Special Air Service

2005
Lieutenant Colonel M.J. Doran
Sheffield University OTC

2006
Lieutenant Colonel S.P. Plummer
Infantry Battle School Brecon

The Green Jackets' Contribution to the Wider Army

AAC, C/Sgt Jim Lawton who retired as a Lt Col having completed his service as Chief Flying Instructor at The Defence Helicopter Flying School, Mario Pampanini and Sgt Bill Kidd, who was commissioned and then transferred to the RAF as a Flt Lt. John Ponsonby transferred to the RAF during his first flying tour with the Army Air Corps and rose to the rank of Air Vice Marshal.

Practical meaning was given to the close links between The Royal Green Jackets and the Brigade of Gurkhas, in particular the 2nd King Edward VII's Own Gurkhas (The Sirmoor Rifles) and the 6th (Queen Elizabeth's Own) Gurkha Rifles, by exchanging captains to serve on secondment. This sensible arrangement allowed British officers from the Gurkhas, who usually spent their early years in the Far East as exponents in the art of jungle warfare, to serve alongside and even lead British soldiers on operations in Northern Ireland. The Green Jacket officers who transferred to the Gurkha battalions offered a wealth of junior command and staff experience from the northern European theatres. Most would serve for two years as operations and training officers, and if they were lucky they would obtain command of a Gurkha rifle company whilst serving in Hong Kong and Brunei. These secondments were much sought after and close connections were forged with Gurkha riflemen that have continued to this day. Amongst those Green Jacket Captains who have served with the Brigade of Gurkhas were Jamie Athill, Christopher Bullock, Tony Berry, Peter Fairgrieve, Jeremy Knight, David Travers, Hugh Patterson and Hugh Willing.

Over the years, many Green Jackets distinguished themselves in the Special Forces, from commanding officers to squadron commanders and troop commanders to troopers. Between 1996 and 2003 alone, the regiment provided a commanding officer, a second-in-command, an adjutant, two squadron commanders, two troop commanders and four troopers. In an account of this character it is not appropriate to cite names, but suffice it to say The Royal Green Jackets was a consistent supporter of 'special duties' in the British Army, and those who serve in The Rifles today continue to be encouraged to volunteer for selection.

FORMER MEMBERS OF THE REGIMENT SERVING THE ROYAL HOUSEHOLD

Lieutenant Colonel Roger Ker – Gentleman-at-Arms
Major Carol Gurney – Gentleman-at-Arms
Bugle Major John Powell – Yeoman Warder
Brigadier Christopher Dunphie – Archer
Major Charles Marriott – Clerk of the Cheque and Adjutant, Yeoman
Colonel Mike Robertson – Gentleman-at-Arms
Lieutenant Colonel Peter Chamberlin – Gentleman-at-Arms

Top: Capt Mario Pampanini, with his wife, Susie, and Sebastian.

Top right: Spot the Green Jacket at the siege of the Iranian Embassy, 1980.

Above: Capt Colin Harrisson in Penang with 2RGJ, being inspected by Field Marshal HRH The Duke of Gloucester, 1966.

The Royal Green Jackets

SENIOR GREEN JACKETS APPOINTMENTS

DEFENCE STAFF

Chief of The Defence Staff
FM Sir Edwin Bramall

Vice Chief of the Defence Staff
Gen Sir Edwin Bramall

Assistant Chief of the Defence Staff (NATO&UK)
Maj Gen Johnson

Chief Defence Intelligence
Lt Gen Foley

Deputy Chief of Defence Staff Intelligence
Lt Gen Sir Richard Fyffe
Lt Gen Sir James Glover

Deputy Chief of Defence Staff (Pers)
Lt Gen Palmer

GENERAL STAFF

Chief of The General Staff
FM Sir Roland Gibbs
Gen Sir Edwin Bramall

Vice Chief of the General Staff
Lt Gen Sir James Glover

Assistant Chief of the General Staff (OR)
Maj Gen Pascoe

Adjutant General
Gen Sir John Mogg
General Sir Roland Guy
Gen Sir David Mostyn
Gen Sir Robert Pascoe
Gen Sir David Ramsbotham

Vice Adjutant General
Maj Gen Wilson

Quarter Master General
Gen Sir Antony Read
Gen Sir Richard Worsley
Gen Sir Edward Jones

Vice Quarter Master General
Maj Gen Worsley

Military Secretary
Lt Gen Sir Thomas Pearson
Lt Gen Sir Roland Guy
Lt Gen Sir David Mostyn
Maj Gen Cottam

Commander Training & Development/ Inspector General Development & Training
Lt Gen Sir Gary Johnson

Director General Intelligence (ROW)
Maj Gen JP Foley

Director Infantry
Maj Gen Young
Maj Gen House
Brigadier Balfour

Director of Manning (Army)
Maj Gen Mills

Director Personal Services
Maj Gen Mostyn

Director General TA & Org
Maj Gen Jones

Director General AT&R
Maj Gen Palmer

PERMANENT JOINT HEADQUARTERS

Chief Joint Operations
Lt Gen Sir Christopher Wallace

Chief Of Staff
Maj Gen Pringle

NATO

Deputy Supreme Commander Europe
Gen Sir John Mogg

UK Military Representative NATO
Gen Sir Edward Jones

Chief of Staff Live Oak SHAPE
Maj Gen Butler

Commander in Chief Allied Forces Northern Europe
Gen Sir Thomas Pearson
Gen Sir Gary Johnson

Chief of Staff Allied Forces North
Maj Gen Hudson

BAOR

Chief of Staff Headquarters BAOR
Maj Gen House
Maj Gen Guy

1st British Corps
Commander 1 (BR) Corps
Lt Gen Sir John Mogg
Lt Gen Sir Roland Gibbs
Lt Gen Sir Richard Worsley

BERLIN

General Officer Commanding
Maj Gen Mostyn

UNITED KINGDOM

Commander in Chief UK Land Forces
Gen Sir Roland Gibbs
Gen Sir Edwin Bramall
Gen Sir Frank Kitson
General Sir James Glover

Deputy Commander in Chief UK Land Forces
Lt Gen Sir Peter Hudson
Lt Gen Sir Frank Kitson

Commander UK Field Army and Inspector General TA
Lt Gen Sir David Ramsbotham

Chief of Staff Headquarters UK Land Forces/Land Command
Maj Gen Alexander-Sinclair
Maj Gen Pascoe
Maj Gen Vyvyan

General Officer Commander in Chief Army Strategic Command
Lt Gen Sir John Mogg

General Officer Commander in Chief Western Command
Lt Gen Sir Antony Read

General Officer Commander in Chief Southern Command
Lt Gen Sir John Mogg

General Officer Commanding North West District
Maj Gen Wilson

General Officer Commanding Wales District
Maj Gen Darling

General Officer Commanding South West District
Maj Gen Acton

General Officer Commanding South East District
Lt Gen Sir James Wilson

General Officer Commanding Eastern District
Maj Gen Hudson

NORTHERN IRELAND

General Officer Commanding
Lt Gen Sir David House
Lt Gen Sir Robert Pascoe
Lt Gen Parker

Deputy Commander
Maj Gen Acton

REST OF WORLD

Commander British Forces Hong Kong
Lt Gen Sir Edwin Bramall
Maj Gen Johnson
Maj Gen Foley

Commander Far East Land Forces
Lt Gen Sir Thomas Pearson

Commander British Forces Gulf
Maj Gen Gibbs

Commander Near East Land Forces
Maj Gen Butler

OTHER APPOINTMENTS

Commandant Staff College
Maj Gen Kitson
Maj Gen Alexander-Sinclair
Maj Gen Wallace
Maj Gen Parker

Commandant Royal College of Defence Studies
Gen Sir Antony Read
Lt Gen Sir Christopher Wallace

Commander in Chief and Governor of Gibraltar
Gen Sir Gerald Lathbury
Sir Francis Richards

Governor of Guernsey
Lt Gen Sir John Foley

Governor of The Royal Hospital Chelsea
Gen Sir Antony Read
Gen Sir Roland Guy

Governor of the Tower of London
Maj Gen Mills

The Royal Green Jackets – Volunteers

The volunteer and territorial battalions of The Royal Green Jackets have a history that is even more complex than that of the regular battalions. For most of the nineteenth century the volunteer and territorial battalions were completely independent of the regular British Army and were confined to the role of home defence. The story starts in the late eighteenth century, within a few hundred yards of the regiment's London home in Davies Street.

Historical Background

In the history of the United Kingdom there have been many military volunteer movements. Public alarm resulting from the violent disorder of the Gordon Riots in 1780 caused many 'armed associations' to be formed to aid the civil power in domestic emergencies. The rise in power of revolutionary France from the 1790s onwards led to the formation of more such associations, together with troops of Yeomanry. In London the response to the threat of invasion by Napoleon's forces was the creation of more armed bodies, such as The Duke of Cumberland's Sharpshooters and the Rangers (Gentlemen Members of Gray's Inn). In 1802 these associations were disbanded , only for 400,000 volunteers to be re-raised in 1803 to supplement the Militia because of an invasion scare. In the event these volunteers were not called upon, but they all practised steadily to enhance their military value, which therefore made it possible for a higher proportion of regular forces to be committed against Napoleon's armies in continental Europe.

The role of the volunteers was therefore unspectacular but vital, given the numerous crises that confronted the fully stretched regular forces. With Napoleon's defeat at Waterloo in 1815 and the long peace in Europe that followed, only one of the Green Jackets' antecedent regiments escaped disbandment, and this by means of a rifle club and royal patronage when the government could no longer offer it official recognition – thus The Royal Victoria Rifle Corps was the only volunteer rifle company existing in England when the volunteer movement was once again revived in 1859 to face a renewed threat from France.

Amidst another wave of national apprehension, vigorously expressed by Alfred Lord Tennyson in his poetic call for volunteers, Riflemen Form, the ranks of the new Rifle Volunteer Corps were swelled rapidly. When the 1859 reorganisation took place, the Victoria Rifle Corps became the Victoria Rifles. Modern territorial battalions can trace their descent directly from these units, including The Victoria Rifles, The Queen's Westminster Rifles and The City of London Rifle Volunteer Brigade – names that survived practically unchanged for a century.

By the summer of 1860 180,000 volunteers had enrolled in spite of the lack of any unified system of recruitment, equipment or terms of service. Even if the military value of such forces was discounted, there is no doubt that the enhancement of popular interest in, and knowledge of, military affairs that it generated were to prove beneficial to the Army and the nation. In 1881 the Cardwell reorganisation of the British Army established the first formal links between volunteers and regular regiments. In London no fewer than twelve volunteer units were affiliated to The King's Royal Rifle Corps and nine to The Rifle Brigade, while The Oxfordshire and Buckinghamshire Light Infantry,

Left: Silver Statuette of a KRRC Rifleman, 1939–45 dress at 56 Davies Street, London home of The Royal Green Jackets.

Far right opposite: Queen Victoria.

Right opposite: Prince Albert.

THE ROYAL GREEN JACKETS TERRITORIAL ARMY FAMILY TREE

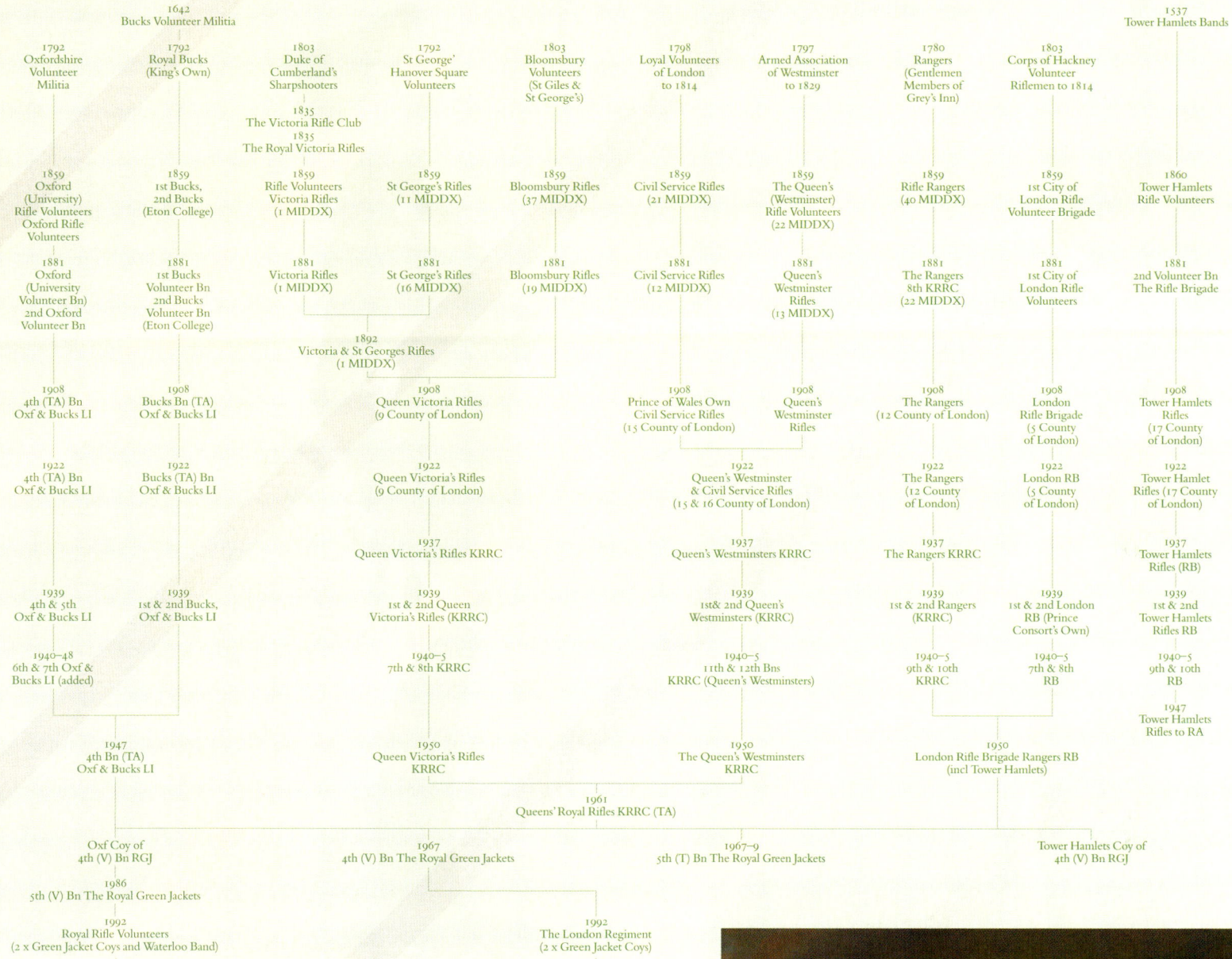

```
                                          1642                                                                                                              1537
                                   Bucks Volunteer Militia                                                                                            Tower Hamlets Bands
    1792          1792          1803              1792           1803           1798           1797           1780          1803
Oxfordshire    Royal Bucks   Duke of           St George'    Bloomsbury    Loyal Volunteers  Armed Association  Rangers      Corps of Hackney
 Volunteer    (King's Own)  Cumberland's     Hanover Square  Volunteers    of London        of Westminster  (Gentlemen     Volunteer
  Militia                  Sharpshooters      Volunteers    (St Giles &      to 1814           to 1829       Members of    Riflemen to 1814
                                                            St George's)                                    Grey's Inn)
                                                1835
                                        The Victoria Rifle Club
                                                1835
                                        The Royal Victoria Rifles

    1859          1859           1859              1859           1859           1859           1859           1859          1859            1860
   Oxford      1st Bucks,    Rifle Volunteers  St George's Rifles Bloomsbury   Civil Service  The Queen's   Rifle Rangers  1st City of    Tower Hamlets
 (University    2nd Bucks    Victoria Rifles    (11 MIDDX)       Rifles         Rifles       (Westminster) (40 MIDDX)    London Rifle   Rifle Volunteers
   Rifle       (Eton College) (1 MIDDX)                         (37 MIDDX)     (21 MIDDX)    Rifle Volunteers            Volunteer Brigade
 Volunteers)                                                                                 (22 MIDDX)
   Oxford Rifle
   Volunteers

    1881          1881           1881              1881           1881           1881           1881           1881          1881            1881
   Oxford      1st Bucks     Victoria Rifles   St George's Rifles Bloomsbury   Civil Service   Queen's      The Rangers    1st City of   2nd Volunteer Bn
 (University   Volunteer Bn   (1 MIDDX)         (16 MIDDX)       Rifles         Rifles       Westminster    8th KRRC     London Rifle    The Rifle Brigade
 Volunteer Bn)  2nd Bucks                                        (19 MIDDX)    (12 MIDDX)      Rifles                    Volunteers
 2nd Oxford    Volunteer Bn                                                                   (13 MIDDX)
 Volunteer Bn  (Eton College)

                                               1892
                                      Victoria & St Georges Rifles
                                              (1 MIDDX)

    1908          1908                            1908                           1908           1908           1908          1908            1908
  4th (TA) Bn   Bucks Bn (TA)                 Queen Victoria Rifles          Prince of Wales Own Queen's    The Rangers     London         Tower Hamlets
 Oxf & Bucks LI Oxf & Bucks LI               (9 County of London)           Civil Service Rifles Westminster (12 County of London) Rifle Brigade  Rifles
                                                                           (15 County of London) Rifles                          (5 County     (17 County
                                                                                                                                 of London)    of London)

    1922          1922                            1922                                          1922           1922          1922            1922
  4th (TA) Bn   Bucks (TA) Bn                 Queen Victoria's Rifles                    Queen's Westminster   The Rangers  London RB       Tower Hamlet
 Oxf & Bucks LI Oxf & Bucks LI               (9 County of London)                      & Civil Service Rifles (12 County    (5 County      Rifles (17 County
                                                                                    (15 & 16 County of London) of London)   of London)      of London)

                                               1937                                             1937           1937                          1937
                                     Queen Victoria's Rifles KRRC                       Queen's Westminsters KRRC  The Rangers KRRC          Tower Hamlets
                                                                                                                                             Rifles (RB)

    1939          1939                            1939                                          1939           1939          1939            1939
  4th & 5th   1st & 2nd Bucks,                  1st & 2nd Queen                         1st & 2nd Queen's   1st & 2nd Rangers 1st & 2nd London 1st & 2nd
 Oxf & Bucks LI Oxf & Bucks LI                 Victoria's Rifles (KRRC)                 Westminsters (KRRC)    (KRRC)        RB (Prince     Tower Hamlets
                                                                                                                             Consort's Own)  Rifles RB

   1940-48                                      1940-5                                         1940-5          1940-5        1940-5          1940-5
  6th & 7th Oxf &                              7th & 8th KRRC                              11th & 12th Bns   9th & 10th    7th & 8th       9th & 10th
 Bucks LI (added)                                                                         KRRC (Queen's Westminsters) KRRC     RB              RB

                                                                                                                                             1947
                                                                                                                                             Tower Hamlets
                                                                                                                                             Rifles to RA

    1947                                       1950                                            1950                              1950
  4th Bn (TA)                              Queen Victoria's Rifles                       The Queen's Westminsters          London Rifle Brigade Rangers RB
 Oxf & Bucks LI                                 KRRC                                           KRRC                            (incl Tower Hamlets)

                                               1961
                                      Queens' Royal Rifles KRRC (TA)

  Oxf Coy of                                   1967                                         1967-9                                       Tower Hamlets Coy of
 4th (V) Bn RGJ                        4th (V) Bn The Royal Green Jackets         5th (T) Bn The Royal Green Jackets                      4th (V) Bn RGJ

    1986
 5th (V) Bn The Royal Green Jackets

         1992                                    1992
  Royal Rifle Volunteers                   The London Regiment
 (2 x Green Jacket Coys and Waterloo Band) (2 x Green Jacket Coys)

                                         2007
                                   7th Bn The Rifles
```

itself a Cardwell amalgamation of the closely allied 43rd Light Infantry and 52nd Light Infantry, gained a volunteer battalion in each of its home counties. In 1899 these affiliations proved their worth when volunteers in their hundreds swelled the ranks of their related regular regiments for the Boer War. Volunteers also served in the mounted infantry and in a composite battalion that became celebrated as The City Imperial Volunteers.

On 1 April 1908 Lord Haldane's Territorial Force was born of countless amalgamations, becoming the Territorial Army soon afterwards. Upon the outbreak of the First World War the existing volunteer battalions became more closely integrated with their regular counterparts and for the first time they fought overseas as complete units. No fewer

The Royal Green Jackets

than fourteen divisions were distributed throughout the country in what King Edward VII described as the 'imperial army of the second line, which lies within the shores of the kingdom'.

Returning to the home-defence role between the wars, the overseas-service principle was revived in the Second World War. Thus it was at Calais in 1940 that a Green Jacket brigade was composed of a regular battalion each of The King's Royal Rifle Corps and The Rifle Brigade, and a territorial battalion of Queen Victoria's Rifles (7th Battalion KRRC). Green Jacket territorial battalions fought with distinction in France in 1940, throughout the actions in the desert of North Africa, in Greece and Crete, in Italy and northwest Europe, and in Burma. Throughout the war the territorial battalions provided trained reinforcements of officers, NCOs and specialists to their affiliated regular battalions.

During the 1950s and 1960s the Territorial Army (TA) endured a succession of reductions as new categories of reserve service came into being, which resulted in a transition from the old TA into the new Territorial and Army Volunteer Reserve (TAVR) with volunteer battalions having a higher commitment than territorial battalions. The result was the creation in 1967 of the new 4th (Volunteer) Battalion The Royal Green Jackets (4(v)RGJ), based at Davies Street, which was produced by merging The Queen's Royal Rifles (itself the earlier amalgamation of Queen Victoria's Rifles and The Queen's Westminster Rifles), The London Rifle Brigade/Rangers and the 4th Battalion Oxfordshire and Buckinghamshire Light Infantry (TA). Detachments, officers and men from the former Oxfordshire and Buckinghamshire Light Infantry (TA) moved into Slade Park, Oxford, and became A Company. B Company, drawn from The Queen's Royal Rifles, was based at 58 Buckingham Gate. C Company was drawn predominantly from the former London Rifle Brigade/Rangers (TA) at 24 Sun Street in the City of London. The battalion's headquarters and its Headquarter Company were established at Davies Street, Westminster. Those former territorials who did not wish to accept the extended training liability and call-out conditions required by the new volunteer battalion helped to form the 5th (Territorial) Battalion The Royal Green Jackets (5(v)RGJ) and the Oxfordshire Territorials, a combination of Oxfordshire and Buckinghamshire Light Infantry and Queen's Own Oxfordshire Hussars territorial units.

Far left top: Queen Victoria's Rifles.

Far left centre: London Rifle Brigade.

Far left bottom: Recruiting poster for The Queen's Westminster Volunteers.

Left: Regular or Territorial, one and the same.

The same year, 1967, saw a contingent from all three battalions, The 4th (Volunteer) Battalion, the 5th (Territorial) Battalion and the Oxfordshire Territorials, present with affiliated cadet units at the Queen's Parade held at Winchester on 25 July 1967, a date now held to be the 'birthday' of The Royal Green Jackets. The entire Green Jacket family was thus on parade together for the first time. In 1969 a further reorganisation resulted in the disbandment of the last two battalions, although in the case of the 5th (Territorial) Battalion its short life was sufficient to provide a Winter Olympics skier, Jeremy Palmer-Tomkinson, and it won the Territorial Army Major Units Shooting Championship.

And so the situation remained until 1 December 1986 when a new 5th (Volunteer) Battalion The Royal Green Jackets was raised. Those two battalions, 4th and 5th, thus claimed descent from the independent volunteers and from the militia of the nineteenth century.

Royal Green Jackets – Volunteers

Above: Nick Eden, Colonel The Viscount Eden, OBE TD, Commanding Officer Queen's Royal Rifles, 1965–7 and 4th (Volunteer) Battalion The Royal Green Jackets 1968–9; and founder of The Royal Green Jackets London Club.

Below right: Captain John Hayter, 4th (Volunteer) Battalion The Royal Green Jackets.

Below: Cripplegate Ward Challenge Plate, London Rifle Brigade annual competitive rifle shooting, presented 1865.

The Early Years

'Death by a thousand cuts' is not a new concept in terms of defence restructuring, and so it was that within two years of its creation the new 5th (Territorial) Battalion, commanded by Lieutenant Colonel John Hanscombe, was disbanded and the new, relatively low-commitment 'cadres' were put in place in both London and Oxford. Meanwhile, 4(v)RGJ, commanded during the reorganisation phase by Lieutenant Colonel Tommy Wallace, had been handed over to a volunteer commanding officer, Lieutenant Colonel Viscount Eden (known to everyone as Nick Eden). In Green Jacket style, led brilliantly to the end by Lieutenant Colonel John Hanscombe, 5(v)RGJ won the Queen's Medal at Bisley (TA) as a fitting epitaph. In London 4(v)RGJ staked a claim to global recognition by entering a car into the London to Sydney Marathon, to be driven by two officers, one a volunteer, George Yanagas, and one a regular, Jack Dill, grandson of the famous Field Marshal Dill.

By 1969, with the regiment newly reduced to two regular battalions (see page 27), the 4th (Volunteers) Battalion was established with three rifle companies and three cadres in Buckinghamshire, Oxfordshire and London. The battalion trained hard in both the UK and Germany and began to establish a reputation for excellence amongst infantry volunteers in London and beyond. The regimental ethos of the Green Jackets was as much a part of the life-blood of the volunteer as it was of his regular counterpart. The battalion was also making its mark on the media – an article in 1971 by the defence correspondent of the *Evening Standard*, Tom Pocock, captured the character and ethos of volunteer soldiering.

In the early 1970s, at the height of the Cold War, the 4th (Volunteers) Battalion was expanded to form a rifle company in Aylesbury (D Company) to replace the former cadre based in Buckinghamshire. In 1971 Lieutenant Colonel Bill Pirie took command of the battalion and Nick Eden moved on to become Volunteer Colonel at London district. Nick, however, had left a legacy at Davies Street far beyond his professionalism and dedication as a commanding officer. He owned restaurants in London, such as Nick's Diner, and with enormous enthusiasm and culinary expertise he established The Royal Green Jackets London Club, which to this day has a reputation for excellence throughout the Army and beyond. Nick's then adjutant (later a brigadier), Colin Harrison, recalls the atmosphere: 'It was a great time and I have huge admiration for the attitude, the enthusiasm, the professionalism and the achievements of TA riflemen. Sharing an office with the Boss was also an interesting experience, usually reserved only for the Guards. Nick Eden was the instigator and founder of the London Club, in which he took a close and very hands-on interest. As adjutant I was frequently summoned to the kitchen, where, whilst he supervised the daily preparation of lunch, he tasked me to carry out certain less-important culinary duties, whilst I sought command decisions and direction on other matters! It sounds extraordinary now, but it all worked, and 4(v)RGJ was a well-recruited and very capable battalion.'

In 1972 Bill Pirie handed over command to Lieutenant Colonel John Cornell. The then prime minister, Edward Heath, visited the battalion and the regiment's club in London. In the Lord Mayor's Show, a number of eyebrows were raised when 4(v)RGJ paraded together with units with which it had trained during the year, because this included a detachment of two open staff cars from the German Army with large black crosses on the side and steel-helmeted soldiers stiff to attention inside. This was probably the first time uniformed German soldiers had paraded in the Lord Mayor's Show.

The early and mid-1970s continued to be exciting times for the battalion. Camps were held in Gibraltar, Stanford, Germany and Canada, together with the usual round of training, recruiting and ceremonial. In 1974, under the command of Lieutenant Colonel John Holroyd, *Tatler* magazine displayed the social face of the battalion in a full-page caricature of the officers' mess. The battalion was visited by civic dignitaries and the Secretary of State for Defence. Camp that year was in Cyprus, where the battalion had just deployed on exercise, with patrols out in the Akamas Peninsula, when a United Nations patrol arrived with the first intimation that all was not well.

81

The Royal Green Jackets

The Reason Why of the Part-time Soldier
Tom Pocock, Defence Correspondent

From the outset, The Royal Green Jackets had no problem in attracting young volunteer soldiers. Writing in the 1960s, defence correspondent Tom Pocock found that in that least conformist of generations, volunteers were just as ready as their peers to buck the trends of the times:

Sun Street, a narrow back street in a shabby part of the City of London, was the scene of an unusual international occasion earlier this month. It was visited by an American military mission led by a major-general in the United States Army. They had come to learn from the British. They wanted to find out why young men in Britain are willing to give up their spare time to train as soldiers.

In Sun Street is the headquarters of C Company, 4th (Volunteer) Battalion, The Royal Green Jackets. They are part of the Territorial Army and Volunteer Reserve which, recovering from the demoralising cuts and changes suffered in the 1960s at the hands of the Labour Government and the Army Board, is now flourishing. Recruiting is so good – many London units are up to their full establishment – that it can be increasingly selective. The 4th Green Jackets are earmarked as immediate reserves for the Army in Germany and, at Sun Street, they say that they would only need two weeks' training in internal security before taking to the streets in Belfast.

These young men are not conformists. Indeed, they are rebels against the conventions of their generation. Through fear of nuclear weapons and horror over Vietnam, the idea of soldiering is as unfashionable now as it was fashionable when Hitler was coming over the horizon.

To find out what sort of young man joins the Territorials, I visited this Battalion and first talked to its commanding officer, a 39-year-old regular soldier, Lieutenant Colonel John Cornell. He commands 552 part-time officers and soldiers in companies based on his headquarters in Davies Street, Mayfair; Buckingham Gate, Westminster; Sun Street, West Ham; Oxford; and Aylesbury. Their average age is 22 and most of them stay with the battalion for about three years.

What are their civilian jobs? 'Almost anything you can think of', said Cornell. 'We have electricians and zoo-keepers, stock-brokers and carpenters, insurance salesmen and civil service clerks.' About 15 per cent have had some military experience as Army cadets, former Territorials or in the Regular Army. A handful have seen active service with the Regulars and have joined so as to combine soldiering with a more settled family life. Why do they join? 'I think many of them get a little message about Queen and Country – although they would never admit to it', thought Cornell. 'There is still the feeling that it is good to do something for your country even if you don't talk about it.'

Next, he believed, came comradeship. Eighty per cent of recruits had a friend already in the battalion and often whole groups of friends joined together. Third, he puts variety. 'It is a complete change. It's something else to do, something different to think about. Whatever your job, this offers a totally new scene.'

At Sun Street two electricians, Garry Hindmarsh, 19, from Stepney, and Richard White, 25, from Islington, were cleaning their machine-gun. White said that his father, who had been a colour-sergeant in the old Territorials, had suggested that if he had little to occupy his evenings, he should give the T.A.V.R. a try. John Meehan, 19, from Tottenham, drives a van as a civilian. Why did he join? Was it patriotism? 'Patriotism doesn't come into it at all. It's soldiering – full stop.' Paradoxically, the principal reason for joining was that by accepting discipline and a professional conformity these young men had found a new freedom … In their generation, they are the odd men out. Their uniforms are for them the gear that expresses their refusal to conform to trends.

'It's the Same Man' by H.M. Bateman.

Uniforms

The uniforms of the former regiments display a wide variety of taste and colour starting with the St George's Volunteers, memorably lampooned in a contemporary cartoon. As the traditions of the Volunteer Rifle Regiment developed, by the time of the First World War the territorials and volunteers were broadly wearing the same uniform as their regular regimental counterparts. The illustration below shows the historical ceremonial dress of the regiments from which The Royal Green Jackets' volunteers (and regular battalions) are descended.

Regiments from which the regular and volunteer battalions of the Royal Green Jackets are descended, in the full dress uniforms of 1914.

The officers 4(v)RGJ. 'With The Royal Green Jackets' by Fred May.

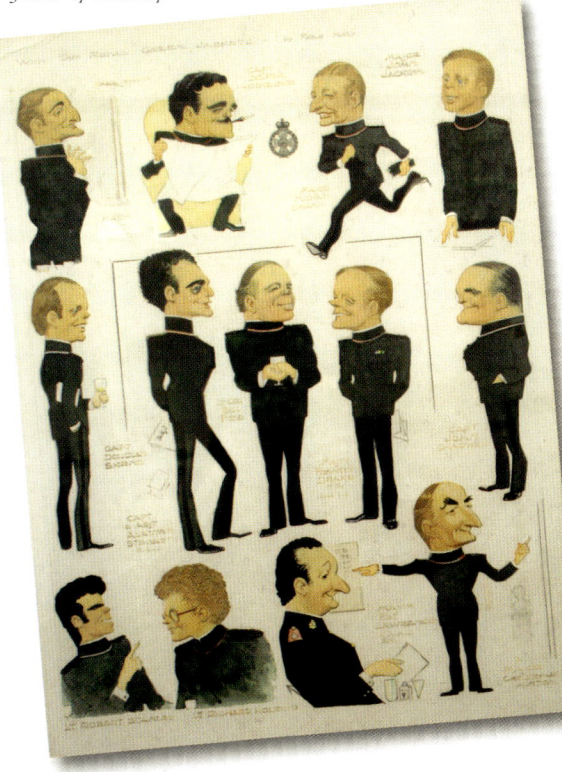

It reported Nicosia in turmoil, President Makarios reputedly dead and Cypriot National Guard officers being arrested. It quickly became clear that this was no exercise play, and gradually the news began to filter in that northern Cyprus had been invaded early that morning by the Turkish Army. A little later that day a Cypriot National Guard patrol appeared in the area and the exercise was brought to an end.

Warrant Officer Second Class (later Major) Gerry Koveny was the sergeant major of C Company. He recalled the colour sergeant driving through hostile territory in order to fill the water bowser, which comprised the company's only supply of drinking water. Having 'got away with it' for a number of round trips, the tap was eventually turned off when the colour sergeant's convoy was stopped and turned around by some very trigger-happy militia. Not quite knowing whether to load rifles with blank or ball ammunition, and reportedly running low on water, the company managed to maintain spirits with at least one 'tea bomb' full of 'brandy sour', a libation well known to all who have served in Cyprus! Camp was brought to an early end, to the disappointment of the riflemen. 'We pitched tents, and loaded aircraft and were only sorry that we were not allowed to do what we thought was our proper job,' recalled one.

After that, and undaunted, the 4th Battalion expanded to five rifle companies by forming G Company in the heart of the regiment's recruiting territory in London's East End. Part of its role was to provide an airportable company in support of 3rd Armoured Division on operations. But what the Ministry of Defence gives, the Ministry of Defence takes away, and in the same year the cadres in both London and Oxford were disbanded, leaving 4(v)RGJ standing alone as the volunteer element of the regiment, with a battalion establishment approaching 700.

It is perhaps worth mentioning why the fifth company of the battalion was christened G and not E or F. The commanding officer, John Holroyd, had spent much time researching the historical records of London's volunteer forces and it was decided to commemorate G Company, 8th Battalion The Rifle Brigade – a battalion that was formed at the start of the Second World War as the 2nd Battalion The London Rifle Brigade (TA). It had a fine record as a motor battalion during the Normandy Campaign in

The Royal Green Jackets

1944 and G Company, 8th Battalion The Rifle Brigade played a conspicuous part in Operation Goodwood – an action used as an example by the Staff College during its annual battlefield tour.

Annual camp was the highlight of the battalion's year, but things were not always guaranteed to go smoothly. In 1976 the battalion went to camp in Germany as part of 19th Brigade's Exercise Clam Fury. TA deployment got off to a storming start when RAF helicopters landed the commanding officer's recce group more than 60 miles (exactly 100 km) from the correct grid-reference and then flew off. That was before mobile telephones, so the Intelligence officer recovered well by marching into the nearest German police station. He explained his plight to incredulous police officers, who connected him with the duty officer at Headquarters Land Forces in the United Kingdom. Eventually reunited with the battalion, it must have been one of the few occasions when positions were dug and occupied before the recce group had even seen them.

At the end of 1977 John Holroyd handed command to Lieutenant Colonel Tony Berry. The battalion strength stood at 725 against an establishment of 720 all ranks, and recruits were still queuing up to join. That year 568 volunteers attended camp and the record shows that two riflemen from G Company were so anxious to attend that they made their own way out to Vogelsang and arrived several days before the advance party. Later in the year, Her Royal Highness Princess Alice visited the battalion at Davies Street.

In 1978 the battalion caused a stir at the Lord Mayor's Show when the dancers Pan's People joined riflemen in the march past. The adjutant, Jamie Robertson-Macleod, was visibly perturbed by Pan's People's version of ceremonial Number One Dress!

By 1980 Tony Berry had handed over command to Lieutenant Colonel Nigel Mogg. D Company won the coveted Courage Trophy Military Skills Competition against thirty-six other teams from London district, and the battalion surprised itself by winning the UKLF Tickle Fitness Competition without apparently breaking into a sweat. Later in the year the battalion took part in the regiment's Freedom Parade in Oxford. The following year the number of training days deemed necessary by a government in search of defence savings was reduced from forty-four to thirty-six per man per year. Camps were becoming more demanding, and that year A, B, C and G companies trained with an armoured battle group in Germany whilst D Company independently took part in an exercise in Schleswig–Holstein with the 381st Panzer Grenadier Battalion. Battlefield tours were by then very much part of a wider military education and that year one tour to Calais included guest speakers from the Green Jacket battalions that had taken part in the fighting.

In 1982 Lieutenant Colonel Christopher Miers took over command of 4(v)RGJ from Tony Berry. The battalion's role in BAOR also changed, from one of 'rear area security' to a much more interesting and demanding role as part of an élite group of volunteer infantry units assigned to operations with an armoured brigade. The battalion duly joined the 12th Armoured Brigade, based at Osnabrück. It was a happy association and one that was to last for many years. Regimentally, of course, 1982 was the year in which the band of 1RGJ was bombed by the Provisional IRA in Regent's Park, killing seven members and wounding a further twenty-four. The Davies Street headquarters of 4(v)RGJ was within earshot of the bombs and the battalion played a significant role in the many counter-terrorist follow-up actions.

The battalion took part in a full-scale divisional field exercise in northern Germany in 1983 with 12th Armoured Brigade. That year there was also a happy rationalisation of the battalion's cherished links with many of the City of London's principal livery companies. Each Green Jacket company established more formal links with the livery companies of their antecedent regiments. Thus, B Company linked with The Goldsmiths' Company, C Company with The Clothworkers' Company, G Company with The Salters' Company and A and Headquarters Company with The Haberdashers' Company. In addition, C Company affiliated with The Grocers' Company, which had previously had links with the Tower Hamlet Rifles. Such historic connections were also strengthened by allowing each of the battalion's companies to wear the tie of the regiments from which they were descended: A Company – 4th Battalion The Oxfordshire and Buckinghamshire Light Infantry; B Company – The Queen's Westminster Rifles; C Company – The London Rifle Brigade; D Company – The Buckinghamshire Battalion (Bucks Battalion); G Company – The Rangers; and Headquarters Company and battalion headquarters – Queen Victoria's Rifles. These details meant a great deal to both the young

Above left: Kit Inspection. The Adjutant 4(v)RGJ, Captain Jamie Robertson-Macleod, inspects Pan's People before the Lord Mayor's Show, 1978.

Below left: Guard of Honour for the Lord Mayor 2006, formed by a combined guard from F and G (Royal Green Jackets) Companies, The London Regiment.

Below: Rifleman, 1802, The Rifle Corps.

84

Above: The Drill Hall, 56 Davies Street.

Below right: Royal Green Jackets, 56 Davies Street.

Below: The London Rifle Brigade, 1908.

riflemen of 4(v)RGJ and the veterans and old comrades of the antecedent regiments, to whom it represented the Green Jacket family firmly 'closing the loop'.

There followed a year of consolidation. In 1984 the battalion went to camp in Otterburn and in the USA, and participated in Her Majesty The Queen's visit to the regiment in Celle. That June, Lieutenant Colonel Peter Lyddon assumed command. Christopher Miers not only left the battalion in good shape but he had also made a major impact on the look and feel of Davies Street – his artist's eye had been put to use to good effect in the redecoration of both the drill hall and mess, and the battalion's many attractive pictures and prints had been re-hung to give a better impression.

Under Peter Lyddon's command the battalion enjoyed a busy time. The focus of training was very much its role in Germany with the 12th Armoured Brigade, with which it trained regularly. The battalion's command group travelled often to Germany to take part in Command Post Exercises (CPXs). At one camp a visit by the Honorary Colonel provided the excuse to re-establish the battalion's links with the brigade mess of 7th Armoured Brigade. The 4th Battalion PMC (President of the Mess Committee) had brought a number of the battalion's pictures from London to adorn the walls, having remembered a previous visit by the battalion when the mess had run out of champagne, the staff this time made the necessary arrangements.

Late in 1985, at the height of the Cold War, came the welcome news of the expansion of the TA. A new 5(v)RGJ was to be raised in Oxfordshire and Buckinghamshire, based on A and D companies of 4(v)RGJ in Oxford, Aylesbury and Bletchley. Preparation for 5(v)RGJ's birth dominated administration and training throughout 1986, though ceremonial occasions also continued with both The Queen's Westminster Rifles and Queen Victoria's Rifles being honoured, with the freedom of Westminster and Marylebone respectively. The battalion's parade through the City of Westminster was followed by a reception at Davies Street.

By the 1980s 4(v)RGJ when in the UK had developed a particular penchant for FIBUA (Fighting in Built Up Areas) training. One visiting senior officer paraphrased the Duke of Wellington's famous comments about the men under his command, when he was heard to comment, 'if they behave like this in the East End, they are truly terrifying'.

On 1 December 1986 5(v)RGJ was born with the seamless transfer of A and D companies of 4(v)RGJ to the new battalion. F Company 4(v)RGJ, the new rifle company in London, formed at its drill hall in the Mile End Road, a former stronghold of the Tower Hamlet Rifles. To the uninitiated, non-Green Jacket observer, the selection of company designations for 5(v)RGJ must have seemed unintelligible. Its newsletter for that year starts with a quotation from a retired officer at a 'frightfully senior headquarters': 'I am little confused, can you tell me where you got D and E companies from, and why you think you are forming a new A Company? And while you are there, perhaps you could tell me where B and C companies have gone. I mean, the Army Board letter was quite clear … !'

Peter Lyddon handed over the infant 5(v)RGJ, hived off from 4(v)RGJ, to Lieutenant Colonel David Innes, and at the same time Lieutenant Colonel Neil Johnson assumed command of 4(v)RGJ. Neil Johnson was a volunteer officer, and at the time a director of Jaguar Cars. His rifle green Jaguar became a common sight around the battalion, serving as his staff car both on visits and occasionally even on exercise in Germany. Peter Lyddon had supervised the foundations of the new battalion with keen interest. The end result was that almost twenty years after the major reorganisation of 1967, The Royal Green Jackets once again had two volunteer battalions to augment the three regular ones. In addition, new TA centres were to be built at Milton Keynes and High Wycombe.

In London, on 26 January 1987, the Lord Mayor and the Corporation of the City of London provided a splendid reception at the Guildhall to celebrate the formation of 56th London Brigade, the Black Cat Brigade. This training brigade included 4(v)RGJ and 10 Para (V) as well as all five of the London public duty battalions responsible for London ceremonial duties. The brigade's direct ancestor, 56th London Infantry Division formed in 1916, included three of the antecedent regiments: Queen Victoria's Rifles, The Queen's Westminster Rifles and The London Rifle Brigade.

Being a supporting element of an operational armoured brigade in Germany, whilst at the same time forming part of what was essentially

The Royal Green Jackets

4(v)RGJ Guard, Lord Mayor's Parade November 1988. Even the horses are in step!

the Household Division in London, presented 4(v)RGJ with a hectic annual training round – albeit one that offered the riflemen tremendous opportunities to train in Kenya, the United States and Canada with the battalions of Foot Guards. Membership of the 'Heavy Brigade,' as the riflemen referred to their brothers in arms, also had its lighter moments. One cavalry officer, chief of staff to his Grenadier brigade commander, was perplexed to discover that the Green Jacket vehicles were not neatly 'dressed by the right' when parked tactically on training areas – it did not take long for a rifleman to present him with a traffic warden's hat. Another Green Jacket exercise initiative of seizing two Chinook helicopters to leapfrog a rifle company behind enemy forces was also considered 'exotic exercise play' by the directing staff from Horse Guards. However, these new relationships worked well, and firm friendships were formed between the riflemen and guardsmen.

During the year Lord Holderness, affectionately known throughout the Regiment as Colonel Richard, achieved the magnificent 'first' of completing twenty-five years' unbroken service as Honorary Colonel of the Queen's Royal Rifles and then of the 4th Battalion. To mark this special event the officers held a 'family' dinner at Davies Street and the new C Company TA Centre in Clifton Street was officially named Holderness House to honour his outstanding service to the regiment. To further mark Colonel Richard's record-breaking stint with 4(v)RGJ, the battalion commissioned Sue Ryder to paint his portrait, at ease in the mess at Davies Street.

The twenty-first anniversary of the foundation of 4(v)RGJ was commemorated in 1988. 'Any excuse for a party' had always been a watchword for London's riflemen, and on 31 March there was a massive party at Davies Street with the Normandy Band Sounding Retreat and bringing sections of Oxford Street to a standstill. The battalion's guests then moved to the various messes to celebrate not only the first twenty-one years of 4(v)RGJ but also, coincidentally, the first 100 years of the regiment's presence at 56 Davies Street, a prestigious location originally provided by the Duke of Westminster for The Queen's Westminster Rifles. Later that year the battalion provided the guard of honour for the incoming Lord Mayor. Turned out in ceremonial Number One Dress and accompanied by the Normandy Band, the event reconfirmed the entire Regiment's relationship with the City of London.

Meanwhile, in Oxford, 5(v)RGJ had been developing in strength and growing in reputation. A public relations team had been formed to introduce local communities to the new battalion, which opened its refurbished battalion headquarters at Slade Park Barracks on 9 March 1987. On 12 May Her Royal Highness The Princess Royal opened the new TA centre at Milton Keynes and E Company was officially up and running, while at High Wycombe a new drill hall was under construction, pending A Company's relocation from Oxford.

The pace of battalion life for 4(v)RGJ was quick. At camp in Germany, to participate with 3rd Armoured Division in a testing Exercise Iron Hammer, half of the riflemen had only recently joined the battalion from their two weeks of training at the Light Division Depot. A measure of the territorials' commitment can be judged from a remarkable photograph taken at the camp at Vogelsang in 1989, which shows six members of the battalion, including the honorary colonel, who between them could boast 176 camps.

In November 1989 the 4th Battalion's regimental dinner attracted the prime minister, Mrs Thatcher, as the principal guest. In the same year Neil Johnson handed over command to Lieutenant Colonel Jamie Daniel and a completely redeveloped Fulham House was reopened as home to B Company. The official programme set the scene thus:

On 8th July 1891, Kaiser Wilhelm II sprung a surprise on his English hosts; as a finale to his State Visit, he would like to inspect one of the Volunteer Regiments about which he had heard so much. Panic ensued. Summoning the Militia [the forerunner to today's Territorial Army] took weeks. They had 48 hours. The Duke of Westminster intervened – his Queen's Westminsters would parade for the Kaiser; and so it was, on 10th July, the Kaiser inspected this Volunteer Regiment in the grounds of Buckingham Palace. No fewer than 790 of the Regiments 1100 men had turned up, ordered by

Left: Colonel The Rt Hon. The Lord Holderness PC DL, Hon. Col Queen's Royal Rifles, 1962–7, Hon. Col 4th (Volunteer) Battalion The Royal Green Jackets, 1967–89.

'The Kaiser'. The portrait carries a plate with the inscription: 'Presented to The Queen's Westminster Volunteers by William II, German Emperor and King of Prussia, in token of His Imperial Majesty's inspection of the Corps at Buckingham Palace, Friday 10th July, 1891.'

speedily printed posters placed all over London. The Kaiser was hugely impressed with the quality of the drill and turnout. On his return to Germany he ordered a new portrait to be painted – for immediate presentation to the Regiment. It is said that he was so taken with the grey uniforms worn by the Volunteers that he ordered the immediate introduction of grey to the German Army.

Sadly, only 23 years later, the Kaiser's troops were to be fighting the British Army. During both World Wars, the famous portrait was turned to face the wall. Now, nearly 100 years on, relations are to be restored. The 4th Battalion of The Royal Green Jackets – the direct descendants of the Queen's Westminsters – have decided to give the Kaiser (or at least one of his relations) another chance to review their troops. The occasion is the re-opening of a new Training Centre at Fulham House, the magnificent Georgian mansion near Putney Bridge. This building will house B Company, and contains every facility needed by a NATO-roled TA Infantry Company. Kaiser Wilhelm's great-grandson, Prince Nicholas Von Preussen, is taking the salute, and inspecting B Company 4(v)RGJ. The Kaiser picture is also here today, but certainly not facing the wall.

Command changed at 5(v)RGJ where in 1989 David Innes handed over to Lieutenant Colonel John Poole-Warren, who was no

Royal Green Jackets – Volunteers

newcomer to the TA since he had been both second-in-command and training major in the 4th Battalion. Another development within 5(v)RGJ was the growing strength of the Waterloo Band. At a time when the numbers in regular bands were being steadily reduced, the volunteer band was flourishing. Within a year of its foundation it had forty-six members, twenty-seven of whom had enlisted into the old 5th Battalion as combatant riflemen in addition to their role as bandsmen. The Waterloo Band was set to go from strength of strength.

The 1990s was an era of downward pressure on budgets and a reduced allocation of training days per man. All of this was accepted with characteristic stoicism by the volunteer riflemen. Indeed, during the previous few years a new Home Service Force (HSF) Company, or H Company, had been formed by the Davies Street-based 4(v)RGJ. H Company contained some real regimental and battalion characters and, as one commanding officer put it, 'had a sort of life of its own'. Meanwhile, despite a bar on women joining the regular infantry battalions, female Green Jackets were emerging in Headquarters Company and in the Waterloo Band, more as a matter of course than an act of policy. It was only some years later that the British Army brought the territorial infantry battalions into line with the regular infantry, thus ending the novelty of female riflemen. Any sceptics were to be silenced by two female 4(v)RGJ teams performing with outstanding success in the Courage Trophy Military Skills Competition.

In 1990 the regiment commemorated the fiftieth anniversary of the defence of Calais, where regular and territorial riflemen had fought side by side with such distinction. A guard of honour from both 4(v)RGJ and 5(v)RGJ joined their regular colleagues in a fitting tribute and a rededication of the memorial at the site of the last stand in the harbour. That year the new TA Centre at High Wycombe was opened by Her Royal Highness The Duchess of Kent for A Company, which continued to develop its association with The Worshipful Company of Furniture Makers by supporting the livery company's activities in the City of London. The 5th Battalion's Home Service Force (HSF) Company, or I Company, was formed and it began recruiting under the slogan 'Riflemen never retire, they join the Home Service Force'.

Right: Davies Street, Bugle Fanfare.

Far right: Training in the TA Centre at Fulham House before a live firing exercise.

The Royal Green Jackets

By 1991 stormclouds were reappearing on the horizon for the reserve forces. The end of the Cold War and the outcome of the defence review Options for Change meant that 4(v)RGJ would lose one of its four rifle companies to conform to a new three-company establishment for TA battalions. Once again the riflemen set about ensuring maximum continuity and minimum disruption. Happily, both the 4th and 5th battalions of the regiment remained in the order of battle. A Home Service Force (HSF) Company also survived.

The reorganisation of 5(v)RGJ fell to Lieutenant Colonel Tim Corry, who assumed command from John Poole-Warren. But as 1991 drew to a close the peace dividend was in peril – Iraq had invaded Kuwait and a coalition was shaping up for war in the Gulf.

By 1992 Lieutenant Colonel Peter Luard had replaced Jamie Daniel as commander of 4(v)RGJ. F Company, at the Mile End Road, was to be closed down, and the HSF Company was absorbed into the battalion with minimum disruption. One bit of good news to come out of the defence review process was that the 4th Battalion was to be one of eight infantry TA battalions to support the ARRC (ACE Rapid Reaction Corps) through a training affiliation with 24 Airmobile Brigade. This meant that the battalion kept all its weapons, and its new role meant the retention of exciting opportunities for high-level training, which was important in keeping the riflemen motivated and the recruiting levels vibrant. Nevertheless, it was with sadness that later that year the battalion said farewell to its relationship with 12th Armoured Brigade with which they had trained long and often during the height of the Cold War for a conflict that, thankfully, never came – and many friends had been made in the process.

Later in the year A Company and the Waterloo Band and Bugles of 5(v)RGJ exercised the regiment's right of the freedom of High Wycombe, exciting the locals with their quick pace and the sounding of the bugles. Another result of Options for Change was that 5(v)RGJ was designated a national defence battalion, with a new role, new establishment and a new chain of command. As with 4(v)RGJ, its HSF Company was disbanded and absorbed into the remainder of the battalion with the three rifle companies in High Wycombe, Aylesbury and Milton Keynes.

As 1993 dawned, 4(v)RGJ's main intention was its integration with 24 Airmobile Brigade. The battalion's successful decade with 12th Armoured Brigade had done much to help it build a reputation as forward-looking thinkers on the employment of dismounted infantry in what was to be a predominantly armoured battle. At the time the battalion was given little indication of what its role would be, but being affiliated to 24 Airmobile Brigade for training purposes was the kind of exciting prospect that riflemen relished. It never turned out like that because the brigade was preoccupied with moving its headquarters from Tidworth to Colchester and taking on two regular infantry battalions and the Aviation Regiment.

True to their rifle traditions the 4th Battalion continued to place considerable effort on marksmanship. Throughout the 1980s its shooting team had consistently collected silver trophies at Bisley but its efforts peaked in 1993 when it won Bisley outright for the first time in the battalion's history. The 5th Battalion's exact role as national defence battalion remained unclear and by the end of 1993 the future size and structure of the TA remained uncertain. Nevertheless, the battalion sponsored an exchange with the US National Guard, and some 200 riflemen visited the United States with the same number of National Guardsmen joining the battalion for training at Worcop. The Waterloo Band of the 5th Battalion, now firmly established, continued to grow from strength to strength, performing in the counties of Oxfordshire and Buckinghamshire, and in London on Horse Guards Parade and at the United States Embassy.

Lack of clarity over the TA did not detract from either battalion's training in 1994. 4(v)RGJ consolidated its links with 24 Airmobile Brigade and took part for the first time in a CPX in Germany with the ARRC. In November Peter Luard handed over command of 4(v)RGJ to Lieutenant Colonel Tom Hamilton-Baillie, and in the same month the battalion provided a guard of honour for the Lord Mayor's Parade and at the Cenotaph for Remembrance Day.

Meanwhile, 5(v)RGJ was wrestling with the continuing fallout from Options for Change. The possibility of re-establishment as a territorial fire-support battalion was gaining currency. In May 1994 Lieutenant Colonel Robert (Bertie) Martin assumed command from Tim Corry. Nearly a year later, in April 1995, the TA was restructured and reorganised; 5(v)RGJ was indeed to become a fire-support battalion, and it was to be assigned to the ARRC.

4(v)RGJ's annual camp for 1995 was held on Salisbury Plain with the entire battalion fitted out with the latest laser simulation equipment. Salisbury Plain was one of the least popular locations for London's riflemen, who tended to find a night out in Amesbury (no offence to Amesbury) scant reward for two weeks' digging into the plain's rocky chalk. The camp, however, turned out to be a memorable one – the riflemen turned themselves into armoured infantrymen in Warrior AFVs borrowed from a regular battalion. A light mobile company was formed using the battalion's own Land Rovers. Battalion headquarters was given armoured command vehicles, and together with a squadron of tanks, 4(v)RGJ's 'battle group' provided the enemy force for a test exercise using the newly issued laser equipment. Many experts forecast disaster. The prevailing wisdom seemed to be that the TA was not skilled enough for armoured infantry work; also, the communications, which required the use of fiendishly complex codes, and the unfamiliar

Left: Annual Royal Green Jackets Carol Service, St George's, Hanover Square.

Left inset: Colin Fox, late 3RGJ Padre, 4(v)RGJ for twenty-three years and subsequently Honorary Chaplain The Royal Green Jackets.

Below: Colour Sergeant Murphy, Mortar Platoon.

Bottom left: Drill Night, fitness training at Davies Street.

Bottom right: TA and Cadets Annual Dinner, Davies Street. Colonel The Rt Hon. Sir Geoffrey Pattie, PC, Hon. Col 4(v)RGJ, 1996–9, and Deputy Colonel Commandant TA and Cadets, 1999–2007, with Brigadier His Grace The Duke of Westminster.

Left opposite: Rifleman 1987 dress presented to 4(v)RGJ by Neil Johnson.

weapons systems of the vehicles would be quite beyond them. After one week of learning the hard way, 4(v)RGJ's 'battle group' very nearly ruined the career of the highly regarded regular commanding officer of the battle group being exercised – an outcome that gave the volunteer riflemen a great deal of pleasure.

In Oxford, meanwhile, 5(v)RGJ was coming to terms with its newly acquired firepower, and the Waterloo Band, originally equipped at regimental expense and initiative, achieved formal recognition as a military band on the established strength of the battalion.

As the structure and roles of both the regular and volunteer forces were in flux throughout the early 1990s, and despite 'overstretch' having entered common parlance, both battalions provided significant numbers of volunteers to serve with regular Green Jacket battalions, other battalions of the Light Division and infantry battalions in general. These attachments were far too numerous to be listed here, but they ranged from the Balkans to BAOR to Northern Ireland. The new Reserve Forces Act (1996) made this flexibility easier to administer, and many volunteers from both battalions, which continued to thrive, were able to find the time and took the opportunity to taste regular service for six months or longer. Some then decided to become regular soldiers and were welcome additions to their chosen battalions. Also in 1996, a combined male and female team commanded by a Green Jacket-badged female officer came first in the Courage Trophy Military Skills Competition, although it was later penalised for being over the combined-team age limit.

The annual camp of 4(v)RGJ in 1996 was held at Sennybridge and the battalion's padre, Colin Fox, impressed all the riflemen by managing to arrange two weeks without rain! No thorough account of the history of the 4th Battalion would be complete without an earnest tribute to Colin's stewardship and ministry as padre over the course of three decades. A former regular officer in the 3rd Battalion The Royal Green Jackets, a tireless and enthusiastic Colin Fox was always to be found with the riflemen. His ministry was real, and is perhaps best exemplified by the baptism of a rifleman at camp at Otterburn in the mid-1980s. No regimental service would have seemed complete without Colin at its heart, carrying on the traditions established by his father, who had been chaplain to Queen Victoria's Rifles.

At the end of the Sennybridge camp came a final change of commanding officers when Tom Hamilton-Baillie handed over command to Lieutenant Colonel Mike Smith; although he did not know it at the time, he was to be the last commanding officer of 4(v)RGJ. Similarly, at 5(v)RGJ Lieutenant Colonel Greg Smith, a territorial officer, had assumed command from Bertie Martin, and the battalion showed great skill with support weapons such as the Milan, mortar and GPMG (SF). In the summer, 150 members of the battalion visited Pegasus Bridge and other battlefields associated with the invasion of Normandy. Named Exercise Ham and Jam, after the codeword sent by Major John Howard to signal that the bridges over the Orne river and the Caen Canal were secure, the tour included a poignant ceremony in the cemetery at Ranville before a march over Pegasus Bridge and a Sounding Retreat by the Waterloo Band on the banks of the canal. A number of veterans were present, and Madame Gondrée, the owner of Café Pegasus, invited the battalion to a champaign reception in her café that evening.

1997 started well for the 4th Battalion with the deployment of a company to Belize. The battalion also had a chance to show off the regiment during a successful 'Meet the Army' day in the East End of London, which was attended by a number of civic dignitaries and Members of Parliament. At the end of the year, one of the battalion's most loyal and dedicated characters left to an emotional send-off – Major Paddy Procter had held every rank from riflemen to second-in-command over twenty-nine years. He received a spontaneous, heartfelt standing ovation from the entire battalion at the Christmas dinner at Lydd camp.

5(v)RGJ's focus was on being operationally fit for its role by 1 April 1997. This was achieved in fine style with a testing exercise at the end of March, when the battalion deployed from RAF Lyneham, landed some thirty minutes later and then, with 1RGJ's Saxon armoured vehicles, deployed to Salisbury Plain where all the support weapons were fired live. The battalion was then declared 'operationally ready' and took its place in the ARRC order of battle. The battalion's tenth birthday was celebrated and its annual camp took the form of a brigade concentration at Sennybridge.

Further change was on the horizon. The Strategic Defence Review, or SDR, had been looming throughout 1997. Few, however, forecast the draconian effect it was to have on the TA in general, and its infantry battalions in particular. A fundamental reorganisation, by the end of 1997 it had become clear that both battalions would cease to exist and that in London two Green Jacket companies, one based in West Ham and the other in Davies Street (with a platoon located in Fulham House, Putney Bridge), would form part of a new multi-cap-badged London Regiment. The Green Jacket rifle companies at Oxford and Milton Keynes were to form a new multi-cap-badged home counties battalion to be known as The Royal Rifle Volunteers.

The Royal Green Jackets

It could have been even worse. The original plan was that just one rifle company would survive from the two battalions. It took an enormous amount of hard work, particularly by Lieutenant General Sir Christopher Wallace, the Representative Colonel Commandant of The Royal Green Jackets at the time, to argue the case for the survival of a 'critical mass' of Green Jacket-badged companies. Just as thirty years previously, these traumatic changes demanded high standards of leadership to maintain morale, motivation and the desire to serve, which was evident: 4(v)RGJ held its camp in Germany and on the way home half of the battalion attended a battlefield tour of Arnhem whilst the other half studied their forebears' exploits at Waterloo, before reuniting at Calais for a memorial service held around the Green Jacket memorial in the harbour. Meanwhile, 5(v)RGJ trained its platoons hard in support weapons. The battalion then exercised the freedom of Aylesbury that October, fifty years after The Oxfordshire and Buckinghamshire Light Infantry had first exercised its right in 1948 – an event that provided a fitting ceremonial high point to the year. Although at the beginning of 1999 both battalions could have been forgiven for taking a downbeat view on life, riflemen-like gallows humour provided most with a coping mechanism.

The 4th Battalion had its first exposure to the London Regiment in its newly amalgamated form at the Longmoor FIBUA complex. Spotting the different regimental attitudes, a rifleman christened this new 'phase of war' as SIBUA ('saluting in built-up areas')! Before the battalion was amalgamated with the old London Regiment, in June 4(v)RGJ held its final exercise as a battalion. The riflemen had requested a battlefield tour to sites where former rifle volunteers had fought; the battalion would visit four First World War battlefields and return via Calais as part of Exercise Last Post. The first stop was at Talbot House in Poperinghe, which between 1914 and 1918 remained just behind the Ypres salient front line. Talbot House, or TOC H as it became known in the military phonetic alphabet of the time, was named after an officer in The Rifle Brigade. It was a place where both officers and men could escape the horrors of battle and trench warfare by relaxing together reading, writing, praying in the attic chapel and walking in the garden. The house is a shrine to the men who fought in that war, and in particular those of The Queen's Westminster Rifles, which developed a close relationship with the house and the family that owned it. The house's contents had been left unharmed by having been put away when Belgium was invaded in 1940, then they were displayed again within twenty-four hours of the Allies liberating the town in 1944. Appropriately, it was during this visit that the battalion presented its padre, Colin Fox, with a First World War communion set from The London Rifle Brigade. Colin Fox was finally leaving the battalion after more than thirty years' service. With the Battalion gathered in the garden, the commanding officer, Mike Smith, presented the gift. The sun was shining as two white doves that had been on the roof of Toc H landed at their feet – it was a magical moment.

The battalion then moved to Ypres where it visited the Menin Gate, Hell Fire Corner and Hill 60, where Lieutenant Wooley of Queen Victoria's Rifles had won the Victoria Cross in 1915. The rapid tour continued via Nonne Boschen Wood and Tyne Cot Cemetery. By late evening the battalion had returned to Calais for its final service around the Green Jacket memorial.

Hard work and play continued right up to the end for 5(v)RGJ too. Battalion and regimental guests attended a Sounding Retreat, cocktail party and families day in May, and the Waterloo Band and Bugles, together with buglers from the Light Division band, played magnificently before they finally marched off the square to 'Auld Lang Syne' followed by the Regimental March. The next day some 500 members of the battalion and their families attended a final party that culminated with a spectacular firework display that lit up the skies over Oxford.

Into a New World

With typical rifleman-like pragmatism the four surviving companies – A, E, F and G companies – of 4(v)RGJ and 5(v)RGJ began working with their new battalions The London Regiment and The Royal Rifle Volunteers. Behind the scenes, however, a great deal of planning and not a little diplomacy was taking place. Charters for the new battalions had to be drawn up and agreed amongst their multi-cap-badged constituents. Major General Andrew Pringle, at the time serving with Christopher Wallace as his chief of staff at the Permanent Joint Headquarters, was charged with this important regimental responsibility, to be conducted in what little 'spare time' was available in that busy operational centre. (He was destined to assume the role of Representative Colonel Commandant from Christopher Wallace.) Outside London, plans for The Royal Rifle Volunteers developed reasonably smoothly, and a charter, incorporating the critical regimental characteristics of all the constituent parts of the battalion, was quickly and amicably agreed. There had been a slight tussle over whether the Waterloo Band of The Royal Green Jackets would lose its Green Jacket identity when it became the band of new unit. A happy compromise was reached whereby the band would remain Royal Green Jackets in every respect but would perform whenever appropriate for all the constituent parts of the new regiment. With that decision behind them the band went from strength to strength under the direction of Warrant Officer First Class (Bandmaster) Morgan.

Within London it looked as if it would take rather longer to reach a consensus. This was due, at least in part, to The Royal Green Jackets' early agreement to retain the name The London Regiment as the name for the new London battalion. It was a name with many historic First World War connections for Green Jacket territorial battalions. Unsurprisingly, there was confusion over whether the then current battalion of The London Regiment, already a multi-cap-badged battalion comprising companies bearing the cap-badges of The Princess of Wales's Royal Regiment, The Royal Regiment of Fusiliers, The London Scottish and The London Irish, and very much the Director of Infantry's exemplar for the future of the territorial infantry, was to be a continuing entity. If that had been the case the Green Jacket element would simply have been absorbed into an existing organisation. The Green Jackets were determined that, as with all other infantry territorial reorganisations underway, it be conducted on the

Bottom left: Pilgrimage to Calais, 1998.

Below: A group from F and G (Royal Green Jackets) Companies, The London Regiment, at annual camp in Romania, 2000.

Royal Green Jackets – Volunteers

Convoy escort near Al-Quma & the site of the Garden of Eden 2004

Above: F (Royal Green Jackets) Company, The London Regiment, on patrol in Iraq, 2003/4, painted by Corporal Matthew Cook, F (RGJ) Company, official War Artist for the Times.

Far right: Lieutenant Colonel James Cunliffe, Commanding Officer The London Regiment, 2000–3.

basis of amalgamation rather than absorption: The London Regiment and the 4th Battalion The Royal Green Jackets, which together would form a new regiment. In that way the two had an equal say in the construction of the new charter. The importance of that became clear when a new 'draft charter', drawn up by the existing London Regiment without any Green Jacket input, was presented for comment to the commanding officer of 4(v)RGJ – one that had everything to do with 'absorption' and nothing to do with 'amalgamation'. To get it right, it fell to Andrew Pringle and his team of company Honorary Colonels, together with Sir Geoffrey Pattie, Honorary Colonel 4(v)RGJ who would become Deputy Colonel Commandant Royal Green Jackets (TA and Cadets) on reorganisation.

There was never any doubt in the minds of the Green Jacket negotiating team as to which route was the acceptable one. It was vital to the individual riflemen to remain 'riflemen' in every respect. Simple absorption put that at risk; even so, it still took a considerable time to agree 'the way ahead' with the other regimental representatives. Eventually, the issues of ethos, dress, drill, cap-badges, letterheads, mess traditions, regimental appointments and a host of other sensitive topics were agreed. The London Regiment was indeed to be a new regiment and not simply the seamless continuation of the old one.

It took a little time for other elements of The London Regiment, all of which are 'heavy' rather than 'light' or 'rifle' infantry in origin, ethos and tradition, to come to terms with the Green Jacket way. The Green Jackets liked to think that their new colleagues had come to recognise some of the advantages, largely as a result of F and G companies regularly showing the way in competitions.

Meanwhile, out in the country A and E companies, which comprised half the strength of their new battalion, had started as they meant to go on – as the backbone of the new Royal Rifle Volunteers. Adding weight to the Green Jacket cause, the Waterloo Band established itself as a leading military band in the district and participated in the spectacular Royal Military Tattoo 2000 on Horse Guards Parade in London.

Towards the end of 2000 Lieutenant Colonel James Cunliffe returned to take command of The London Regiment. An end to a simmering 'rearguard' regimental battle was in sight. Despite the new charter, any insistence on strict adherence to Green Jacket regimental differences and traditions in the two Green Jacket companies had not always proved easy. James was a regular Green Jacket officer and had previously been adjutant of the 4th Battalion – he understood the volunteer ethos well. Both The London Regiment and the Green Jacket companies within it were safe in his hands. The concept of a partnership of equals was quickly reinforced with the proper acknowledgement to regimental traditions, ethos and differences for each of the differently cap-badged companies in the battalion. The London Regiment settled down happily in its reorganised form, and F and G companies retained their professional dominance within the battalion – the Green Jacket spirit remained safe in their hands.

As the regiment and its territorial elements entered the new millennium The Royal Green Jackets had four strong volunteer rifle companies all situated within 40 miles (65 km) of Davies Street. To a casual observer the dispositions looked remarkably like the way 4(v)RGJ was organised between 1967 and 1986.

As pressure on the regular army increased, with operations in Iraq and Afghanistan, 2003 saw the mobilisation of Territorial Army personnel to support their regular colleagues. Green Jacket Territorials were to undergo two months of training before deploying on a six-month tour of duty in Iraq as part of Cambrai Company of the London Regiment. Further deployments followed for Green Jacket territorials in both Iraq and Afghanistan involving personnel from A (RGJ) and E (RGJ) Companies of The Royal Rifle Volunteers, and F (RGJ) and G (RGJ) Companies of The London Regiment. Amongst those mobilised was Corporal Mathew Cook of F (RGJ) Company who also acted as the official War Artist for the *Times* and whose work has subsequently been acquired by the Imperial War Museum.

The period 2003–7 witnessed large-scale mobilisation of the TA. It was clear that support to the Regular Army from the Territorial Army was no longer simply desirable: it was essential. As recounted in Chapter 12, by 2007 all four Green Jacket territorial companies are once again happily together in the same battalion and have become Riflemen of 7th Battalion The Rifles. As this book draws to a close 7Rifles is deploying a 140-man company to volatile southern Afghanistan for a six-month operational tour in Helmand Province.

91

The Royal Green Jackets Cadets

There were more than 2,000 cadets in the Combined Cadet Force (CCF) and Army Cadet Force (ACF) who wore a Royal Green Jacket cap-badge. As such they were very much part of the Green Jacket family. Their interests were overseen by Sir Geoffrey Pattie, Deputy Colonel Commandant The Royal Green Jackets (TA and Cadets). He chaired regular meetings of the Regimental TA and Cadet Council, where representatives of the TA companies, the cadets and the regular battalions met together and arranged mutual support for each other. A much closer bond between the units resulted.

Cadet Sgt Mark Flanagan, one of the senior Cadets in the Merseyside ACF 2RGJ Detachment, 2005.

The regular battalions invariably provide instructors to assist at cadet annual camps and the inter-cadet force competitions, which are arranged on an annual basis. Each year a TA and Cadet Dinner is held at Davies Street at which Green Jacket officers and NCOs from the TA and the various cadet forces dine together. After-dinner speakers have included the Duke of Westminster. The Oxfordshire Royal Green Jacket Battalion, Army Cadet Force, was an established part of the Royal Green Jacket family for many years. Colonel Bob Hordle, its commandant, is responsible for ensuring that cadets are trained to the standards set out in the Army Proficiency Certificate Syllabus for Cadet Military Training. He also has a duty of care *in loco parentis* for the 700 cadets who are in his charge, which involves a variety of responsibilities:

> *The cadets attend one of twenty-five cadet detachments, in the city of Oxford and in towns and villages throughout Oxfordshire. The cadet battalion organisation is similar to that in the Army or TA: in our case we have four companies, each with five to eight platoons (detachments). Each detachment is split into four training cells called 'Stars': Basic, One, Two and Three Star. Four Star training is carried out with the assistance of the County Training Team made up of regular Army personnel, culminating in a one-week course at annual camp, at the end of which the cadets pass out with their Four Star Award.*
>
> *Detachments are commanded by adult cadet officers or senior adult cadet NCOs. The detachment commander is supported by two or three serjeant instructors. Typically, a detachment parades once per week, but some do two nights – especially if they are large, say over twenty-five cadets – in order to get through the training programme. Army Cadet Force adults are trained at Frimley Cadet Training Centre, and officers have to pass the Westbury Territorial Commissioning Board to gain their 'Type B' commissions.*

The Royal Green Jackets Cadets

OXFORDSHIRE ACF – NORMANDY 2007 BATTLEFIELD TOUR

Above and right: Oxfordshire ACF, newly-badged as The Rifles. Some 14,000 Cadets spread throughout the country became badged to The Rifles on 1 February 2007.

The Oxfordshire (RGJ) Bn ACF runs an annual 'Ham and Jam' battlefield tour to Normandy, to visit the 1944 D-Day beaches and participate in the commemorations of the actions of the 2nd Bn Oxfordshire and Buckinghamshire Light Infantry. The tour takes place between 1 to 7 June each year, and 2007 saw the ninth tour and the first wearing the new Rifles cap-badge. A maximum of seventeen cadets can attend, and in recent years there has always been a waiting list. The tour visits the US, British and Canadian beaches and the US and several British Military Cemeteries, thus learning of the magnitude of Operation Overlord and the sacrifices and cost of war in human terms. The 5 and 6 June are spent in participating in uniform at official French/Oxf & Bucks LI ceremonies at Ranville, Herouvillette and Escoville, plus the 7th (LI) Para ceremony at Benouville. It is these ceremonies, the appreciation of the French for their liberation and meeting the veterans of 1944 that have the most marked affect on the cadets, making them fully appreciate the events in Normandy during 1944. Oxfordshire ACF now also provides the buglers at these ceremonies to play Last Post and Reveille. In addition, the tour holds its own ceremony at Bayeux Military Cemetery, laying a wreath in memory of all who lost their lives during the Second World War. The tour is organised by Major Alan Hames, assisted by his wife and two sons, former cadets, now adult instructors.

Cadet LCpl Melissa Higgins of the Merseyside ACF 1 RGJ Detachment, the top shot in her company, 2005.

Cadets join aged twelve and leave at eighteen years nine months if they stay the full term. The cadets come from all walks of life. Some join from disadvantaged backgrounds, some may have been in trouble with the police, but whatever their weaknesses or strengths we recruit them and 'inspire them to achieve', to become better citizens, and to develop a real sense of community spirit.

Certainly, the sense of military discipline, and the skills learned through the training, band membership, Duke of Edinburgh's Award Scheme and NVQ/EDEXEL Scheme, help to make them more confident young people, and more attractive to future employers, including the regular Army. Adventurous Training, trips abroad, charity work and community work make the cadets more rounded, understanding and sympathetic youngsters. I believe the annual regular Army recruitment of ex-cadets comprises nearly 30 percent of the total intake.

The Army Cadet Force is sponsored by the Army, which supplies our uniforms and equipment, and our funding. As the Army's youth movement it has the largest 'green footprint' in many, if not all, of the sixty

93

The Royal Green Jackets

BUCKINGHAMSHIRE ACF
OBSERVATIONS OF AN HONORARY COLONEL, BRIGADIER DAVID INNES

The Army Cadet Force (ACF), the Army's youth movement, thrives in Buckinghamshire and the Army cadets of The Royal Green Jackets, and now The Rifles, are the largest uniformed youth movement in the county. There are nearly 500 of these young people based in twenty-two cadet detachments spread from Marlow in the Thames Valley and High Wycombe in the Chilterns northwards to the young and growing city of Milton Keynes. These extremes show the variety of the county both geographically and demographically. In some ways it is remarkable that one locally based youth organisation embraces such different areas, but this is one of the strengths of the movement and the same will be true elsewhere in the country. The Battalion or County Headquarters, and therefore the coordinating centre of the Bucks ACF, is in Aylesbury, for many years a centre for the Territorial Army in the county, and it is a mark of the success of the movement that in 2004 Battalion Headquarters moved into a new purpose-built headquarters, named Viney House after Major Elliot Viney DSO (of the Buckinghamshire Battalion [TA], the Oxfordshire and Buckinghamshire Light Infantry, and one of Buckinghamshire's most famous sons in recent times).

Cadets detachments meet twice a week for two hours and, on average, cadet activities take place somewhere on two weekends a month, occasionally more frequently. Most regular soldiers would be surprised at the numbers of young people on these occasions who dash home from school, don their boots and combat kit and a Green Jacket beret before spending an evening in the classroom or perhaps doing some practical training on a local area. Evening activities include learning about weapons, radios or First Aid, preparing for the next stage of the Duke of Edinburgh's Award or the coming weekend's competition, sporting activity or adventurous training expedition.

The initial attraction for many young people to join the Army Cadet Force (ACF), the Army's youth movement, is the opportunity to wear military uniform and to participate in outdoor pursuits and activities that many schools have difficulty in providing. Very few start with an ambition to join the Regular Army or the TA. Equally, very few have any difficulty in adapting to the Army's way of doing things – they readily accept the military rank structure and the hierarchy of supervision that applies in the ACF, and many respond magnificently to the opportunity to exercise some responsibility themselves. Many of the young people who join (they can now do so from as early as the age of twelve) have no previous family connections with the Armed Forces, but rather are encouraged to join by their school friends or by their interest in the military appearance of the movement. For some it is the physical training or sporting aspect that appeals, or simply the opportunity to do something different. In 2003 a cadet band was started in the Bucks Cadet Battalion, and this provides an interesting and unusual challenge for some. Most cadets are boys – female cadet numbers are limited to a percentage of the local unit – but the number of girls in the ACF is generally increasing, and in Buckinghamshire the girls are proving themselves good attenders and good, too, at some of the skills, such as shooting and handling weapons, at which boys might be more expected to excel. In the past, the Battalion's female contingent has produced several highly successful Lord Lieutenant's Cadets, as well as a female cadet Regimental Sergeant Major; additionally, female cadets have gained some outstanding Duke of Edinburgh's awards. It is also of note that the ACF syllabus is designed for all levels of ability – a number of our cadets attend special schools but compete well within the cadet movement.

The supervision of youth in corporate and mixed gender activities is becoming increasingly difficult for the adult instructors who volunteer for service with the ACF – there are about four permanent administrative staff in cadet battalions, everyone else is a volunteer. Over recent years legislation and regulation have imposed considerable restrictions upon the way in which young people are supervised and, to further complicate matters, the Army has imposed its own dimension on this. The result is that it is very difficult to find adults who are willing to commit to voluntary service with the movement because the demands made upon them are so strict. In many ways it is remarkable that anyone is prepared to take on responsibility for running a cadet detachment. This is likely to involve a building, maybe weapons and stores too, with a twice-weekly evening commitment and accompanying paperwork

High morale and companionship. Some of the Merseyside ACF Cadets from the 1 and 2RGJ Detachments on a training weekend at their HQ at Altcar, 2005.

The Royal Green Jackets Cadets

Cadet Rachel Duffy, a new recruit in the Merseyside ACF 2RGJ Detachment, 2005.

– all for no pay and few allowable expenses. When still serving and presiding at the Territorial Army Commissioning Board at Westbury, I always made a point of telling those being commissioned into the Reserve Forces about the additional responsibilities that cadet officers are obliged to take on through having to act *in loco parentis* for the minors in their care.

For me, one of the important motivators in attracting young people to organisations like this is the sense of belonging to something that is bigger than themselves. Too often this is lacking in their education or school life: many do not belong to sports teams or to other youth organisations, such as the Scouts or Guides, and to be part of something that is community based and enables people to contribute outside their own families can be of remarkable importance to young people today. Within local communities the cadet movement is playing an increasing part, particularly in terms of contributing to the Outreach initiative, which seeks to demonstrate to youngsters who are judged to be 'at risk' in their communities for whatever reason, the advantages of supervised, challenging group activities. Such young people may turn to crime or to vandalism if their energies are not channelled constructively, and frequently we find that young people who meet cadets and participate in these Outreach weekends are subsequently attracted to join themselves. Cadets are now also much more in the public eye than hitherto, regularly participating in church parades in different parts of the county and playing a supporting role at numerous functions.

Quite apart from the interest in shooting and wearing military uniform, numerous other activities appeal to the young people who become cadets: adventurous training, military music, sport and other group activities elsewhere in the UK – or even abroad – can have great appeal for young people, and the opportunity to represent their own cadet battalion is a particular draw. Each October the Lord Lieutenant presents cadets from all three services, including the local CCF contingents, with locally earned awards, and some remarkable personal success stories emerge. Perhaps unsurprisingly few of these successes are reported or achieve any visibility at all, even locally. On these occasions county-based Sea, Army and Air Training Corps cadet units (as well in fact as local CCF contingents) each nominate their highest achievers – certainly their smartest and most alert – as the Lord Lieutenant's Cadet. Those chosen accompany the Lord Lieutenant during the year at a variety of county functions, often having the opportunity of meeting members of the Royal Family.

One of the most important advantages that youngsters gain through service with the cadets is contact with each other and with adults who may bring to a young person's life a totally different perspective. This makes youngsters much more socially aware and may open the eyes of cadets to other possibilities in life. By no means all cadets stay the full course between the ages of twelve and eighteen, but they will all be marked by it and will retain some reference point to that period in their lives and may come back to it later. Personal development is key to success in the cadets. Those who show promise achieve cadet rank and added responsibility within the movement, while those who stay until their final year play a major part in running the organisation and administration of their detachments. There is no doubt that parents who see the development of their offspring in the ACF are often amazed at the change in their approach and motivation. One of the most satisfying things for anyone who has ever trained other people is to see growth and development in an individual when achieving in a new and unfamiliar arena.

The annual highlight for any cadet unit is Annual Camp – normally two weeks at the end of July – when a half or two-thirds of the total strength of the Battalion concentrate at one of the Army's training camps around the UK. Frequently this will give access to a major training area, such as Thetford in Norfolk or Dartmoor in Devon, but it may also take the Battalion away to other more remote parts of England and Scotland. For up to 25 per cent of cadets this may be the first time they have been away from home on their own, and for some it will be their only holiday. The regular battalions of the Regiment provide assistance and instructors to cadet camps wherever possible, cementing the bond between regiment and affiliated cadet movements. Camp activities vary from the purely military to adventure training. Biking, canoeing, abseiling, hiking, orienteering, access to helicopters, clay pigeon shooting and more can often be seen in cadet camp programmes.

The cadets identified themselves with The Royal Green Jackets, proudly wearing the cap-badge of the Regiment. Cadet units received visits from regular soldiers, several of whom had been cadets in the past. The Regiment arranged an annual schedule of senior officers who visited the cadets at camp and saw them training, feeding back observations and recommendations for further support to The Royal Green Jackets Deputy Colonel Commandant (TA and Cadets), Sir Geoffrey Pattie. Bucks ACF contingents participate in Cadet Sunday church services and small parades in different parts of the county every year.

With The Royal Green Jackets now merged into The Rifles, that identity and affiliation between the Regiment and the cadets passes seamlessly to The Rifles with the wearing of the new Rifles cap-badge. Appropriate parades were held to mark the change of affiliation and the adoption of the new cap-badge.

The Royal Green Jackets

counties in which it is represented. A true testimony of how well that money is spent can be seen at annual camp when at least 250–300 cadets carry out their training and testing to earn their Star badges. The regular Army visitors and civilians alike are invariably struck by the cadets' alertness and smartness, their professional attitude towards their training, and the way they confidently and cheerfully speak up when engaged in conversation. The Army Cadet Force is indeed a force for good.

In 1859 Octavia Hill started the Army Cadet Force in London, and if she were alive today she would be proud of the growth of her youth movement: some 42,000 cadets nationally, with numerous cadets in other countries around the world. If she had a dream of what the future held in store for the ACF, she could never have dreamt how integral to the community the Army Cadet Force has become.

Above: City of London School CCF annual five-day ski trip, 2007.

Top: Cadet Instructor Sgt Rachel Evans at the Southport Air Show and Military Display with a potential future recruit, Aaron (age three), 2005.

Affiliated Cadets

Combined Cadet Force:
- Bloxham School, Banbury, Oxfordshire
- City of London School, Victoria Embankment, Queen Victoria Street, London
- Downside School, Downside Abbey, Stratton-on-the-Fosse, near Bath, Somerset
- The Oratory School, Woodcote, near Reading, Berkshire
- Radley College, Abingdon, Berskhire Oxfordshire
- Rutlish School, Watery Lane, Merton Park, London
- Shiplake College, Henley-on-Thames, Oxfordshire
- St Edward's School, Oxford
- Winchester College, Winchester
- Harrow School Rifle Corps (CCF), Harrow on the Hill, Middlesex

Army Cadet Force:
- *Buckinghamshire*
  The Buckinghamshire Cadet Battalion The Royal Green Jackets
- *Hertfordshire*
  The Royal Green Jackets Platoon (No 2 Company) Hertfordshire ACF
- *London*
  City of London and North East Sector ACF No 23 Group
  Middlesex & North West London Sector ACF
  1st Cadet Battalion (KRRC) Royal Green Jackets
  Greater London and South West Sector ACF
- *Merseyside*
- *Northern Group*
- *Nottinghamshire*
  A (Robin Hood Rifles) Company
- *Oxfordshire*
  The Oxfordshire Royal Green Jackets Battalion ACF

Schools:
- College of Languages, Cobham
- Kings' School ACF, Winchester
- Royal Alexandra and Albert School ACF, Reigate
- Seldon High School ACF, South Croydon
- St Joseph's College, Croydon

Above and below: Oxfordshire ACF, Normandy battlefield tour, 2007.

96

1st Cadet Battalion King's Royal Rifle Corps

The Cadet Battalion has a long and proud history, and uniquely has been awarded the battle honour 'South Africa 1900–2'. Founded on 4 November 1894, and with the permission of HRH the Duke of Cambridge, Colonel-in-Chief, affiliated to The King's Royal Rifle Corps with the title '1st Cadet Battalion The King's Royal Rifle Corps', the Cadet Battalion enrolled 1,400 cadets in the first five years of its existence. Following the call in 1900 for volunteers for the South African War, in response to which it sent 100 senior cadets to serve with the City Imperial Volunteers, it has worn to this day the same miniature King's Royal Rifle Corps black cap-badge on a scarlet background. The cap-badge carries the Cadet Battalion's own battle honour 'South Africa 1900–2'. The award of the battle honour followed recognition by King Edward VII of the battalion's service in the war, and was recognised in Army Order 151 in 1905. Along with the Battle Honour and its cap-badge came the right for all cadets in the battalion to be called riflemen.

The First World War once again saw the Cadet Battalion offering its services. The offer was declined, but the cadets were encouraged to join the various London TA battalions. Almost to a man, all eighteen-year-old cadets enlisted; 400 to the 6th City of London Regiment and 100 to the 7th London Regiment. Numbers were to swell as the war progressed, with over 8,000 ex-cadets from the battalion eventually serving. Many decorations were won including 3 VCs, 4 DSOs, 12 MCs, one DCM, one MM, one Legion of Honour and one Croix de Guerre.

Shooting has always formed a major part of the battalion's training. Much use has been made of Bunhill Lodge at Bisley, which the Cadets manage on behalf of the Trustees. The lodge proudly displays The Royal Green Jackets badge and forms the centre for cadet shooting at Bisley. It is the last building on the common to have a regimental association. The 1st Cadet Battalion King's Royal Rifle Corps looks forward to the patronage of The Rifles whilst continuing to guard its KRRC history and the unique and much loved cap-badge.

Far right: 1st Cadet Battalion King's Royal Rifle Corps on parade, 1900.

Right: 1st Cadet Battalion King's Royal Rifle Corps cap-badge showing the battle honour, 'South Africa 1900–2'.

Below: Bunhill Lodge, Bisley, home to Green Jackets shooting for many years, now in the care of The Rifles Cadets.

Sgt Monaghan, 1st Cadet Battalion King's Royal Rifle Corps

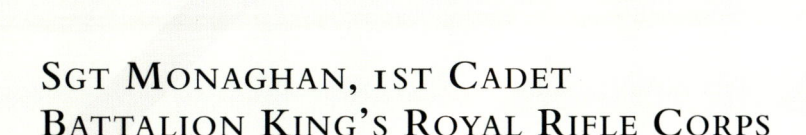

Sgt Monaghan completed his service in September 2004, having attained the upper age limit for cadet service. His shooting prowess was remarkable. He won three 'Cadet 100' small-bore badges and three 'Cadet 100' full-bore (Bisley) badges. In his final year of cadet service he won the National Small Bore Title with a score of 397 out of 400. He went on to lead the victorious ACF team in the .22 Cadet Inter-Services shoot, and at Bisley he won the Individual National Title at the Inter-Services Cadet Rifle Meeting, the Rifle Brigade Cup for the top ACF cadet and the Aggregate Cup. This was the first time that both full- and small-bore titles had been won by the same cadet in the same year. Sgt Monaghan went on to captain the ACF Team beating both the Sea Cadets and the Air Training Corps.

Sergeant Monaghan.

COUNTER-INSURGENCY: FROM GREEN JACKETS BRIGADE TO ROYAL GREEN JACKETS

The early 1960s was a period of considerable operational activity for the three regiments that were to become, on 1 January 1966, The Royal Green Jackets. The 'Confrontation' in Borneo was to ensure that all three partners came together having had recent experience of operational soldiering in the jungle. Both the 43rd & 52nd and The Rifle Brigade had undertaken anti-terrorist operations in Cyprus, Kenya and Malaya in the 1950s; the 60th Rifles, however, had seen no active service since Palestine in 1948, and therefore the Borneo experience was to be of particular value for 2nd Green Jackets, The King's Royal Rifle Corps (or the 60th, as it was still universally referred to). Patrolling with a live round in the chamber and the possibility of action, no matter at how low a level, concentrates a soldier's mind and sharpens his professionalism and self-confidence. It is for this reason that the inch of medal ribbon on the left chest is valued – or, perhaps, that its absence is felt. At the beginning of the 1960s the younger generation of riflemen in the 60th lacked this, and felt it.

In July 1963 2nd Green Jackets, commanded by Lieutenant Colonel Giles Mills, was mobilised at Colchester and flown hastily to British Guiana (now Guyana) in South America where trouble was brewing following a ten-week national strike. The speed with which the battalion deployed and its evident alertness and professionalism did much to ensure that the situation was contained. 'Swift and Bold' (Celer et Audax, the regimental motto), the battalion's show of strength persuaded potential trouble-makers that violent insurrection would be dealt with firmly. By January 1964 the battalion had returned to England without firing a round in anger; even so, it was a taste of operational soldiering for the riflemen of the 60th, as well as exposure to tropical heat and humidity. These would shortly prove to be immensely valuable.

Since November 1961 3rd Green Jackets, The Rifle Brigade, had been stationed at Dhekelia in Cyprus, first under Lieutenant Colonel Gris Davies-Scourfield and then under Lieutenant Colonel Hew Butler. Although the troubles initiated by EOKA (Greek for National Organisation of Cypriot Fighters), which had torn the island apart in the 1950s, had subsided, fresh disturbances were never far beneath the surface. The mistrust between the Greek and Turkish communities, and the ever-present fear among the latter that Greece might seek to annex the island, erupted periodically in public disorder. Usually these were minor and local outbreaks, but on 22 December 1963 violent hostilities resumed in earnest with inter-communal strife in Nicosia and Larnaca. The latter posed a particular problem for the British troops because most of the married men's families lived there, and it was felt that the presence of British troops in the area, albeit only moving peacefully between married quarters and Dhekelia, might in some way inflame the situation. The battalion was, in effect, frozen; no movement was allowed in to, out of or within Larnaca. Colonel Butler sent a few married men to rejoin and reassure their families, but with the battalion confined to barracks some 5 miles (8 km) away it was understandable that many families felt isolated and unprotected in an inter-communal 'war zone'. Several of those personnel with the

1st Battalion The Rifle Brigade, Mau Mau uprising, Kenya, 1955–6.

Counter-Insurgency

Above: 2nd Green Jackets, King's Royal Rifle Corps, British Guyana, 1963.

Right: Cyprus, 1963. Rfn Finch and Rfn Cobb, 3rd Green Jackets, The Rifle Brigade, with a Greek Cypriot policeman.

families in Larnaca were caught in crossfire, and bandsman Baldwin was killed. On Christmas Eve Colonel Butler was authorised to send the Reconnaissance Platoon, under Captain Jeremy Clowes, into Larnaca in an armoured patrol to move those in the most dangerous areas nearer to safety. The situation in the town was extremely delicate, so this had to be undertaken with sensitivity and tact. Two days later C Company, under Major Mike Tarleton, established two posts in Larnaca from which to keep the two sides apart. Shooting continued, and riflemen occasionally came under fire, usually mistakenly rather than intentionally, though one man was wounded.

By now Major General Peter Young, who had commanded the 43rd & 52nd in the 1950s and was now GOC Cyprus, had taken control of the situation and established a Green Line between the two communities in Nicosia, where the worst of the trouble was taking place. On 29 December he ordered the 3rd Green Jackets, The Rifle Brigade, to hand over Larnaca to The Sherwood Foresters, newly arrived from England, and for the battalion to move into Nicosia. Throughout January and February 1964 the riflemen held the ring between the two bellicose sides – tact, humour, patience and professionalism kept the lid on a simmering pot. Although there were murders and frequent outbursts of shooting, outright warfare was avoided. By the end of March an uneasy peace existed, the United Nations had deployed a peace-keeping force (United Nations Peacekeeping Force in Cyprus, UNFICYP) and the battalion had been withdrawn to its Dhekelia base. UNFICYP then awarded its troops a campaign medal, which was not offered to those riflemen who had taken the strain initially.

Meanwhile, 1st Green Jackets, 43rd & 52nd, had been in the Far East, in Brunei and Borneo. In April 1962, after a tour of duty at Warminster as the demonstration battalion, 1st Green Jackets, under Lieutenant Colonel Tod Sweeney, had deployed to Minden Barracks, Penang. The primary role of the Malaya-based battalion

99

The Royal Green Jackets

was to reinforce the Hong Kong garrison in the event of an insurrection. Although that would be largely an urban counter-insurgency task, jungle warfare skills had to be learned following the recent experience of combating the communist-led terrorist insurgency known as the 'Emergency'. Malaya had gained its independence in 1957, and the so-called Emergency had lasted from 1948 until 1960 – a campaign that had involved The Rifle Brigade throughout 1956 and 1957.

Peace and stability in the region seemed assured. Then, on 8 December 1962, a revolt broke out in the oil-rich sultanate of Brunei, a British Protectorate on the northern coast of Borneo. 1st/2nd Gurkha Rifles was flown in from Hong Kong that day, and on 9 December 1st Green Jackets was put on immediate notice to move there from Penang. After a rapid move to Singapore, the battalion embarked on HMS *Tiger*, bound for Labuan island. Major David Mostyn commanded Letter B Company:

> *It was the most remarkable mobilisation. From no notice at all, on a peaceful Sunday afternoon, with the second-in-command on leave in the UK, the adjutant in Singapore, the signals officer up on the Malay–Thai border, with officers, NCOs, men and families dispersed throughout the island (and me in between the first and second chukkas of a polo tournament at Ipoh). From beaches, sailing, trekking, sight-seeing, etc, the battalion had been mobilised, with its full first-line scale of equipment and ammunition, had moved by ferry to the mainland, then by road and rail to Singapore, and had embarked and sailed in HMS Tiger – all within thirty-six hours.*

Twenty-four hours later the battalion disembarked, not at Labuan as expected, but at Miri, a small oil terminal some 40 miles (64 km) down the coast, which was thought to be at risk. There the battalion found that although the situation was under control, the rebels had attacked the small *kampong*, or settlement, of Bekenu, a few miles inland from Tanjong Batu, which was about 15 miles (24 km) further down the coast. Having captured the police station and the local government offices, the insurgents had taken several hostages and seized the police arsenal, which included one light machine gun. The battalion was ordered to recapture the *kampong*, release the hostages and, if possible, regain the weapons. Colonel Sweeney tasked Mostyn's Letter B Company to undertake this. The Shell Oil Company offered a small craft and a rudimentary map that showed Bekenu was some 5 miles (8 km) inland on the north bank of the Sibuti River. The country in between – devoid of contours, streams or tracks – was 'unexplored'. Major Mostyn made his plan of attack:

> *I was determined not to sail my force up the Sibuti River and attempt a direct amphibious landing at Bekenu. That ploy had been tried by others at Limbang. The rebels had opened fire with a captured LMG [light machine gun] and the assault force had had a number of casualties. I decided, therefore, to disembark the company, less one platoon, at the small coastal village of Tanjong Batu, from where there was said to be a path east towards Bekenu. I ordered Nick Shaw and 6 Platoon to sail quietly up the river in the launch and hide up in the rushes short of Bekenu, to provide flanking fire support when we attacked and to control the river.*

> *At 17:00 on 12 December the rest of the company landed at Tanjong Batu and set off across country, led by a Police Field Force guide. The first mile, through mangrove swamp and paddy, was appalling. During a halt we heard that the only bridge over a stream was held by the rebels so, as surprise was essential, I decided to take a longer, circuitous route. We pressed on, through thick jungle and swamp, crossed a small river by using two native dugout canoes as ferries, and eventually reached the pepper garden just west of Bekenu. By now it was 09:30 and we had been going for sixteen hours. Having contacted Nick Shaw on the radio and heard that he was in position, I ordered H Hour for 09:45.*

Top: Supplies being dropped to 3GJ(RB)to Nibong Base, Borneo, 1965.

Top right: 2nd Infantry Division flash.

Above: Jungle patrol, Borneo, 1965.

Right: Merv Sprague (1GJ) in Borneo, 1965.

Counter-Insurgency

At H Hour we advanced through the pepper garden in open order, with Robert Hay-Drummond-Hay's 7 Platoon on the left, company HQ in the centre and Bob Mullard's 5 Platoon right. Behind, as my reserve, was my company second-in-command, Peter Blaker, who also commanded 8 (Support Weapons) Platoon. We breasted a small rise and saw the kampong below us. Then the shooting started; 12-bore solid shot from the rebels – surprisingly, and thankfully, they did not use the captured LMG. As we returned fire and charged, the rebels fled, attempting to escape by the river, where they were caught by fire from Nick's platoon.

We had just released the hostages unharmed and liberated the rebel flag (which now hangs in the RGJ Museum), when a beaming Chinaman tapped me on the shoulder. 'Welcome to Bekenu, sir, and how many will there be for lunch?' Having established that we had had no casualties, I replied 'Ninety'. Six of the rebels had been killed, another six captured, some wounded, and a further ten or so had escaped into the jungle. Following the Bekenu action about another 100 surrendered in the area.

Left: Tropical heat and humidity were a constant presence.

Below: 13 Platoon 3GJ(RB), commanded by Robert Pasley-Taylor, on return from an operation, Borneo 1965.

Although Bekenu effectively marked the end of the Brunei revolt, greater trouble was in store. In 1963 the Federation of Malaysia was born, comprising Malaya, Singapore (later to secede), Sabah (North Borneo) and Sarawak. The inclusion of Sabah and Sarawak was strongly resented by Indonesia, which controlled the largest part of the island immediately to the south, the southern and central areas known as Kalimantan, and had long coveted the northern areas of Sabah and Sarawak. Indonesia viewed the new federation as a threat to its own territorial ambitions. The revolt in Brunei, which lay between Sabah and Sarawak, heralded an undeclared war that was to become known as the 'Confrontation'.

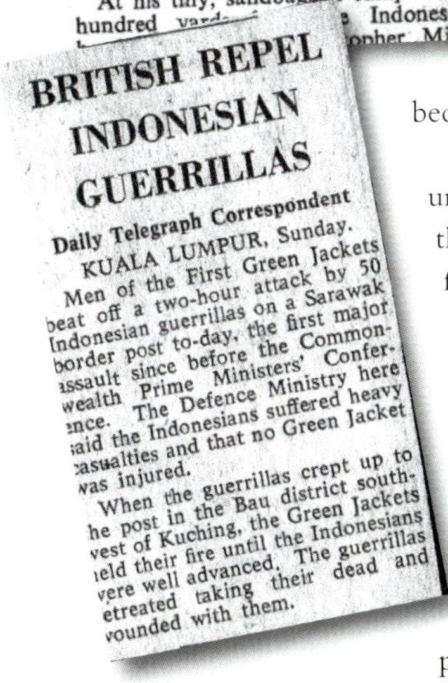

Early attempts to stir up trouble were largely unsuccessful; 1st Green Jackets stayed in Sarawak for three fairly uneventful months, tasked with searching for rebels and intercepting any Indonesian attempts at infiltration. Before too long raiding parties of Indonesian regular forces, or parties trained by them, began to operate against towns and villages across the border in the north. The aim of the parties seemed to be to penetrate ever more deeply and with increasing strength until main centres such as Kuching, the capital of Sarawak and only 25 miles (40 km) from the border, could be threatened and perhaps even over-run. Malaysia, with relatively small and unsophisticated forces, quickly called upon British and Commonwealth support. The resultant Borneo campaign was to involve all three of the regiments of The Green Jackets Brigade that would soon become The Royal Green Jackets. It would be impossible here to detail the activities of all three battalions over the next three years, so this account will outline only some of the main components and significant stories of the campaign.

In *The Jungle is Neutral* Colonel Spencer Chapman gave an account of his experiences in the Malayan jungle during the Second World War. Neutral the jungle may well be, but only after you have mastered the business of living in it. There is the tropical heat, which ensures that your clothes are always wringing wet, either with sweat or when the daily torrential downpour soaks you to the skin within a minute. The terrain is rugged and nearly mountainous, but covered by dense jungle, deep valleys and fast-flowing streams, all of which have to be crossed without giving your presence away. For a five-day patrol, it is necessary to carry everything you will need on your back. There are the problems of living in the jungle: no talking, no smoking, no washing (which means getting used to the reek of sweaty bodies), often no cooking, no bed (except the ground), no roof (except the hastily erected poncho), the smell of damp and rotting vegetation, the quiet alternating with jungle noises – and the tingle between the shoulder-blades when, as you lie in ambush, even the jungle noises stop and you feel the presence of another being moving in the area. In the jungle it is necessary to remain constantly alert in order to be able to respond to a sudden, unexpected clash with a hidden enemy. Add the leeches, snakes, red ants and a mass of other unattractive creepy-crawlies with which the jungle abounds and the environment is arguably as far removed as is possible from life in London, Birmingham, Liverpool or Oxford, where so many of the young riflemen who served with such distinction in Borneo hailed from. Soldiers who have lived entirely in towns and cities have to be taught to listen out for and recognise any unnatural sound, to look for and take in the detail of what they see, to identify the signs left by the movement of human beings through virgin jungle, and above all to get, as quickly as possible, on neutral terms with the jungle. Jungle soldiers must be supremely fit and expert at weapons' handling – slow and stealthy when moving, yet instantly ready to be quick and decisive in action. There is no room for passengers on jungle operations; it is infantry soldiering par excellence.

With a large area of jungle to dominate, battalions were deployed with permanently manned patrol bases well forward – to within a few thousand yards of the Indonesian border, in fact. The aim was to provide a springboard from which patrols and ambushes could be mounted against any Indonesian incursions and in which riflemen could live in comparative safety and with a reasonable

101

The Royal Green Jackets

degree of comfort, such as a bed, cooked meals and showers. Usually sited near border villages, for which they could provide protection, the base was also the focal point for gathering intelligence about the enemy over the border. Although, particularly in the early stages of the campaign, platoon-size bases existed, experience suggested that company-size bases were preferable because they enabled a platoon to go out on patrol without having to leave half its men behind guarding the base. The correct balance between offensive operations and base life was difficult to achieve, as had been shown at Plaman Mapu when the defensive requirements of a Parachute Regiment company base had been neglected and a strong Indonesian attack was mounted when most of the company was out on patrol. The base would have been overrun but for the extreme gallantry of the sergeant major and a few soldiers.

Lieutenant Colonel Edwin (affectionately known as Dwin) Bramall, who commanded 2nd Green Jackets, The King's Royal Rifle Corps, on two tours in Borneo (May–September 1965 and January–June 1966, as 2RGJ), described these company bases:

> Bases had to be prepared to withstand attack by a battalion group supported by mortars. Much attention had, therefore, to be paid to field works, fields of fire and defensive devices. All troops slept protected by overhead cover, or at least by thick blast walls, and all were within easy reach of their firing trenches where sentries manned LMGs, fixed-line GPMGs [general purpose machine gun] and the normal range of illuminations. All trenches were linked by telephone to a central command post. To the observer the finished article looked like a cross between a sector of a World War I trench system and a 'Wild West' fort occupied by the US Cavalry in some past Indian war.

Responsibility for running a company base usually fell on the company sergeant major. Sergeant Major Ron Cassidy of A Company, 3rd Green Jackets, The Rifle Brigade, which served in Sarawak from June 1965 to January 1966, explains:

> With the company commander, Major Mike Carleton-Smith, concentrating on operations, it was my job to run our base at Nibong, which was situated on a small hill in primary jungle about 2,000 yards [1,800 m] from the border, near a Dyak village. My remit from the company commander was to improve the base defences and make sure that all ammunition and grenades, which remained in the trenches on a permanent basis, were in first-class condition. This was not easy in the permanently damp conditions, but, as our testing was to prove, everything – Claymore mines sited in the barbed-wire surrounding the base and machine-guns in the sentry boxes – worked. Dawn and dusk 'stand-to' gave the platoons the chance to test-fire their weapons. At the same time our gunners could test their 105 mm howitzer and 4.2 in mortars, which lived at Nibong to support operations along the border. Firing 2 in HE [high explosive] mortar bombs from one end of the base to the other was soon discouraged as being too hazardous!
>
> Improving the trenches, bunkers and sleeping accommodation, all of which were underground, was a never-ending task, rather like painting

Above and left: Patrolling the rivers and riverbeds.

Counter-Insurgency

Right: Serudong Ulu, D Company 2RGJ base, Sabah, Borneo, 1966.

Below: 2RGJ, Sabah, Borneo, 1966, Platoon Base '291'. L–R: Lieutenant Mick Yasa, 9 Platoon Commander (a Fijian, joined as a rifleman, promoted to Corporal, attended Mons Officer Cadet School and commissioned. Now a Baptist Minister in New Zealand.); David Barnet, D Company; Vere Hayes, 9 Platoon Commander Designate.

the Forth Bridge. In order not to call on the platoons, who were either out on operations, or, if in the base, mounting the twenty-four-hour guard or resting, I had 150 Dyaks who were paid to work in the base.

All resupply came in by air, fixed-wing or helicopter – rations (fresh and compo), ammunition, defence stores, the colour sergeant's and NAAFI stores. Even fresh eggs arrived unbroken by parachute, a tribute to the RASC [Royal Army Service Corps] packers and dispatchers. Our DZ [drop zone] was in a clearing down the hill – after an airdrop it was all hands to the wheel to get everything carried up to the base as quickly as possible. Mail, the biggest morale booster, came in daily by helicopter.

Living on top of a hill, water should have been a problem. It wasn't; the solution was rifleman Reed! Give a rifleman an insoluble job and you will usually be rewarded with an excellent result. He pumped it from the river to tanks in the base and then ensured that it was purified. The only problems arose when the river was in flood and his two-stroke engine submerged. Hot water – Colour Sergeant Bill Taylor and I had learnt about that in Kenya! It was always available.

The Royal Green Jackets

"I STILL SAY IT'S ONE OF THE ROYAL ULSTER RIFLES ON THE SCROUNGE."
Cartoon drawn by Jak of the *Evening Standard* after visiting the Regiment at Bukit Knuckle in Sarawak
Reproduced by kind permission of the Editor of the "*Evening Standard*"

To make life better for platoons when they came in from operations we ran a canteen. Beer – a maximum of two cans per man per day. At one stage copious amounts of Coca-Cola were drunk. The company commander applauded this, until it emerged that the colour sergeant's rum reserve was disappearing at the same speed! Doubtless it was the same riflemen who always managed to 'lift' the eggs from the chickens and ducks I kept in the base!

There is a well-known military saying – 'Any fool can be uncomfortable'. We weren't. We lived a hard but remarkably comfortable existence for six months at Nibong. But leaving was not a wrench – we had been away from home and families for a full year.

Offensive operations could involve small reconnaissance patrols, ambushes of platoon or company strength, or attacks on located enemy positions, sometimes just over the border. Reconnaissance patrols would visit local *kampongs*, where they would seek to win the 'hearts and minds' of the local inhabitants (the medical officer often played an invaluable part in this); any information acquired from the locals might be of help in mounting an offensive operation. Given good information and a sound intelligence assessment, probably at battalion or company level, an ambush would be aimed at intercepting an Indonesian incursion. Unlike the Malayan Emergency, where a successful ambush might involve just a few terrorists, most of whom would flee rather than stand and fight, an encounter in Borneo might involve a company-strength force, the majority of whom, if not caught in the killing area, would mount a swift and strong counter-attack, perhaps supported by mortars. The ambush party had, therefore, to secure its flanks and rear and be prepared, having sprung the ambush, to pull back quickly through a series of pre-arranged rendezvous points (RVs), often held by other sections or platoons. Ambush teams would invariably have call on nearby artillery and mortars, probably sited in the nearest company base, which could bring down almost instantaneous supporting fire to cover the withdrawal of the ambush party or to harass a retreating enemy. Further back, helicopters would be on alert to bring in more troops to conduct follow-up operations quickly.

Ambushing was an exhausting and nerve-racking business, requiring a very high level of professionalism.

Above: River patrol, C Company 2RGJ, Serudong Laut, Sabah, Borneo, 1966.

Right: Serudong Ulu, D Company 2RGJ base, Sabah, Borneo, 1966. Note the Sioux helicopter of the 2RGJ Air Flight.

Opposite: Cpl Michael, C Coy 3GJ(RB).

Counter-Insurgency

point, and place 'panjis' (short, sharpened bamboo stakes stuck in the ground and grouped closely together, pointing towards the enemy) so that an enemy counter-attack quickly, and painfully, ran into them. He had also to lay down exactly how the ambush was to be sprung – perhaps the first burst of fire from the LMG gunner lying beside him, the detonation of the first grenades or Claymores, or, at night, the initiation of illumination. All this had to be carried out without leaving any signs that troops had been moving in the area or were concealed nearby.

For an ambush to be successful the initiative, obviously, has to lie with the ambusher – the first indication the enemy should receive is when it is hit by devastating fire. Once set, ambushing in Borneo required the very highest levels of self-discipline from every rifleman involved. A man who moved just a few inches, sniffed or coughed at the wrong moment could alert an approaching enemy. This might not just compromise the ambush but it could lead to a situation where the initiative lay firmly in the hands of the enemy. The best description of Borneo ambushes comes from those involved in two actions which are well known in Green Jacket annals.

Having returned to Penang in March 1963, 1st Green Jackets was given little time to rest before being sent back to Borneo for a second four-month tour in August. That was followed by another four months in Penang before the battalion returned for its third Borneo tour, in May 1964, now under the command of Lieutenant Colonel David House. Taking over an area from the 1st Division of Sarawak, the battalion was to have an eventful and highly successful tour, of which perhaps the high point was the action at Stass in late July 1964. Now commanding Letter B Company was Major Michael Koe:

I took over the Bau sector from 2/2 Gurkha Rifles on 14 July. Bau was about 15 miles [24 km] south of Kuching, and my sector covered about 25 miles [40 km] of border, along which were a series of Dyak kampongs, close up to the Indonesian border and about 7 miles [11 km] apart. The country was largely primary or secondary jungle, with open swampy areas. Movement had to be by helicopter or on foot. My three platoons were deployed forward, near the border kampongs of Stass (7 Platoon under Peter Chamberlin), Serikin (6 Platoon under Richard Hume Rothery) and Bukit Knuckle (5 Platoon under Christopher Miers). The platoons carried out daily patrols from their bases, both to dominate the area and to establish good relations with the locals.

On 18 July, a night attack on Bukit Knuckle was beaten off by 5 Platoon, with several enemy casualties. A few days later we had 'hard' intelligence of an imminent attack on Stass. I alerted Peter Chamberlin and brought forward David Roberts's 11 Platoon, from Letter C Company, to put out an ambush on the track from Stass to the border.

For two nights nothing happened, except that it rained almost unceasingly on 11 Platoon in its ambush position. At about 02:30 on 30 July the enemy attacked Stass. Second Lieutenant Peter Chamberlin, commanding 7 Platoon at Stass, takes up the story:

Three hundred and sixty-three days after commissioning and my baptism of fire! I was sound asleep at 02:30, having waited up till after 01:15 in anticipation of attack, when peace was shattered by a

Above: 2RGJ Recce Platoon, field firing, Malaya, 1966.

Left: Resupply by Wessex helicopter, 2RGJ Recce Platoon base '281', Sabah, Borneo.

The most usual site was a track likely to be used by an enemy infiltration force. In selecting the killing area the ambush commander had to carry out a careful reconnaissance to ensure that the maximum number of weapons (rifles, machine guns, grenades and Claymore mines) could cover the killing area. He had then to site flank-protection positions, in case the enemy did not come down the expected track. If his ambush was to be conducted at night, he had to place illumination flares so that the killing area was floodlit but the ambush party not blinded. And he had to select the withdrawal RVs, details of which must be clearly understood by all. He could then bring forward the ambush party, position every man where his weapon could best cover his allotted arc, set out his grenades or Claymore mines, with wires running to the detonation

105

deafening outburst of fire. Rushing from the command post to see what was going on I very nearly had my head taken off by a 2 in mortar light fired by my platoon sergeant, Sergeant Green. Thereafter a sense of exhilaration and euphoria as we riddled every possible hiding place with fire, including 3 in mortar fire using a helmet as the mortar baseplate, in order to reduce the range to 80 m [260 ft] so that we could engage anyone on our perimeter wire. The mortar was soon completely buried!

I have no idea how long the firefight lasted, but it became pretty clear that the enemy's fire was too high and thus ineffective. I must admit that I was thrilled by the discipline of the riflemen and the effectiveness of our fire. Eventually the opposition broke off the attack and withdrew. When the din had ceased we watched and waited. We had had no casualties, but everyone was on a high. And then at about 04:00 the amazing sound of 11 Platoon opening up, and the excitement of relaying David's fire-control orders to the gun at Serikin. Quite a night!

About half a mile away Second Lieutenant David Roberts and 11 Platoon heard the battle at Stass:

It was a very dark night and not raining, for once, so it was very startling when, at 02:30, a sudden and tremendous firefight started at Stass. I had sited our ambush at a 'Y'-track junction, with one arm of the 'Y' and the stem coming from Stass and the other arm going to the border. The main ambush position was between the arms of the 'Y', which gave us a good killing area, but posed the risk of our being attacked from the rear. So I sited an oval-shaped ambush, with my group facing forward and Sergeant Walker's facing the rear.

The pyrotechnic show from Stass was magnificent. After it died down our thoughts turned to the remote chance of the enemy using our track back to the border. I had almost given up hope when, at 04:12, we heard footsteps and whispered chatter and saw a pencil torch. Clearly they were coming round the rear of our position and would then turn into the killing area. Absolute silence and steadiness were essential – and were delivered. Time seemed almost endless – one rifleman later explained his steadiness as 'Rigid with fear!' I counted more than twenty enemy, and when I felt that the last of them was clear of our rear group and there was a solid body of them in the killing area, I sprung the ambush. Flares, grenades and small-arms fire shattered the night. A mere 5 m [16 ft] from the enemy, very close-range LMG fire from Rifleman Maltby and Rifleman Lewis killed those in the centre, while others died when they ran into exploding grenade-necklaces. There was some return fire and Rifleman Cowan was unfortunately hit by a ricochet.

As I expected a counter-attack from the leading part of the enemy, who had already passed through the killing area before I detonated the ambush, I pulled the platoon back quickly to a pre-arranged RV where we could more easily resist any assault. I then called down artillery fire on the ambush site and the border track. The first two rounds exploded in the trees almost above our heads, which called for some very speedy signal work by Lance Corporal Gibson. Dawn enabled us to move forward again and search the debris, which was done very thoroughly and professionally, revealing four bodies. This score later increased to six killed, with five more enemy wounded and nine missing.

Above left: 'Bukit Knuckle', 5 Platoon 1 GJ (43rd and 52nd) base, Borneo, 1964.

Above top: Captain Christopher Miers, soldier and artist.

Peter Uden was an eighteen-year-old rifleman who had only joined the battalion and 11 Platoon four months earlier:

I was, with Rifleman Gordon Bailey, the right-hand cut-off group, beside a small hut at the track junction. At about 04:00 I heard footsteps splashing in the muddy track behind me and low voices talking excitedly. They seemed to take forever to pass – I could hear some in the killing area while there were still others behind me. I had a slightly panicky thought that if the ambush was sprung now we would be surrounded. I remember trying to hold my breath in case they could hear my breathing. All this did was increase the pounding in my ears until I felt sure they could hear that!

Then the platoon commander sprung the ambush. The noise was terrific. By the light of the flares I could see movement and I fired a full SLR [self-loading rifle] magazine. When the flares died out the firing ceased. Shortly afterwards the platoon commander pulled us back and called down artillery fire. After dawn we returned to the ambush area, which we cleared, and then took the bodies back to 7 Platoon's base. I remember as we went through the perimeter wire the commanding officer, Lieutenant Colonel David House, was standing there with a big grin on his face. He shook hands with each one of us as we went past.

Above: Lieutenant David Roberts, 11 Platoon Commander (left) and 2nd Lieutenant Peter Chamberlin, 7 Platoon Commander (right), both 1 GJ (43rd and 52nd).

The enemy force was estimated as at least thirty strong. David Roberts's platoon, from which he had omitted those with coughs or other ailments that might compromise the ambush, amounted to about twenty. In mid-1965 it was announced that for their actions that night Second Lieutenant Roberts had been awarded the Military Cross, while Sergeant Walker and Rifleman Cowan had had a Mention in Dispatches. Major Koe summed it up:

Back at Bau we had listened to the action with growing excitement. It really was a classic operation. Both platoons performed outstandingly well and dealt the enemy a real blow. My only regret was that, while I was delighted by David Roberts's Military Cross for 11 Platoon's part in the action, the inevitable rationing of awards prevented Peter Chamberlin from receiving some recognition on behalf of 7 Platoon.

In October 1964 1st Green Jackets returned to Penang yet again. In February 1965 the battalion handed over to 2nd Green Jackets before returning to the UK and onwards to Berlin. In Germany, the emphasis on ceremonial was a marked contrast from jungle operations.

With intensive army patrolling and ambushing dominating the area north of the border, Indonesian incursions were becoming few and far between. But if the British Army lowered its guard and reduced force levels, the Indonesians still had the ability to turn the tap on again. They were operating from secure bases sited just a few miles south of the border, and the British and Commonwealth forces were then not allowed to operate there. Policy was therefore changed and a decision was taken to attack these bases; undermining Indonesian confidence in their own safety should force them to withdraw deeper into Kalimantan, making it more difficult for them to mount offensive operations into north Borneo. And so the British Army quietly went onto the offensive. These 'Claret' operations were kept on a strict 'need to know' basis, and they were only publicly acknowledged some years later. They involved both 2nd and 3rd Green Jackets; the former, commanded by Lieutenant Colonel Bramall, was to have just three months in Penang in which to train for jungle operations, before moving in early May 1965 to Borneo. The battalion's most notable operation, one of a sequence of actions mounted against enemy bases south of the Sarawak–Kalimantan border, occurred in August 1965.

D Company, commanded by Major Bob Pascoe, was ordered to ambush a track that ran beside the Sekayan River to the enemy base at Mankau. Although the track ran along the west bank of the river, Lieutenant Colonel Bramall considered, from earlier experience, that it would be unwise to cross this spate river because of the risk of being cut off. The ambush was therefore to be sited on the east bank, about 5,500 m (6,000 yards) over the Indonesian border. Taking all three of his platoons, Major Pascoe moved across country, avoiding tracks, until he reached an escarpment about a mile short of the river. Here he left Lieutenant Kit Brinkley's 16 Platoon, to provide depth and to secure the withdrawal route. At the foot of the escarpment, he established his firm base, with Lieutenant Richard Hill's 15 Platoon, an artillery forward observation officer and his mortar base-plate. He then took forward the main ambush force, Lieutenant Mike Robertson's 14 Platoon, which he sited before returning to his firm base. Robertson takes up the story:

I don't remember being particularly excited or apprehensive as we descended into enemy territory. Heavily laden down with food and ammunition, soaked as always in the jungle, trying to map-read off air-photographs, we slipped and slid, swore and grabbed handfuls of prickles as we tried to keep upright and hack our way through almost impenetrable, dripping jungle. Eventually we hit the river at exactly the right place. I remember feeling quietly chuffed, having had serious doubts on the way.

I sited the ambush on the only possible place overlooking the path on the far side of the river. It was far from ideal – only just enough cover and on a small lip on the edge of the river, which saved the killing group from being exposed on a forward slope. And I sited cut-off groups towards the kampong and behind us. The platoon was organised into two patrols, one under Corporal Nobby Winkworth, the other under the incorrigible Corporal Pat Kirby – both really good riflemen. With them and Sergeant Danny Hunt, I had as good a team as one could

wish for. Danny Hunt, with his quiet sense of humour, was a real pragmatist and excellent at keeping even the doziest rifleman (and the platoon commander!) up to the mark. The two patrols took turn and turn about in the ambush site, while Danny, Rifleman Martin (my runner), and I were just above and behind the killer group.

Time ticked by – first one day, then the next, until we felt that we should soon have to pull out, not least because having taken two days to reach the ambush position we had by now eaten most of our rations. But clearly information from battalion headquarters indicated that the enemy were still expected. We stayed put.

I remember looking up blearily in the stifling heat at the path we had stared at for so long, and suddenly, there was a man – in bright green fatigues, carrying a weapon, entering stage right. My heart raced as I tugged the communication cords to alert the others – and another figure appeared. The ambush was to be sprung by my shot; but at who? How many were there? Was this a section? A platoon? I hoped not more than that as there were only nine of us in the killer group. Who should I shoot at? Where would the commander be travelling? – perhaps, like me, behind the lead scouts to control the patrol? I sensed the others tensing and I fired at number three, now well in view on the path. He was hit, but total silence as he fell – then suddenly the noise was overwhelming – more figures, a stream of firing and shouting across the water. Shots were coming back now, but high, mostly from the jungle to our right. Then suddenly they found us and we were flat on our faces. But the riflemen were terrific, firing exactly as trained and driven by the rush of it all. I remember seeing an Indonesian .5 in Browning heavy machine gun being brought up and sited behind a tree. I suppose I was trying to control the fire fight, though I don't really remember that, while Danny Hunt was trying to locate the Browning before it found us. We yelled at Martin to get up and run to a tree – that drew the fire and Danny Hunt located the Browning and silenced it with a well-aimed shot from the M79 grenade launcher. But more men, now running forward towards us, into the river – how many for goodness' sake? More firing and terrible noise. Time to go; but how?

We threw white phosphorus, got up, ran, zig-zagged back to deeper cover and bigger trees, knees like jelly, mouth totally dry, heart-rate 500 to the minute – total adrenaline! Was everyone there, was anyone hurt? And then a mortar started firing at us. But no Rifleman Martin – had he not heard us? Danny Hunt and I told the platoon to head back to the first RV. They set off while we went back to the scene. We found Martin behind a tree. It was clear he had been hit and there was still a great deal of shooting going on. No time to check where he was hit or by what, just a mad rush back to the others carrying him as best we could.

The events that followed are still something of a blur, except the total calm of Bob Pascoe and the quiet efficiency of Danny Hunt. With the enemy still coming, we had to pull back as fast as possible, especially as Martin had been hit a number of times. We must get him back over the border quickly for helicopter evacuation. We dropped off stay-behind parties to protect our rear, but the enemy had lost enthusiasm for the pursuit. Carrying a stretcher uphill in jungle is almost a platoon task, but eventually we slipped and slid our way over the border, where a heli-pad had been cut and we sent Rifleman Martin on his way – a brave and uncomplaining rifleman.

Counter-Insurgency

It later transpired that Robertson's small group of nine men covering the killing area had taken on an Indonesian company of some 120 men. Fourteen of the enemy were killed in the action. In due course it was announced that Lieutenant Mike Robertson had been awarded the Military Cross and Sergeant Danny Hunt a Mention in Dispatches.

In late December 1964 3rd Green Jackets, stationed at Felixstowe under Lieutenant Colonel Mark Bond, was dispatched at ten days' notice for a year-long tour of Hong Kong and Borneo. Arriving in Sarawak in late June, the battalion was to have a relatively uneventful tour compared to the other two battalions. But in October a patrol of two platoons under Captain Mark Scrase-Dickins mounted a successful attack on an Indonesian base:

I took two platoons over the border and carried out a very detailed recce of the Indonesian base at Boenkang. At the time it was unoccupied so I was able virtually to enter the base, but there was the odd civilian about so we withdrew, planning to return later. When I did return, with 7 Platoon under Alastair Stewart and the Recce Platoon under Sergeant Cameron, we found that the clearing around the huts had been considerably extended, but we were able to get into position undiscovered. The enemy consisted of a force of about platoon strength. A communications failure made things a little difficult, but Alastair opened fire at exactly the right moment and we met little opposition. I remember that Corporal (as he then was; later Lieutenant Colonel) Bill Logden was particularly effective. We then withdrew through the back-up platoon and brought 105 mm artillery fire down on the area. We hoped that the Indonesians would mount a follow-up and we were ready for that, but they confined themselves to some desultory mortar fire which did not cause us any problems, so we withdrew over the border. It transpired that in the attack we had killed eight and wounded five, and that the subsequent artillery fire had caused another two casualties.

On 2 January 1966, the day after it became 3rd Battalion The Royal Green Jackets, the battalion handed over its operational responsibilities to the Durham Light Infantry, and by mid-January it had returned to Felixstowe.

By the 1980s Mark Scrase-Dickins had left the British Army and become the political counsellor in the British Embassy in Jakarta, where he became friends with General Benni Moerdani, commander-in-chief of the Indonesian Armed Forces. During 'Confrontation' Moerdani had commanded a battalion of Indonesian Special Forces, formidable troops of a very different calibre from the regular army. He revealed his respect for, and admiration of, the professionalism of all three Green Jacket battalions, which he had come to know well.

'Confrontation' actually served as one of the foundation stones of the new regiment because so many of the young officers, NCOs and riflemen who grew up and learned their trade in the Borneo jungle were to become the backbone of The Royal Green Jackets' officers' and sergeants' messes. Their experience, self-confidence and professionalism were to prove invaluable just a few years later when all three battalions of the new regiment found themselves in rather different forms of jungle – the concrete ones of Belfast and Londonderry.

Above: Setting out on a clearing patrol around a company base.

Right: Lieutenant Mike Robertson and Sgt Danny Hunt 14 Platoon, 2nd Green Jackets, KRRC, withdrawing from the ambush of an Indonesian company, Sarawak, 1965.

Left: C Company 2RGJ, Sabah, Borneo, 1966, Rifleman Boarer (left) and Corporal Curtis (right).

109

NORTHERN IRELAND 1969–2007

During the last thirty years of the twentieth century 'The Troubles' in Northern Ireland dominated the domestic political agenda of the United Kingdom, and the province provided the setting for most of the British Army's operational activity. Every infantry battalion, with the exception of the Gurkhas, served there on a regular basis; and so, too, in one guise or another, did most of the other elements of the Army and the Royal Marines, as well as the helicopter forces of the Royal Air Force (RAF) and the Royal Navy.

When The Troubles started in 1969, 1RGJ deployed first into the western counties of Ulster and subsequently into Belfast. In 1998, when the Good Friday Agreement was signed, 1RGJ was again in Belfast. It was another nine years until the campaign officially ended, in July 2007. Over the decades battalions of the regiment deployed to the province on six residential tours of either twenty-four or thirty months, and on twenty-four roulement tours of either four or six months. During that thirty-year period, there were only four in which there was no Green Jacket battalion serving in Northern Ireland. And while the battalions often operated alongside each other, or indeed deployed elements under the command of another Green Jacket battalion, on two occasions – in 1972 and 1991 – all three battalions were there at the same time. It is perhaps worth noting that while the campaign itself was very much a rifleman's war, the regiment also provided a significant number of senior commanders in the province – two General Officers Commanding (GOC), two Commanders

Above: 1RGJ patrol leaving Albert Street Mill, Lower Falls, Belfast, 1971.

Above right: 2RGJ, Londonderry, 1971.

Right: Early days, rural patrol.

Top: Recovering a casualty, 2RGJ Londonderry, 1971.

Land Forces (CLF) and twelve brigade commanders.

The impact of these tours on the development of The Royal Green Jackets as a regiment was profound, and their value equally significant. Most importantly, it developed the cohesion of the regiment and confirmed the very real benefits that could come from the 'large regiment' concept (see Chapter 2). In 1969, only three years after the establishment of The Royal Green Jackets, most ranks were still, if not in a 43rd & 52nd, 60th, or Rifle Brigade mindset, certainly in 1st, 2nd, and 3rd Battalion mode – with their loyalty owed more to the battalion than to the regiment. Through shared experiences and natural cross-postings between battalions, riflemen, whether officers or other ranks, began quickly to see themselves as part of a regiment, and only temporarily as a member of a particular battalion. This came about for three main reasons: first, the gradual disappearance from the regular battalions of anyone who had served in the antecedent regiments; second, as a result of the battalions serving alongside each other and even, on occasions, being under the command of another Green Jacket battalion; and third, as a result of the ease with which postings took place between battalions, which offered value in both operational and personal terms. There can be no doubt that R Company not only benefited enormously from its six weeks under the command of 1RGJ in the Lower Falls, Belfast, in 1971, its men also recognised, as perhaps they had not done before, that the members of 1RGJ were not only very capable and effective, but were also similar in every respect – and were actually pleasant people! The cross-fertilisation, which inter-battalion postings encouraged, meant that the knowledge and the experiences of each battalion were more widely spread and more generally implemented.

Riflemen will have their own stories and memories of their postings and attachments to other battalions, but it is likely that all will recognise the value of the sense of familiarity that a common regimental ethos and culture meant to them. It is also worth noting the similar benefits that accrued to the Regiment from its association with, or at least exposure to, other units whether in the Army, Royal Marines or Royal Air Force; when you depend on another organisation – whether it be RAF or Army Air Corps (AAC) helicopter support, the bomb disposal capability provided so gallantly by the Ammunition Technical Officers, armoured cars from the Royal Armoured Corps, or another headquarters – you quickly come to appreciate that their standards and their commitment are similar to your own. At the same time the battalions benefited hugely from the secondment of a variety of officers from other regiments, arms and corps, who brought with

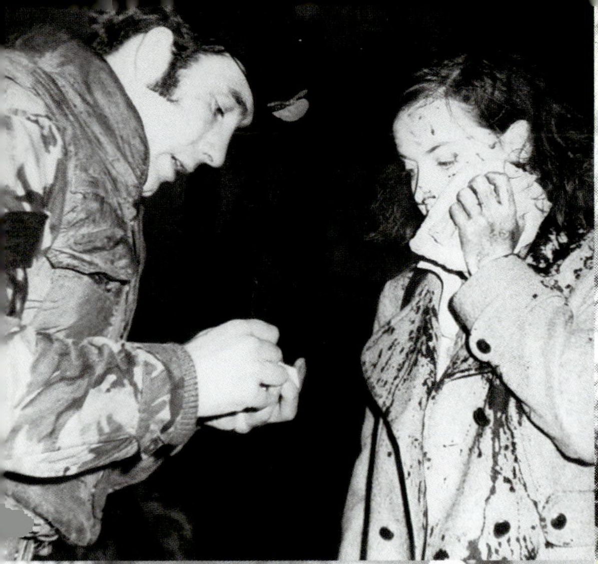

GREEN
JACKETS

WANTED
for murder
and torture of
Irish prisoners

Northern Ireland 1969–2007

Above: Belfast, 1972.

Above top right: Rural bomb disposal, clearing a booby-trapped lorry.

Above right: Brigadier Frank Kitson, late RGJ, Commander, 39 Infantry Brigade, Belfast, and Lieutenant Colonel Roly Guy, Commanding Officer 1RGJ, Lower Falls, Belfast, 1971.

Below right: The yellow card, orders for opening fire, carried by all soldiers on operations.

Opposite: The Riflemen's war. The Riflemen and their young NCO and officer leaders bore the brunt of the campaign from 1969 to 2007.

them their distinctive attitudes, experiences and understanding. And, of course, the process was reciprocal, as the Royal Marines' company sergeant major clearly recognised when his operations room in North Howard Street Mill, Belfast, was invaded in 1989 by a 3RGJ close-observation platoon Junior NCO in a cut-off T-shirt, combat trousers and zippered boots. On being asked what 'the –' he wanted, Corporal Garnett suggested, 'cup o' tea, Sergeant-Major?'

The second major impact was on the professionalism of the regiment, and not just in the rifle companies. Deployments to Northern Ireland put the whole battalion on an operational footing, and this meant that all its procedures and activities were continuously being tested. From the families' office to the motor transport platoon, from the orderly room to the medical centre, procedures were scrutinised and improved. The regiment developed operational experience in considerable depth as the Northern Ireland tours started soon after the ending of 'Confrontation' in Borneo, where all three battalions had deployed widely. At the same time, training improved. Before 1969, training for battalions in the UK had little real focus other than as a general strategic reserve. As the need for both specialist and more general training became necessary on a continuing basis to meet the real operational demands of service in Northern Ireland, the level of individual and sub-unit capability, tactical awareness and wider understanding became greater. With this professionalism came a greater sense of corporate confidence. The turnover in riflemen was as great as ever during these years – many only served for three years; often a platoon would contain half or fewer of the riflemen who had deployed with it a year before. Yet even so, its operational ability seemed unimpaired. Battalions acquired a corporate knowledge and experience from continuous Northern Ireland operations, all of which fed through into a wider and sustained operational capability and professionalism.

This development was accompanied by an equally significant, if less welcome, one: the increasing isolation, if not alienation, of the military from civilian society. This happened slowly and was due to various factors: in the 1960s, social attitudes among younger people became more anti-militaristic than for some time previously; the start of The Troubles elicited considerable sympathy among sections of the broader UK population for the underdog, the less privileged Northern Irish Catholics, with an associated distrust of the actions of the Stormont government and, by extension, that at Westminster; and the growing threat of terrorism on the British mainland meant that personnel in military uniforms were no longer seen in public, and that military garrisons were increasingly isolated behind screens of barbed wire, becoming places where the public rarely went. The Army came to be seen more and more as another arm of government rather than 'society' in uniform; as a result, there was an increasing divergence between military values and ideals and those of society at large. This had an adverse impact on recruiting and often on the opportunities for post-Service employment. Civilian society increasingly failed to appreciate or understand military standards and values.

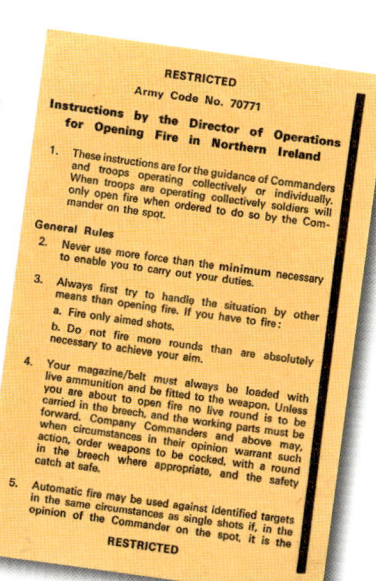

Finally, it is worth emphasising that the

113

The Royal Green Jackets

nature of operations in Northern Ireland played to the strengths of the Green Jacket way. From the outset, in 1969, decision-making on operations took place at the lowest level; patrols were routinely commanded by Junior NCOs or the youngest officers, and in the event of a 'contact' decisions had to be taken quickly and without immediate advice. Thus the value of the thinking rifleman, who was encouraged to 'do everything that was necessary and nothing that was not', came into its own once again. The campaign was made for riflemen and Junior NCOs; it is they who have been recognised and who will be best remembered for their achievements during it. They carried the risk on a daily, if not hourly, basis; they showed incessant alertness; and they ensured that, throughout the campaign, the regiment was considered a professional, effective and versatile force.

Beginning as a protest to demand civil rights, the situation in Northern Ireland escalated rapidly from an anti-government campaign into a terrorist war. In 1971 Corporal Bankier of 1RGJ was one of the first soldiers to be killed in action on the province's streets. A further 650 soldiers were to be killed and 6,307 wounded or injured before the campaign came to an end. Bankier was a corporal bugler, one of the best in the battalion, who was shot by a sniper whilst leading his section in the Markets area of West Belfast. In the early phases of the campaign the Army had deployed to protect the Roman Catholic population from violent Protestant Loyalist mobs, and the 'Angels of the Falls Road' were much in evidence in 1969, bringing tea and sympathy to 1RGJ during their Belfast commitment, but before long the Irish Republican Army (IRA) had capitalised on the political uncertainty in the province to initiate a bloody terrorist campaign against the British presence. The IRA campaign endured for nearly thirty years, until the Good Friday Agreement in 1998.

Throughout it all the role of the Army was to support the police (the Royal Ulster Constabulary) in maintaining law and order. This subordination of the Army to the police, a fundamental article of civil–military relations, was initially perhaps honoured more in theory than in practice, because the police had been largely removed from the streets following the deployment of the Army in 1969. However, in 1976, with police morale restored and large numbers of new recruits trained, 'Police Primacy' became the declared policy and an

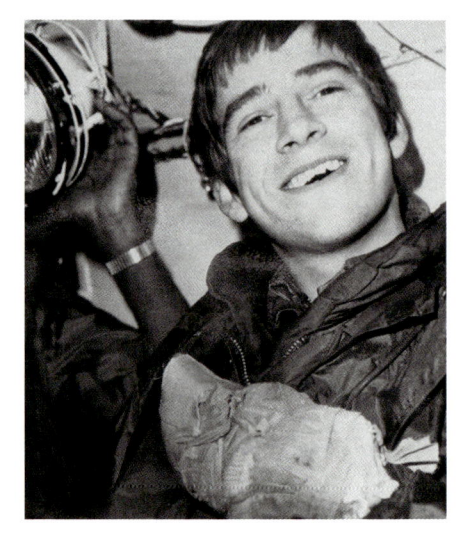

THE COST OF REPUBLICAN TERRORISM

1RGJ, THREE OP BANNER TOURS AMONGST MANY CONDUCTED BY ALL THREE BATTALIONS

1971, Belfast, Lower Falls

Cpl Bankier	Killed	Gunshot wound (GSW)
Rfn Walker	Killed	GSW
Cpl Kneller	Wounded	GSW
2/Lt Daniell	Wounded	GSW
Rfn Wagstaff	Wounded	GSW
Cpl Fairhurst	Wounded	GSW
Rfn Courtney	Wounded	GSW
Rfn Hawkins	Wounded	GSW
Rfn Taylor	Wounded	GSW
Rfn Nixon	Wounded	GSW
2/Lt Dixon	Wounded	GSW
Rfn Harvey	Wounded	GSW

1972, Belfast, Andersonstown

L/Cpl Card	Killed	Gunshot wound (GSW)
Maj Johnson	Wounded	Bombed
L/Cpl Rowledge	Wounded	Bombed
WOII Osmand	Wounded	Bombed
Capt Logdon	Wounded	Bombed
L/Cpl Harrison	Wounded	Bombed
Rfn Day	Wounded	Bombed
Rfn Willett	Wounded	Bombed
Rfn Lawrence	Wounded	Bombed
Cpl Rathbone	Wounded	GSW
L/Cpl Austin	Wounded	Crash injuries (ambush)
Rfn Marshall	Wounded	GSW
L/Cpl Frampton	Wounded	GSW
Cpl Cheetham	Wounded	GSW
Rfn Vaxley	Wounded	Riot lacerations
Rfn Edwards	Wounded	Riot lacerations
Rfn Critchley	Wounded	Riot lacerations
Rfn Hall	Wounded	GSW
Rfn Penford	Wounded	GSW

1973, Belfast, Lower Falls

Rfn Vehya	Wounded	Bombed
Rfn Featherstone	Wounded	Bombed
Rfn Clayton	Wounded	GSW

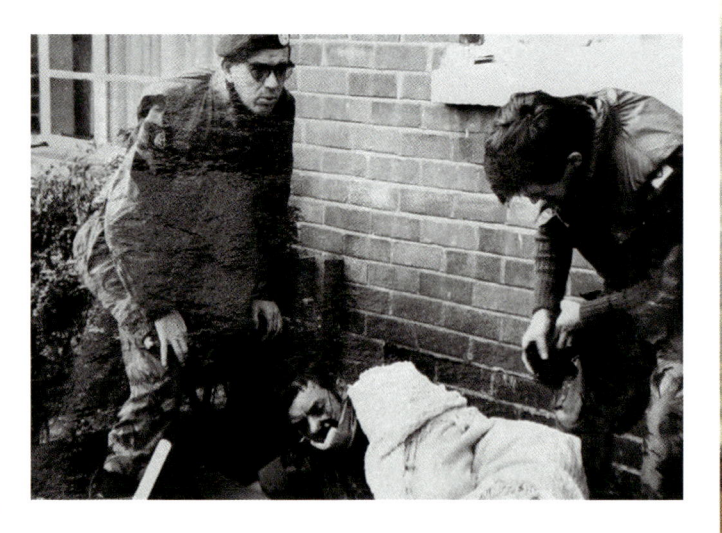

Above left: Lance Corporal Harrison, 1RGJ, being treated by Sergeant 'Doc' French and the Regimental Medical Officer, Captain Kenny Brown, Belfast, 1972.

Above: 'Aggro Corner', Londonderry, 1971. Well-known particularly to 2RGJ.

Opposite left: Rifleman Penford, 1RGJ, cheerful, despite having been shot in the hand.

Opposite right: Rifleman Lawrence, 1RGJ, wounded but alert.

increasingly close relationship developed between the RUC and The Royal Green Jackets. Operational success depended upon close links between the battalion Operations and Intelligence staff and the RUC, who provided the Intelligence support. The RUC went out of its way to develop a smooth working relationship with battalions deploying to Northern Ireland; its personnel would visit pre-Northern Ireland training, brief the battalion on the operational situation, dispel as many myths as they could and ensure that the unit was as prepared as possible for its deployment. Riflemen, being largely drawn from the big cities, were on familiar terrain in the urban jungle.

And what was the level of success? Northern Ireland was a campaign in which the Army's role was to assist the RUC in creating an environment in which the terrorist would find it increasingly difficult to operate; the aim was not to achieve the military defeat of the terrorists, it was to try to develop the confidence of the population in the intentions of their government so that they would isolate and therefore fatally weaken the terrorists themselves. Thus the number of rounds fired, the number of terrorists arrested or killed was not necessarily an accurate measure of 'success'; nor was the number of casualties or the amount of damage sustained a fair reflection of 'failure'. Indeed, it could be argued that the two most devastating blows that the regiment suffered during the course of the campaign – a culvert-bomb ambush in South Armagh in 1981 that killed four riflemen and their RCT armoured personnel carrier driver, and the Regent's Park bombing in 1982, when the IRA placed a bomb under the bandstand and blew up the band of the 1st Battalion – may well have done more to persuade people of the moral bankruptcy of the IRA, and therefore helped to create a less accepting environment for the terrorist, than more transparent 'successes' in which terrorists were killed or arrested.

R Company 3RGJ

R Company formed up in Netheravon on 2 August 1971. On 6 August it was ordered to come to seventy-two hours 'notice to move' to Northern Ireland with effect from 11 August. The company recovered to Netheravon on 10 December, moved to Shoeburyness in the New Year and formed the nucleus of 3RGJ when it reformed as a battalion on 15 January 1972, a mere six months after having been reduced to company strength as a result of ill-conceived defence cuts. Peterborough noted in the *Daily Telegraph* on 17 August 1971 that R Company might well have created something of a record 'by being formed, operationally deployed, and coming under fire all within ten days'.

The reasons for the reorganisation of the regiment in 1971, for the existence of R Company and for the reformation of 3RGJ, a mere six months after its reduction to company strength, were related in Chapter 2. The intention here is to outline R Company's brief but distinguished tour in the Lower Falls area of West Belfast in 1971, an area then composed of mean streets with back-to-back terrace houses, derelict areas and the notorious high-rise blocks known as Divis Flats.

While the company remained in the due-to-be-demolished Albert Street Mill base throughout, and operated in the same area – the Lower Falls – the tour was divided into two very distinct parts: the first under the command and in support of 1RGJ, the second under the command of 3rd Battalion, The Queen's Regiment, but with operational responsibility for the Lower Falls. The initial phase under command of 1RGJ was a godsend. Most of the members of R Company had been deployed to Northern Ireland with 3RGJ for their short, three-week emergency tour the year before but very obviously had had no time since the formation of the company to do any subsequent training.

It had arrived expecting riots, box formations, CS gas and normal, if modified riot drills. Instead the company found that

Above: 'The Leeson Street Patrol', R Company 3RGJ, Lower Falls, Belfast, 1971.

Below: Lower Falls, Belfast, 1971.

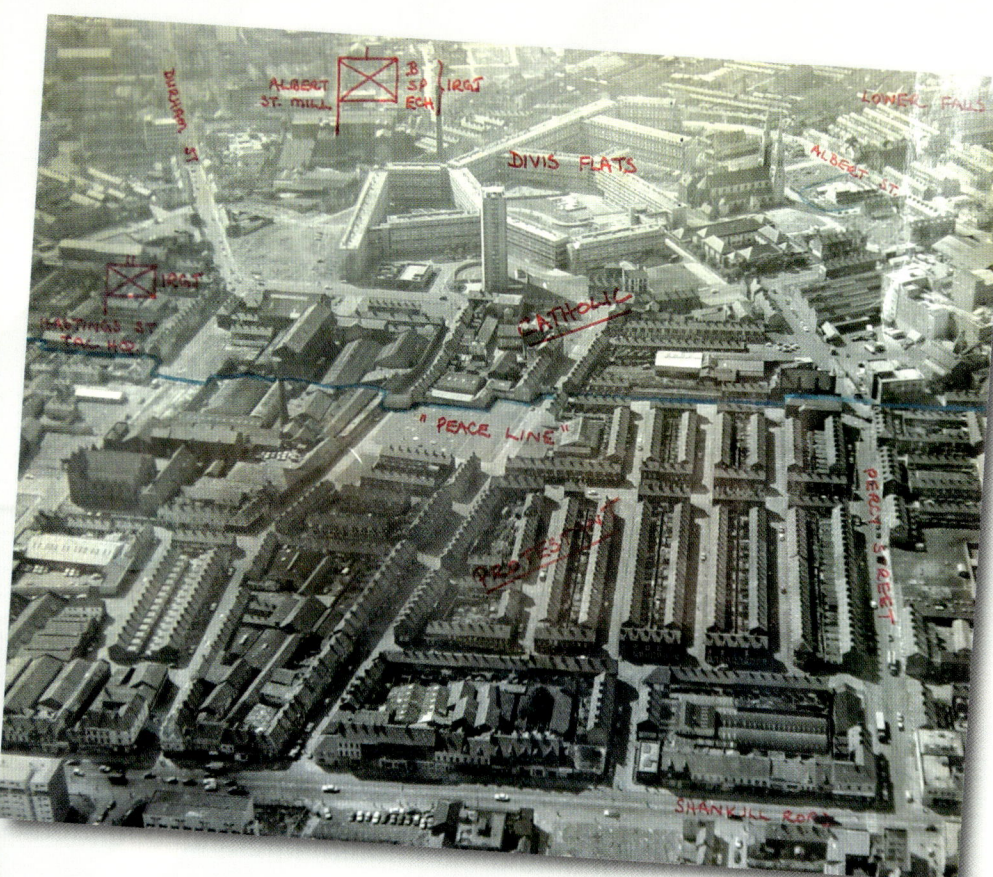

Above: The Lower Falls area of Belfast, 1971 – completely rebuilt and unrecognisable today.

Bottom right: Corporal Chris 'Rocky' Gates, 2RGJ, 'Echo OP', Londonderry, 1972.

1RGJ's area was the home of the gunman and sniper, and in consequence tactics were far more military than police.

Thus for the first month of its tour, until 1RGJ left in the second week of September, the company was able to 'understudy' the battalion and to learn from its experience. Riflemen were rotated through the platoons of B Company and Support Company, accompanying them on operations, undertaking a large number of the guards and duties in order to release 1RGJ for more offensive activities and getting to know the area and the ways and means of dominating it.

And dominate it in their own right the riflemen of R Company subsequently did. The Lower Falls had been, and would continue to be for some considerable time, a centre of Provisional IRA (PIRA) activity, and this fact determined the nature and extent of the company's operations. Within days of assuming responsibility for the Lower Falls from 1RGJ, the company was engaged in a major operation that extended throughout the area: it lasted three hours, and involved at least seven gunmen, of whom two were wounded, and the expenditure of more than fifty rounds of ammunition, which was a considerable amount in an operation where single, aimed rounds could be fired only at a clearly identified target. It was an indication of how the company intended to impose its will on the area, and as such it proved an effective and decisive action. It became known in R Company – rather grandiosely – as the 'Battle of Leeson Street'. Terence Cuneo subsequently captured the atmosphere in the picture of the operation he painted for the regiment.

The pace of life in the company was intense. Riflemen would expect to undertake at least two planned patrols at either section- or platoon-level every twenty-four hours, depending on the operational situation. There were, in addition, immediate reserve commitments, as well as guards and duties and unscheduled operations, which occurred on a regular basis. One such was the Cape Street shooting in which two IRA women – one a senior officer on its 'command staff', the other her younger sister, a 'volunteer' – were shot dead as they drove through the Lower Falls while engaging a patrol through the back window of a car. This incident brought into relief for the first time a dimension to operations in Northern Ireland that would assume greater and greater importance in the years to come – public relations and liaison with the media. Facts have no objective reality in counter-terrorist operations; perceptions are just as important, if not more so. On this occasion, time and trouble previously devoted to the press was rewarded in a more favourable and balanced reporting of the incident.

Tactics changed to suit the situations. The female vigilantes, using their dustbin lids to warn gunmen of the presence of patrols, were finally run off the streets, and the stoning of the various protective sangars was finally halted by a combination of psychological operations and clerical pressure. Water-cannons, containing coloured dye, were brought in with limited success to counter the painting of the street walls by the locals – often daubed white so that they would act as a canvas on which the riflemaen stood out as inviting targets while they patrolled. Civilian cars were used by riflemen in mixed dress in an attempt to infiltrate areas unnoticed. So, while the level of violence declined as the domination of the area by the company became more and more pronounced, the pace of the riflemen's life did not reduce. As a result R Company achieved a level of professionalism and self-confidence that not only had a real impact on the effectiveness of their operations in Northern Ireland, but was also of great value when the company returned to England in 1972 to became the core of the newly reformed 3RGJ in the New Year. By August that year, R Company was back in West Belfast as part of the battalion. 3RGJ was back in business, and serving alongside it in Belfast was 1RGJ, whilst 2RGJ was deployed in Londonderry. Operation Motorman, the breaking of the so-called IRA 'No Go Areas' controlled by the IRA, was underway and all three battalions of the regiment were involved.

The Royal Green Jackets

OPERATION HUNTSMAN

The first phase of internment took place throughout Northern Ireland on 9 August 1971. It was followed by serious rioting and the erection in the cities and towns of street barricades. Within a week, in Londonderry there were at least twenty-seven such 'obstructions' in the Bogside alone, most of them reportedly booby-trapped and manned in one way or another by 'vigilantes' who only allowed sympathisers into 'their' areas. At the same time the roads leading out of Londonderry to the southwest were controlled by the 'IRA', and all the city's essential services – rubbish collection, mail, the fire brigade – were at a standstill. Commander 8 Brigade determined to mount a brigade-sized operation in an endeavour to return the city to as near to normality as possible.

Then on a resident tour in Ballykelly, 2RGJ was selected to design the operation and to lead it. The commanding officer decided to infiltrate his battalion of four companies into position with the aim of removing the 'obstructions' in the Brandywell and Bogside, and thus open up the roads out of the city. At the same time he anticipated having to take on and defeat at least seventy street hoodlums and a significant number of gunmen. The colonel believed – rightly as it turned out – that he would need to encircle the area if he was to outflank both elements. The companies moved into position, apparently undetected, during the night of 17–18 August, initially by vehicle with the aid of a very effective yet simple deception plan, and then by the application of some very basic if somewhat arduous infantry skills. By first light on 18 August – 'a simply glorious morning with a breathtaking sunrise over the Foyle' – everyone was in position and ready to go. The initial assault on the 'barricades' was met by stunned inactivity. After a brief respite the gunmen appeared, but after a further ninety or so minutes the battalion had achieved utter domination with – so the press claimed – three gunmen dead, three wounded and two captured. Subsequently, the battalion continued into the Bogside and by early afternoon it had cleared the entire area.

It had been an impressive performance by a well-trained and operationally experienced battalion. It demonstrated that the disciplines learned in more conventional operations could be applied just as effectively to counter-terrorist operations – a well-thought-out-plan, clear direction, a high level of basic infantry skills, cooperation and coordination with other arms, maintenance of the aim and domination of the 'enemy'. The commanding officer concluded his report of the operation as follows: 'I stood by the barrack gate as the trucks drove in and more than one load were singing the Huntsman chorus – part of the Regimental March. Morale was very high. The battalion had carried out what amounted to a battalion attack, as the spearhead of a brigade operation, after a difficult night infiltration march, and it had worked. The unbelievable tragedy of it all was that it had taken place in the United Kingdom.'

HQ Support Company 2RGJ, Operation Motorman, Londonderry, 1972.

The question as to whether or not a tour had been a success in relation to the overall aim would probably have been one best addressed to the IRA – and one best answered by the local population, who would have said that a tour that deterred the terrorists whilst reassuring the population and improving the security situation – which was always the aim of the Green Jacket battalions – was a 'success'. To achieve this it was essential to operate in a way which did nothing to alienate the population. At the heart of operational planning lay a finely balanced assessment of short-term gain versus long-term success.

The intensity and nature of the campaign varied. Operations developed in response to the threat and covered the full range of counter-terrorist activity – from crowd- and riot-control tasks in the initial stages, to deliberate offensive military operations. In scale these varied, from large-scale, battalion-sized – or even brigade-sized – operations such as 2RGJ's Operation Huntsman to clear the Bogside in Londonderry, through to intensive company-sized operations such as B Company 1RGJ's attack on an IRA-held bakery in the Markets area of West Belfast, both in 1971, and R Company 3RGJ's tour that year in Belfast's Lower Falls, where company-sized operations were the norm; or platoon-level operations, such as the Keady incident in 1979; to section-level operations, such as an ambush in South Armagh in 1981 conducted by 1RGJ in which Lieutenant Corporal Dean was killed and Rifleman Moore was seriously wounded.

Normally, however, most of the time was spent patiently patrolling, both on foot and in vehicles; in gathering information that would enable Intelligence-led operations to

Before and after – the Bandstand, Regent's Park, 20 July 1982.

be mounted; in reassuring the local population; in what riflemen called 'stags', which meant sentry duty or radio watch; in urban and rural searches; and in mounting vehicle checkpoints. All such operations, no matter what their precise nature, were to be conducted at all times within the rule of law. The civil law applied as elsewhere in the UK and every soldier was issued with the 'Yellow Card', a digest that identified the situations in which lethal force could be used legally. Further emphasising ultimate civil control, the RUC was to endorse the concept of operations, and the battalions would ensure that these were, as far as possible, based on Intelligence. Any operation, though, still relied for its effectiveness on personal qualities and professional abilities: a mixture of clear direction from the HQ, positive and immediate judgement by the commander on the ground, and alertness, resilience and decisiveness down the chain of command. Ultimately, it was the riflemen who shouldered the principal pressures; who, day after day, had to show the necessary alertness in both defensive and offensive operations – like Rifleman Pope who, on a routine patrol along the border during 2RGJ's tour in 1989, found a well-hidden command wire, thereby foiling a particularly elaborate improvised explosive device (IED) attack. It was the rifleman who had to possess the mental and physical resilience – following day after day of sustained alertness – to be ready in an instant to impose their will on a situation, such as Lance Corporal Fryer of 1RGJ in 1992 who in the spate of three months had been involved in a Lynx helicopter crash, an exchange of automatic fire in Strabane, an IRA grenade attack and a major engagement with a terrorist so-called 'active service unit' (ASU) in a stolen car.

It should be borne in mind that a terrorist was active as a terrorist only for the short period that he or she was engaged in an act of terrorism; for the remainder of the time he or she was a civilian member of the population like anyone else and had to be treated as such until there was the evidence to arrest them and bring criminal charges. It was therefore extremely enervating for the riflemen to be patrolling on a regular basis among those whom, from Intelligence gathered, they 'knew' to be terrorists but whom they could not touch until sufficient evidence had been gathered to permit an arrest. Evidence and Intelligence are not the same thing; evidence has to hold good in a court of law.

And it was the riflemen who, day in day out, had to show decisiveness and determination. In 1971, during just a short period in the Lower Falls area, corporals Hansford and Thompson of R Company 3RGJ in different incidents, captured a senior IRA officer, took possession of 10 pounds (4.5 kg) of gelignite, caught one of Belfast's most wanted gunmen hiding under a bed and uncovered a newly formed IRA 'company', which was consequently quickly rounded up – all as a result of their immediate reactions in different incidents. As Major (later Brigadier) Christopher Dunphie, commanding R Company, wrote: 'It is the standard of the soldiers on

Belfast scene, 1972, painted by Elizabeth Kitson, wife of Brigadier Frank Kitson, late RGJ, who commanded 39 Infantry Brigade, Belfast.

The Royal Green Jackets

the streets which determines the degree of success achieved. It was the regiment's good fortune to have soldiers whose characters, personalities and backgrounds lent themselves so well to such operations.'

Training for deployments to Northern Ireland was initially pretty ad hoc – if it took place at all. But over time the variety and the sophistication of pre-tour training developed significantly. Typically, a battalion, whether in the UK or BAOR, organised, both mentally and physically, for a tour of Northern Ireland about three months before its deployment. The organisation of the battalion had to be fundamentally restructured, courses arranged and equipment familiarisation begun. There were specialist courses, principally for the variety of Intelligence requirements, but also for medics, search teams, electronic counter-measure (ECM) operators, helicopter handlers and many others. Individual training took place within the platoons and companies, followed by Northern Ireland Training and Advisory Team (NITAT) familiarisation packages, which included RUC and other presentations. Battalions then deployed for two weeks to either the Cinque Ports Training Area (CPTA), in the UK, or to Sennelager, in BAOR, where they underwent both individual and collective training in a simulated (urban or rural) Northern Ireland environment. If the deployment was to be to a rural area, such as along the border or to South Armagh, then the battalion went out into the countryside to practise the many specific drills and procedures that were needed to combat the sniper and the bomber. Local knowledge was essential if one was to win people over and deter terrorists – 2RGJ spent a day at an agricultural college in order to familiarise with farming activities and issues. The regiment tended always to have at least one officer or Senior NCO in either the UK or BAOR Teams. Training at CPTA benefited always from the support and guidance on the Lydd and Hythe ranges of the two redoubtable retired riflemen, Dougie Maber and Reg Trimblick. The NITAT professionals ensured that operational lessons were taught and absorbed – their exercises were designed always to address the worst-case scenarios and were so real that after one deployment to Northern Ireland 1RGJ reported: 'so effective was the training that when the serials from PIRA's "main events list" began to occur, there were many who were half expecting the traditional umpire debrief at every juncture.'

Operations lasted twenty-four hours a day, seven days a week. Roulement units deployed for four, or later six, months, while

Top left: B Company 1RGJ, resting after mounting a company attack on Inglis Bakery in the Markets area of Belfast, 1971.

An Incident at Keady, 1979

Over three decades a large number of successful contacts have taken place in Northern Ireland where riflemen have displayed the imagination and professional skills for which they have traditionally been noted. An unexpected, but not unforeseen, engagement in Keady during 2RGJ's tour in 1979 is a typical example of the ability of the riflemen on operations. It is taken from the annual *Regimental Chronicle* for 1979 and is told in the words of the platoon commander, Philip Mostyn:

At 19:25hrs that evening [9 June 1979] we saw from the ops room on our recently installed closed-circuit television, a cattle-truck and car pulled up in the market place. The angle of the lorry looked wrong for a mortar attack and so, fearful of setting a pattern by investigating too many 'suspicious' lorries, we decided to ignore it. We watched an exchange of words between the drivers of the two vehicles and then saw both vehicles drive southwards down Victoria Street. With keener interest we watched the lorry reverse behind a house and park on the precise spot that we had tipped as a favourite for a mortar base-plate position. When the passengers leaped out and ran to the other side of the lorry, I was convinced that a mortar attack was about to take place. In lieu of a reply to my tasking of 1 Section, which was in the immediate area, we saw small puffs of smoke emerge from unseen weapons behind the lorry.

Having just completed a vehicle checkpoint, Corporal Barnfield was taking his section, in two mutually covering groups, across some rough, boggy ground to Victoria Street. Lance Corporal Mitchell was climbing over a gate onto Victoria Street when he noticed a small gathering of people watching something beside a house some 50 m [55 yards] up the road. When they saw him, the spectators rushed inside and Lance Corporal Mitchell's suspicions were sufficiently aroused for him to cock his weapon. Looking up the road he found himself staring at a masked gunman backing up the side of the lorry, feeling behind him for the door of the cab. Shots were exchanged and Lance Corporal Mitchell dropped behind cover, only to have to move immediately because he could not see his target.

By this time a considerable weight of fire was coming from the back of the lorry and Rifleman Ashort, moving up behind Mitchell and finding himself unable to see what was happening, ran up to the side of the house beside the lorry to adopt a more useful fire position. By the time that they had reached their new positions, the lorry was pulling away. For want of a more specific target, they both fired as rapidly as possible into the back and side of the lorry. Lance Corporal Mitchell heard screams as the lorry pulled away.

Having passed through the centre of the town the lorry was driven out towards the border. Later in the evening, one dead and two wounded terrorists were admitted to hospital in Monaghan, south of the border. 2 Section, elsewhere in the town at the time, crossed the path of the escaping lorry about a minute too late. One might wonder how much more complete the success would have been.

Northern Ireland 1969–2007

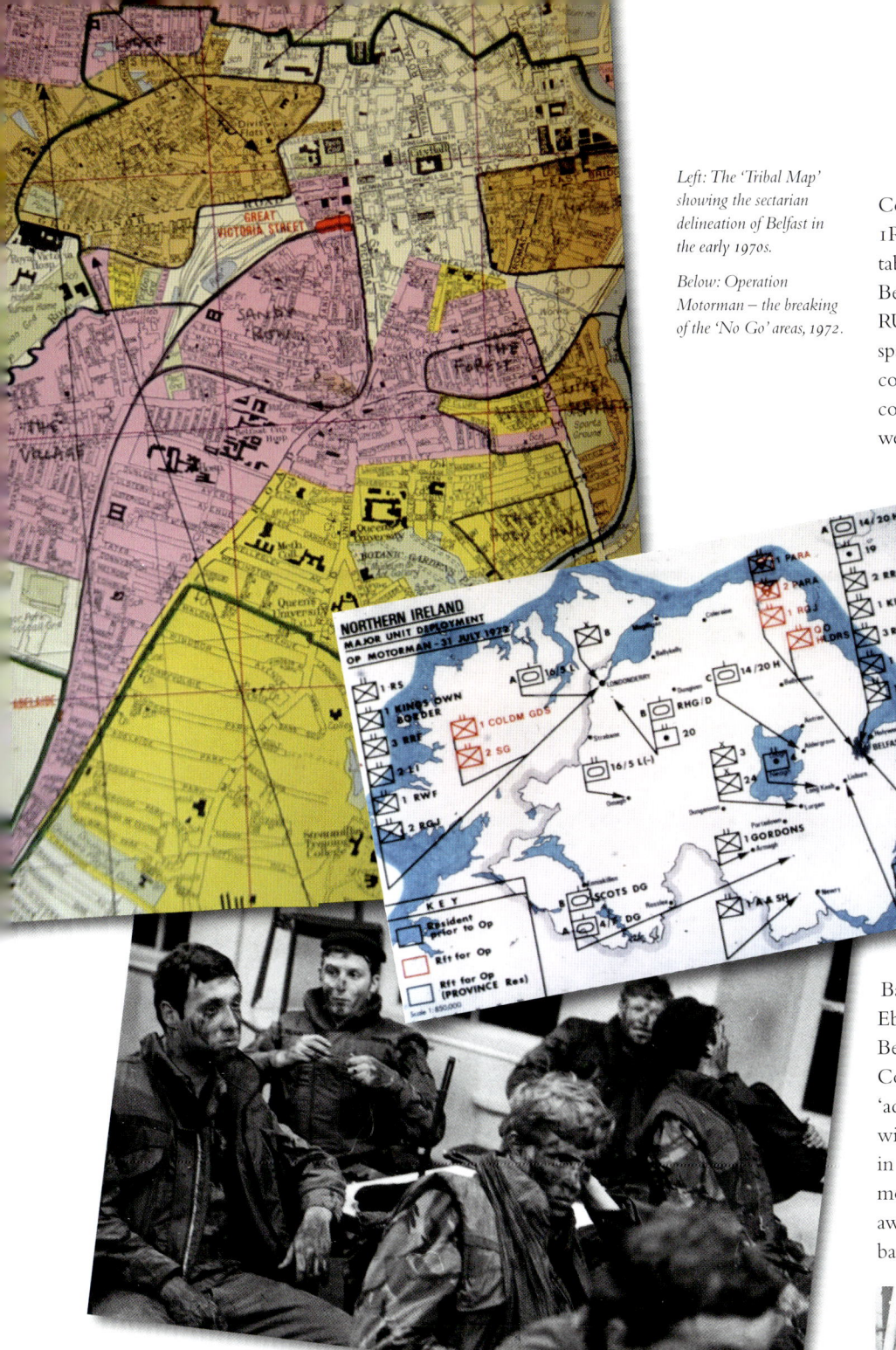

Left: The 'Tribal Map' showing the sectarian delineation of Belfast in the early 1970s.

Below: Operation Motorman – the breaking of the 'No Go' areas, 1972.

Above: Exhausted riflemen await yet another briefing for yet another patrol.

Right: The Bugles/Assault Pioneer Platoon, 1RGJ looking forward to improved accommodation after surviving an IRA mortar attack on Newtonhamilton Police Station, South Armagh, May 1981.

In the derelict Albert Street Mill, in the Lower Falls in 1971, R Company slept forty to a room. In Fort Monagh on the Falls Road 1RGJ slept thirty to a room in three-tier bunks with no lockers, tables or chairs. In the tiny Andersonstown Police Station, West Belfast, where 1RGJ Battalion Headquarters collocated with their RUC counterparts in 1972, the operations officer shared a minute space under the stairs with the second-in-command for the complete duration of the tour. In Londonderry little consideration could be given to tactical issues in the choice of bases, so few sites were available. In 1971 the Bligh's Lane base in the heart of the Creggan Estate consisted of an old factory and three Twynam huts and could not have been situated in a worse defensive position, bordered on two sides by a wide green and overlooked on two by the terraced houses of the estate and St Cecilia's School (a gunman's paradise). The Mex Garage base – a burnt-out petrol station adjoining a dairy – alongside the Foyle River was a dangerous location amidst hostile Bogsiders and flak jackets had to be worn at all times, even in the living accommodation.

Conditions for the resident battalions were considerably better – while they were in barracks, at least. Once they deployed the situation was not far different from those of the roulement units. There were six permanent barracks in Northern Ireland and by 2004 the Royal Green Jackets battalions had served in all of them: Aldergrove, outside Belfast, hosted 1RGJ in 1981–3; Shackleton Barracks, in Ballykelly, 2RGJ in 1970–2; Ballykinler 2RGJ in 2004; Ebrington Barracks, in Londonderry, 3RGJ in 1978–80; Holywood, Belfast, both 1RGJ (1999–2001) and 2RGJ (1995–7); and Omagh, County Fermanagh, 2RGJ (1991–3). These were all officially 'accompanied' tours – that is to say the married soldiers deployed with their wives and families and were housed in married-quarters in or close to the barracks. During these twenty-four- to thirty-month tours anything from 50 to 70 per cent of the time was spent away from home and out of barracks on operations. All of these barracks had most of the modern facilities one might expect to find

resident units were stationed in Northern Ireland for two years and typically developed a three- or four-week roster with one company deployed in an operational role, one on training, one on guards and duties, and one on leave. The deployed troops existed – lived is too generous a word – in conditions that could only leave an observer in admiration of them for their commitment and robustness. Tours were usually nasty and brutish; anyone with experience of having deployed to the Falls or Andersonstown bases in Belfast, or to the City bases in Londonderry, will recognise familiar things in Rifleman Moore's comments about life in Crossmaglen: 'the whole place reeked of sweaty bodies, stale air, and rotting rubbish … It was amazing how the soldiers endured the intolerable smoke-filled environment and got along with each other … Fights only rarely broke out.'

121

in any British Army barracks in Europe, with the additional provision of much better local education. Strangely, security was never a particular issue for the families; living behind wire of some sort tended to be the extent of their restrictions. They came and went as they chose and took local jobs. In Omagh in 1992 fifty-eight out of the 172 wives were in some sort of part-time employment. Local facilities were as available to them as to local residents, but most of the recreational activities tended to be within the battalion and the barracks. The key to living a relatively normal life was to be aware of the security situation and to know where, and where not, to go. Terrorist activity was largely confined to specific areas of Northern Ireland, and these were to be avoided. The extent to which the families contributed to the effectiveness and morale of those deployed cannot be sufficiently emphasised; whether as part of a resident battalion or the rear party of a roulement battalion, the families formed an integral part of the overall battalion capability. The families organised holiday activities, kindergartens and community centres. Among the rear parties, in the days prior to the internet and mobile telephones, the wives met weekly to discuss the battalion's doings with the aid of a map, photographs and a cassette-tape recording produced in the battalion; over time, this progressed to a weekly video recording. All the while, activities were developed, from coffee mornings and film shows to concerts and a families' camp on the Baltic coast.

Even within the province there were many opportunities for off-duty activities. The resident battalions, with their reasonably fixed programmes, were often able to conduct more and better training than when based on the mainland. It was particularly important that the support weapons' platoons were able to train to maintain their expertise. Adventure training became a welcome relaxation from operational activity – one which often seemed to include such marginally demanding pursuits as shooting, with Bill Brownlow (ex-Rifle Brigade and later Lord Lieutenant of County Down), or fishing. The roulement battalions had less spare time, being continuously deployed and responsible for a specific area of operations, but in the early years most of them ran discotheques in their bases (until security became too much of an issue), which provided the riflemen with some well-earned relaxation and helps to explain the very welcome presence of a large number of Irish wives in the battalions. Many a young nationalist or loyalist girl in the early 1970s who had hurled abuse or worse at the manned barricades earlier in the day would appear at the discotheque that evening and hurl herself equally passionately into the fray there. Female Royal Military Police (RMP) searchers would ensure no one attended with anything threatening hidden under their mini skirt. It took some years for the discotheques to be banned, a decree much to the disappointment of the soldiers.

Above left: 3RGJ, South Armagh, 1992. A Platoon Commander briefs his Section Commanders.

Above right: Capt Ron Cassidy, commanding the rear party, 1RGJ, in Celle, Germany, 1973. Looking after the families at the home base was an essential part of any operational tour.

Bessbrook Mill, South Armagh; the busiest heliport in Europe.

Northern Ireland 1969–2007

When the battalions first deployed to the province, the riflemen were genuinely keen to help the disadvantaged and alienated nationalist communities. It is too easy to forget, by concentrating on the profile of subsequent military operations, that during the first two years of The Troubles the Army was deployed in a low-key mode to react to civil disturbances. Throughout the campaign one of the Army's principal aims was to win the 'hearts and minds' of the local population. In the Falls Road in 1969 1RGJ initiated a series of community relations projects, principally in an attempt to bring the two communities together. Most battalions tried in one way or another to generate some form of community activity, whether it was the boy scouts in South Armagh, to which 2RGJ devoted a good deal of energy in 1978, or the Magnet Club in Belfast, which 1RGJ first organised in 1969.

Some forty years later the future of Northern Ireland remains very much in the hands of those same communities. The Royal Green Jackets gained a great deal as a result of its many deployments to Northern Ireland, and if its presence helped to create a sense of confidence and purpose in the communities, the regiment's dead and wounded will not have been in vain.

Bands and Bugles

The bands and bugles were, from the outset, an integral part of every battalion's capability. As combat riflemen, the bugles tended to deploy to Northern Ireland as formed platoons within a rifle company, while the bands tended to remain with the rear party and to visit Northern Ireland as the occasions required. The first Green Jacket to be killed in Northern Ireland was Bugle Corporal Bankier. Whilst in the province a band would perform 'community relations' concerts, concerts for the various headquarters, and, of course, visit and play at all the battalion locations. Bands were a much-appreciated boost to morale in theatre and a highly valued resource for the rear parties. A band's members would also help out with guards and duties, although they did not, as a rule, go on patrol – not out of reluctance to do so, but rather because they lacked the tactical awareness and pre-training required. In the early 1970s one bandmaster, when called for a meeting in battalion HQ, strolled along the Falls Road, in the very heart of nationalist West Belfast; unable to locate the Springfield Road RUC Station, he walked into the Beehive Pub, a then notorious watering hole popular with republicans, to telephone for directions!

The event that will always be most associated with the Green Jackets' bands is the bombing by the IRA of 1RGJ Band whilst it played to the public enjoying the sunshine in London's Regent's Park on 20 July 1982. Six members were killed instantly – Band Sergeant Major Graham Barker, Sergeant 'Doc' Livingstone, Corporal John McKnight, and bandsmen George Mesure, Keith Powell and Larry Smith. Bandsman Heritage died of his wounds two weeks later; everyone else on the bandstand that afternoon was injured, some very seriously.

It was an appalling act, and the whole regiment rallied round to assist Warrant Officer First Class Little, the bandmaster who was himself wounded in the attack, in rebuilding the band and its reputation for excellence, while at the same time arranging for a fitting tribute to those who had died. On 5 October the following year this tribute took place when Prime Minister Margaret Thatcher, accompanied by the Colonels Commandant, unveiled a memorial at the very bandstand where the incident had occurred. The reconstituted band played a piece by Sir Arthur Bliss entitled 'Reconstruction' and, at the end, 'High on the Hill'. A remembrance ceremony has been held there every year since.

Below: Sergeant Lewis, trombonist, wounded by an IRA bomb during a band concert in Regent's Park, 20 July 1982. Seven members of the band were killed, the rest wounded.

Bottom right: Padre Colin Fox leads the annual commemoration service held in Regent's Park on 20 July every year.

Germany and the Cold War Years

The British Army of the Rhine, or BAOR as it was usually termed, comprised the main peacetime element of the British Army from the end of the Second World War until 1994, some four years after the fall of the Berlin Wall had heralded the collapse of the Soviet Union and the end of the Cold War. The bulk of the army was based in Germany, trained and prepared to counter any attack across the Inner German Border (IGB) by the forces of the Warsaw Pact. With the end of the Second World War, manpower reductions eventually resulted in there being just two British divisions in West Germany, based in the north of the country.

Amongst the units deployed in the former Wehrmacht barracks of Lower Saxony and North Rhine Westphalia at that time were 1RB and 2RB as elements of the 7th Armoured Division and the 2nd Infantry Division. By the early 1950s these two divisions had been reinforced by 11th Armoured Division and 6th Armoured Division to form 1 British Corps, or 1(BR) Corps, a formation within NATO and subordinated to Northern Army Group (NORTHAG). The NORTHAG area of responsibility was roughly from Hamburg to Kassel and from the border between East and West Germany, the 'Inner German Border or IGB, to the borders of The Netherlands and Belgium. In addition to the British Army, Corps were assigned to NORTHAG by Belgium, Germany and The Netherlands.

By 1966 there had been many changes in manpower, equipment and organisation within BAOR, which consisted of three principal elements: the main fighting force of 1(BR) Corps with its headquarters at Bielefeld; the British Rear Combat Zone, with its headquarters in Dusseldorf, responsible for the resupply of the fighting formations; and the British Communications Zone, with its headquarters at Emblem in Belgium, tasked to receive reinforcements from the UK into the ports and docks of northwest Europe and coordinate their onward forward movement to 1(BR) Corps. A fourth and final element was the Berlin Infantry Brigade, part of the Allied Control Council in Berlin not subordinated to NORTHAG but reliant on 1(BR) Corps for peacetime administrative support, and assistance if it came to war.

Over the years the strength of BAOR varied between 25,000 and 60,000 troops. It was commanded by a four-star general with his headquarters at Rheindahlen. The commander was double-hatted as Commander NORTHAG, his wartime role, and co-located in Rheindahlen with Headquarters RAF Germany and 2nd Allied Tactical Airforce. Withdrawal from east of Suez during the 1960s and 1970s, combined with a declining British economy and rising inflation, created downward pressure on the defence budget. There was a drive to reduce

Left: NORTHAG Corps emblems.

Right: Gas gas gas – training in NBC dress state 'black'.

Below: BAOR principal elements schematic layout.

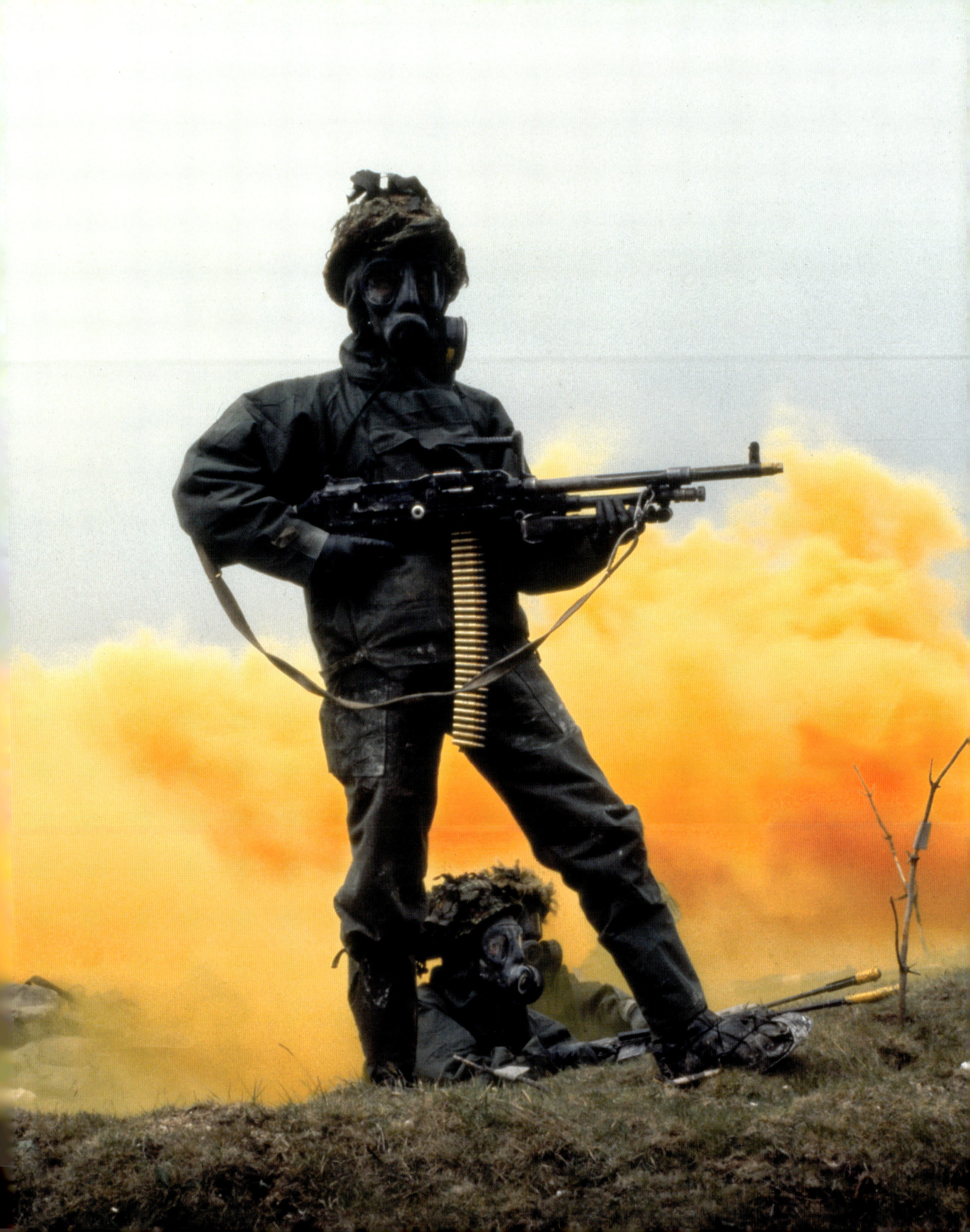

The Royal Green Jackets

manpower yet retain capability, which spawned many Defence Reviews and reorganisations. Experiments such as the removal of the brigade level of command, with units grouped into 'task forces' in Germany and 'field forces' in the UK, operating directly under divisional headquarters, were tried but soon proved unworkable.

By 1980 1(BR) Corps, as the main fighting force of BAOR, comprised four divisions and corps troops. There were three armoured divisions in Germany – 1st, 3rd and 4th – with the 2nd Infantry Division (rear based in the UK from January 1983) tasked to reinforce 1(BR) Corps in the event of war. The order of battle (orbat) of the armoured divisions changed frequently over the years, but essentially each consisted of three brigades with differing numbers of infantry and armoured units. Brigades had their own integral artillery, logistics and signals units, with the latter forming the nucleus of the brigade headquarters in the field and the vital radio-relay stations that ensured communications forwards to units and back to division. Divisions had heavy artillery, air defence, long-range reconnaissance, Army Air Corps helicopters for liaison and mobile anti-tank defence, supply, repair and signals units grouped together in divisional troops. Back in the UK the primary role of many units, in the event of war was the further reinforcement of 1(BR) Corps.

In the 1960s an Airportable Strategic Reserve, formed around 3rd Division in the UK, was busy with the campaigns resulting from the withdrawal from the UK's overseas territories. By the 1970s the British government had declared that the defence effort would 'in future be concentrated mainly in Europe and the North Atlantic area', (statement on the Defence Estimates presented to Parliament February 1968). 3rd Division was consequently assigned to NATO, initially as the United Kingdom Airmobile Force, but further reorganisations soon followed. By the 1980s the Division was stationed in Germany, as an armoured division, whilst the 2nd was returned to the UK as 2nd Infantry Division based in York from where, in 1983, it assumed the role of reinforcement of BAOR with one regular and two Territorial Army (TA) brigades. The regular brigade was 24 Airmobile Brigade equipped with more than fifty Milan anti-tank missile posts, ready to be flown into blocking positions astride any deep armoured breakthrough. The TA brigades, which included both 4(v)RGJ and 5(v)RGJ amongst their units, were enthusiastic but lightly equipped and usually given a static defence task to hold vital points such as the bridges over the Weser River.

Mechanised Infantry

For much of the Second World War the British infantry suffered from a lack of mobility in armoured operations. Until American half-tracks were made available infantrymen relied either on their feet, on soft-skinned lorries incapable of cross-country movement, or on Bren Gun carriers, tracked vehicles that lacked power and protection, and were capable of transporting only two or three men into battle. In Normandy this lack of protected mobility was a significant factor in Montgomery's failure to make headway in the fighting around Caen that culminated in Operation Goodwood, the second British attempt to breakout to the east from their sector in the Normandy bridgehead. Michael Carver, later to be Chief of the Defence Staff and a distinguished military historian, was then in command of an armoured brigade, and he severely criticised Monty for not having learnt from the El Alamein battles that, 'you cannot in open country move infantry up to support armour in lorries. Soft-skinned vehicles are no good.'

By the end of the war the lesson was understood, and the concept of mechanised infantry was embraced by the British Army. The debate over whether the infantry should have protected mobility only – the 'battlefield taxi' – or a vehicle that allowed them to fight from under armour without dismounting – the 'infantry fighting vehicle' – was to continue throughout the Cold War. Whilst the British opted for a vehicle in which the infantry rode to battle under armour, dismounting to fight, other nations preferred vehicles with integral firepower that enabled the infantry to stay mounted for as long as possible. By 1966 and the creation of The Royal Green Jackets, the equipment on issue to the British Army of the Rhine (BAOR) was the family of Armoured Fighting Vehicles (AFV) 432, more commonly known as armoured personnel carriers (APCs) or

Above: Debussing for the attack.

Below left: British Carrier Universal Number 1 Mark II.

Below right: American M3 Armoured Personnel Carrier.

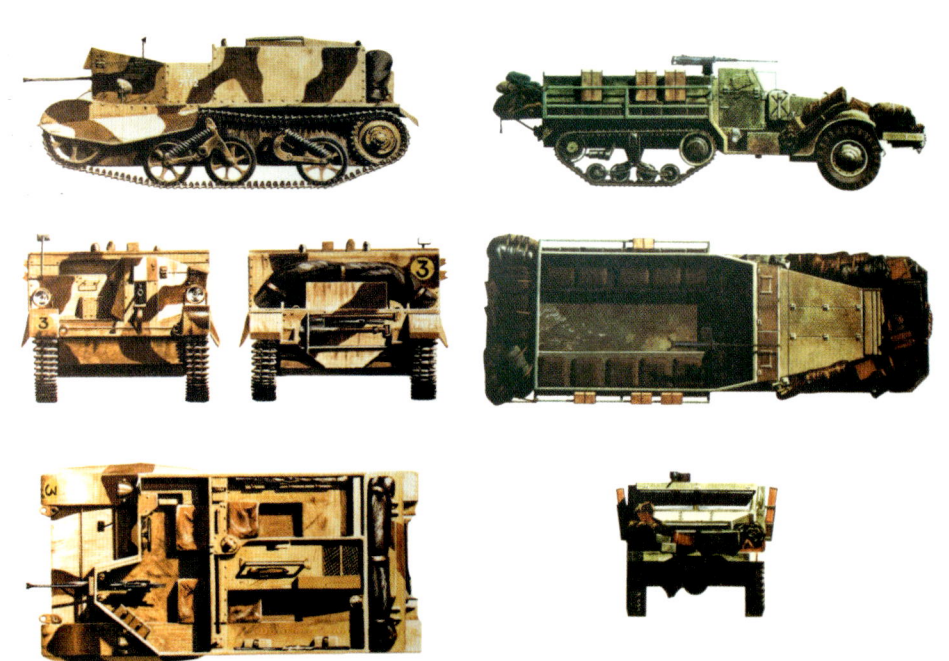

just plain 432s. Initially fitted with petrol engines, a diesel version was introduced only slowly from the late 1960s.

The 432 was to remain the standard infantry vehicle until the late 1980s when the army was re-equipped with an Infantry Fighting Vehicle (IFV) christened Warrior. By then there was a standard joke that the APCs were older than the riflemen driving them. Vehicles became an integral part of every battalion stationed in Germany, with each section having its own 432 to maintain, each platoon commander having his own headquarters vehicle and each company commander his own pair of command vehicles. Various adaptations of the basic vehicle were produced: some mounting mortars or anti-tank guns and missiles; others for use as radio relay-stations; some as ambulances; and versions such as specialised engineer, artillery and recovery vehicles. Mechanised companies had fitter-sections of Royal Electrical and Mechanical Engineers (REME) attached to them from the battalion's Light Aid Detachment (LAD), a company-sized group of REME skilled in all aspects of first-line repair and recovery of vehicles. The size of the battalion's vehicle fleet and natural manpower wastage rates meant that a continuous stream of drivers from within the rifle companies had to be trained. This was done by battalion instructors, usually grouped together in a Driving and Maintenance (D&M) Wing. QTOs (Qualified Testing Officers) then assessed the learner drivers and granted licences for both tracked (A) and wheeled (B) vehicles. The problem of driver training was at its most intense when a battalion first arrived in Germany and it could be quite a shock to the system (see page 128).

The difficulties that 2RGJ found in 1967 with the availability and serviceability of the APCs – and the insistence from on high that, problems not withstanding, the battalion would participate in the planned exercise schedule – were not unique. In Iserlohn, 3RGJ under Peter Hudson arrived in May of the same year to find their expected vehicles had not been issued; the outgoing unit had handed in their Saracen wheeled-APCs, but by mid-June only seventeen 432s had arrived to replace them. The promise of a total of twenty-seven vehicles by early July allowed rifle companies seven each with which to train before beginning a battalion test exercise set by 20 Armoured Brigade in late July. As usual the riflemen rose to the occasion, met the challenge and in September participated successfully in two weeks of divisional training with a full complement of vehicles.

Right: The interior of a section 432 as troops dismount.

Below (clockwise): Wombat mounted on the 432; 432 command vehicle (showing the poles for the command post extension); Warrior 2RGJ Warminster; 438 recovery vehicle; 81mm mortar firing from the back of a 432.

2RGJ's Experiences When They Left the Far East, 1967

As recorded by Major Anthony Karslake

When rumour that our role was to change from jungle battalion in Penang to mechanised battalion in Münster crystallised into fact, the memories of old motor-battalion warriors went back to a previous life in Münster in the 1950s. Being optimists, we knew, of course, that the new FV432 was just an updated half-track and the only problem with mechanised tactics and administration would be imparting our knowledge to the uninitiated.

Reality was rather different. Even before we left Penang there had been talk of the battalion being 'thrown in at the deep end' by having to perform on a brigade exercise within weeks of our arrival. At that distance it seemed quite a good idea. The problem of getting ready would be solved by sending the drivers on conversion courses at the Motorised Transport (MT) School at Bordon during block leave, while most of the officers would do a 'familiarisation course' so that they could hold their own in technical talk and supervision with their drivers.

It was only at Bordon that the problem, far from being solved, became apparent. First, the FV432 proved to be as different from a half-track as the latter was from an ox-cart, so the APC commander needed to be pretty knowledgeable about such basic subjects as track tensions and coolant levels, and nothing short of a formal course could prepare him for his new task. The contrast with the time when a new subaltern in a motor battalion was told by his company commander 'here is a scout platoon; go away and train it' was stark. Grease-removing soap was even to be found in the officers' mess.

The next problem was the drivers. A generous number had been allowed on the courses in anticipation of the loss of those who proved to be incompatible with tracked vehicles. Notwithstanding this, the battalion arrived in Münster with the bare minimum of qualified drivers; one cut finger and a vehicle would be off the road. That was not all; BAOR had invented a further hurdle in the shape of the 'matrix test', multiple-choice questions on German road laws and signs. The number of available drivers was instantly decimated and it was said that the situation was only retrieved by some drivers retaking the test so many times that they knew all the possible answers by heart.

Just as despair at ever getting on the road set in, it emerged that there was no driver problem because there were no APCs to drive. As the battalion was moving in, all the FV432s developed a sort of muscular dystrophy in something called the 'metallistic coupling'. There were no spare parts in Germany and little prospect of improvement for several weeks. The fact that the officers and NCOs could not pass the matrix test now scarcely seemed to matter.

It turned out that all the APCs in the brigade were similarly affected, and the chances of the brigade exercise taking place were minimal. In the end, though, the REME doctors were persuaded that they had been over-cautious and the disease was cured by simple decree. Exercise Fug Fury, as it was quaintly named, took place as planned around the notorious Grosses Moor, and the battalion received many polite comments about its performance. Which all goes to show that it is wrong to panic and optimists are best after all.

Cross-country practice on Dorbaum training area near Munster, 2RGJ 1967.

Germany and the Cold War Years

1RGJ
1966–7 Berlin
1970–74 Celle
1987–92 Osnabrück

2RGJ
1967–71 Münster
1980–6 Minden

3RGJ
1967–1968 Iserlohn
1975–77 Berlin
1982–87 Celle

Above: Complete Equipment Schedule (CES) check Oxford Barracks, 1968.

Above right: D Company 2RGJ post exercise wash-down, 1968.

Bottom: Front Gate and Battalion HQ, Oxford Barracks, Münster.

Life in BAOR

Although life in BAOR offered many material advantages to the troops garrisoned there – such as duty-free goods, cars, cigarettes and alcohol, plus an often generous Local Overseas Allowance (LOA) to compensate for the higher cost of living – it was not a universally popular posting for the riflemen. Somehow they found it hard to reconcile the mechanised infantry role and endless rounds of make-believe exercises with that of 'proper soldiering'. They often took time to settle to the routine and constant maintenance demands of the battalion vehicle fleet. Whilst the armoured corps might spend most of its time greasing nipples on the tank park, for a rifleman this was simply not what he had joined up for. The decision in 1969 to deploy the British Army to Northern Ireland in support of the Royal Ulster Constabulary was, to most, an absolute godsend – proper operational soldiering at last. As the situation in Ulster deteriorated, infantry battalions were sent there increasingly frequently on emergency roulement tours of four-and-a-half months or longer.

Despite the dangers and the family separation involved, these tours provided a welcome focus throughout the 1970s and 1980s; they kept many infantry skills alive and were invaluable in developing leadership and initiative at junior levels – all in the finest traditions of the regiment. The regiment thrived on these operational deployments and looked forward eagerly to the next time they could park the 432s in the garages and head off to Ireland.

Green Jackets were familiar with life in Germany well before 1966. In 1945 1RB and 2RB had been stationed there with the 43rd in Berlin. In the following twenty-one years, throughout the various amalgamations and reductions leading up to 1966, Green Jacket battalions were to spend thirty-one years between them soldiering in BAOR, in what had become West Germany. During this time they were stationed in towns and cities that their successors in The Royal Green Jackets were to come to know well – Osnabrück, Iserlohn, Münster, Minden and Celle – with the then 1KRRC posted to Sennelager for six years, a training area that would feature prominently in the BAOR annual training cycle. In 1966, as The Royal Green Jackets came in to being, 1RGJ found itself in Berlin and 3RGJ in Iserlohn. A posting to Germany was, by then, a regular feature of life for all infantry battalions, and in the next twenty-three years, up to the end of the Cold War, the three battalions of The Royal Green Jackets were to spend a total of thirty-three years stationed in BAOR or Berlin.

Battalion life revolved around the barracks and garrison where the battalion was stationed. Most accommodation for the single riflemen was in large company blocks that also housed the offices, stores and armouries. Initially, the barrack rooms were spartan, but over the years they were upgraded and modernised, in a refurbishment programme entitled Operation Humane, into a series of small, self-contained flats. Cellars were often converted into company clubs which sold duty-free alcohol; although the profits from that swelled the coffers of the company account, it all too frequently proved a nightmare to run for the company second-in-command and worse still to audit. Over-consumption of alcohol in the towns was the primary cause of disciplinary problems, usually ones involving skirmishes with the German Politzei or the Royal Military Police. The company clubs served a useful purpose in keeping matters more 'in house' and under stricter control. Most families lived in married quarters, or in 'patches' amongst – but distinct and separate from – the local German community. Although infantry units moved frequently, each garrison tended to have a large British civilian presence that was more permanent and that staffed the infrastructure of schools, shops, cinemas, hospitals and broadcasting services that developed over the years. Military-run bus services took children to school and wives to the NAAFI where they could buy quintessentially British goods such as teabags, Marmite, Cheddar cheese and bacon. It was easily possible, and sadly not uncommon, for families to spend three or more years in West Germany without learning more than a few phrases of the language.

For the more adventurous there was plenty to do. Money went further than in the UK. In 1966 a Grade III rifleman on a six- to nine-year engagement received – in pounds, shillings and pence, as then was – an amount of £1.3s.9d a day (or about £1.20p for the younger reader) equivalent to a purchasing power of £15.27p in 2006; a captain on appointment £3.2s.6d (£3.12p) equivalent to £40.19p in 2006 and the commanding officer £6.6s.6d (£6.32p) equivalent to £81.35p. (Calculations taken from the website, Measuring Worth.) To this was added a variable rate of LOA of several shillings/pounds a day (dependent on a comparison of the cost of living in Germany and the UK, and the prevailing Deutschmark/Pound Sterling exchange rate). By 1989, when the Berlin Wall came down, the equivalent rates of daily pay were Grade III rifleman £26.33 (£45.28p adjusted), captain £47.44 (£81.58p) and commanding officer £84.39 (£145.12p), but by then there were automatic deductions made for food and accommodation. A couple of decades on these seem small rates of pays but a car was comparatively cheap to buy and petrol was bought using duty-free coupons.

Acquiring a car was a primary objective for many riflemen. Constant tours in Ireland helped them to save the money required, and when these tours emptied the barracks for months on end, the square was often used as a secure parking lot for the single soldiers' cars, presided over by the rear party. Touring the camp with his RSM just prior to departing for Ulster, one commanding officer commented that there must be 'five million deutschmarks' worth of cars parked on the square'. 'No Sir,' replied the RSM, 'its only half a millions' worth of car – the rest is debt!'

Winter sports were activities that really took off in popularity after the purchase by 2RGJ of a ski hut in Steibis, Bavaria (see pages 64–5). Steibis was shared within the regiment and later across The Light Division. It allowed large numbers of riflemen to experience the delights of downhill and cross-country (or langlauf) skiing at heavily subsidised rates, and it contributed significantly to the regiments successes in BAOR skiing championships over the years (see pages 63–5). Other adventurous training pursuits were readily available: dinghy and offshore sailing, canoeing, free-fall parachuting, rock climbing – the list was lengthy, with only the pace of life and the commitments the battalion had to meet preventing many from enjoying more of them.

Despite such commitments, life in BAOR was very much what battalion members and their families made of it. Inevitably, it did not suit everyone, but for many it was their first, and perhaps only, experience of living in a foreign country. One had to become accustomed to a more regulated Germanic lifestyle, which involved respecting the 'quiet' hours between noon and three pm, not hanging out washing on a Sunday or cutting your lawn at the weekend after midday on Saturday, and clearing your own path and the pavement of snow in winter. Relations with the local communities were excellent, and the freedom of several towns was bestowed on battalions over the years. The riflemen, of course, joked that they had the freedom of any town any Friday night! Many a commanding officer found himself explaining his riflemen's sense of humour to brigade commanders, with varying degrees of 'understanding'. Expected to have the qualities and toughness to turn out and fight the Warsaw Pact to the death, the chain of command never really appreciated it when the same qualities were exhibited rather too freely in the towns of North Rhine Westphalia.

Green Jacket bands were always popular in Germany and were closely identified with *Jäger* traditions because of their green uniforms, bugle calls and speed of marching. They could always be guaranteed to draw a crowd and a cheer. This was particularly so on one memorable occasion when Sounding Retreat at the Weser Stadium in Minden. It was a very damp evening with cold, humid air rolling off the river into the arena. The band and bugles were marching at their fastest, whether to impress or finish early was never quite clear, but at every halt the combination of warm musicians and cold air caused them to vanish in a swirling cloud of steam. As Sunset was played, the bandmaster appeared to be conjuring music from a mystical, wraith-like being, before the Regimental March was struck up and the bugles burst out, leaving behind them a vapour trail through which the rest of the band streamed.

Top: A typical officers' married quarter patch in Germany.

Above left: Inside the NAAFI.

Above right: Celle, winter 1972. Most rifleman's accommodation in Germany was in these 'Hitler' blocks.

Grape Picking
As remembered by Rifleman Alan Payne

Helping to bring in the grape harvest was a popular activity for many riflemen in the late 1960s and early 1970s. Harvesting got them out of barracks and out of uniform and able to sample life with a German farming family. They relaxed after work in the local gasthaus and got paid for doing it. One rifleman recalls his memory of the experience:

> In autumn 1970, 2RGJ were allocated thirty places in the numbers being sent to help gather in the grape harvest in the Mosel valley, part of a scheme to integrate riflemen and German civilians, whilst providing a welcome break from barrack life. Competition for vacancies was fierce, fuelled by the knowledge from the previous year that although the work was hard the pay was about DM300 per week – plus all the wine you could drink. Four of us from the recce platoon were chosen and after an early breakfast and with a subaltern in charge, we climbed into a bus, travelled through the day and arrived at the small hamlet of Osann, where we were shown into the village hall full of grape farmers. We were asked to line up and something akin to a slave auction took place with the farmers walking up and down feeling our muscles and judging who could carry heavy weights. One by one we were picked and two of us were led away by a farmer, Theo Muller, with the biggest hands I had ever seen. I was happy to be with a friend, but the thought did strike me that if he needed two of us he must have a lot of grapes to pick!
>
> At his farm we were introduced to his family, shown our billets and warned of an early start. True to his word, 6:30 saw us up and by 7:00 we were down in the cavernous cellar under the farmhouse where, after a very large glass of schnapps, we set about preparing all the equipment for a day of grapepicking. Breakfast followed and then we were off. Transport was a tractor and trailer (carrying a glassfibre container the size of a small swimming pool) that Theo drove like a demon with the two of us perched precariously on seats on the mudguards.
>
> In daylight the one thing you notice about the Osann area is that nowhere is flat, in fact it's all steep – very steep! The whole region was a mass of grapevines as far as the eye could see, and each farmer owned sections in different parts of the area, rather than in just one place, in order to give the wine a uniform taste. Theo showed us how to cut the grapes from the vine and place them in a large plastic bucket with straps, like a rucksack, which we were invited to carry to the trailer and unload once it was filled. When full the bucket weighed about 70 pounds [32 kg] and whether you were moving up or down, the slatey, slippery soil made for hard going.
>
> Every day was a carbon-copy of the first, except on Saturday when all the farmers congregated at the gasthaus, bought the drinks, and we all enjoyed a good night out with rather more schnapps than was wise! During the second week Theo invited us into the part of the cellar where last year's harvest resided in giant hogsheads waiting to be bottled. He removed three small rubber tubes from the wall, handed one to each of us, removed the bung from the top of the first barrel put in his tube and took a good mouthful. He invited us to do the same and it was only after we had taken a good few 'glugs' that we noticed Theo had spat his drink into the gutter after appreciating the taste. The cellar contained fifty barrels, all of which we were invited to sample. To this day I cannot recall how many we managed to try, although the number nine sticks in my mind along with the difficulty we had climbing the stairs back out of the cellar!
>
> The second week passed all too quickly and the work seemed to get harder but the promise of a village-wide party on the Saturday night kept our spirits up. However, on the Friday word came from Münster that the recce platoon was to return the next day to attend a ZB 298 radar course starting on Sunday. To miss the party was a blow but as we held out our hands for the pay after our two weeks of hard graft, worse was to come. The subaltern in charge of the trip had instructed the farmers that they were only to pay us DM100 a week instead of the DM300 they normally shelled out, as we were receiving military pay. It was not a happy bunch of riflemen that arrived back in Münster, but the memories of those two weeks still make me smile.

A rifleman helping in the grape harvest – Bernkastel Moselle, vintage 1969. Let's hope his beret hadn't dropped in the vat.

The Royal Green Jackets

stretched back to Antwerp and the Channel coast. It would be along these lines of communication that reinforcements and supplies from the UK would flow in the event of war. Within NORTHAG, the British were flanked by a German corps to the north and a Belgian corps to the south.

Planning for the defence of West Germany was a continuous process. The very fact that it was dynamic, and being amended as circumstances and weapons changed gave it credibility. The plan for 1(BR) Corps flowed from the mission and tasks allotted to it by NORTHAG, and that plan formed the basis for the subsequent divisional, brigade and unit General Deployment Plan (GDP). The infantry in 1(BR) Corps might have found themselves facing many different tasks: fighting a delaying action as part of the covering force; defending the best tank approach across the Hanoverian Plain in the 'pin table battle'; or supporting armoured regiments delivering 'counter-strokes' on ground of their choosing against deep thrusts by Soviet ground forces. Green Jacket battalions filled several different

The General Deployment Plan

In the event of war BAOR came under NATO operational command. The defence of western Europe was vested in three commands: Allied Forces North, Central and South (AFNORTH, AFCENT, AFSOUTH). 1(BR) Corps, as a formation within NORTHAG, a part of AFCENT, had responsibility for a sector that stretched from a line north of Hanover to a line north of Kassel, and extended from the IGB to a line just west of Soest. The balance of the units in BAOR, those not in the 1(BR) Corps order of battle, formed the support for 1(BR) Corps and guarded the rear areas that

Left: 2RGJ. Freedom of Minden Parade, 1982.

Below: 1 (BR) Corps exercise Spearpoint 80 schematic, superimposed over a BAOR road map.

Bottom left: Chocks and chains. ENDEX – loading the train at Emmerthal near Hameln, 1967.

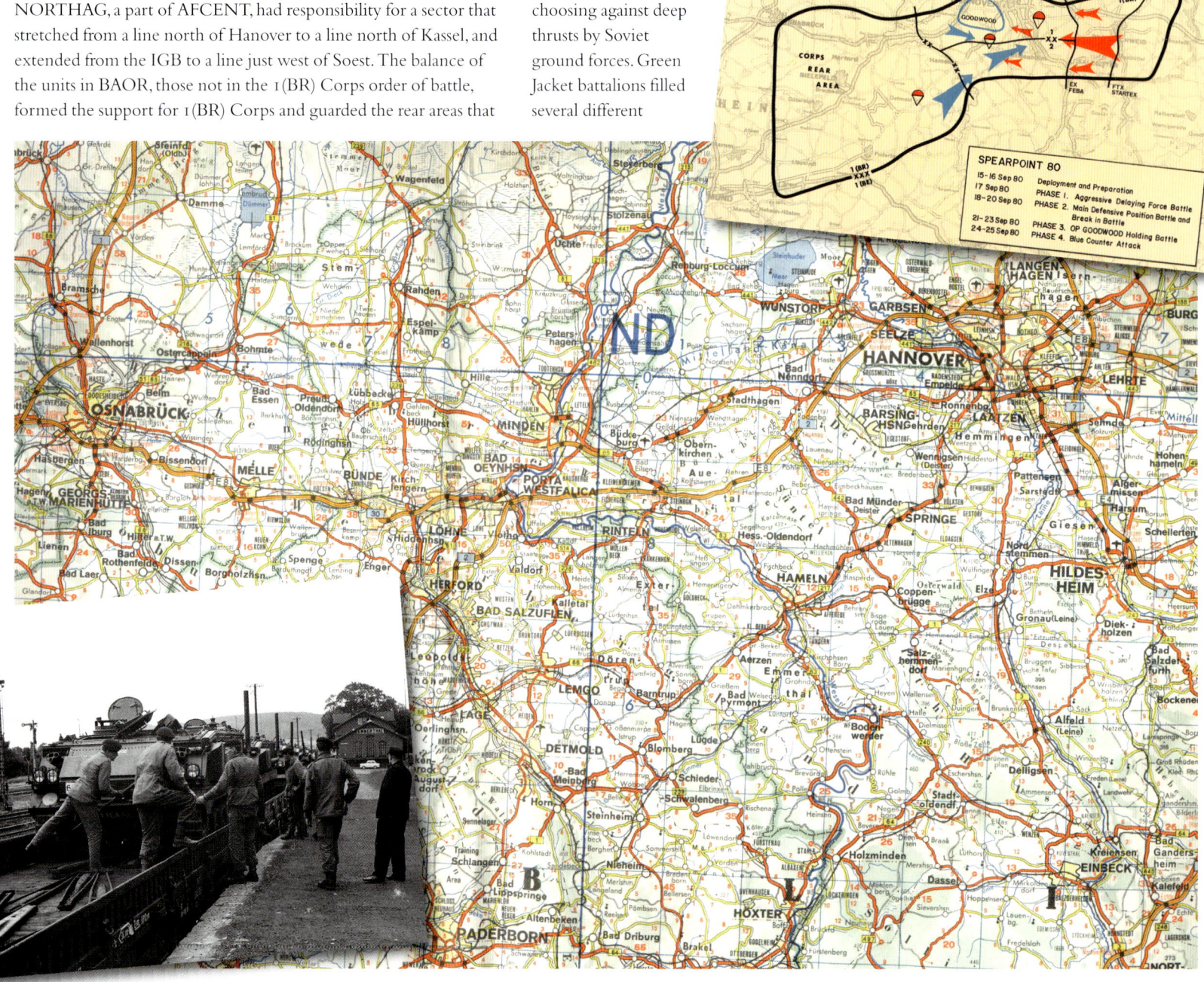

132

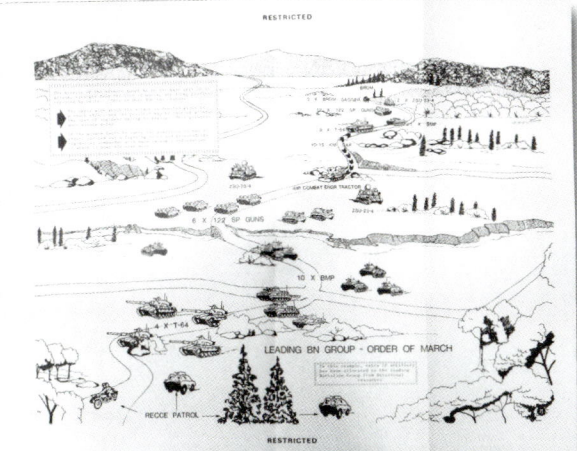

Above: Contact *handbook on Soviet tactics, issued by 1 (BR) Corps.*

Top right: Early days, early errors. A disconsolate Christopher Dunphie watched by Rfn Fox, 1967.

Centre right: RSM Potter, Mike Robertson and APC driver dug in at Soltau, 1981.

Below right: An O group at Soltau, 1969. Peter Treneer-Michell, Peter Lyddon and Sgt Mitchell.

positions in the order of battle over the years, depending on the role of the division of which they were a part.

All GDP documents were 'Top Secret' and kept securely within battalion HQs. It was usual for 'staff rides' to be held annually at corps, division and brigade levels, when commanders and their supporting staff officers went into the field to review plans on the ground, revising and redrafting them if necessary. The threat from Soviet espionage was real and taken seriously. Map boards were kept covered in the field against the possibility of being photographed by satellites, vantage points were swept and guarded by RMP, and discussion in *Gasthauses* was forbidden. On leaving 4th Armoured Division, after two years on the staff during which time he was intimately involved in the division's battle plan, Philip Mostyn, a keen amateur painter, presented one of his watercolours to the headquarters. It was entitled '4th Division Vital Ground Grid 674961', which meant that it had to be entered in the register of Top Secret documents and was only allowed to be hung behind curtains in the headquarters' keep. One wonders where it is now!

Amongst the other important roles that would have fallen to the infantry in time of war was that of the Nuclear Convoy Escort (NCE) battalion, filled by 2RGJ from Münster in 1970. This was a highly sensitive task, guarding tactical nuclear munitions during their outloading from secure sites and their delivery to the artillery units destined to fire them. The sites were established in several places across the 1(BR) Corps area, and although it was a regular chore for all units to provide the static guard, acting in the NCE role was a specialised duty that required the battalion to work closely with US custodians and dedicated Royal Corps of Transport regiments. Efficiency and strict adherence to and understanding of the duties and responsibilities of the NCE role were checked frequently and culminated in annual procedural inspections with lengthy acronyms – ADM NSI AOT would confound anyone not steeped in the jargon of the NCE; it stood for an annual assessment of training in escort duties, security procedures and firing drills for atomic mines entitled the 'Atomic Demolition Munition Nuclear Surety Inspection and Annual Operational Test.'

Another annual task that was sometimes allotted to the Regiment and would surely have been suicidal if it had ever been attempted for real was to form part of an Allied battlegroup ordered to 'open' the corridor through East Germany to Berlin in the event of the Soviets trying to impose another blockade of the city. The

The Royal Green Jackets

battlegroup comprised a US tank company and two batteries of French artillery alongside, and under the command of, a British infantry battalion. It formed up at Sennelager for Exercise Treaty and spent a week practising convoy drills and actions using the ring road round the training area as a simulated 'Berlin Corridor', which was suitably 'blocked' at various points, necessitating its clearance by negotiation, a show of force or an actual attack. In some respects it was a foretaste of what many riflemen would later find themselves doing in Bosnia or elsewhere. It was a high-profile, symbolic bit of training that attracted the attention of senior NATO officers; for the participants it was a tactical and administrative experience, and if you were attached to the French a gastronomique one too!

Training

BAOR was certainly a hectic posting. The year was divided neatly on wall-planners in many offices into individual- and company-level training for battalions from January to March. Brigade-level Command Post Exercises (CPX) were held in the spring along with the corps level signals units' CPX; weapon classification and field firing took place in the summer, along with the corps' CPX; and in the autumn there was the Field Training Exercise (FTX). Into this framework had to fit battlegroup training, conducted in Germany or Libya before the establishment in Canada of the British Army Training Unit Suffield (BATUS). The excellent, realistic training

Left: 2RGJ drawn up for the film Battle Group, *1970. David Mostyn and Philip Smith leading the way.*

Below: SACEUR, Bernard Rogers, lunching with 3 Platoon, 2RGJ Exercise Treaty, 1983.

Germany and the Cold War Years

provided there by the 'Medicine Man' series of all-arms, live-firing exercises was the envy of most NATO forces, and it compared with the very best available to the US military. There was also Nuclear, Chemical, Biological (NBC) training; flotation training for drivers and vehicle commanders; the Brigade and Battlegroup Trainer (BBGT) at Sennelager, to work up battle procedures at command level, support weapons concentrations, tasks in support of the Regular Army Assistance Table (RAAT) and, if any time was left over, the demands of 'normal' battalion life. Various specialist skills had to be maintained as well, and in one area 3RGJ excelled. As was the case in all Green Jacket battalions, 3RGJ employed its bugle platoon as sustained-fire machine-gunners, combining their specialist rifle regiment skills at bugling with an operational skill. Under Bugle Major Powell they won the BAOR GPMG(SF) competition in four successive years.

In an equipment-heavy mechanised battalion routine maintenance and inspections took up considerable time and could not be ignored. Fitness For Role (FFR) inspections, with a plethora of supporting inspections, were annual events. The riflemen invariably rose to the challenge as noted by Lieutenant Colonel David Mostyn commanding 2RGJ in 1970: 'We have just had our FFR report, which is an extremely good one. The day itself went well, with one or two notable triumphs for the riflemen. Our brigadier, a cavalryman, had ordered one of the companies to parade "ready for war with magazines loaded." Now we had just been issued with the General Purpose Machine Gun and almost the first man the brigadier inspected was one such gunner.

'How many magazines have you got rifleman?'

'None, Sir,' came the immediate reply.

'The brigadier, John Stanier, thereupon embarked on a fearsome tirade on preparation for war that left all except the rifleman shellshocked and surveying the ruins of once-promising careers. "Why haven't you got any magazines?" came the question finally. With a deadpan expression, clearly and loudly the rifleman replied, "Our GPMGs are belt-fed Sir". The brigadier was gracious enough to send over to the officers' mess for a bottle of champagne there and then!'

Readiness for war was also tested in the form of call-out exercises codenamed 'Quick Train'. These required a unit to be assembled in barracks ready to deploy to their GDP positions within two hours. In later years this became known as the Operational Readiness Test (ORT), or Exercise Active Edge, and entailed the unit collecting its first-line ammunition holdings from brigade stocks and the deployment of units to holding areas well away from the likely targets that a barracks was expected to become in time of war.

Busy it certainly was. It is no wonder that commanding officers sometimes despaired of having the time to enjoy command. Looking back on his time in Germany, first as Intelligence Officer in the 43rd & 52nd and then Commanding Officer 2RGJ in Münster, David Mostyn wrote:

My overriding memory of life in BAOR, generally, was one long exercise and such a very crowded programme that one never really had time to do anything properly. And when it wasn't exercises it was some other extraneous activity like making a recruiting film, or running the BAOR rifle meeting, or acting as enemy to someone else's division, or having the Colonel Commandant, C-in-C BAOR, corps commander, divisional commander, brigade commander, or even perhaps the chaplain-general or the Royal College of Defence Studies, to visit. It went on and on, and every

Bugle Major Powell (above) ready to march on with the Band and Bugles and (right) collecting the BAOR GPMG (SF) Cup from Martin Farndale, Commander 1 (BR) Corps.

Flotation training in different guises
Far left: Into the Weser at Hameln with a 432.

Above: A Stalwart swimming the Weser.

Left: Rfn Abbott and Corporal Chen-See keep smiling during flotation training.

135

time a commanding officer took issue with his bosses he was told to get on with it or else – I experienced this personally when commanding 2RGJ in 1970. Then there were the annual Fitness For Role inspections, the twice-yearly Operational Readiness Tests, the brigade, division and corps' signals exercises et al – as every commander at every level tried to prove himself. In retrospect, and having seen them close-to in Berlin, I think we vastly overrated the Russians when we were in BAOR. But one has to say that at the end of the day it gave us forty years' peace.

Major exercises at division, corps and above took place approximately every four years. In the 1960s many of these were based on the use of tactical battlefield nuclear weapons. This meant much time waiting out of contact, interspersed with lengthy but rapid moves, often at night, with the riflemen confined to the back of their APCs for hours on end. As deterrence theory in the 1970s came to rely on conventional defence and 'no first use' of nuclear weapons, exercises began to involve the riflemen more and more. Corps' level exercises Spearpoint (1980) and Lionheart (1984) saw 2RGJ enjoying both sides of the game, being the enemy Red or Orange forces in 1980, and then part of friendly Blue forces four years later.

Imagination improved as resources became greater, but in the financially lean 1960s and 1970s major exercises had been a great disappointment to the riflemen. Michael Haines, a 4(v)RGJ officer attached to 3RGJ for a divisional FTX in 1967, illustrates the point:

The major comment I have on the exercise itself is that it seems a shame to assemble 20,000 men and their vehicles for two weeks and exercise them in such an uninspiring way. Until the penultimate day no real use was made of the mobility that a mechanised infantry battalion can command. On the day in question the battalion advanced some thirty miles [48 km] clearing quite heavy opposition on the way, much to the profit and enjoyment of all concerned. All the rest of the time the battalion was either in defence or in reserve, waiting for the enemy breakthrough that never came. This was probably due to the profligate use of nuclear strikes made by both sides, which may have made sense militarily, but certainly ruined an exercise at least partially designed to test the efficiency and mobility of a largely armoured division.

I was greatly struck by how much life in an APC battalion differed from the simple life of the infantryman that I knew, where we were sacrificed on the twin altars of shooting and physical fitness. These old religions have now given way to the new gods of signalling and driving – at both of which the battalion excelled. In passing, I must comment that although my voice procedure was awfully inadequate for the battalion net, I was every bit a match for HQ Guards Brigade!

Throwing a track was always a problem.

3RGJ Battle Group officers, BATUS, 1986.

Above: Cold weather training, Sennelager, 2RGJ, 1968.

Top right: The dust on the wibbly-wobbly way, near Reinesehlen Camp, Soltau.

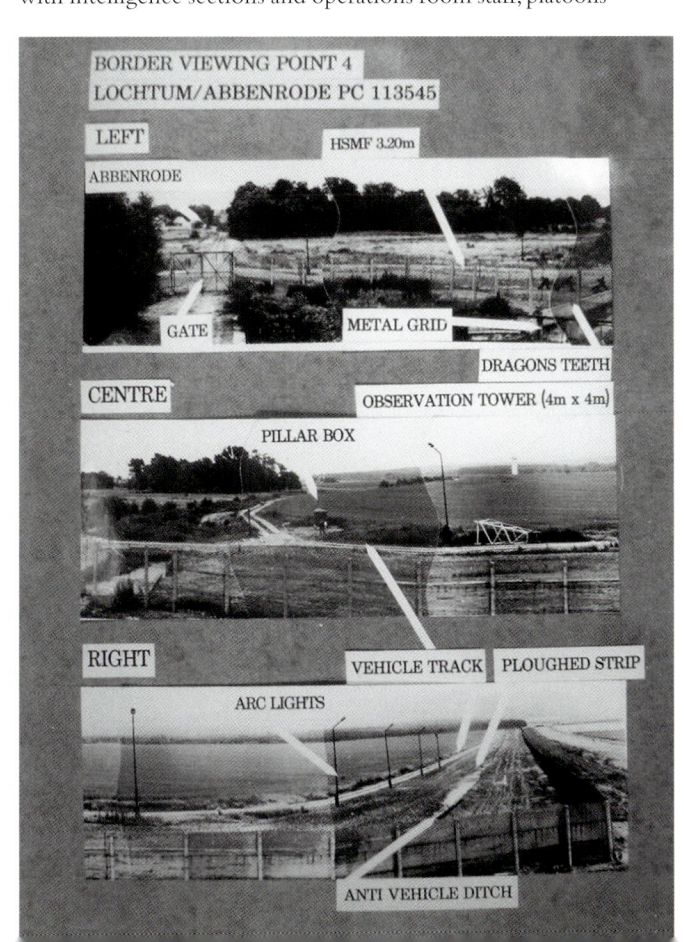

Panoramic montages of the IGB, showing the variety of obstacles dividing Germany.

For the infantry in Germany The Troubles in Northern Ireland and the requirement to support the Royal Ulster Constabulary added another layer of complexity and commitment to the BAOR training year. The role played by the regiment in Ulster is covered elsewhere (see Chapter 9), but suffice it to say here that from 1969 to 1989 Green Jacket battalions completed eight emergency tours in Ireland whilst serving in BAOR, each imposing tremendous strains on organisation, administration and training. Planning for deployment on an 'Op Banner' emergency roulement tour began some six months before the advance party deployed. Specialists had to be selected and trained for intelligence, photographic, close-observation and liaison duties; companies had to be reorganised with intelligence sections and operations room staff; platoons restructured into 'four-man bricks'; and, most importantly, a rear party had to be selected.

The latter had the unglamorous but essential role of guarding the barracks, looking after the families, maintaining the vehicle fleet, an endless round of inspections and starting-up engines in conjunction with the Light Aid Detachment (LAD). In the early 1970s there seemed to be a stark divide in BAOR, the infantry on the one hand, struggling to maintain mechanised infantry skills in the widest sense between tours in Ireland, and the cavalry on the other, unencumbered by the need to confront republican terrorism and leading a more traditional lifestyle of exercises, sport and 'fun'. There was never much allowance made for the infantry, which was expected to hit the ground running on the streets of Belfast, the fields of Armagh or the plains of Hanover. 1RGJ had a particularly difficult spell in the early 1970s when completing four full Ireland tours in four successive years. Nevertheless, operational tours in Ireland were regarded by many as a welcome break from the surreal world of 'deterrence' and the threat from the Warsaw Pact. Parking up the APCs for six months was to be enjoyed.

Border Patrols

Apart from tours in Ulster the nearest those serving in BAOR came to an 'enemy' was patrolling along the IGB. This regular operational task usually involved a platoon in Land Rovers or, later, CVR(T) armoured reconnaissance vehicles in a one-week deployment entailing a series of patrols along specific lengths of the IGB. The 870 mile (1,400 km) IGB was the reality of the 'Iron Curtain' – wire fencing, watchtowers, pillboxes, bunkers and death strips overseen by the East German border guards of the Nationale Volksarmee (NVA). In 1980 these guards were a mixture of regulars and highly trusted conscripts completing their two-and-a-half-years' military service. Despite the East German authorities spending some £3 million per mile on the border defences, an average of about thirty people a year managed to escape across the IGB, usually arriving in the West with nothing more than the clothes they stood up in.

Soviet personnel were also occasionally sighted within West Germany, because just as there was a British Observer Mission (BRIXMIS) stationed in Potsdam in East Germany and operating from Berlin, so too there was a Soviet Observer Mission (SOXMIS) in the West, stationed in Lübbecke, which carried out regular patrols throughout the 1 (BR) Corps area. If the Soviet personnel's distinctive cars were spotted they had to be reported in accordance with the instructions on BFG Form 66 and detained if they were in a restricted area. Correct procedures had to be followed or retribution would be exacted against BRIXMIS in Berlin.

The Royal Green Jackets

Breaking the Rules at Spandau Prison
Recalled By Lance Corporal Peter Uden

After the Nuremberg Trials (a series of trials that ran from 1945 to 1949) the top convicted Nazi war criminals were incarcerated in Spandau Prison, situated adjacent to Smuts Barracks in the British Sector of West Berlin. The internal security and administration of the prison and its inmates was run on a civilian quadripartite basis, under the military government. External security was the responsibility of the military personnel of the four occupying powers and was rotated among them, a month at a time.

The prison guard had to man a guardroom, a main gate and five watchtowers. When it was the British turn we furnished a platoon, with the lieutenant and sergeant as the commander and second-in-command, three JNCOs as NCOs in command of reliefs, and three 'stags' of six men. The orders for the guard were comprehensive, very comprehensive as I remember, and seemed to cover every eventuality from not talking to the prisoners up to nuclear war. The changeover of guards between nations and the changeover of stags was always done with a lot of ceremony and bull (to the Green Jacket mind any way).

1st Green Jackets, 43rd & 52nd, transposing whilst there into 1RGJ, were stationed in Berlin from April 1965 to April 1967. When we arrived in Berlin from the Far East there were three remaining inmates in the prison: Baldur von Schirach, Albert Speer and Rudolf Hess. During 1966 von Schirach and Speer were released, leaving Hess as the sole inmate.

The watchtowers at the prison were mutually supporting to the left or right except for No. 3 tower right at the back of the prison, which was unsighted from the other towers. This was okay during daylight but became quite spooky at night, especially with lurid tales of previous sentries who had committed suicide in it. This was not helped by us being told that Hess had lost his marbles by this time and had developed a penchant for screaming and howling at night, which was clearly audible to the sentry in No. 3 tower.

Above: Soldiers from the 1st battalion, The Royal Highland Fusiliers take part in the international changeover of the guard at Spandau Prison in Berlin, May 1985.

Right: Hitler's right-hand man, Rudolf Hess, the sole inmate of Spandau Prison from 1966 until his death in 1987.

At the back of the prison, overlooked by No. 3 tower, between the outer perimeter wall and the internal massif of the prison proper, Hess had developed a small vegetable plot and there was a straight line path, worn quite deep, where he would rapidly march up and down during his exercise periods.

On the day in question, in 1966, I was the JNCO in command of reliefs, the guard commander was Lieutenant 'Diddy' Hughes and the sergeant was Dave Conway. It was mid-morning, and we were in the guardroom relaxing between stag changes when a member of the prison staff came to the guardroom with a German workman. The workman had to do a small plastering job on No 3 tower and I was to escort him. Off we set with me unlocking and locking doors and gates as we made our way to the rear of the prison. As we came within view of No 3 tower I could see that Hess was out on his patch with a warder in attendance. Nothing wrong with that I thought, but I was worried in case there was something in the orders to cover this eventuality, which I could not remember.

The warder and the workman obviously knew each other and hailed and greeted each other. The workman then veered off our selected path to go and talk with the warder and I trailed along behind. I had already established that the workman did not speak English and my German at this time was pitiful. I felt that I was rapidly losing control of a situation that could have dire consequences (for me). The warder was American, a huge man getting on for seven feet tall, his height accentuated by the floor-length cloaks that the warders all wore. He and the workman were having a conversation in German, which I could not follow, and I became aware that Hess had stopped his exercises and was making his way over to us.

I now knew that this was definitely not according to the rules and was desperately trying to think of a way to resolve the situation. By this time Hess was standing alongside me and staring at me intently. He also was very tall, but not as tall as the warder. My overriding impression was of eyes which were very dark and very deep set, and a huge pair of bushy eyebrows. Here was I, Lance Corporal Uden, standing next to the bogeyman, Hitler's deputy, and wanting the ground to open and swallow me up. On a scale for dropping a clanger this seemed to me off the Richter scale. At this point Hess spoke to me and said, 'Nice weather we're having,' or some other banality, in a clear but slightly accented voice. I gulped and some sort of strangled noise came out of my throat. This was a waking nightmare. However, on hearing Hess speak or noticing my extreme discomfort, the warder abruptly finished his conversation with the workman and led Hess away.

The workman picked up his bucket, made his way over to No. 3 tower, did the plastering job and we returned to the guardroom without further incident. I wrestled with my conscience about whether to report it or not. I did not and for the next few hours, days, weeks waited for the summons to explain myself. Gradually the experience and the expectancy of retribution faded, but I remember avoiding Spandau Prison guard like the plague for the rest of our tour in Berlin!

After the death of Rudolf Hess in 1987, Spandau Prison was demolished to prevent the building becoming a Nazi shrine. A large NAAFI was erected on the site, which British troops immediately named 'Hescos'.

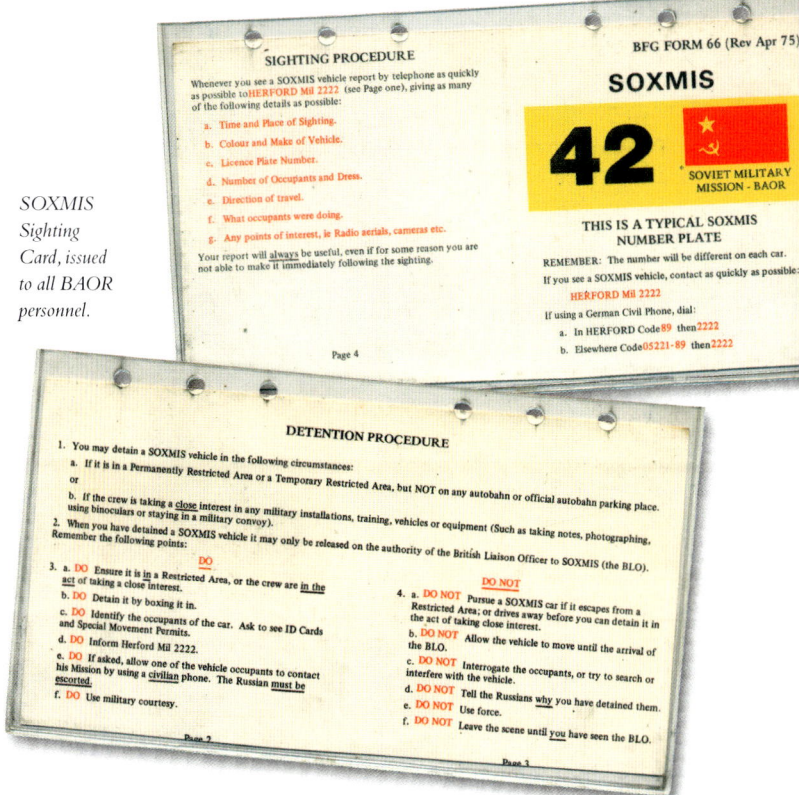

SOXMIS Sighting Card, issued to all BAOR personnel.

Berlin

For those 13,000 Allied personnel stationed in its garrison, Berlin was a western island 100 miles (160 km) behind the Iron Curtain. The British brigade and the headquarters staff of the British sector accounted for 3,000 overall, equal to that of the French; the US contingent at 7,000 strong was the largest. The Royal Green Jackets served twice in Berlin, 1RGJ in 1966–7 and 3RGJ in 1975–7. Several senior officers also filled appointments in command and on the staff, including General Sir David Mostyn, GOC Berlin 1980–2, and Colonel Peter Lyddon, Chief of Staff (COS) Berlin Brigade in November 1989 when the Berlin Wall came down.

For many riflemen the Berlin posting was not particularly to their liking. Duties were frequent, and in many ways service life in Berlin was not dissimilar to a spell of public duties in London. For the junior officers, too, the range of duties to be performed was lengthy: battalion orderly officer, alert platoon commander, Spandau Prison guard commander, military train commander and tour guide on coach trips around East and West Berlin on Saturday mornings. Nevertheless, there were plenty of perks to be enjoyed: the night life of Charlottenburg, 'grotty Charlotty' to one and all; amazing concerts, both classical and rock; multinational cuisine; international-standard sporting facilities; and access to the Post Exchange (PX) in the US sector and the French Economat with its regular supplies of cheese and wine. There was also the weekly FRIS – 'fresh rations issue' – from the rations that were stockpiled in the event of another blockade by the Soviets. These rations had to be turned over regularly thus providing all service families with a regular supply of heavily subsidised fresh food delivered to their doors each week.

When not engaged in ceremonial or guard duties, the Berlin Brigade trained to defend the Allied sectors of the city in the event of a Soviet attack. Fighting in Built Up Areas (FIBUA) was practised and readiness was tested in a series of exercises called 'Rocking Horse', which was announced by wailing sirens and

The Royal Green Jackets

BERLIN CEREMONIAL

An aspect of military life in Berlin where the riflemen invariably stole the show, out of novelty if nothing else, was the ceremonial involved in national and allied parades. Their quick pace required other marching contingents to be held back until the way was clear. Then, with a flourish of bugles, the riflemen would be 'released' to applause from the crowds. In 1976 3RGJ provided a guard for the Queen's Birthday Parade on the Maifeld alongside contingents from The Royal Regiment of Wales and 1st Battalion, The Parachute Regiment. As the *Chronicle* for that year records:

The Royal Regiment of Wales arrived with Taffy the Goat; The Parachute Regiment produced Bruneval the Shetland Pony. Now this is the sort of challenge that no rifleman can resist. Nor could Captain Ron Cassidy and Corporal Fletcher who was in charge of the battalion pig farm. Charlie, our tame half pig, half wild boar, appeared suitably dressed in a Rifle Green coat but squealing loudly because of the heat of the tarmac on his trotters, as the battalion formed up. This caused a considerable stir, but as some battalion wag put it 'we were only poking charlie at our neighbours'. Charlie was fallen out before we marched on and as ever the riflemen took over and performed splendidly. Whilst the battalion was much amused by its own little joke, the other battalions on parade found it more difficult to appreciate.

Charlie and Cpl Fletcher in mufti and on parade.

THE BERLIN TRAIN AND CORRIDOR

Taking a car to Berlin entailed a 100 mile (160 km) journey from Checkpoint Alpha, just outside Helmstedt, south of Hanover, to Checkpoint Bravo in the city's US Sector. A full briefing before the journey meant a thorough check of the travel documents and gave you details of the route, the procedure in the event of a breakdown, the speed to travel (62 miles per hour, and if you arrived significantly earlier or later by not adhering to the speed limit, woe betide you!), the protocol at the borders that were dual controlled (no contact with the East Germans, how to address the Russians), and what to look out for and report on if seen, such as convoys or troops on exercise. It was certainly an exciting trip the first couple of times it was made, and the thought that after Checkpoint Bravo came the infamous Checkpoint Charlie of spy film fame added spice to it. But after a few journeys the tedium and the bad roads made it into more of an endurance test.

A less taxing way of entering or leaving Berlin was by train. Every day after the 1945 peace the *Berliner* made the 145 mile (230 km) return run from West Berlin's Charlottenburg station to Brunswick, carrying passengers and a fifteen-strong crew, including a signaller, a four-man armed guard, a courier and half-a-dozen civilian dining car staff. Come rain or shine, empty or full, the *Berliner* was needed on a daily basis to exercise Allied rights of free access to and from Berlin. It was 'commanded' by an officer from the duty battalion who was assisted by the Train Conducting Warrant Officer and an interpreter. Carriage doors were secured to prevent access or exit on the journey, and strict rules were applied that prohibited the use of binoculars or cameras. If you referred to the guide that was available to passengers, there were some interesting sights to be seen along the route. The train was an easy and relaxing duty, though it was a long day of around fifteen hours. For the passengers the trip to Brunswick was a pleasant one offering the opportunity for a few hours shopping with a light breakfast and three-course lunch on the way out, tea and a three-course dinner on the way back – and all for £1.

There was access to Berlin by air, road and rail. Flying into Berlin was no different from arriving at any other international city, but travelling by road or rail meant going through procedures and observing protocol – making use of the Berlin train and corridor – that had been refined to an art form over the years since the end of the war.

Above: The Berlin train itinerary, menu and tickets.

Inset: Boarding the Berliner for a day out in Brunswick.

Germany and the Cold War Years

Right: John Foley (right) greeting General Snetkov, Commander-in-Chief Group of Soviet Forces Germany, at the Soviet War Memorial in West Berlin, 1987.

Below: The BRIXMIS RAF Chipmunk over the Teufelsberg, West Berlin. The white 'golfballs' on the Teufelsberg are part of a Western electronic listening station gathering intelligence from Warsaw Pact radio transmissions.

Above right: The BRIXMIS House in Potsdam.

British Armed Forces currency (BAFs), used in the British sector of West Berlin.

required the battalion to muster and deploy at any time of the day or night, without warning.

Training with allies was enjoyable enough, and certain duties were shared with them, most notably the guarding of Spandau Prison, in the British Sector, where Rudolf Hess was serving his life sentence for Nazi war crimes. As one of the four powers controlling the city, Soviet forces also undertook this task, which made it a particularly sensitive area of protocol and one in which any mistake could have significant diplomatic repercussions.

BRIXMIS

Few people knew about the British Commanders-in-Chief's Mission to the Soviet Forces (BRIXMIS), and fewer still what it did. Established in September 1946, BRIXMIS was designed as a liaison mission to help foster good relations between the British and Soviet occupation forces. It was based in Berlin, and the reciprocal Soviet mission was at Bunde, West Germany. As the Cold War intensified, BRIXMIS's real role became more that of intelligence gatherer. Much of the mission's time was spent collecting intelligence on the Group of Soviet Forces Germany (GSFG) and East Germany's NVA. Numbering around eighty all ranks (60 per cent Army, 40 per cent RAF), the mission was commanded by a brigadier with a group captain as deputy. Green Jackets were well represented. Brigadier, later General Sir, Thomas Pearson was chief of mission in 1960–1 and Brigadier, later Lieutenant General Sir, John Foley in 1987–9. General Pearson's son Johnnie, also a Green Jacket, joined BRIXMIS in the 1970s, provoking a typical Soviet response, 'So, Captain Pearson, do we conclude from this that in England espionage is a family business?' After a demanding course at the Intelligence Centre – learning equipment recognition, photography and reconnaissance tradecraft – new members joined the mission, which was organised into sections including liaison/operation touring (liaison officers and NCOs were called 'tourers'), intelligence, technical, photography and administration. Tour officers learned Russian and German.

Operational tours combined boredom and routine with excitement and fright. Travelling across East Germany (except in restricted areas), touring teams of a tour officer (photography), tour NCO (recognition) and tour driver (security) gathered intelligence on Soviet and NVA military and air force garrisons, equipment and deployments. They also used high-performance cross-country vehicles, Nikon cameras and a variety of image intensifiers, video cameras and night-vision goggles. No communications equipment was carried nor were any weapons that did not fit with the overt

The Royal Green Jackets

The Fall of the Wall

If any one event can be said to symbolise the ending of the Cold War it must be the day the Berlin Wall was breached. Colonel, later Brigadier, Peter Lyddon was chief of staff at Headquarters British Sector Berlin and one of three riflemen serving in the city at the time:

Thursday 9 November 1989 was a routine day for the chief of staff of HQ British Sector Berlin. I had the usual series of meetings with diplomatic colleagues in the British Military Government (BMG) in the morning, and calls to my opposite numbers in the US and French sectors in the afternoon. That evening Nicky and I had been invited to a wine tasting in the officers' club followed by dinner. The next day the wall in the British Sector became the focus of large crowds and the world's media. 'As we were sampling the red and white wines, announcements were being made on the radio and television by the East German press officer, Herr Shabowski, that DDR citizens were to be allowed unrestricted travel to the West. The timing of this was totally unexpected; the influx began immediately through the existing crossing points and by midnight the first revellers were dancing on top of the wall at the Brandenburg Gate! I was fortunate enough to witness these unforgettable scenes in the company of Mr Donald Lamont, the number two in the BMG and his head of security, Mr Arthur West.

On Friday the three commandants held an extraordinary meeting of the Allied Kommandatura (the supreme legal authority in Berlin), which was attended by the three ministers and the sector chiefs of staff and, inter alia, took an important decision to allow the West Berlin Police to enter the 'Unterbaugebeit' (a narrow strip of land immediately adjacent to the wall), that hitherto had only been accessible to allied military policemen. That evening the DDR officials announced nine new crossing points in addition to the thirteen that had previously existed; the Glienicke Bridge, scene of many spy exchanges, was one of the nine. In the early hours of Saturday morning the West Berlin police were now able to assist their eastern colleagues by controlling the situation right up against the wall on the western side. On Sunday the focus of attention switched to Potsdammer Platz, the old centre of Berlin – and previously one of the starkest views of the no-man's-land that existed between East and West, when it was opened, allowing a stream of Trabant cars to cross.

The fall of the wall in November 1989 and the events that followed over the next few months in 1990 changed the course of history in Europe. The Allies provided much-needed security and logistics; in the end the number of refugees that wished to stay in the West was not significant. The ensuing pace of change was staggering. Monetary union took place in June and unification on 4 October. The Allied commandants, the epitome of the Cold War command in Berlin, departed shortly afterwards. On 22 December the Brandenburg Gate was opened to pedestrians.

9 November may have started as an ordinary day in the office, but the events that followed changed all our lives. I was not the only Green Jacket fortunate enough to be in Berlin at that time: Robin Steel was on the Staff of HQ British Sector and Phillip Scofield working in HQ Allied Staff Berlin.

Top: Peter Lyddon, COS HQ Berlin (British Sector) with (left) Mr Arthur West, Police Liaison Officer, and (right) Mr Donald Lamont, Deputy Head of the Berlin Mission, at the Brandenburg Gate during the night of 9/10 November 1989.

Above: East and West Berliners celebrate on top of the Wall at the Brandenburg Gate on 10 November 1989.

Left: Major General Haddock, US Commandant, speaks at the ceremony to mark the removal of the military police post at Check Point Charlie on 22 June 1990.

During the Cold War, the twenty divisions of the GSFG were the prime target for the intelligence collection effort in Whitehall. BRIXMIS's legitimate ability to observe and photograph at close range, and its continuous presence over forty-four years, created a pool of unequalled knowledge. Most intelligence came from routine, methodical collection, but occasionally a 'scoop' (or first sighting) was achieved, as John Foley recalls:

When I was chief we were urgently tasked to get an Explosive Reactive Armour box, recently introduced onto the Soviet tanks – by a stroke of luck one of our sharp-eyed tour NCOs spotted one on a tank firing-range and grabbed it. More often, scoops were surprises. A good example was the find of an SS-23 ballistic missile unit – the tour was immediately detained but the tour officer had shot some film thinking it was an SS-21 unit. On analysis it was revealed as SS-23 – until then no one knew the Soviets had deployed SS-23s in East Germany.

Throughout the Cold War the liaison function of the mission continued, and although tours did experience detentions and incidents it was not in the interests of either the Soviets or the Allies to impose draconian restrictions on the missions. The motif chosen for the BRIXMIS necktie was, appropriately, a mission restriction sign (one that, of course, was invariably ignored). The mission closed in October 1990, upon German reunification, with a party organised by Major Crispin Beattie, the last Green Jacket to serve with BRIXMIS. BRIXMIS must rank amongst the most professional and cost-effective military intelligence collection organisations of the Cold War.

The final words on life in BAOR belong to Christopher Wallace who spent much of his service in BAOR, commanding at battalion and brigade level before assuming command of 3rd Armoured Division just as the Berlin Wall tumbled:

I was first posted to Germany, or to be more precise West Germany and the British Army of the Rhine, in 1967. I was the Intelligence Officer in the 2nd Battalion, The Royal Green Jackets, newly arrived in Münster from Penang, Malaysia. After a few months in England learning how to drive AFV 432 armoured personnel carriers, we were obliged, rather reluctantly, to cast aside our knowledge of jungle warfare in favour of our new role as mechanised infantry. For me, it was the start of what was later to total over ten years' service in Germany, first as a battalion officer and subsequently as a battalion, brigade and divisional commander. There was, of course, something surreal about the Cold War and about service in BAOR, with the forces of NATO and the Warsaw Pact, each armed with nuclear weapons, lined up in opposition on either side of the Inner German Border. Whilst the possibility of conflict between East and West was always present, it seemed improbable – or so we hoped – that the Soviet Union would ever initiate a war that threatened Armageddon. Quantitatively, if not qualitatively, the odds seemed stacked against us. However, it was not our job to worry about preparing to fight a war, which privately we feared we might not win. On the contrary, the better prepared, the better trained and the more professional we were, the more likely – or so we were told – that NATO's strategy of deterrence would succeed. War would not be required. And so we trained hard, on exercise

Christopher Wallace Adjutant (left), and Bill Williams, Technical Quartermaster. Exercise Iron Hand, 2RGJ, 1968.

liaison role. Many hazards nevertheless faced the tours because both the Soviet and East German forces would chase them, attempt to ram or block their vehicles and lay ambushes. East German Stasi (secret police) surveillance teams, called 'narks', routinely tailed tours, and all the time they were at risk of being arrested or detained, for an alleged infringement of touring rules. If this happened, protocol required that the local Soviet *kommandant* was called; meanwhile, the crew sat tight in the locked vehicle until he arrived and checked their passes, which would have been issued by HQ GSFG (Group of Soviet Forces Germany) and conducted an investigation into the incident.

Apart from vehicle-mounted tours, BRIXMIS also used an old Chipmunk trainer aircraft manned by an RAF crew to fly low-level sorties in the Berlin Control Zone to collect invaluable intelligence on the large Soviet garrison. The cover story was that they were carrying out aircrew refresher training for members of RAF Gatow (part of the British sector of West Berlin).

The Royal Green Jackets

Left: Cross-country skiing on 'Army planks'.

Below left: Minimal exposure in minimum temperatures was essential.

areas such as Soltau and Sennelager, to hone our individual and collective military skills. There were also frequent exercises, entitled 'Quick Train' and later 'Active Edge', to test our preparedness, at all times of the day and night, to move swiftly from our barracks to pre-designated deployment areas. Such activities all added to a prevailing sense of competitiveness in which battalions, and their commanding officers, vied to be the best in the brigade, brigades vied to be the best in the division, and divisions vied to be the best in the corps. The annual exercise cycle, involving command post exercises in the early part of the year and full-blown exercises with troops in the autumn, both established and destroyed reputations. To manoeuvre armoured formations around the battlefield successfully was perceived to be the acme of military skill. Thus – or so it was thought – aspiring generals had to be posted to Germany if they were to stand a chance of reaching the top. There were few Green Jackets to whom the 'hothouse and make believe' environment of BAOR truly appealed. Most riflemen preferred to be on their feet in the open rather than entombed in the back of an APC. And what they really wanted was to be on real operations against a real enemy. Given the choice, the majority would opt for the dangers and discomforts of Northern Ireland rather than a posting to Germany. As a result, battalions in Germany were often undermanned. But there were compensations – the married men enjoyed living allowances, better quarters and a quality of life, which led some later to marry and settle in Germany. There was also plenty of opportunity for single men who were so minded to engage in sport, travel and adventurous training. BAOR has since been retitled BFG (British Forces Germany) and the Cold War is history. As a divisional commander at its conclusion, I admit to considerable surprise that it ended so abruptly, with the Soviet Union, crippled economically by the cost of sustaining the Cold War, disintegrating at the end of 1991. Although some now say, with the benefit of hindsight, that the collapse of the Soviet Union was inevitable, that is certainly not the way it seemed when I arrived in BAOR in 1967.

Soldiering in the UK in the Cold War years

Although this chapter has been focused on BAOR in the days of the Cold War there were aspects of life in the UK that were bound up in the same business of 'deterrence'. The role of the Allied Forces Mobile (Land), AMF(L) was the ground defence of NATO's flanks in Norway and Turkey in the event of war with the Warsaw Pact. To form the UK contribution to this force, one infantry battalion from the Army was dedicated to the task, along with supporting arms and services, with the UK focus being on the northern flank of NATO. In 1992 the newly merged 2RGJ, stationed in Dover, prepared for its tour of duty as the UK infantry element of the AMF(L) – a role that required its men to learn the personal and tactical skills that would enable them to operate 20 miles (32 km) beyond the Arctic Circle in temperatures well below freezing. For the average riflemen – who had only seen snow occasionally, dashed outside to build a snowman as soon as it fell and then watched from the warmth of his bedroom as it melted away – learning to live in a snow-hole for several weeks on end was quite a challenge!

NORWAY and the AMF(L) role

Pre-Arctic training was very tough, supervised by Royal Marine Arctic Warfare Instructors. Each company had to select a number of officers and NCOs to become trainers and the rest of the battalion had to get to what was described as 'mountain fit'. They also had to get used to cross-country skiing, which for a couple of months involved the whole battalion cruising round the barracks on elongated rollerskates while carrying enormous rucksacks. The training paid off when the battalion arrived in Norway for the first time on Exercise Hardfall, the name given to AMF(L) winter deployment training from November to March annually, although spills and thrills were frequent. Skiing on issue skis, that the riflemen christened 'Army planks', with a Bergen and a rifle slung across the chest, is not easy and many faces subsequently bore the scars of damage caused by coming into contact with the SA80 sight in a tumble. Plunging into the waters of a frozen lake to learn how to climb out onto the ice after falling in, enduring a 'survival night' in minus 20 degrees centigrade without a sleeping bag, having to bag and carry your own bodily waste, and overcoming the physical and mental effort needed to live and fight in such conditions, are all experiences not quickly forgotten. On their initial deployment, and despite the lack of Arctic training, the men of the battalion came first and second in the 15 km (10 mile) ski and shoot race, rising to the challenge in true Green Jacket style and beating teams from Norway, Germany, Italy and Holland.

One feature of the multinational nature of the AMF(L) was the round of parties to entertain the other contingents. This became something of a beauty contest and competition was steep, with some almost regarding it as the measure of their success in the AMF(L) rather than their contingent's performance on training. The form was a cocktail or dinner party, which 2RGJ quickly realised meant that it would be unable to compete on the usual terms, so it provided a 'full English' breakfast instead! Greeted with bemusement initially, this quickly won an appreciative following among the other commanding officers and staff personnel who were used to a slice of cheese and a lump of heavy bread with which to start their day.

The 2RGJ tour with the AMF(L) lasted from 1992 until 1995, and although the battalion only exercised for two winter seasons a great deal was learned from the role. It also had the unique experience of being under the command of two Green Jacket brigadiers concurrently, Vere Hayes in Dover, for administration and training, and David Innes in Bulford, for operations. The challenges and requirements of survival and soldiering in the harsh environment north of the Arctic Circle are many, but not least among them is the need for excellent personal administration. That the challenges were met successfully and cheerfully by 2RGJ is testimony to the professionalism of the riflemen, working in conditions they had never before experienced – and for most of them will probably never wish to again!

UK Public Duties

Some postings in UK offered other challenges, public duties being a particular challenge for riflemen. Over the years, from a variety of barracks and suitably drilled by long suffering Household Division Drill Sergeants, riflemen deployed to London to mount guard at Buckingham Palace and elsewhere. They always aroused the interest of tourists with their different drill, dress and marching pace, which sometimes caused consternation. One hundred and forty paces to the minute seems to fall between a very fast walk and a slow trot for a horse, making the task of escorting the incoming guard to St James's Palace somewhat tricky for mounted policemen. 'Watch out Ladies and Gentlemen' one was heard to remark to a group of spectators crowding the Mall as he cleared the way for 3RGJ, 'this lot are on roller skates.' When the Green Jackets Guard stood at ease after every movement during the Changing of the Guard ceremony, it was not unusual for Household Division and Infantry of the Line units to join in, causing disruption in the ranks opposite much to the amusement of the riflemen.

Cpl Clarke, Rfn Bentley and Rfn Dyer, tackling a blaze in South London.

Green Goddesses

The 1970s saw many industrial disputes, and the Armed Forces were sometimes called on to keep essential services running whilst politicans and unions sought a resolution of their differences. Refuse collection and provision of ambulances fell to the Services at various times, and in 1977 a strike by firemen saw the army deployed with RN and RAF units as fire fighters throughout the country. 1RGJ was in Dover and 3RGJ in Caterham at the time. Together they covered south London.

Operation Burberry – Fire Fighting 1977
As recalled by Major John Taylor, 3RGJ

In November 1977 the Fire Brigade Union called a national strike over a pay dispute and the Government decided that the Armed Forces should provide fire-fighting cover for the whole of the United Kingdom. At the time the 1st Battalion, based at Dover, was preparing to move to Hong Kong and the 3rd Battalion, at Caterham, was about to alternate Public Duties with training for its next Northern Ireland tour. As existing fire stations were heavily picketed by striking firemen, companies from both battalions established ad hoc fire stations in TA centres in South London and drew up their 'Green Goddess' fire engines from Home Office depots. These venerable machines had been mothballed awaiting the Third World War but proved reliable and ideal for virtually untrained crews. The riflemen warmed to the challenge of yet another, but completely different task, and a welcome alternative to Public Duties or Ulster training. There was some trepidation as to the public's response which it was feared might be hostility or derision, but such fears swiftly proved unfounded as support blossomed for riflemen doing the same job as firemen but with rudimentary equipment and less pay. On arriving at a fire near a Camberwell street market, the Green Goddesses were greeted with a standing ovation, and shortly afterwards the Company Commander was presented with an upturned hat brimming with silver and notes. But much had to be learned the hard way. The fire-engine crews had only been trained in their individual drills, and at a major fire at King's College Hospital one night Green Goddess crews continued to arrive and deploy their equipment until the approaches were choked with a mass of vehicles and a spaghetti tangle of hoses. The fire was eventually extinguished but it became clear that a robust command and control system needed to be developed based on sound military principles but with advice from fire officers. In the early days large amounts of water were used on even small fires and no doubt there was as much damage to property from flood as fire. But the riflemen soon became adept at the economic and precise use of water and in such precautions as turning the gas off well before a spark reignited the fire with a loud roar. All riflemen like a bit of excitement and it was often a case of 'keep the fire going till we get there!' Forcing the Green Goddesses through the rush hour traffic of South London or driving along pavements in a Land Rover fitted with siren and blue flashing light, usually following a police motorcycle escort with 'Go Places with the Royal Green Jackets' sticker on its windscreen, was exhilarating enough even before arriving at the blaze. With the move to the Far East imminent, the 1st Battalion handed over their areas of responsibility to the Parachute Regiment after three weeks. The 3rd Battalion, rotating companies between the contrasting demands of fire-fighting and Public Duties, continued its deployment in South London for six weeks until the end of the strike in January 1978 by which time they had dealt with over 500 fires, of which 280 were extinguished by the company in Camberwell.

Soldiering Around the World

The change in the frequency and intensity of operational tours since the Cold War, when being on the 'front line' in Germany dominated the lives of professional soldiers, is stark. The Cold War years proved routine, bordering on mundane, for most of the Regiment, and even when deployed on an operation much soldiering tended to be uneventful in comparison to operations TELIC in Iraq and HERRICK in Afghanistan in the twenty-first century. But, training was intense, varied and demanding, and tours in Northern Ireland, whether on the streets of Belfast and Londonderry or in the fields of South Armagh and Fermanagh, were frequent. Often operating under the eye of an ever-present, intrusive media and detached from his platoon commander, the 'strategic corporal' was born in Northern Ireland, where decisions at Section level could have far-reaching consequences. This has been significant in many of the operations described in this chapter and important in the ongoing war fighting deployments that end it.

Just as those who experienced the Second World War imbued a proper understanding of soldiering in the Cold War generation – the subalterns of that conflict becoming the brigadiers and generals of the late 1960s and 1970s – so too the Cold War generation has passed on to today's riflemen the same essential qualities of professionalism and leadership, the ethos and 'fighting spirit', and the ability to take the knocks that has come so obviously to the fore in operations from the first Gulf War, with the UN and NATO in the Balkans in the 1990s and onto Sierra Leone, Iraq and Afghanistan.

The Cold War dominated over half of the forty-year life of The Royal Green Jackets and, although those years are epitomised by the armed stand-off that divided Europe, the battalions served a total of thirty-seven years (excluding postings as resident battalions in Northern Ireland) outside BAOR and Berlin between 1966 and 1989. After the fall of the Berlin Wall, and the draw-down of the Army based on the Continent, postings to Germany were less frequent and the Regiment found itself more often stationed in the UK.

During the lifetime of The Royal Green Jackets battalions found themselves stationed in England or overseas on many occasions. Whilst 'home-based' battalions served their turns in Ulster on a regular basis, and life was often no less hectic than in BAOR, these were postings the riflemen relished. Overseas training opportunities were many, and away from the armoured personnel carriers that dominated their lives in Germany they got back to 'proper' infantry soldiering with many memories to cherish of exercises and adventures in places such as Fiji, Jamaica, Kenya, the USA, Canada and Belize – some of which fulfilled the promise of the recruiting posters. Postings to Hong Kong, Cyprus and Gibraltar fell into this category, though even there two years was enough for most riflemen.

3RGJ at Wainwright, Canada.

Hong Kong, 1979

As far as the Chinese were concerned, 1979 was the Year of the Goat, but the massive influx of refugees seeking to escape from Vietnam by boat and on foot across the border from communist China meant that as far as the battalion in Hong Kong was concerned it would be the 'year of the illegal immigrant'.

Operation Culex, the name given to anti-illegal immigrant operations, started in March; by the end of May all the armed forces

Soldiering Around the World

Above: The Hong Kong skyline and the Star ferry.

Below: Training in the humidity of the jungle in Belize.

in Hong Kong, including The Royal Hong Kong Regiment, were deployed in support of the police.

By that time the battalion had been given responsibility for the southeast third of the colony, which included part of the Kowloon mainland. Initially, battalion tactical headquarters deployed into Sai Kung police station, with Letter B Company in Man Yee police station and a composite company from A and C Companies, together with Support Company, in Erskine Training Camp, Clearwater Bay Peninsula. As the crisis grew, life became hectic and there were continuous changes in deployment. Letter B Company was deployed at short notice to the island of Lama to deal with the refugee ship *Skyluck,* whose inmates, after four months anchored offshore, had cut their moorings and consequently run aground on the north of the island – 3,000 'boat people' were rounded up and handed over to the police.

REGIMENTAL POSTINGS, BRITAIN AND OVERSEAS

1RGJ	2RGJ	3RGJ
1967–70 Tidworth	1966–7 Penang	1966–7 Felixstowe
1974–8 Dover	1973–5 Catterick	1970–1 Tidworth
1978–80 Hong Kong	1975–7 Gibraltar	8/1971–1/1972 R Company Netheravon
1980–1 Hounslow	1977–9 Tidworth	1972–5 Shoeburyness
1983–7 Tidworth	1986–8 Warminster	1977–1979 Caterham
	1988–1991 Dover	1980–2 Oakington
		1987–8 Colchester
		1989–91 Gibraltar

25 July 1992
The 1st, 2nd & 3rd Battalions merged into two battalions.
The 2nd & 3rd Battalions redesignated as 1st & 2nd Battalions

1RGJ	2RGJ
1993–6 Cyprus	1992–5 Dover
1996–9 Bulford	2001–3 Warminster
2002–7 Weeton	2005–7 Bulford

Above: Training with alternative transport in the arid climate of Dol Dol, Kenya.

147

The Royal Green Jackets

Oman and Dhofar, 1960s–90s

Green Jacket officers and NCOs served in Oman from the late 1960s and well into the 1990s, in varying numbers and positions either as 'loan-service' or 'contract' officers, within the Sultan's Armed Forces (SAF).

Perhaps the principal reason for loan-service in the 1970s and 1980s was the prospect of some real action as opposed to continuing constabulary duty in Northern Ireland or more garrison assignments in Germany. As Christopher Kemball said:

In early 1972 my eye caught a memo offering a two year secondment to the Sultan of Oman's Armed Forces, then in the middle of an armed insurgency … With the prospect of endless tours of Northern Ireland and not much else … I found the prospect very appealing, particularly as we were offered promotion and the opportunity to fight in a guerrilla war.'

Earlier loan-service officers, such as Simon Theobalds, served with the Trucial Oman Scouts in the Gulf States, but by 1970 Whitehall had responded to Omani requests for military assistance to quell a communist rebellion and SAS squadrons deployed on operations and to train local militias. Green Jackets who worked with the SAS at the time included John Foley, Arish Turle, Simon Adamsdale, and Mark Whitcombe. Other Green Jacket officers on secondment returned to encourage individuals to apply for loan service with stirring tales of action on the jebel. Mike Smith recalls:

I was 'recruited' for service with SAF by Graham McKinley who returned to Celle in 1972 and gave us a terrific insight into life and operations in a part of the Middle East which I had some difficulty finding on a map.

Graham had joined Northern Frontier Regiment in 1970 and had been decorated for holding Salalah against the rebels. The war in Dhofar in the early 1970s saw the fight taken to the enemy.

Operation Simba established a base deep on the jebel at Sarfait. Life there was spartan with constant shelling. Christopher Kemball and Charles Vyvyan recall:

We lived in rock sangars and were regularly shelled and mortared in the evening. At night, we patrolled out into the wadis to interdict resupply while other units attacked adoo positions in the centre of the country.

Our tactics were straightforward … we would set up an ambush … and with luck surprise an adoo formation … there would be a fierce exchange of fire while they attempted to recover their dead and wounded (a matter of honour for them).… Instead of bugging out we stayed put calling up air and artillery support ready for the usual counter-attack. We then hit them hard generally coming off best thanks to our firepower although the adoos' standard of shooting and fieldcraft was far superior to ours.

The war was officially won in December 1975, but SAF continued to patrol on the jebel. Companies were generally deployed for three or four months, and Mike Smith described the sheer enjoyment of operational autonomy:

We were left alone by battalion HQ and as a 26-year-old company commander with my own mortar fire support, and the occasional company of an SAS team, I was very much lord of all I surveyed and enjoyed myself hugely. Woken one night by firing on the perimeter of my position I felt duty bound to fire everything in the armoury – such opportunities were few and far between on Salisbury Plain!

Where else in the British Army at the time could these experiences be matched and so much enjoyment be had? Even in the 1980s it was still possible to patrol where nomadic families had never seen a Western face. Green Jackets who were in Oman then included Jolyon Jackson, Paul Luckhurst, Jeremy Russel, Johnny Schute and Richard Thompson.

Perhaps the longest-serving Green Jacket in Oman was Bill Logdon, who was on loan service from 1977 to 1979, returned as a contract officer in the late 1980s to command a SAF battalion (the only Green Jacket to do so) and then worked in various staff positions before retiring in 2000.

Finally, the war in Dhofar was not without casualties. Tim Taylor, who, received the Sultan's Commendation Medal, was killed in 1971 and Don Nairn in 1979. Ex-Bandmaster Major John McTomney died of a heart attack in 1976, and other Green Jackets were wounded or injured including Bill Foxton who lost a limb while destroying a 'blind' mortar bomb. Bill was met at Salalah airport, on 'casevac' by a Green Jacket contract colleague who with typical Rifleman humour asked: 'Hello Bill, decided to throw your hand in?'

Above: Roger Luscombe in the mountains of Dhofar.

Below inset: Charles Vyvyan taking the evening air on his sangar. Note the thickness of the overhead cover.

Below: The base at Sarfait on the jebel.

Bottom: LCpl Hughie Vernon 22 SAS (ex 2RGJ) instructing local militia in Dhofar.

Above: The border crossing point at Man Kam To. The actual border is the far side of the river.

Right: Support Company 1RGJ quick reaction force (QRF) led by Sergeant Oates.

Far right: Parade Programmes 3RGJ, Gibraltar, 1989.

Bottom right: The Monday morning ceremonial 'Changing of the Convent Guard', Gibraltar, 2RGJ, 1975.

By the beginning of November the crisis had passed, and UK-based battalions that had been deployed to Hong Kong as reinforcements returned home. 1RGJ still had two companies deployed, one under operational control of the 7th Gurkha Rifles at Man Kam To and one at Man Yee. The former manned observation points along Hong Kong's border with China, whilst the latter deployed platoons into four- or eight-man observation posts overlooking the coastline and were kept supplied by air. With one small adjustment to the area covered, this remained the deployment until February 1980 when the battalion was relieved of its operational responsibilities in order to prepare for the move back to Hounslow and public duties in London. It had been a busy ten months. A minimum of two companies had been continuously deployed and more than 8,000 illegal immigrants had been caught, including some in Stanley Fort, the battalion's barracks.

Gibraltar, 1975–7; 1989–91

When 2RGJ arrived on 'The Rock' in 1975 they were the first Green Jackets to serve there since the RB in 1922. When 3RGJ left Gibraltar in 1991 they were the last British Army regular battalion to be stationed there. A posting to Gibraltar provided a haven from the rush of life in Germany and the UK but, although a true sunshine posting, the lack of any real operational role and the constant round of ceremonial duties could soon pall without a determined effort by the chain of command to make life interesting.

The main military task during the 2RGJ tour from 1975 to 1977 was to keep watch over the frontier with Spain, which continued to lay claim to the colony. The border between the two countries had been closed in 1969 and was to remain closed throughout the battalion's tour of duty. One platoon was permanently allocated to border security – but as the last shot in anger had been fired across it in 1783, the duty was never likely to be too arduous.

For 3RGJ over the period 1989–91, since the border with Spain was by then open, this task had ended. However, the attempted attack on the Gibraltar Resident Battalion by PIRA in 1989 necessitated the maintenance of a relatively high operational profile. Ceremonial tasks took hard work and careful preparation, but Rifle Caps and black accoutrements over Summer Whites combined with the distinctive speed and movements of Green Jacket drill presented a dashing effect that won many plaudits for both battalions. Those who live in Gibraltar became, over the years, connoisseurs of ceremonial drill, and Peter Browne commanding 3RGJ was amazed to be told by one veteran spectator that he 'had compared video recordings of the 3RGJ Guard Mount with that of 2RGJ in 1977 and found several differences!'

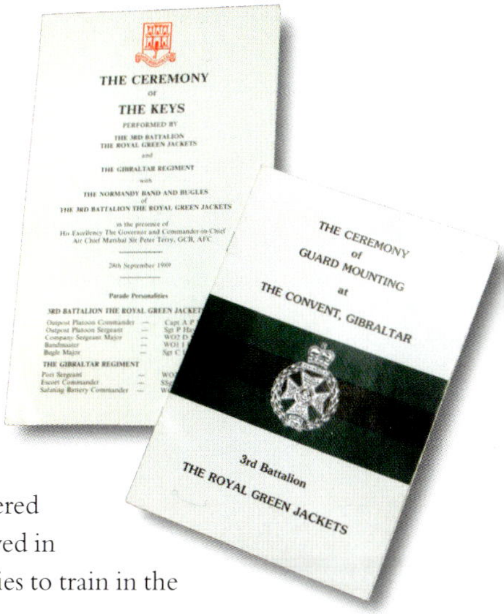

Considerable enterprise, energy and effort were put into finding varied ways to train in the confined spaces of The Rock, including the construction by 2RGJ of an imaginative series of ranges in the small local training area and the tunnels beneath it. These were designed by Major Dougie Maber, ex-RB, who had created the Hythe and Lydd complex of ranges so familiar to those completing Northern Ireland pre-deployment training. Sadly, neglect and a lack of funds had rendered them derelict by the time 3RGJ arrived in 1989, but the ability to send companies to train in the UK was compensation for their loss.

The Royal Green Jackets

An interesting coincidence occurred in the summer of 1990 when a fire broke out in the scrub of the Upper Rock. 3RGJ was called on to put it out and noted that the call to fight the fire came to them on 10 August, exactly the same day as a similar call had been made to 2RGJ 14 years earlier. The *Chronicle* of that time had noted that 'putting out a scrub fire is a pretty hazardous operation at the best of times, but on a 45 degree slope it becomes highly dangerous', and in August 1990 3RGJ found themselves in complete agreement.

Sport – especially water sports – sailing, exercising with visiting TA units, seizing opportunities to train with any visiting Royal Navy ship, completing career courses and the performance of varied ceremonial duties – from the changing of the Guard at Government House to the Ceremony of the Keys and the annual Queen's Birthday Parade – filled the programme. It was a happy posting and one to be enjoyed, but at the end of two years most Riflemen were glad to leave. As 2RGJ recorded in 1977:

> We were very fortunate to have been posted to The Rock in 1975 but by September 1977 we were undoubtedly keen to leave and get on with some more realistic training. Some people will dislike any posting but certainly the majority left with affection for Gibraltar. The people of the colony had been good to us – and we to them too. The fact that we emerged with absolutely no trouble in the town having occurred says as much for our relations with the local people as it does for the excellent behaviour of the riflemen.

The Subalterns of 2nd Bn The Royal Green Jackets (Gibraltar 1977)

Belize, 2RGJ, 1973–4

Ten years and one month after 2nd Green Jackets King's, The Royal Rifle Corps had completed an emergency deployment to British Guyana, the Regiment found itself in that country once more, but it was now called Belize. Guatemala had a long-standing territorial claim to the area, showing it on maps as a province. Since British Guyana had become the self-governing colony of Belize in 1964, Guatemala's attitude had been aggressive. Shortly before 2RGJ deployed in 1973, Guatemala mistook a UK exercise in the region for a force build-up, and in response it made various overt warlike preparations. The Belize garrison was therefore increased from a company group to a reduced-battalion with a force HQ and supporting elements, including Harrier aircraft.

Commanded by Peter Welsh, the battalion deployed in August 1973 for a four-month tour, leaving A Company behind in Catterick. The main role of the battalion was to deter, and if necessary counter, any threat by Guatemala to invade or annex any part of Belize. The battalion was split between two locations: Battalion HQ and a company in Airport Camp alongside the international airport, and the other rifle company in Holdfast Camp,

Far left: The Officers vs Sergeants annual cricket match (the Sergeants won), Gibraltar, 3RGJ, 1990.

Opposite: Jamaica exchange training, Exercise Red Stripe, 2RGJ 2003. From top left clockwise: Rfn Timms weapon cleaning in the jungle; the heat of the day when the fish won't bite; patrolling the river line; L Cpl Glazebrook leading the dive; Major Khan RMO 2RGJ displaying a good catch – but the fish have got smaller since '73 (see opposite).

Left: Anthony Stansfeld, RGJ commanding the Army Air Corps flight supporting 2RGJ, holding an 80lb Tarpon he had caught, Belize, 2RGJ, 1973.

Below: Rifleman Mileson in the jungle, Belize, 4(v)RGJ, 1997.

Left: No two Subalterns ever dressed the same. Standing L–R: Neil Baverstock, Martin Rigby, Robert Bolton, Peter Pelly, Jolyon Jackson, Simon Ffennell. Sitting L–R: Toby Heppel, Philip Howell, Greg Taylor, Mark Boringdon, Alex Nall. Gibraltar, 2RGJ, 1977.

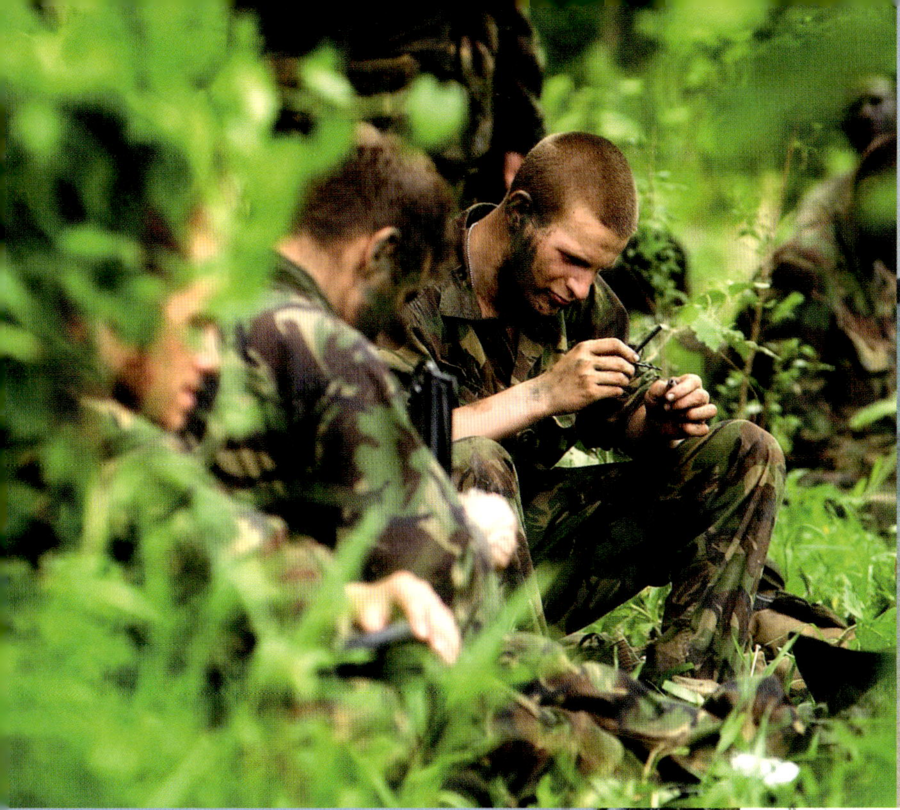
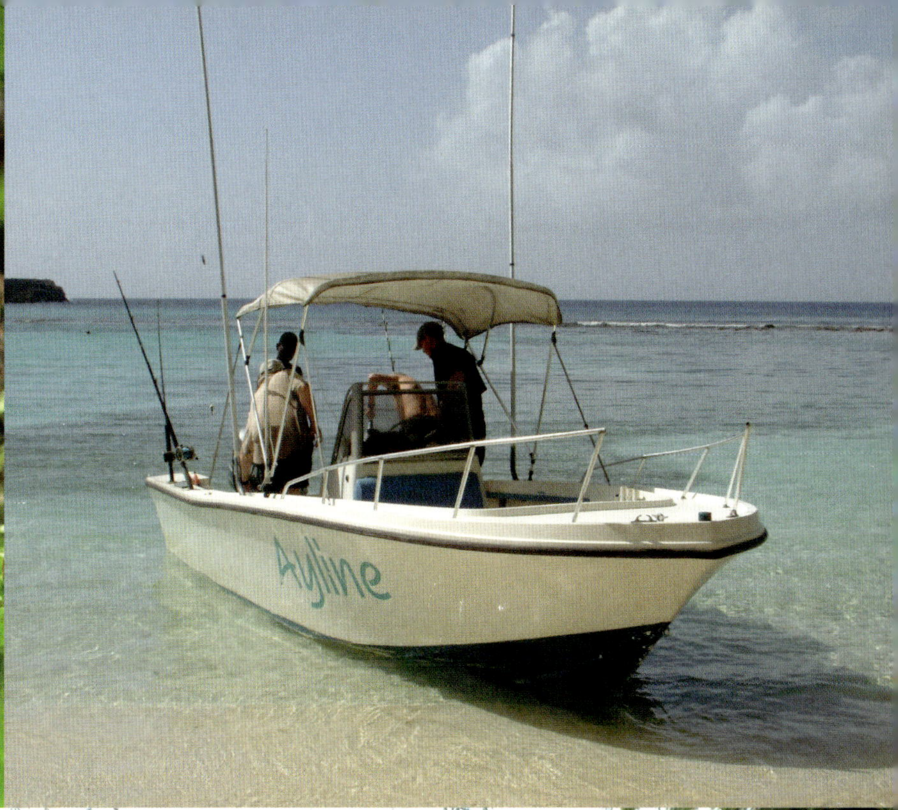
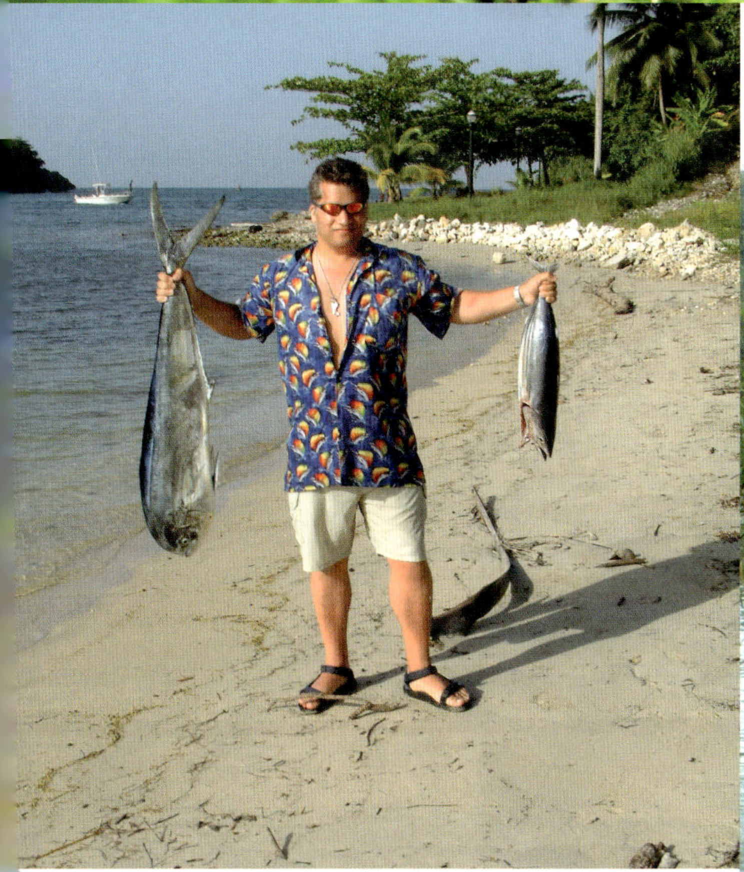
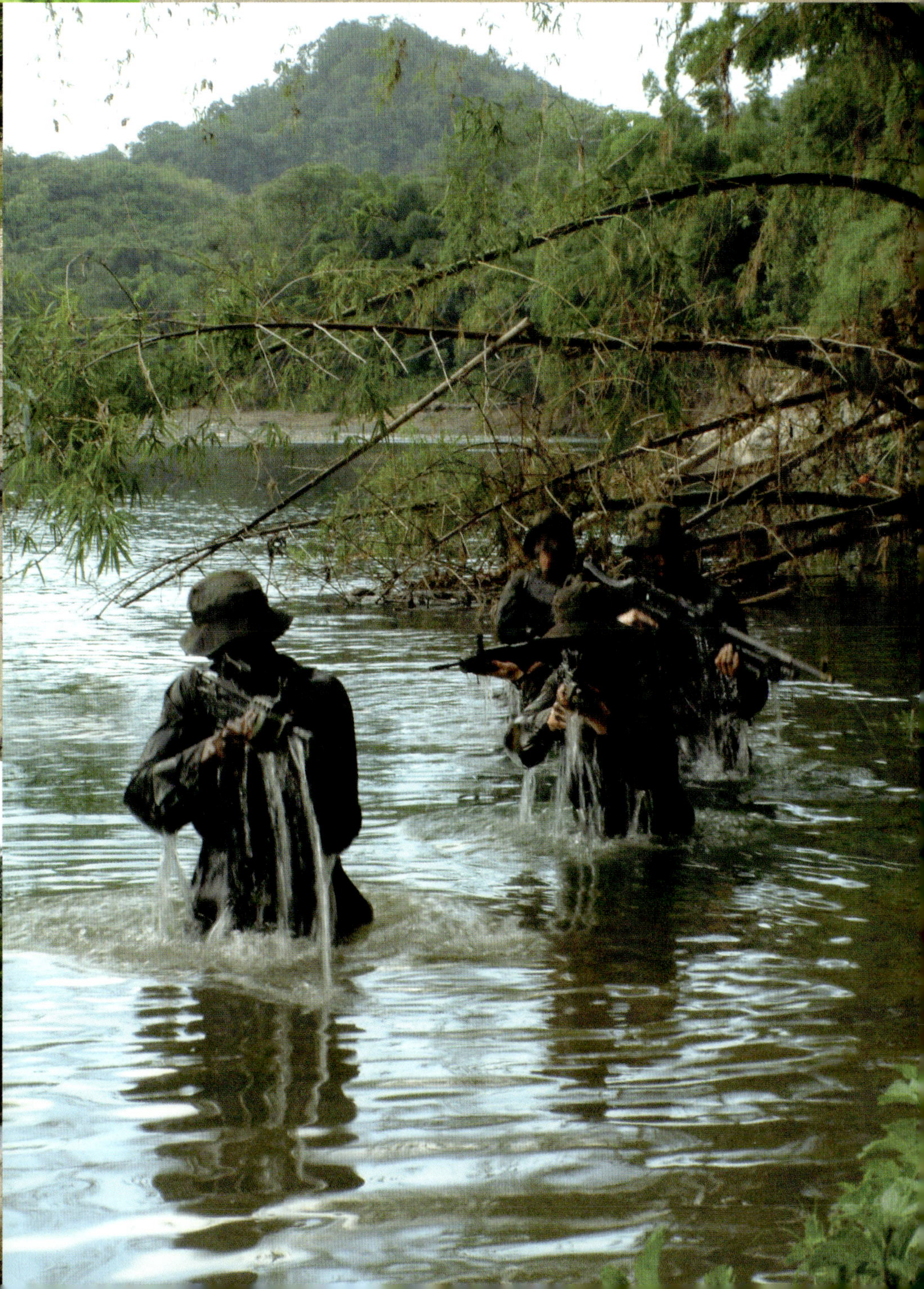
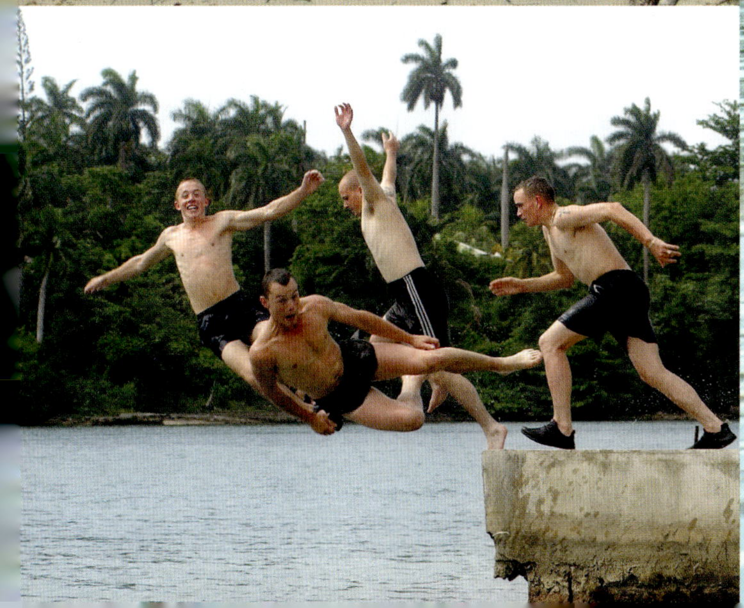

about 75 miles (120 km) away and 15 miles (24 km) from the Guatemalan border. Companies rotated through Holdfast Camp every six weeks in order to provide variety and to make use of the opportunity to carry out jungle and other training. A tour in Belize provided excellent training as well as opportunities for diving, fishing and other adventurous pursuits, most notable of which was the ascent of Mount Victoria by Second Lieutenant Jamie Vyvyan and Corporal Croucher. Adding a rather different dimension to an operational tour, the commanding officer was married on 16 February in an 'atap' shelter in Airport Camp.

Operation Agila, Rhodesia, 1979–80

In 1965, following the breakdown of talks with the UK Labour Government led by Harold Wilson, the Rhodesian Government led by Ian Smith made a Unilateral Declaration of Independence (UDI). This sparked the isolation of the country and a bitter war between white and black Rhodesians. On one side there was the Rhodesian Security Forces (RSF), which considered it an insurgency; on the other side there was the Patriotic Front (PF), an alliance between the ZAPU (Zimbabwe African People's Union) and ZANU (Zimbabwe African National Union) parties, each of which had its own military wings (ZIPRA and ZANLA) and considered the conflict a war of liberation. At the Commonwealth Conference in 1979 agreement was reached on setting up talks to resolve the question of the future of Rhodesia. Subsequently, the two sides met at Lancaster House, London, and negotiated a ceasefire and arrangements for free elections.

To oversee this agreement, the United Kingdom set up a Commonwealth Monitoring Force (CMF) of some 1,300 personnel drawn from various Commonwealth nations, commanded by Major General Acland, to monitor the official ceasefire from 00:01 hours on 29 December 1979 to 00:01 hours on 6 January 1980, and subsequently to remain in place until after the results of the elections had been announced at the beginning of March – this was Operation Agila. The CMF set up two parallel organisations, one to work with the RSF Combined Operations HQ in Salisbury, Rhodesia, and a small staff to work alongside the PF with liaison officers from either ZIPRA or ZANLA (or both) in charge of operational areas as a 'PF Commissioner' who controlled a number of RV points and assembly points. The plan was that fully armed PF troops would emerge from the bush, report to the RVs during the official ceasefire and then be moved to the assembly points and held there until the end of the election. This was not without risk, as the reactions of the various groups were as yet uncertain. Finally, there was a number of Border Liaison Teams (BLT), which monitored the main crossing points between Zambia, Botswana, Mozambique and South Africa. Overall, it was a complicated operation with many moving parts in the plan, great distances and difficult communications. Fifteen officers and NCOs from 2RGJ and twenty-two from 3RGJ took part in Operation Agila.

On arrival in Rhodesia the fifteen members of 2RGJ deployed on Op Agila were split up and dispersed: Lieutenant Colonel Peter Treneer-Michell, commanding officer of 2RGJ, Major Nick Magnall and three NCOs formed a monitoring team in Bulawayo responsible for Matabeleland, with Captain Robin Steele running a subordinate HQ. JOC. RV teams were provided by Captain Guy Fetherstonhaugh, Warrant Officer Second Class Winkworth, Colour Sergeant Sawyer and Colour Sergeant Bartlett. The task was to identify any breach of the ceasefire agreement by either the RSF or Patriotic Front (PF) Forces. To do this they were required to 'act in a spirit of co-operation with the RSF and PF, referring to higher authority only in circumstances where reasonable agreement cannot be reached'.

The time was filled with briefings at JOC HQ and visits around the area, either with the Rhodesian brigade commander or to the various Commonwealth sub-units. Breaches of the ceasefire and incidents between ZIPRA and ZANLA did occur, but thanks to goodwill and compromise the operation was a remarkable success.

The tour ended with some of the assembly points – at which guerrilla forces had agreed to gather – being turned into training camps to integrate the PF and RSF into the new Zimbabwe Army. In time this arrangement developed into the British Military Advisory and Training Team (BMATT), an organisation that remained in the country for more than twenty years, until 2001. When BMATT finally left, its commander, Brigadier Vere Hayes, deputy commander, Colonel Nick Mangnall (who had served with the original monitoring force), and chief of staff, Lieutenant Colonel Peter Luard, were all Green Jackets.

THE MULTINATIONAL FORCE AND OBSERVERS (MFO), SINAI, 1982

CAPTAIN JAMES BOWDEN

The signing in 1979 of the Camp David Agreement between Egypt and Israel provided for the peaceful return of the Sinai Peninsula to Egypt. The provision of a UN force to monitor this was vetoed by the Soviet Union and so the Multinational Force and Observers, or MFO was established.

I served with the MFO for the second half of 1984. There were eleven contingents then, and the British contingent was one of the smallest, some thirty-seven officers and mainly SNCOs filling administrative and security posts in the Force HQ. I was the admin officer, effectively the adjutant, of the contingent or BRITCON. Sergeant Ollie Brown, also from 3RGJ, was the camp commandant's assistant. We were all based at a comfortable former Israeli air force base close to the north coast.

The Force worked remarkably well, given the diversity of the contingents and the relative lack of experience at that time of multinational peace-keeping operations, for which much of the credit must to go to the Force's first two commanders. It helped that money was not short, but I think the key to success was that contingents were encouraged to maintain their distinctive national characteristics while having to integrate operationally, administratively and socially into the overall force structure. In this way, the strengths of each were effectively harnessed.

BRITCON made an impact out of proportion to its size. Its commanders adopted the approach that everything would be done absolutely correctly but with style and a little eccentricity – ideal for a Green Jacket. This won us the particular trust of the Force Commander and the admiration of other contingent commanders.

CEASEFIRE IN RHODESIA, 1979–80

LIEUTENANT COLONEL J.R. CUNLIFFE

High up on the southwestern border of Rhodesia and within sight of the mountains of Mozambique, the tiny village of Rusitu was the temporary RV point manned by myself, then a Lieutenant, Sergeant Bill Bailey and eight corporals from 3RGJ.

We had deployed from Salisbury in armoured trucks, led by an armed police escort and a mine-detection vehicle along the dirt tracks. Once they had departed we were alone in the bush armed only with rifles, wondering how long we could withstand any attack if things went wrong. Within a few hours we had raised the Union Jack, sprayed the abandoned buildings with insecticide, erected our signals mast and set to work clearing up and sandbagging the rooms.

However, guerrilla distrust of the security forces was intense, particularly in the Eastern Highlands. We were lightly armed, felt vulnerable and were undoubtedly nervous, wondering what would happen next. With no sign of anybody for the first few days and reports of large numbers of fully armed ZANLA and ZIPRA arriving at other RV points around the country, the situation seemed hopeless. So rather than wait for ZANLA and ZIPRA to come to us, we went looking for them.

Eventually, after a difficult and sweltering afternoon of searching Corporal 'Angel' Brown and I finally made contact with the ZANLA guerrillas in a hill-top fortification. We returned to the RV, relieved and exhausted, just before last light.

The next morning, armed with mortars, rocket-launchers, heavy machine-guns, assault-rifles, most with bayonets attached and bulging ammunition packs, a group of 200 guerrillas emerged from the bush, clambered aboard buses and, accompanied by the Green Jacket team, were driven to their assembly point on the southwest border with Mozambique.

We stayed there for the next two months, which was a period of excitement, tense situations, political manoeuvring, logistical headaches and, above all, plenty of talk (usually over cups of tea). The ZANLA guerrillas had little conventional organisation; they had come to the camp in the clothes that they stood up in (plus weapons and ammunition) and urgently needed food, shelter, medical help and the hundred-and-one things that such a field army needs in a static location.

Regular early morning muster parades at 05:30 were a memorable feature. Breaking into a sweat, singing war chants with fervour and clutching their AK-47 assault rifles, which had come to symbolise the revolution, 1,000 ZANLA guerrillas poured onto a clearing in the bush to be paraded and counted. Attitudes could change from warm and friendly acceptance to gun-waving anger, sometimes in the space of a few minutes. Tact, diplomacy and even brinkmanship averted numerous serious incidents, but every rifleman was well aware that he was very much in the front line.

By the time the election came in early March, the guerrillas took their turn to vote. Fifty heavily armed guerrillas at a time trotted up to the Monitoring Force camp, reluctantly deposited their weapons and made an orderly queue to vote.

It was a gruelling two months, and most Commonwealth troops were keen to get home, but it had been exciting and challenging, leaving us with a great sense of achievement.

Top right: Patriotic Front guerrillas emerging from the bush.

Below: The multi national team at the Assembly Point.

Right: Deploying on one of the excellent 'tar' roads. Note the roll bars fitted to the vehicles.

BATTLE OF KOPHINOU

The village of Kophinou occupied a strategic position that both Turkish and Greek Cypriots wished to control. It was a flashpoint that was monitored by the UN. After several months of tension Greek forces launched three simultaneous assaults on the Turkish positions around Kophinou ignoring the UN presence.

All 1RGJ's observation post positions were caught in the crossfire. Corporal Savage refused to move his section from Grenadier Hill. On Tango Hill the post's administration area was looted, but a Greek officer lost his thumb to a rifleman's sword (bayonet) when he tried to interfere with the section radio, and Corporal Bradford remained in place. Corporal Devine's section on Radio Hill had a worse time. Direct hits landed on the administrative area, their possessions were looted and two riflemen were relieved of their weapons. Throughout all these actions the posts continued to send accurate information that provided comprehensive reports to UN HQs and resulted in a ceasefire at 22:00 hours., Under threat of invasion by Turkish forces, and with Turkish planes regularly overhead, a lasting ceasefire and the withdrawal of Greeks troops was eventually secured.

Above: Cpl Devine in his OP position at Kophinou.

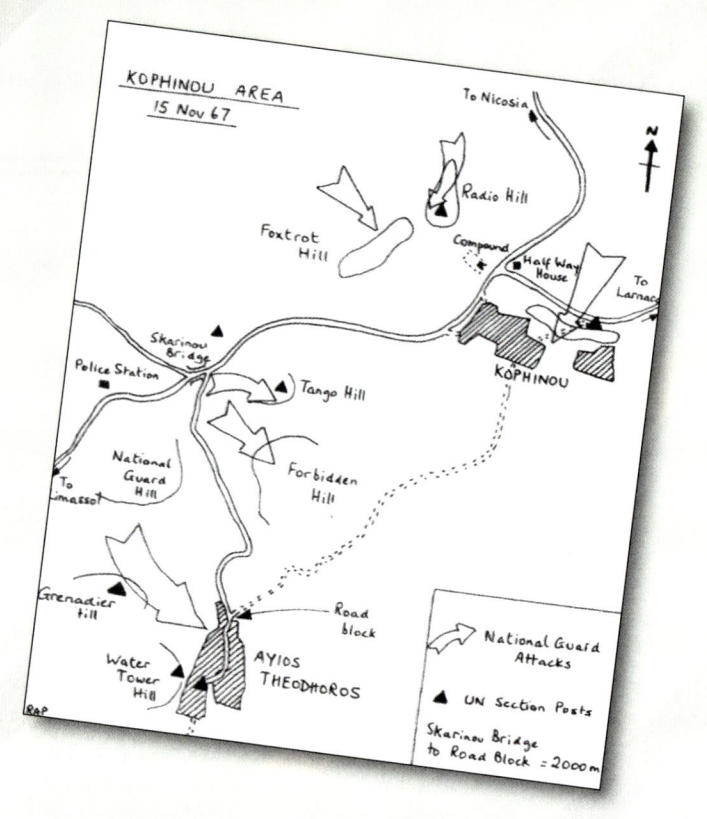

Left: Sketch map of the Turkish assault.

United Nations Force In Cyprus (UNFICYP)

UNFICYP is one the longest running UN operations, dating back to 1964. Battalions of The Royal Green Jackets served four times with UNFICYP: 1RGJ in 1967–8 and 1976, and 3RGJ in 1970–71 and 1980. Prior to this, battalions of The Green Jackets Brigade had served in Cyprus as part of the British Garrison as 1RGJ was to do in 1993. The UN mission was there because inter-communal strife broke out between the Greek and Turkish communities only three years after independence in 1960. The UN regarded the situation as a threat to international peace and security, and at the request of the new Cypriot government, a UN force (UNFICYP) was deployed to the island. It had the traditional peace-keeping tasks of observation, monitoring, reporting and negotiation in order to prevent outbreaks of violence, thereby establishing the conditions for a political settlement to be negotiated.

The force's capacity to intervene and prevent serious outbreaks of violence was limited by the UN mandate, which permitted force to be used only in self-defence. When it first deployed, UNFICYP was scattered throughout the island, interposing itself at the many flashpoints where the Greek and Turkish communities coexisted in a mosaic of minority communities. The difficulties of the task were highlighted by the experiences of 1RGJ in 1967–8, which included 'the Battle of Kophinou'. Following the overthrow of President

Soldiering Around the World

Makarios, which was supported by the Greek military junta on the mainland, and then the Turkish invasion in 1974, the task became more straightforward as the two communities were then separated by a UN 'buffer zone' known as the Green Line. It was then UNFICYP's task to patrol and police the line, tackling incidents that had the potential to derail the peace process.

UNFICYP, 1RGJ, 1967–8

1RGJ was warned of its six-month unaccompanied tour in early June 1967 and was deployed in November. The same plane that arrived with the incoming Green Jacket companies departed that evening with the outgoing companies of The Duke of Wellington's Regiment. Breakfast, briefings and the issue of UN berets, insignia and ID photographs left only an hour for hand-over. The battalion's mission was to prevent a recurrence of fighting, to contribute to the restoration and maintenance of law and order, and to secure a return to normal conditions. Asking a lightly armed peace-keeping force to prevent a recurrence of fighting is, we now know through experience, an impossible mission. And so it proved. Commanded by Frank Kitson, the battalion was responsible for the southwest part of the island, an area some 75 miles (120 km) long and 20 miles (32 km) wide. The tour was dominated by the Battle of Kophinou and its aftermath.

The reality of the incident at Kophinou was twenty-seven dead and many wounded. General Grivas was removed from command by the Greek government and the majority of Greek troops were removed from the island. Six years of relative peace followed until another Greek gamble turned the island into turmoil in 1974.

UNFICYP, 3RGJ, 1970–1

The 3RGJ tour in Cyprus, from October 1970 to April 1971, occurred a mere seven months before the battalion was 'reorganised' into a single company represented by R Company. Commanded by Jimmy Glover, the battalion was responsible for the zone consisting of Limassol and Paphos districts, with five platoons earmarked to operations and three to low-level training. Generally, it proved to be a quiet tour. The battalion's view was expressed in the Regimental *Chronicle* at the time:

Top right: The Colonel Commandant, General Sir John Mogg, talking to Rifleman Holmes, 9 Platoon C Company 1RGJ Cyprus 1968. On the left Tim Hartley, looks on and on the right Sergeant Walters waits to be inspected.

Left: The national flags of the UNFICYP contingents.

Below: Rfn Norcott in his observation post, Cyprus, 1RGJ, 1968.

The six-month United Nations tour had been a reasonably happy one. The riflemen had either worked hard … or had been in interesting or attractive surroundings. There had been no serious incidents or violence. but a succession of minor problems, had occupied our attention and efforts for considerable periods. Although we, had by our presence, helped to keep the peace, it had been impossible to make any real progress in helping in a return to normal conditions.

1RGJ, 1976

1RGJ was the first of the Royal Green Jacket battalions to deploy on an UNFICYP tour following the Turkish invasion of 1974. By then UNFICYP had been redeployed to man positions along the six-sector demilitarised or 'buffer' zone that split the island in two, the Turks to the north and the Greeks to the south. The battalion occupied Sector 2, some 16 miles (25 km) long and varying in width from one to two miles (1.5–3.5 km). A contingent from Denmark was to the west and contingents from Austria, Canada, Finland and Sweden to the east.

The UN required only two companies and a battalion HQ, hence half of battalion HQ, led by the commanding officer, Edward Jones, with B and C companies, commanded by Major Alastair Stewart and Major Kit Owen, and an element of HQ Company, all deployed under the UN flag. The other half of the battalion was deployed to maintain the security of the Eastern Sovereign Base Area under the battalion's second-in-command, Major Peter Blaker, together with an additional company from the resident battalion in Episkopi – 3rd Battalion The Royal Anglian Regiment – and two troops of Ferret scout cars from The Royal Scots Dragoon Guards.

The landward side of the Eastern Sovereign Base Area's perimeter faced the Turkish Army forces, who were NATO allies – it was ironic that it was they who shot at and hit one of the armoured cars. Apart from the incident at Avlona (see page 156), the battalion's time was taken up with routine and largely unexciting UN tasks of observation work, patrols, escorts for farmers, firefighting, and meetings with Greek and Turks alike.

3RGJ, 1980

The last UNFICYP tour conducted by the regiment was 3RGJ from May to November 1980. The battalion was split between the UN and the Eastern Sovereign Base Area, as had been 1RGJ four years before, but the rifle companies rotated after three months so everyone got a UN medal. The commanding officer, John Foley, with half of

The Royal Green Jackets

Avlona

The Greek Cypriot population of Avlona abandoned the village following the 1974 Turkish invasion. The Turks had a defensive position to the north with two standing patrols in the village that gradually increased to a garrison of sixty men. The UN's demilitarised zone patrol track passed through the centre of the village with an observation post to the south and a daylight only standing patrol to the west. As part of the policy of returning life back to normal in the demilitarised zone, farmers were allowed to farm their own lands if they could prove themselves to be the owners.

Towards the end of March 1976 demobilised Turkish soldiers masquerading as refugees began to repopulate the village and farm the land that was Greek owned. Meetings failed to resolve the situation. Greek farmers were escorted back and C Company prepared to evict the Turks. Scuffles and stone throwing resulted in Turkish forces opening fire over the heads of C Company causing all the civilians to take cover. A simultaneous withdrawal of both sides was then negotiated. The mundane incident was over – a pointless and frustrating experience, but one that demonstrates the sort of petty incidents that troops have to deal with on peace-keeping operations, where showing restraint and keeping a cool head remain paramount.

Left: Rfn Osby and Atherton on farm escort duty, Cyprus, 3RGJ, 1980.

Below: GSM and Cyprus UN Medal.

battalion HQ, elements of HQ Company and a rifle company – S and A companies, commanded by Major Peter Browne and an exchange officer, Major Vince Kennedy from Princess Patricia's Canadian Light Infantry – were based in St David's Camp, whilst B Company and R Company – commanded by Major David Godsal, and Major Rupert Ross-Hurst – were based in the box factory.

As it had for 1RGJ in 1976, life revolved around the observation of ceasefire lines, the provision of escorts for Greek Cypriot farmers in the UN buffer zone and patrolling. All farming in the buffer zone was controlled by a special team of Sergeant Brian Edwards and Sergeant 'Nippy' Hawker, two honest and incorruptible NCOs. This was important because farming was big business, with bribes not unknown. They were directed in their work by the Sector Economics and Humanitarian Officer, Captain Jamie Gordon. Despite the 1976 agreement, which stated that both protagonists had to agree to a new field being farmed, more than 150 fields had been opened.

Cyprus Garrison

For most Riflemen Cyprus was synonymous with UNFICYP and a six month unaccompanied tour there wearing the blue beret of the United Nations, but in 1993–5 for 1RGJ stationed in Alexander Barracks as part of the garrison it was a sunshine posting to rank alongside Hong Kong and Gibraltar.

Life on the island was full. One company was assigned to Garrison Duties, a Reinforced Infantry Company was required as part of the defence of the Falklands Island with a further 'platoon plus' in South Georgia. Training opportunities were many with company and battalion exercises in Jordan and Kuwait welcome chances to experience working with other nations in desert conditions. Sport, sailing and shooting filled in any spare moments as did the inevitable round of visitors and ceremonial duties that are the lot of any garrison unit in such a place.

Peace Support Operations

Everyone understands the term 'war-fighting'. The term 'peace-support operations' is less well known, but it describes the doctrine that emerged in the 1990s to deal with the complex tasks then becoming increasingly commonplace. This doctrine divided such operations into 'peace-keeping' – the UN operations in Cyprus was a typical such mission – and 'peace-enforcement', the much more messy and complex experience of what was required in the Balkans.

Peace-keeping assumes there is a peace to keep and that the opposing sides consent to the UN (or UN authorized) force operating under a Chapter 6 UN mandate authorising the use of force for defence or protection only. Peace-enforcement requires a Chapter 7 UN mandate authorising the use of force, if necessary, to achieve the mission. To confuse the two forms of operation and deploy under a Chapter 6 rather than a Chapter 7 mandate into a situation where consent is absent or minimal – where, in reality, there is not yet a peace to keep – will invite disaster or international embarrassment as was illustrated in the Balkans.

Programmes for UNFICYP UN Medal Presentation Ceremonies, 3RGJ, March 1971.

Bosnia, 1992–2001

The United Nations attempts to bring peace to the Balkans in the early 1990s produced many lessons for the international community and prompted an examination of the accepted doctrine for the conduct of 'peace-keeping'. British Army units deployed to join the United Nations Protection Force, UNPROFOR, in late 1992 with the mission of escorting humanitarian aid convoys from the Croatian coast to central and northern Bosnia. Adopting a robust approach when attempts were made to hinder their operations

Soldiering Around the World

MULTINATIONAL FORCE IN THE LEBANON, 1983

Lt Col D.H Godsal MBE

In August 1982, following the Israeli invasion of Lebanon, a 4,000-strong multi-national force (MNF) of US, Italian and French troops deployed to Beirut to oversee the withdrawal of the Israelis and Palestinians. By 10 September with the job complete the MNF withdrew only to return almost immediately following the assassination of the Lebanese President-elect, Bashir Gemayel and the subsequent slaughter of well over 1,000 people in the Palestinian refugee camps that sparked a resumption of interfactional fighting. This time the British Government was asked to contribute.

The French, Italian and American contingents were each 1,700 to 2,000 strong. The British contingent (BRITFORLEB), in November 1983, numbered some 116, consisting of an armoured recce squadron equipped with Ferrets and mine-plated Land Rovers, commanded by what is best described as a small brigade headquarters located in a derelict four-storey block of flats on high ground in the southeast of the city. When selected in February it was safely out of the way, but later it was surrounded by all the different factions. Some 250 yards to the East was a D30 battery, which was a regular target for mortars and artillery. We were also directly under the flight path of the 16 inch shells from the USS New Jersey on their way to the Bakar Valley.

When I arrived there had been eleven different contingency plans for evacuation, involving both war and peace scenarios, using ships, helicopters and ferries. In January, in light of the situation and changes to our support we rationalised these down to two – Plan A was for 'endex' under peacetime conditions, taking everything with us, and Plan B was 'go now' with everything we could salvage.

The Plan B 'execute' order came at 0200 on 8 February, a year to the day after BRITFORLEB had arrived in Beirut. The initial plan to move out at 0330 was changed to 0830 and by 1845, just after dark, 60 helicopter sorties, with stores and vehicles underslung, had transferred BRITFORLEB on board RFA Reliant. It is remarkable what can be achieved under operational conditions, without the constraints of peacetime rules, regulations and health and safety margins. We sailed to Cyprus and in order to 'conform with our allies' maintained part of the force on board RFA Reliant, with the majority at Akrotiri

I returned to Beirut the following week in order that HMG Ambassador could continue to be accompanied by a member of BRITFORLEB at the various meetings and to show that we were poised to redeploy if necessary (I was known as BRITONELEB!). I spent a fascinating three weeks, based with the DA in the embassy, able, in plain clothes, to see far more of the city than had been possible before. At the end of March the operation was ended and BRITFORLEB ceased to exist.

I came away from the experience with great respect for the young soldiers; it can be extremely difficult to operate in a hostile environment such as Beirut without being able to take positive military action. It also taught me about 'flexibility', both with operational planning and logistics – I wrote the orders for our evacuation on a single sheet of paper!

Right: Srebrenica, east Bosnia, April 1993.

armoured infantry units in Warrior vehicles were largely successful in getting convoys through.

The conflict between Bosnian Croats, Serbs and Muslims dragged on until the end of 1995 when a combination of battlefield successes, diplomatic pressure and the intervention of NATO air power brought all sides to the negotiating table at Dayton, USA. The peace that followed was overseen by a strong international ground force with a peace enforcement mandate based around the British-led Allied Rapid Reaction Corps, the ARRC. Known by the acronym IFOR (Implementation Force) the NATO-led force deployed across Bosnia to replace UNPROFOR. The first Green Jacket battalion to serve in Bosnia was 1RGJ as part of IFOR in 1996, but several Green Jackets served earlier with UNPROFOR as individuals wearing the blue beret of the UN. Four tours in the Balkans, first to Bosnia with IFOR and SFOR, later to Kosovo with KFOR, were made by 1RGJ and 2RGJ over the period 1996–2001. For the most part the tours passed quietly with occasional periods of tension and excitement.

The Royal Green Jackets

Left: On the road to Sarajevo, winter 1992–3.

The Race To Titov Drvar, 2RGJ, April 1998

In April 1998 2RGJ deployed to Bosnia as part of Multi-National Division (Southwest) MND (SW) responsible for enforcing the Dayton Peace Accord in the area of the Vrbas Valley. Part of the Accord involved enabling displaced persons to return to the homes they had occupied before the conflict started in 1991. Often, this was in the face of acute hostility from those who had 'ethnically cleansed' them previously, and there was particular friction being caused in Titov Drvar, in the Canadian Battle Group area, as the battalion deployed into theatre.

In Germany the last words from the commanding officer were that Bosnia was quiet and that the greatest dangers to the battalion were minefields and traffic accidents, but only a few hours after arriving elements of 2RGJ found themselves loading operational stocks of ammunition into their Warriors and preparing to depart as quickly as possible to assist the Canadians in Titov Drvar, 100 miles (160 km) away to the west.

CHIEF OF STAFF UNPROFOR, 1993

Brigadier G. de V.W. Hayes CBE

In April 1993 I joined UNPROFOR for a six-month tour with the UN as Chief of Staff (COS) in what was then called Bosnia Hercegovina Command, or BHC. I was principal staff officer to a UN force of 13,000 troops from ten different nations and my commander was a French general, Philippe Morillon.

Troop-contributing nations in the force shared command-and-control in a multinational effort; there was no one lead nation to give direction, coherence and authority to the staff effort. Nations filled staff jobs in numbers and importance proportionate to the size of their overall commitment to BHC; they supplied the functions on the UN shopping list for the establishment of the mission in accordance with their capabilities and availability of resources, making for a mixed bag. As COS BHC, I worked for a Frenchman who had a Spanish deputy; my deputy COS (DCOS) was a Belgian, the assistant COS (ACOS) G3 Ops Canadian, ACOS G2 (Intelligence) French, ACOS G4 (Logistics) Swedish and ACOS G1 (Administration) Spanish. The civil affairs adviser was Russian, the convoy operations leader Dutch and the HQ administration was run by a Dane (roll-mop herrings for lunch every day!).

The HQ was located in a disused hotel, built for the winter Olympics in 1984. In the main hotel all ranks slept four or more to a single room, with a few lucky enough to be only double-bunked. The hotel had its own power and water supply and a platoon of superb Norwegian engineers to maintain, alter and improve the conditions. Colonels and above had the luxury of a room to themselves in a nearby gasthaus but were reliant on civilian services for water and power; candles were a necessity and if the water came on you stopped what you were doing and rushed to fill the bath or flush the loo.

Communications were always a problem. Getting through to Forward HQ in Sarajevo relied on a Motorola net, notoriously temperamental, or a rather fragile civilian satellite link that worked through an exchange in Atlanta, Georgia, USA. If this went down at a weekend it stayed down until Monday, and once, after some heavy rain, when the Mississippi broke its banks and flooded the exchange half a world away, it made it impossible for us to call Sarajevo 20 miles (30km) down the road.

CNN was an essential real-time information link and was always live in the ops room. On one occasion I was called in to look at the 10:00pm news bulletin that told me I was required to broker an agreement with the Serbs over withdrawal from Mount Igman by midday the next day. I was grateful for the warning since it came four hours ahead of the UN chain of command and my meeting was to take place some six hours drive away.

Whilst it is easy to criticise and smile at this, we should remember that the UN can only be as effective as its members will allow, and that the UK is no better or worse than others in having its own agenda and interests to defend in such an international forum.

The confused situation of alliances and conflicts facing UNPROFOR across Bosnia, summer 1993.

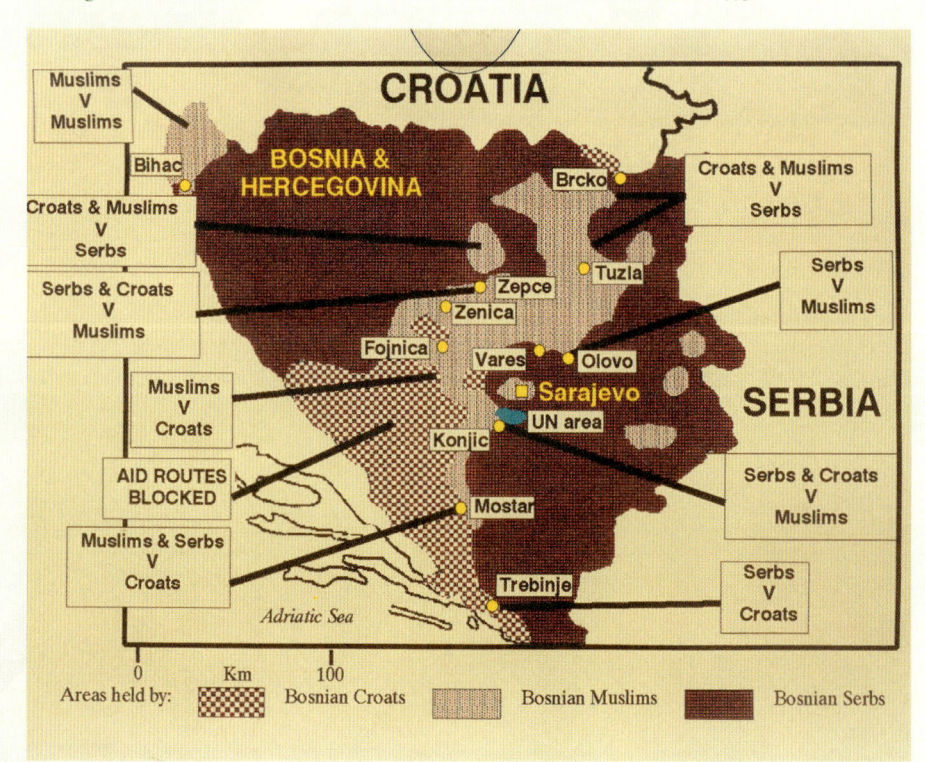

158

UNPROFOR – SECTOR LIAISON OFFICER, PERSONAL REFLECTIONS
NOVEMBER 1994–MAY 1995, LIEUTENANT ALEX BARING

'You can speak French, can't you?'
'Yes.'
'Right, we'll be sending you to Bosnia. You'll be working direct to the brigadier in Gorni Vakuf.'
'Er, okay, wasn't he the bloke I failed on his annual personal weapon test on Operation Grapple training?'
'That's the one. Have fun.'

The regular morning O Groups (Orders Groups) at UN Sector Southwest in Gorni Vakuf were depressing because they lacked orders. For thirty minutes (forty if a Spaniard was involved) the brigadier would listen to intelligence, met (weather), political, aviation, civil aid, engineering, and other reports from UN officers seated around a huge map table. Armed with the latest information, he was able to do … nothing – except remind people of the timings of his next O Group.

This was Bosnia. This was UNPROFOR. 'Before arrival, I imagined that the UN was viewed as saviours, protectors and providers. In Bosnia I felt, at best a spectator, at worst a supplier. Our grandiose idea of UN freedom of movement would be checked by a couple of drunken soldiers with a piece of string across the road. Our food sustained armies; our vehicles, effortlessly hijacked, were resprayed and driven openly, without fear. Locals would watch our engineers build mountain roads and then complain when aid convoys slowed traffic All sides viewed us as cowards. I felt embarrassed, but more often angry.

My job was that of Sector Liaison Officer, based initially in the Bosnian Croat town of Tomislavgrad. Liaison proved difficult. The local Croat militia (HVO) had nothing to say to us; they were busy fighting a war. The problem was that we did not have much to say to them either. I spent days, weeks, months familiarising myself with the area, a three-month Land Rover safari with my driver, Marine Rowland – who, thankfully, had a great sense of humour. We would count tanks, try to get through roadblocks and generally make our presence felt, at all times desperately trying to get ambushed by bandits so that we could justify some 'self-defence', but to no avail.

Half-way through our tour I was flown by helicopter to an empty hotel on the outskirts of Banja Luka, a large town 100km [60 miles] behind Serb lines. My mission was to liaise with the Bosnian Serb Army during the opening stages of a peace plan. We expected to stay for ten days – we came out after six weeks.

We kept in touch with our HQ in Gorni Vakuf every day by satellite phone and HF radio. The term 'nothing to report' featured heavily. We listened to the World Service, tracking the breakdown of the peace process; isolated liaison teams were being used as pawns by the Serbs to increase pressure on the UN. During the following month the Bosnian Serb Army cancelled our extraction each week. Not surprisingly, we became very good at chess and ran out of brew kit. Eventually we were allowed a road resupply to exchange our signaller and dead batteries, and bring in more money. They left us a Land Rover and mail (including a mess bill), but we were still not allowed to leave. The resupply team told us that the same thing was happening to the other three liaison teams deployed to Serb territory.

Finally, after six weeks, the UN protested by expelling the Bosnian Serb liaison team from our HQ in Gorni Vakuf. The next morning the electricity was cut, our radios were jammed and the hotel sealed on every floor by armed militia and military police. Our general arrived and gave us two hours to pack our Land Rover and leave the Republika Srbska. I was delighted and looking forward to eating some vegetables.

My tour in Bosnia can be summed up in two words 'immense frustration' – a team of keen, professional soldiers reduced to spectating a war, misunderstood by all sides, and often having to bow down to miserable peasant militias. Nearly every day I must have said to myself 'do something – or get out – but don't just sit and watch'.

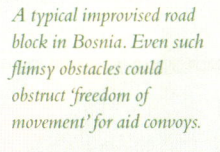

A typical improvised road block in Bosnia. Even such flimsy obstacles could obstruct 'freedom of movement' for aid convoys.

The Royal Green Jackets

Below: An Armoured Infantry company on the move in Warrior vehicles.

Below right: A SAXON vehicle from 2RGJ, Bosnia, 2001.

Right: Rfn Diamond and CSgt Pyle familiarising themselves with the ground, IFOR, Bosnia 2RGJ, 1996.

The Recce Group flew in by helicopter and was met in person by Major General Cedric Delves, the newly arrived commander of MND (SW) who had assumed command from Major General Andrew Pringle only minutes before the rioting began. He gave clear instructions to Major Dick Ovey:

'Have you been in Northern Ireland?'
'Yes, Sir.'
'Good, then you'll know what to do!'

The 1RGJ road convoy of fourteen Warrior Infantry Fighting Vehicles rolled into Titov Dravar at 07:00 on 25 April after an overnight drive. The swift and professional response by the battalion and their sudden, unexpected arrival in the area was enough to ensure that there was no more trouble and the situation quickly stabilised.

Operation Mosque, 2RGJ, October 2001

In the early 1990s the ancient mosque in Banja Luka was destroyed by the Bosnian Serbs, but six years after the Dayton Peace Accord of 1995 had brought peace to Bosnia the remaining Muslim community of the Republika Srpska planned to lay and consecrate the foundation stone of a new mosque to be built on the original site. Given the political significance of this act many leading diplomats came from Sarajevo for the ceremony, including the American and Turkish ambassadors.

On their third tour in the Balkans in as many years, 2RGJ expected a long, hot, uneventful summer. The battalion deployed two companies to oversee the situation. The stone-laying ceremony was seen as little more than a matter for the local police that might see a few hardline Serb nationalists mount a small protest, but on the day feelings ran high and stones began to be thrown. A small crowd of 500 rowdy Serbs quickly grew to 5,000 angry, rioting people with the police struggling to control them. The crowd identified and turned on the battalion's small command group and, in the ensuing mêlée the commanding officer, Henry Worsley, and his interpreter were separated from the others and trapped in a building, along with a frightened Turkish ambassador. The situation causing concern up the chain of command, questions were asked about how 2RGJ intended to rescue the ambassador, and it was suggested that two Warrior companies be used.

Fortunately, Lieutenant Colonel Worsley was able to use his mobile telephone to reassert command and stop any premature action by the battalion – and shortly afterwards the president of the Republika Srpska arrived to calm the angry crowd. The police restored a semblance of order and the diplomats were shuttled away to safety. It had been a timely reminder that the underlying political and religious tensions of the Balkans could boil over all too easily.

Kosovo, 2RGJ, 1999

In September 1999 2RGJ found themselves in Kosovo. Back in the Balkans only ten months after leaving Bosnia and a tour of duty with SFOR – the NATO Stabilisation Force – the battalion was now a part of KFOR – the NATO deployment in Kosovo. The task of reducing inter-ethnic violence between Albanians and Serbs was reminiscent of the early days of tours in Northern Ireland; many of the same joint police/military structures were put in place and proved successful.

The major incident, apart from the fire in Headquarters R Company accommodation that caused several casualties, one of the most severely burned being CSgt Logan, was the incident on the Austerlitz Bridge over the River Ibar.

The bridge was on the route from Mitrovica (Serbian) to Pristina (Albanian) and was the focus of much inter-ethnic tension. This came to a head following the beating of an Albanian family living in Mitrovica who were forced to abandon their home and flee across the bridge to the Pristina side of the river. This was a commonplace occurrence but this time the Albanians decided that enough was enough. It was time to make a point to NATO, exercise their right to freedom of movement and march in numbers across the Austerlitz Bridge whether that provoked confrontation with the Serbs or not. They planned a large scale demonstration of 50,000-60,000 people, whilst KFOR (2RGJ in the lead) prepared to prevent any violence by blocking the Austerlitz Bridge. A few days later, starting with a trickle, the demonstration began. The crowd quickly swelled to several thousand pressing forward towards the bridge where 3 Platoon, a 'thin green line', linked arms to create a physical barrier to their progress.

The 3 Platoon line broke under the pressure of the crowd, with several riflemen and NCOs being trampled underfoot, but not before reinforcements had been able to take up positions behind them, barring the route to the bridge. The confrontation lasted all day with tear gas being fired and continual calls to the crowd for calm from the Commanding Officer, Nick Carter. With no arrest capability, the riflemen resorted to pushing, talking, shouting and pulling constant offenders and ring leaders out of the crowd in front of them, running them along the outside of the line and pushing them back into the crowd in a different area.

By nightfall the Albanians began to make a slow departure from the area knowing they had made their point and caught the attention of the international media. The incident did make world headlines and, alongside the reports of the Albanian grievances, the restraint and professionalism of 2RGJ received recognition and admiration.

Andrew Marr, *Daily Express*:

'The behaviour of the British troops in separating ethnic Serbs and Albanians was completely superb, a display of discipline, coolness and tactics that showed the Army at its best.'

Left: CS gas being used to try to control the crowd on the Austerlitz Bridge, Mitrovica, Kosovo, 2RGJ, 1999.

Above: On patrol in Pristina, Kosovo 2RGJ, 1999.

Above inset: Newspaper cutting on the operations conducted in Mitrovica by 2RGJ in 1999.

The Royal Green Jackets

Sierra Leone, Operation Silkman, 1RGJ, 2001–2

In May 2000 Sierra Leone hit the headlines after more than thirty years of independence when a brutal civil war threatened the safety of British citizens in Freetown, the capital. A UN military force in Sierra Leone, sent to restore order and disarm rebels, had all but collapsed, with 500 peace-keepers effectively being held hostage. An operation to evacuate UK citizens was mounted at short notice. A Joint Task Force Headquarters commanded by a brigadier was deployed to Freetown to command the operation, supported by an 'over-the-horizon' reserve of Royal Marines afloat with the Royal Navy.

The UK agreed to assist the emerging peace process by creating an effective Sierra Leone Defence Force. An International Military Advisory and Training Team (IMATT) and a UK short-term training team (STTT) were set up. Soon afterwards a number of personnel were taken hostage by a rebel splinter group and a successful hostage rescue operation was mounted direct from the UK.

On the command-and-control side of these actions, in the Permanent Joint Headquarters, Major General Andrew Pringle oversaw the deployment as the chief of staff/director of operations until May 2001, with Colonel Jamie Gordon as his deputy for operations. Brigadier Nick Parker was the commander of the Joint Task Force from April to November 2001. 1RGJ provided companies for the STTT and force protection from October 2001 to January 2002, tragically losing two riflemen when a vehicle overturned on a patrol.

British involvement in Sierra Leone during 2000–2 must be deemed a success. The rebels never resumed their offensive, which allowed the UN to re-establish a presence throughout the country. A comprehensive disarmament programme was agreed in May 2001. By January 2002 the whole country was once again under the control of the newly trained Republic of Sierra Leone Armed Forces, and elections were held in May 2002.

The Gulf Conflict, Operation Granby, 1RGJ, 1990–1

In the early hours of 2 August 1990, under the pretext that members of the 'Provisional Free Kuwait Government' had asked Saddam Hussein to rescue the country from the rule of the Al-Sabah royal family, a force of 100,000 Iraqis crossed the border into Kuwait. Within six hours, and without taking casualties, they had seized their key strategic targets and were in control of the country. Saddam Hussein declared the situation irreversible.

Bottom left: Sierra Leone, 1RGJ, 2001.

Above: Jungle operations, Sierra Leone, RGJ, 2001.

Below: A Warrior of the Milan platoon, 1RGJ attached to 1 Staffords battle group shortly after cessation of hostilities, Kuwait, 1991.

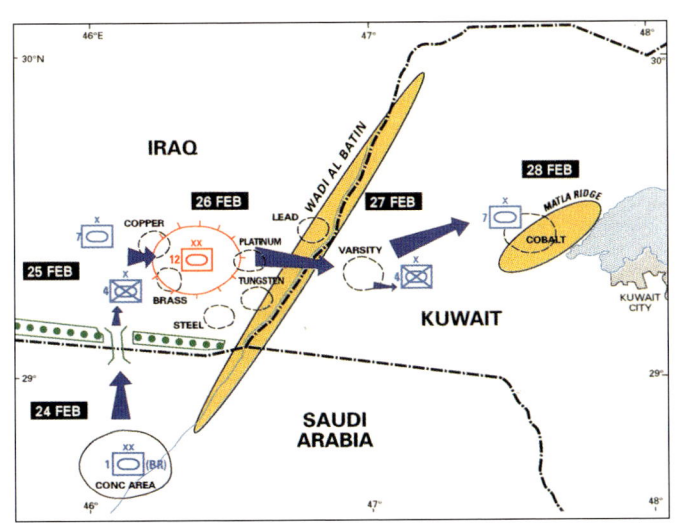

Left: Schematic of the battle plan for 1 (UK) Armoured Division in Operation Granby.

Top right: Three of the four officers reunited after the fall of Kuwait. L–R: Ben Woodley, Sebastian Willis-Fleming, Tom Thicknesse.

On the same day the UN Security Council met in emergency session, unanimously condemned Iraq's actions and demanded a withdrawal. Kuwait's ambassador to the UN appealed for military help, and on 8 August Britain's Secretary of State for Defence announced that British Forces were to prepare to deploy to the Gulf region under the codename of Operation Granby. These forces were to join a multinational 'coalition of the willing' led by the United States to protect Saudi Arabia and to liberate Kuwait.

The Allied build-up of troops to prepare for the liberation was entitled Operation Desert Shield, and it started almost immediately. By the end of 1990 there were more than 500,000 troops, including 45,000 UK forces, in the region. Combat operations to recover Kuwait, entitled Operation Desert Storm, began on 16 January 1991 with airstrikes.

On 24 February the ground operation started, ending some 100 hours later with the total destruction of the Iraqi Army as a fighting force and the objectives of the UN Security Council Resolution achieved. Although Green Jacket battalions were not deployed to the Gulf as formed units, 1RGJ provided seventy reinforcements, mainly from the support weapons platoons, most of whom were attached to 1st Battalion The Staffordshire Regiment battle group in 7th Armoured Brigade, the Desert Rats, whilst others deployed as liaison officers or to bolster the brigade staff. The 1RGJ contingent did not get away unscathed – Captain Toby Tennent, working in the Step Up HQ of 1 Staffords, was badly wounded in the legs in a 'friendly fire' incident when a nearby Warrior AFV was hit by a Challenger tank round during action on Objective Platinum. On a happier note, Corporal Bill Tyson was awarded a Mention in Dispatches for his actions with the Milan anti-tank platoon.

INTERPRETING IN THE CONGO – OPERATION DETERMINANT, 1996

CAPTAIN ALEX BARING

Mr Mobutu's domestic problems could not have come at a better time as far as I was concerned: a series of rather unpleasant duties were looming so a quick trip to join the operation to evacuate UK nationals from the Congo, seemed an excellent alternative but getting to Brazzaville to join the Joint Forces HQ proved to be a problem I got as far as Dakar with the RAF, but the C-130 went 'unserviceable' and there I stuck for several days despite my best efforts to hitch a ride from anyone.

By the time I finally made it the crisis was over, but as one of the HQ's three French speakers, there was plenty of work still to be done, not least coordinating the draw-down with local authorities and liaising with the rest of the multinational force based around the airport.

One of my first tasks was to tie in with the Belgian contingent on the other side of the airport – at last a chance to put my French to good use. 'Bonjour. Comment ça va? Je suis l'officier Britannique.' Blank looks all round, then, 'Would you mind if we use English – we're Flemish and don't speak French'.

After a week I returned to the UK with the remainder of the force and missed all the action again: the French who stayed behind were soon to find themselves calling in the Foreign Legion as Brazzaville, not Kinshasa, descended into anarchy.

Mike Smith and Alex Baring serving with MONUC, the UN Mission in the Congo. Operation Determinant, 1996.

Far left: Examining the wildlife, Falkland Islands, 1RGJ, 1994.

Left: Port Stanley, Falkland Islands.

Below left: Coming ashore and preparing to 'tab', Falkland Islands, 1RGJ, 1995.

The Falkland Islands, 1984–5; 1987–8; 1994–5

Although formed units of The Royal Green Jackets did not take part in the 1982 campaign, many subsequently garrisoned the Falkland Islands (including South Georgia). 1RGJ deployed as a full battalion from October 1984 to March 1985; a company group based around B Company of 3RGJ deployed from November 1987 to March 1988; and company groups formed on D and then C companies of 1RGJ deployed in 1994 and 1995, respectively, direct from Cyprus – a dramatic change of topography and climate, which was reported in the *Chronicle* as 'going from 36 degrees centigrade to minus 36 degrees centigrade in 24 hours'. Brigadier Jamie Gordon spent 2003 in the islands as Commander British Forces, sixteen years after his sojourn as B Company's second-in-command in 1987.

A tour in the stark grandeur of the islands and their distinctive clear light presented great training opportunities and the rare chance of independence for the command team many miles from home. The task of deterring or reacting to any Argentine aggression gave it focus, purpose and an operational edge, whilst the terrain and the rapidly changing weather conditions offered a different challenge when patrolling. Riflemen made the most of the field-firing, the chance to see the abundant wildlife at close quarters, the community relations tasks and, of course, the fishing – there was something for everyone.

INTO AFGHANISTAN

LT COL HENRY WORSLEY

If someone had said to me in 1980 when I joined the Army, that twenty years later I would deploy to Bosnia with a Czech BMP (a Soviet-era infantry fighting vehicle) company under my command, and that six years after that I would be one of the first British soldiers deployed to southern Afghanistan, I would have thought them utterly mad – on both counts. But that is exactly how it turned out.

On 26 January 2006 as Dr Reid announced that the UK would deploy troops to Afghanistan I was listening to hm via the BBC in Lashkar Gah, the capital town of Helmand province. But so too were a number of UK journalists who had pre-empted the broadcast and arrived early to get first-hand stories. There was significant media interest as soon as the story broke, and I found myself, as the senior soldier in Helmand, giving interviews to print, radio and TV reporters. I explained as best I could what the UK soldiers were going to do, how we would do it and with what. But I also made it clear that I did not expect it to be an easy start. Whilst the vast majority of the Afghans would be delighted to see our soldiers, the Taliban would have a different welcoming party, and we should expect some stiff opposition. It would have been militarily naïve of me to have painted a more kindly picture and rather surprisingly I was asked to 'tone down' my forecast by the media suits in the MoD.

As the forward eyes and ears, and reporting to a small advance party in Kandahar who were writing the cross-government plan for Helmand, I set about preparing the ground for the task force's arrival by informing as many Afghans as I could of how we would do our business, where our priorities would lie and how we intended to help. But I was also eager to listen to their needs and expectations. I soon learnt that what they craved above all else was to be safe – safe from the Taliban first, but also safe from a predatory police force and safe from the grip of the opium poppy. They longed to have faith in their police and army and gave unanimous praise to the UK for sending their soldiers to help deliver it. However, at one such talk it was made clear to me by a finger-pointing tribal elder not to forget that 'the only difference between you and the Russians is that you bring development and reconstruction'.

To spread my message I set out with fifteen soldiers and six armoured Land Rovers to travel to the thirteen districts of Helmand to talk and to listen to the governor and his staff, the district chiefs, the

Henry Worsley and a local, Afghanistan, 2006.

police chiefs, the mullahs, the tribal *shuras* (gatherings of tribal leaders and power-brokers), the nomads and as many of the general population as I could. I received extraordinary hospitality, as enshrined in the Pashtunwali code (the tribal code of honour, customs and laws), wherever I and my soldiers visited. I was always keen to speak to as many people as possible about the pending arrival of the British troops and the reconstruction effort. Interestingly, I soon learnt that the Afghans thought that the troops were coming solely to eradicate the poppies. I explained that this was not the case – much to visible relief from some of the more wily members of the audience!

I made many lengthy but exhilarating journeys across the gravel plains of the desert, often with a night stop-over hidden in a wadi. Waking at dawn to the distant sound of goat's bells as they trudged off in search of sparse grazing and to just pick up the call to prayer from a far-away minaret is a memory impossible to erase from my mind.

As I left Afghanistan the main body of the UK troop deployment was starting, and it was obvious to me that we would be in for a rough ride against the Taliban.

An Airborne Rifleman in Afghanistan, 2006
Brigadier Ed Butler, late RGJ, Commander UK Task Force, April–October 2006

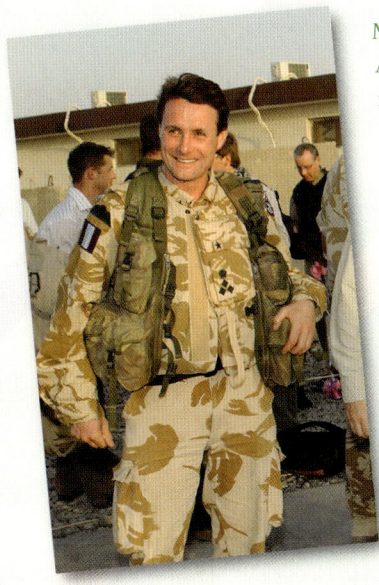

My six months as Commander British Forces Afghanistan, in 2006, was the most challenging and risk-intensive command tour I have undertaken. Over six bloody and ferocious months in Helmand province, the UK Task Force was involved in just under 500 contacts, with some half-a-million rounds of small arms being expended. Nearly 13,000 rounds were fired from our light guns and mortars; we saw the blooding of the Apache helicopter – over 20,000 30 mm rounds and forty-five Hellfire missiles unleashed. Over 100 CASEVAC missions were flown to extract some 170 casualties; very sadly, thirty-three of my force were killed.

Hundreds of Taliban were also killed and injured, but not once was any of the force in danger of being defeated. By the end of the summer the Taliban had been tactically beaten, resorting to a conventional, attritional fight. In my judgement the Taliban seriously underestimated the professionalism, courage and self-belief that Tommy Atkins has shown over the centuries.

The long, hot summer of 2006 convinced me that all elements of the UK Armed Forces are now operating and currently delivering success in a changed world – what we call the 'contemporary operating environment' of the twenty-first century. This used to be the preserve of the Special Forces' community, but is now an environment where the well-honed skirmishing skills, experiences and characteristics of the rifleman are required – and flourish. 'Equally essential for survival and success are those alley-cat skills and rifleman-initiative, developed over the generations.

There are no longer definable front lines or a safe rear area: every member of the battle group must be a 'fighter first'. From clerk to commanding officer, man or woman, they must be able to fight out of an ambush – survive and win a firefight that might last half a day n ot just a few minutes.

To deliver continual operational success remains the domain of the thinking rifleman. Commanders in Afghanistan are required to identify and manage risk to a much greater degree than has been the case before on conventional operations. Risk in the heat and sands of Afghanistan is all about achieving tempo and maintaining the initiative, balanced against time, security (force protection) and resources. Understanding and managing ambiguity and uncertainty at all levels of command was at a persistency that I have never experienced or witnessed before and many commanders were at the edge of their abilities. Decisions on the ground made by junior ranks had strategic consequences as never before. Today's Green Jacket (nay Rifle!) has to be both a strategic corporal as well as a warrior-diplomat. But the domain of the 'contemporary operating environment' should be second nature to the modern-day rifleman and Green Jacket/Rifles officer; in many ways it is no different from the environment of the Peninsular campaigns.

Top: Preparing the ground – a typical briefing on the road in Helmand, Afghanistan, 2006.

Above: Ed Butler, camp Bastion, Helmand Afghanistan, 2006.

Right: Sunrise on the Afghan Plains, Helmand, 2006.

Into the Future: Rifles Once More

The improving security situation in Northern Ireland was the catalyst for further reductions in infantry manpower. Some radical proposals were put forward to meet the need for greater flexibility from reduced resources. For the infantry the recommendation that the Arms Plot should be ended was the most significant factor in the proposals on how infantry numbers could be reduced.

The Arms Plot

The Arms Plot, the periodic rotation of infantry battalions and armoured regiments through different locations with differing operational roles, was designed for two purposes. First, it ensured that differing experiences were spread throughout the infantry, and second it avoided fixing a battalion in one of the less desirable locations for long periods. By moving battalions on a two to six year cycle individuals (particularly the officers and Senior NCOs) gained vital experience in all the many and varied roles that the infantry were required to undertake. Importantly, it also ensured that there was a fair chance of an operational tour for battalions when opportunities were limited. Its major disadvantage was that at any one time approximately eight battalions were either moving or re-rolling, and sometimes both at the same time, and thus unavailable for operational deployment.

Moving locations and changing roles was a major undertaking in terms of training and logistics. Quite apart from the domestic upheaval for families and single riflemen, the handover and takeover of equipment and barracks was time-consuming, painstaking work involving detailed planning, many checks and much paper. For a simple move, without a significant change in the equipment held by a battalion, an Arms Plot move might take a few months. If the change of location required the conversion of the battalion to an armoured role with Warrior Armoured Fighting Vehicles or the slightly less demanding 432 Armoured Personnel Carrier the period would be extended considerably. Then, of course, there was the time it took to become accustomed to the new role and operating procedures before the battalion could be safely declared operationally effective. Putting an end to this Arms Plot movement would, it was concluded, maximise the infantry's operational capability and availability. In other words, more could be done by the infantry with less. It was an attractive option for the planners.

Continuing improvement in the security situation in Northern Ireland at the turn of the century heralded the chance to end Operation BANNER, as the Northern Ireland deployment was known, and the requirement for the permanent commitment of battalions to the support of the police. Without the need to rotate battalions on a regular basis through operational tours in the Province, the number of battalions could be reduced, the planners quickly concluded, without affecting the 'overstretch' experienced by the infantry; this proved to be a decisive factor in the June 2004 Army Board decision to abandon the Arms Plot, reduce the infantry order of battle by four battalions and reallocate some of the manpower savings.

However, it was also realised that ending the Arms Plot was likely to have a dramatic effect on those battalions and regiments that found themselves in the less desirable locations when movement ended. As has been said, one aim of regular movement was to avoid a long time being spent in such places by any one battalion. The prospect of permanent basing would therefore be a threat to the regimental system if the infantry structure and organisation were not reviewed at the same time in a way that would permit soldiers to move between battalions of the same regiment. The Light Division for a long time had been working well as two – two-battalion – regiments, in this respect, and on the face of it there was therefore no pressure for change.

Changes to the Light Division

Inevitably, the proposed reduction in infantry battalions caused another scramble for survival, particularly among the single-

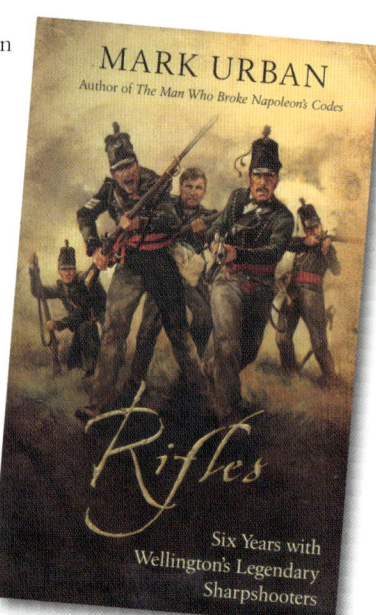

Mark Urban's book, Rifles, *captures the exploits of 1st Battalion 95th Rifles in the Peninsular War.*

Into the Future: Rifles Once More

Above: 'Turning the Pages', Book of Remembrance, Winchester Cathedral.

Right: Recruiting poster for The Rifles.

battalion regiments that this time found themselves under threat. The Devonshire and Dorset Regiment (D&D), concerned about their future, approached the Light Division with a view to joining The Light Infantry as their third battalion. In a decision that was to have far-reaching implications, this request was agreed by the Light Division Council in August 2004 on the understanding that this was an internal arrangement and would not alter the 'no change' position that the Division proposed to adopt in the initial stages of the forthcoming infantry reorganisation. The key points put to the Army Board were:

- The Light Division should remain in its current configuration with a view to moving to a closer integration, perhaps one Regiment when appropriate.
- That the D&D should be incorporated into The Light Infantry to become D&D LI.
- Being joined by the D&D would not be at the cost of losing any of the Division's core recruiting areas.

The Light Division Council felt that they were in a very strong position to adapt to the post-Arms Plot environment. Since the formation of the Light Division in 1968 mutual support between The Light Infantry and The Royal Green Jackets in the form of cross postings, joint NCO cadres and operational reinforcement had developed to the benefit of both regiments. However, there was also some disquiet amongst the Green Jackets that a precedent had been set by admitting to the Light Division a regiment that did not share the rifle and light infantry traditions and heritage.

In December 2004 the Army Board decided that The Light Infantry would receive a third battalion, but, to everyone's surprise, it was announced that this was to be based on a merger of the D&D and the 'Glosters' element of the Royal Gloucestershire, Berkshire and Wiltshire Regiment (RGBW). At the same time, a separate study into the Territorial Army decided that the decisions made as a result of the Strategic Defence Review (1998) would be reversed and 4(v)RGJ, The Royal Green Jackets Territorial Battalion, would be revived with two companies in London and one each in Oxford, Milton Keynes and Reading. On the face of it this was a satisfactory outcome, but there was significant disquiet across the Regiment that the introduction of a third battalion in The Light Infantry would unbalance the divisional structure and possibly even undermine the Green Jacket ethos by stealth.

There were strong and differing views throughout the Regiment. There were plenty who felt that the Green Jackets could continue to operate as a separate two-battalion regiment with a strong and unique identity within the Light Division. There were others who felt that we should move more quickly, combining The Light Infantry and The Royal Green Jackets into a single, new, large regiment structure ensuring the Rifle Regiment ethos was embedded into it from the outset. Each model had risks and benefits. One essential need was to ensure that once the Arms Plot had stopped, and battalions had settled into their final fixed locations, there remained opportunities for all ranks to gain

The Royal Green Jackets

Left: Green Jacket Fighting Cock by Bryn Parry, late RGJ.

- That a defined regimental culture and ethos should be agreed first with The Light Infantry and then with the joining Regiments.
- That this culture should promote:
  – A national Rifle Regiment where Regional identity recognised by, but not linked to, Regular battalions
  – A distinctive operational approach
  – Complete integration with the TA.
- That following agreement a Regimental Charter be produced and endorsed by the Army Board before any further change took place.
- That once the Charter was endorsed an implementation plan be developed and executed by the new regimental hierarchy dealing with the supporting detail and policy.

The assumption then was that this new regiment would be a Rifle Regiment; and on these conditions The Royal Green Jackets would be prepared voluntarily to merge their identity into it. This was a voluntary action, there being no pressure from the Army Board since the Regiment already measured up to future infantry requirements as 'a large regiment of two battalions or more'. Opinion was understandably coloured by the risk of the Green Jackets being reduced in any future cuts to a single battalion regiment or made subject to a forced merger as other regiments enlarged.

Equally, there remained concerns, fuelled by past experience, that by adopting a structure comprising five regular battalions the Regiment would be setting itself up as an easy target for future reductions. Losing cap-badges was an emotive and politically sensitive subject. Had this not been the case The Royal Green Jackets, structured by the founding fathers for the future as long ago as 1966, and paradoxically exactly replicating the infantry requirements of 2007, could have survived to this day as a regiment of three regular battalions.

The Formation of The Rifles

With the measured approval of the former Colonels Commandant the serving Colonels Commandant then took the decision to proceed and put in hand two strands of work. The first was a five-step process towards integration with The Light Infantry, each step representing a decision point, a common position with The Light Infantry being the first and the most important. The outcome was the production of a Light Division Directive, based on agreed Rifle and Light Infantry principles, which formed the basis for discussion with all parties. The new organization should be recognizable and distinctive with an agreed philosophy and approach. The Royal Green Jackets argued strongly for a Regiment that had national (rather than regional) roots. The intention was to have a strong collective identity across the whole Regiment, to operate the chain of command in a fashion that embodied partnership and mutual trust, and to have the appearance, customs, modus operandi and ethos of a Rifle Regiment. This last point was essential if The Royal Green Jackets were to merge their identity.

Finally, it was felt that the new Regiment should be operationally distinctive, able to share experience across the Regiment, combine training skills and integrate Regular and Territorial more effectively than before. The riding instructions for this work stated:

For this process to work we must believe that we are at a decisive moment in our history similar to the conditions that resulted in the

operational experience by moving between battalions. Cross-postings across all battalions in either case would be both desirable and essential if variety and opportunity were to be achieved and the Regiment was to attract high quality officers and recruits.

The Colonels Commandant

The Former Colonels Commandants Committee comprises in effect an advisory panel rather than an executive body, but despite the absence of any form of written charter, it would be an unwise Regimental Colonel Commandant that failed to take due attention of their views! At a meeting of the former Colonels Commandant on 11 February 2005 it was decided to articulate, and then agree, a Green Jacket view that would form the Regiment's position in negotiating the future structure of the Light Division. The circumstances were complicated further when representation by the RGBW, which was understandably disappointed that their Regiment was to be split, resulted in the Army Board revisiting their earlier decision, and in March 2005 directing that the whole of the RGBW should be merged with the D&D before joining The Light Infantry with the excess manpower being absorbed across the whole of the rest of the Light Division. The mould having been broken, the Light Division was now set to absorb not one but two regiments, each with strong but different traditions from the rest of the Light Division.

The work requested by the former Colonels Commandant resulted in a Regimental Position Paper submitted to them in June 2005. There were strongly held views in discussion but, the Army Board decision having been made, the meeting concluded that 'at sometime in the future, with no date fixed and under certain conditions, The Royal Green Jackets would be willing to join in forming a new five-battalion regiment to replace the Light Division. The conditions were:

Into the Future: Rifles Once More

Top left: Button of the 95th Rifles, Peninsular War, 1808–14.

Top right: Cap-badge of The Rifles, 2007.

Above left: Cap-badge of The Royal Green Jackets.

Above right: Cross belt plate and rifleman's belt plate of The Rifles, 2007.

formation of the Experimental Corps of Riflemen. We are considering the creation of something new that, while it can feed on the traditions of our past, is forward looking and will be designed for a future operational environment that will continue to develop and may be difficult to define. There will be plenty of uncertainty, we cannot let this stifle change, but we must be pragmatic in our approach and consider the short-term risks of taking bold steps, particularly the incoherence of many of the other related initiatives that are taking place concurrently.

The work progressed satisfactorily, and by November 2005 all the regiments involved had agreed to form a new Regiment entitled The Rifles. It would be a regiment of five Regular Battalions (with 1RGJ becoming 2Rifles and 2RGJ becoming 4Rifles) and two Territorial Battalions (with 4(v) and 5(v)RGJ becoming 7 Rifles). The Regiment's Charter was agreed in November 2005, and in June 2006 the Principles for The Rifles were also signed. These conformed to the conditions set by the former Colonels Commandant, and The Rifles were formed on 1 February 2007 as the first truly large infantry Regiment in the Army of the modern era with battalions deployed in a variety of roles providing the widest possible opportunity:

1Rifles at Chepstow to join the Royal Marine Commando Brigade.
2Rifles at Ballykinler in the light role.
3Rifles at Edinburgh in the light role.
4Rifles at Bulford in the mechanised role.
5Rifles at Paderborn, Germany in the armoured role.

Once again the Green Jackets were taking brave and innovative steps ahead of the rest of the army and a new and exciting chapter had opened up in the history of the Rifle Regiment.

The Royal Green Jacket Legacy to The Rifles

The Rifles have inherited from The Royal Green Jackets the rich and unique legacy of rifle regiments of the British Army. Indeed, it is true to say that many of The Rifles' new customs and much of its ethos has been directly adopted from those of The Royal Green Jackets. This legacy can be divided broadly into three areas; the distinctive outward appearances and customs of a rifle regiment, its characteristics and its ethos.

Rifle Regiment Customs

Rifle Green Uniform

The RGJ rifle green ceremonial uniform jackets, headdress and blazer recalls the original camouflaged green uniforms of the former rifle regiments from which came their nickname of 'Green Jackets'. This rifle green uniform continues forward into The Rifles with the addition of thin red piping at the base of No. 1 dress collars, and scarlet collar and sleeve cuffs overlaid with black braid on Mess Kit jackets and band parade uniforms. This is very similar to the uniform of the 60th, which retained scarlet in memory of their red-coat origins, but now represents as well the red-coat background of the other founding regiments of The Rifles.

The Rifle

The original Green Jacket rifle regiments were armed with rifles, hence both the term 'rifle regiment' and 'rifleman' to reflect their specialist role. The first rifles were shorter and lighter compared to the muskets used by line infantry and required a longer sword-bayonet to compensate for close-quarter fighting hence the term 'sword' in place of bayonet in rifle regiments to this day. Just as the Oxfordshire and Buckinghamshire Light Infantry (43rd and 52nd) chose to become riflemen, so now The Light Infantry, Devon and Dorset Light Infantry and the Royal Gloucestershire, Berkshire and Wiltshire Light Infantry have chosen to become riflemen and adopt these terms as well.

The Bugle

In their original role as rifle regiments Green Jackets adopted open order tactics and skirmishing, fighting well forward of the main infantry formations. Individuals often found themselves beyond the range of the human voice and needed an efficient way of signalling to control battlefield manoeuvres and drill. The bugle provided the appropriate way of passing orders, and a complex system of calls was developed, many of them still in use today. For rifle regiments the bugle remains the equivalent of the drums or bagpipes of other infantry regiments, hence 'Sounding Retreat' rather than 'Beating Retreat' will continue to be used by The Rifles.

Regimental Colours and Battle Honours

Rifle regiments carried no colours as they traditionally operated in open order, making maximum use of the ground for cover, and thus did not need them as a rallying point or to indicate their position on the battlefield. Battle Honours were carried on the cap-badge of the 60th and Rifle Brigade, and thus in 1966 a selection of these battle honours, together with those of the 43rd and 52nd, were displayed

169

on the new RGJ cap-badge. A similar badge design displaying the shared battle honours of the founding regiments now forms the basis of The Rifles badge worn on the crossbelts of officers and warrant officers, and on the belt buckle worn by all riflemen.

Cap-badge

The bugle horn was the distinctive symbol used by all light troops and was incorporated into the badges of all former Rifle and Light Infantry Regiments. It was also the cap-badge of The Light Infantry. It was at the centre of the RGJ cap-badge but was used 'alone' as the cap-badge worn on a boss on the sidehats of officers and WOs and the collar dogs on No. 2 Dress for all ranks in the Light Division. Combined with a crown the bugle horn now forms the cap-badge of The Rifles.

The Crossbelt

Adapted originally from light cavalry style, the RGJ officers' black crossbelt carried a whistle to pass on orders to dispersed riflemen in the same manner as the bugle, and a large version of the cap-badge carrying representative battle honours. The Light Infantry adopted the black crossbelt for officers in the 1970s, and the RGJ crossbelt design is now being carried forward into The Rifles. Their new crossbelt will carry a large version of The Rifles belt badge and an 'Inkerman whistle' with chain on the front, and a pouch with The Rifles bugle horn cap-badge on the back.

Rifle Drill

Rifle regiment drill descends from the original need for dispersed riflemen to move rapidly and easily across the battlefield with the minimum of orders. Carrying rifles at the trail rather than in the shoulder and all drill movements automatically starting and ending in the 'at ease' position typify rifle drill. Rifle pace, a quick march at 140 paces to the minute compared to the standard Army 120, and a double march at 180 paces to the minute rather than a slow march, are based on the original Rifle and Light Infantry Regiments, which frequently on outpost duty, needed to move around the battlefield faster than other infantry units, and often at the 'double'.

Green Jacket Characteristics

Self-discipline

The principle of self-discipline based on mutual trust and respect for individuals between all ranks, a brotherhood of fellow rifleman, was the foundation of Green Jacket leadership and discipline. It was marked by a lack of formality, a relaxed efficiency in doing business and an easy relationship between all ranks – 'Once a rifleman always a rifleman' defined the creed. This ethos called for a very high standard of basic training if 'relaxed efficiency' was to result. When soundly based and combined with the natural humour and irreverence of most riflemen, especially the Cockneys, Brummies and Scousers from the inner cities, RGJ battalions exuded an aura of confidence, with an atmosphere in which rifleman of all ranks were seen as trusted individuals bound together by a relaxed but deeply professional and operationally focused common sense of purpose.

Professionalism

The Royal Green Jackets took pride in striving for professional excellence and skill both in the art of warfare and in their style of military leadership. It was encapsulated by the Green Jacket focus on 'the fighting thinking rifleman' who 'does everything that is necessary and nothing that is not'.

Above: Locations of the regular battalions of The Rifles.

Left: Briefing for the next operation – getting the details right and making sure the riflemen understand their part in it.

THE CHARTER OF THE RIFLES

The Army Board has directed battalions to group into larger regiments to meet the operational and organisational demands of the future. In light of this, Her Majesty The Queen has graciously approved the formation of a new regiment. The Devonshire and Dorset Light Infantry, The Light Infantry, The Royal Gloucestershire, Berkshire and Wiltshire Light Infantry and The Royal Green Jackets recognise the profound impact of the Army Board's decision. They elect to join together to form a wholly new regiment called The Rifles; comprising seven battalions, five Regular and two Territorial, as well as other Territorial, Cadet and Association elements. They do this after thorough and careful consideration, of their own free will, to ensure the continued excellence of their service to The Crown. The four Founding Regiments will combine to form The Rifles from the Light Division.

The Rifles will take their inspiration from the Founding Regiments' Light Division ancestry, including their Line Regiment History. The Rifles will hold to the qualities advanced by General Sir John Moore and displayed by the finest of infantry regiments. They will demonstrate the values of independent thought and action, leadership, self-discipline, fortitude and steadfastness. The Rifles will strive for excellence and be known for their fighting spirit and strong sense of decency. They will be forward looking, at the forefront of military thought and determined to set the highest professional standards. The Regiment will give a place to all and anyone prepared to soldier loyally and effectively.

The Rifles will cherish and foster their links to the counties, cities and towns from which they come; and which underpin their strong sense of national identity. This new Regiment will be organised, operated and commanded so as to bring unity, professionalism and a sense of pride to all those who step forward with The Rifles.

| Lieutenant General
Sir Cedric Delves
KBE DSO
Col DDLI | Lieutenant General
RV Brims CBE
DSO

Col Comdt Lt Div & Col LI | General Sir Kevin
O'Donoghue KCB
CBE

Col RGBW LI | Major General NJ
Cottam OBE

Regt Col Comdt RGJ |

25th November 2005

Officer Quality

For the RGJ it was the quality of the officers and their leadership ability that were the key to success combined with the strength in depth of the warrant officers' and sergeants' mess. This difference was key, especially in a rifle regiment, where historically initiative, intellect and quickness of thought were essential qualities for officers when operating away from the 'Line'. RGJ officers have always taken pride in being forward-looking and innovative, responsible for major developments in Army thinking and practices. The Regiment's reputation as a successful elite, one that produced a disproportionate number of high-ranking officers, was gained through the extraordinary success and contribution made by its officers to the wider Army as has been illustrated elsewhere in this book.

Marksmanship

The introduction of the rifle and the skirmishing role naturally led to a tradition of marksmanship with Green Jackets being the sharpshooters of the Army. Thereafter for many years Green Jackets dominated Army shooting competitions and have always seen marksmanship as one of their core values. In recent years the RGJ were at the forefront of the renewal of sniping skills in the British Army. The emphasis on professional marksmanship is a core characteristic of a rifle regiment that will be inherited by The Rifles.

Ethos

Our legacy in this area is perhaps the most important as it is key to the way that the RGJ operated so successfully, and the basis we hope of the ethos of The Rifles. To quote from the regimental policy booklet *The Green Jacket Way*:

What then is the Regiment's ethos? It is to do with officers who really know and care for their riflemen: a leadership style based on absolute professionalism, self discipline, mutual trust and loyalty; a spirit of self reliance embodied in our historic tradition of the 'fighting, thinking rifleman'; a forward looking attitude; a level of competence and military effectiveness which are second to none; and knowledge that all of this comes through hard work and getting the detail right, but without making a meal of it.

It is the way that one does it that really marks a rifleman as different – and that is with a light touch; a sense of humour; style and a spirit of adventure; but without pomposity, without fuss and without any form of rigid formality. It is based on mutual confidence, mutual

The Royal Green Jackets

respect, mutual affection and a love of soldiering. The Green Jacket way combines a light touch with a tight grip; a difficult trick to pull off if relaxed efficiency is not to descend into relaxed inefficiency.

This ethos was well described by then Lieutenant Colonel Bramall, now Field Marshal and as such the senior serving soldier of both The Royal Green Jackets and The Rifles, who wrote the original *Leadership the Green Jacket Way* on the formation of The Royal Green Jackets in 1966:

In The Green Jackets we rightly put the emphasis on self discipline rather than the imposed variety favoured by some others. We seek, by good leadership, example, explaining what we are doing and generally treating those under us with humanity and commonsense, to evoke a loyal response and produce the sense of responsibility needed. This is a policy to be proud of and it has proved to be extremely effective. The end product is more deep seated because it is based on the individuals own will power, and it usually creates a fine atmosphere of trust and mutual respect which manifests itself in a sensible adult approach to problems and a marked absence of crime.

This then is The Green Jacket way – pride in fighting qualities and professional skill, intelligent and humane discipline, sympathy and understanding between all ranks and concern for the individual, for his welfare and for that of his dependants.

Conclusion

The lessons of past achievements, the example of illustrious predecessors and the many traditions based on them deserve to be remembered, but they are no substitute for an attitude of mind that always sees the future as an opportunity. For over 200 years Green Jackets have been at the forefront of adapting to technological and organisational change in the British Army. When the RGJ found themselves once more at a point in history where change was required, the Regiment stood ready again to seize the opportunity in a proactive and forward-looking spirit. The birth of The Rifles brings a resurgence in the British Army of Riflemen, inheriting the best of all their founding regiments and bringing to the Army a large body of men that will be trained to act, think and operate as Riflemen. With five regular and two Territorial battalions there will be more riflemen serving in the Field Army than at any time since World War 2. There will also be some 14,000 Rifles cap-badged CCF/ACF cadets, a third of the Army's total cadet strength. They too will be imbued with The Rifles' ethos.

A mix of rifle regiment customs and an ethos that combines professional leadership, innovation, self-discipline, mutual trust and an empowering of the individual, a formula that proved so successful for The Royal Green Jackets, is what we bequeath to The Rifles. We can take pride in what the Regiment achieved and also pride that our legacy will be carried on as the core foundation on which The Rifles will build and model their future. Perhaps our greatest legacy will be found in the years to come, when The Rifles, with strength in numbers, attitude and style, professionalism, rifle ethos and reputation, will be at the forefront of the British Army in every way. The conditions are in place for The Rifles to forge the most powerful reputation.

'Success to The Rifles!'

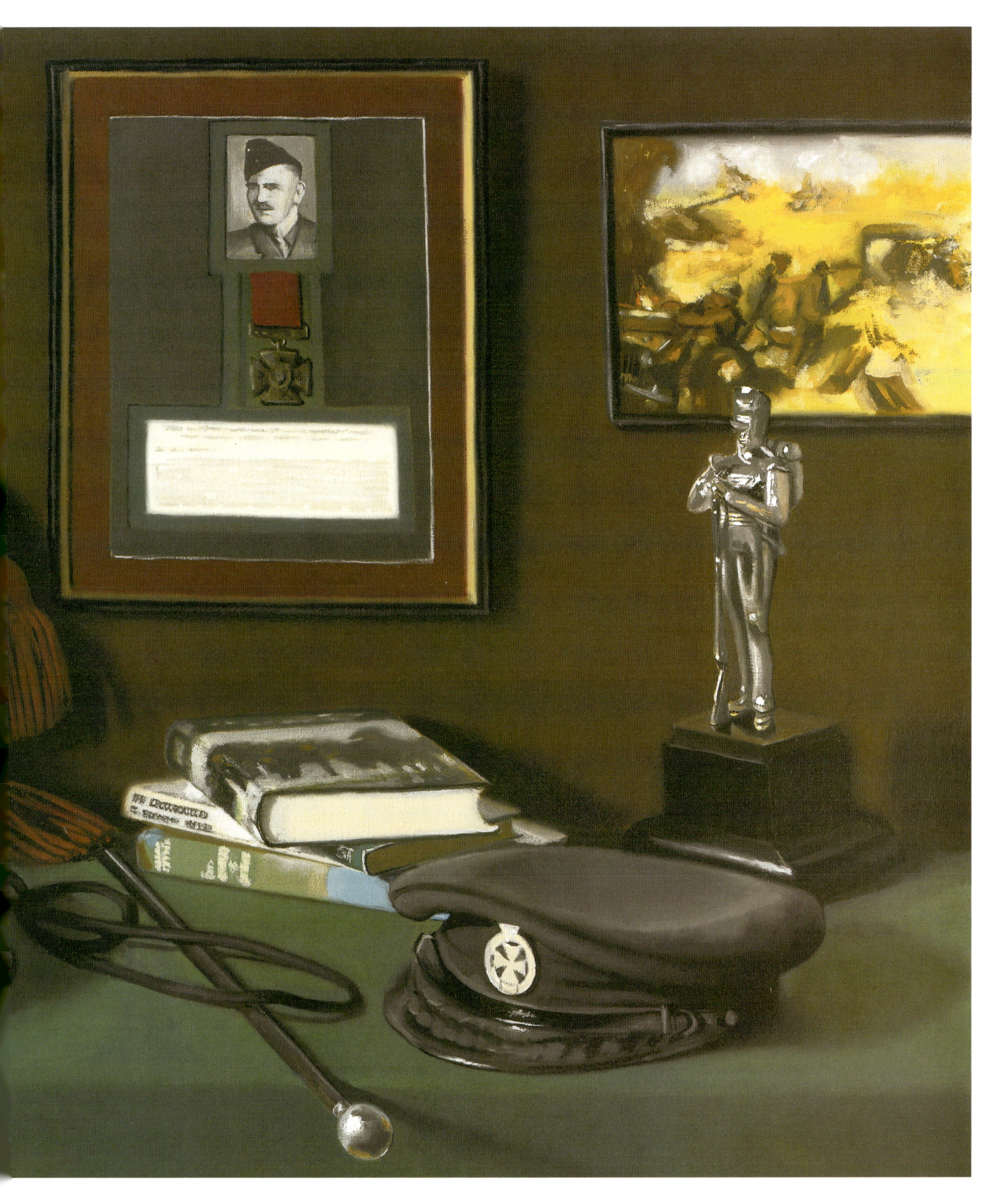

'Once a Rifleman …'

Operations in Iraq: The Royal Green Jackets to The Rifles – 'Forged Under Fire'

Just as The Royal Green Jackets came into being, in a period when all three battalions were on operations in Borneo, so the 1st and the 2nd Battalions of The Royal Green Jackets have evolved into the 2nd and 4th Battalions of The Rifles whilst conducting operations in Iraq.

1st Battalion The Royal Green Jackets/2nd Battalion The Rifles
Major Quentin Naylor MBE, OC B Coy 2Rifles Battle Group, Basra City Battle Group, 25 November 2006

2Rifles deployed to Iraq in October 2006 as 1st Battalion The Royal Green Jackets, holding their inaugural parade of The Rifles at Basra Palace on 1 February 2007, when the battalion became the 2nd Battalion The Rifles, in a short ceremony on the exposed HLS of Basra Palace. For a brief period on parade the riflemen did not wear their helmets and body armour, despite the pervasive threat of indirect fire, as if to show that The Royal Green Jackets, and all the other antecedent regiments forming The Rifles, would move on confident and undeterred by the enemy.

Operation TELIC 9 also saw the introduction of the AFV 430 Mk III Bulldog armoured personnel carrier into service. This was as a result of the government's drive to improve protection from roadside bombs that had been plaguing the aged wheeled Snatch fleet. Seven months later, when 2Rifles have fought with it, from it and around it in the shanties of Basra City through quite intense and demanding combat they have emerged as a strong new battalion. Some examples of the sort of operations conducted by the battalions are described below.

Battle at ORANGE 1

It wasn't long before 1RGJ in their new Bulldogs were proven in contact. There had been a number of skirmishes in the days after the Battlegroup had arrived in the city, not least when the Recce Platoon, under Captain Ed Smith, had caught an enemy improvised explosive devices team in the south of Al Quibla, but 6 and 7 December 2006 were days when Bulldog and 1RGJ really proved their credentials. The resupply convoys in and out of Basra City were major operations in both timing and manoeuvre – securing routes so as not to advertise intent, deceiving the enemy, drawing enemy pockets away. The first packet of the Convoy had received a lot of fire from insurgent rocket propelled grenades, and B Company had been tasked to provide depth. In this case 'depth' simply meant providing an alternative target to draw fire away at the southern end of Al Quibla, a notorious insurgent hot spot. This tactic worked as the first vehicle (B22) was hit by 2 rocket propelled grenades as it entered the southern streets of Al Quibla, quickly identifying a prepared enemy position and destroying it with Underslung Grenades (UGL) and 7.62 mm machine gun fire. A dismounted follow up was conducted by 6 Platoon (B20), against strong opposition from a series of defended houses. Bulldog was manoeuvred as a firing platform and the pintle-mounted GPMG, and Corporal Spamer commanding B21, plus Minimi LMGs from his top cover proved a great platform for getting a lot of fire down quickly to support a dismounted follow-up.

All seemed to be going well, until the prop shaft on one of the vehicles broke. The contact that ensued lasted almost two hours. The company kept on the offensive throughout to buy both the space and time to allow the convoy to go past (we didn't want them to switch targets to the more vulnerable HETs and Snatch vehicles in the convoy) and also to recover the broken-down vehicle. Yet as much as the Platoon and Company Headquarters manoeuvred to attack options, the enemy battled hard against them, using cars and sometimes police cars to regroup and insert reinforcements. A Warrior Platoon from B Company 1 Staffords manoeuvred in to pin one of the enemy pockets down, but the enemy attempted to block

'Forged Under Fire'

routes to prevent the withdrawal of the stricken vehicle. The Iraqi Police Service were seen to be moving people around and consistently 'dicking' (reporting the presence) the Multi National Forces. Eventually recovery was affected, and the enemy pockets closest to the Company Headquarters destroyed with a lot of accurate fire.

Once both packets of the convoy had passed unaffected to the south the withdrawal was started under an intense weight of fire from all directions. A resupply from the Company Serjeant Major, WO2 Youngs, between vehicles was carried out to replenish turret stocks and the company moved out in a devastating hail of fire from pre-prepared enemy positions. The lead Bulldog (B22) took two direct rocket propelled grenade, hits knocking out the commander, Corporal Nunn, and starting a fire in the back of the vehicle. Rifleman Ratu, a gargantuan Fijian, tried to close the mortar hatches as one was hit by an rocket propelled grenade. Once he had regained consciousness a few seconds later he put the fire out, revived his commander and signalled to the Officer Commanding, Major Quentin Naylor, that they were able to continue. (Rifleman Ratu was subsequently awarded an MiD for his actions.) Further into the move Corporal Simon Brown REME, commanding the Recovery Warrior (C24B), was seriously injured with a gunshot wound to the head. In the ensuing evacuation of Corporal Brown, the actions of Lance Corporal Wilson (a REME mechanic) the CSM and a medic, LCpl Garry, were instrumental in saving the life of Corporal Brown. (Lance Corporal Wilson was subsequently awarded the Military Cross for his actions.) All those who took part in this demanding contact grew confident in both the mobility and protection afforded by Bulldog and in their ability to locate and engage the enemy under fire. It was a true baptism of fire.

Opposite: 6 Pl, B Coy on patrol near PINK 16. LCpl Baleamoto dismounted left and Sjt Marriott right. Rfn Bruckshaw gives top cover.

Right: Rfn Ratu, B Coy.

Below: WO2(CSM) Dave Youngs, CSM B Coy.

The very next day 5 Platoon B Company was ambushed with rocket propelled grenades, heavy machine guns and small arms fire. A lead Warrior was hit by an improvised explosive devices, and again Bulldog manoeuvred to draw fire away from a convoy. Operating at range the firepower available was outstanding with the top cover well placed to identify and engage multiple firing points. Once the convoy had passed, 5 Platoon called on American F-16 fighter planes to fly low to allow them to break contact.

The above gives a taste of the sort of engagements faced by 1RGJ/2Rifles almost on a daily basis. The battlegroup averaged four contacts per day, from the quick pot-shot to the multi-weapon company sized firefight. Contacts were short in duration but intensely fierce, and with little or no warning. The insurgents were prepared to initiate fights when the local population was unaware, and so there were few 'combat indicators' for the commander.

The tempo of operations was punishing. The planning for strike operations and the major resupply convoys was meticulous, and the Battlegroup Chief of Staff, Major Bill Wright, and the Operations Officer, Captain Andrew Ridland, were operating within a constant planning cycle. Some strike operations had days notice, whilst others were at immediate notice. Yet, from the Commanding Officer down, every rifleman knew that each time a patrol went out of the door, it had to be the performance of a lifetime.

On 30 December 2006 1RGJ was involved in a protracted battle in the Timinyah District of Basra City. Operation PHOENIX had carried out two simultaneous strikes against enemy indirect fire crews, and both A Company and Chindit Company (attached from 1st Battalion the Duke of Lancaster's Regiment), with B Company in support, had managed to detain a number of known militia, complete with mapping indicating indirect fire targets. But on one of the target

The Royal Green Jackets

areas the Jaish Al Mahdi insurgents (JAM) sought to deny extraction routes, and a find of unstable munitions meant that ATO (Ammunition Technical Officer or bomb disposal) was required on the scene. It was clear that Major Chris Job's Chindit Company had stirred up a hornets' nest and were soon engaged in a pitch battle with insurgents in Al Timinyah. Bulldogs from B20 were tasked to escort ATO and moved straight into a contact battle where Chindit Company were engaging a number of insurgents attempting to place improvised explosive devices. As it approached the drop off point one of the lead Bulldogs was hit by an improvised explosive devices and another insurgent attempting to lay an improvised explosive devices was killed. Once ATO had been delivered onto target the platoon had to 'satellite' in support of Chindit Company's Warriors to deter follow up attacks and buy them some space, by destroying a number of enemy, whilst ATO hurried through his task. Warriors from C Company 1 Staffords, under Major Mike Ross, in the north of the city also came south to assist, and one of the Warriors was hit by 4 rocket propelled grenades as it arrived. Women were seen to be smuggling rocket propelled grenades and ammunition under their hijabs and the enemy seemed set for a protracted battle. Yet the ultimate impact of Warrior and Bulldog standing and fighting toe-to-toe with the militia had a significant deterrent effect on JAM.

Striking at the Heart of the Enemy

Throughout the long months of January and February 2007 the commanding officer kept the battalion relentlessly on the offensive, but with a mind firmly fixed on the endgame, the creation of Iraqi Security Forces capable of maintaining security. Operation SINBAD, the zone by zone reconstruction project in Basra City, was drawing to a close, and the insurgents seemed determined to claim credit for the work. Indirect fire on the Basra Palace increased, and as a result the tempo of strike operations increased to detain insurgent leaders. As 1RGJ became 2Rifles on 1 February 2007 the battlegroup was a battle-hardened and focused body of riflemen, up to any challenge and continually seeking to be unpredictable. On a number of occasions the impact of fourteen armoured vehicles arriving at a target house and then gaining explosive entry (or using the vehicle themselves to effect entry) was sufficient to deter insurgents from escaping or other insurgents taking on the multi-national forces as they sought to strike targets in the dead of night.

March saw the first loss of a rifleman, with Rifleman Daniel Coffey killed by enemy action whilst on patrol in the north of the city on 27 February 2007. He was serving with C Company, under Major Michael Foster-Brown, in the Shat Al Arab Hotel. The end of March saw re-organisation in the city with the closure of the Shat Al Arab Hotel and the return of 1 Staffords battlegroup back to the UK. C Company was re-subordinated back to 2Rifles, and B Company 1 Staffords, after a hard 5 months, returned to their Regiment. The Old State Building was handed over to a platoon of Iraqi Military Police, and Chindit Company found a new home in Basra Palace with the rest of the battlegroup. The battlegroup was re-organised, and B and C Companies each donated a platoon of Bulldog to Chindit Company, which in turn provided Warrior platoons to each company. The Battlegroup was thereafter comprised of three identical companies, making an operations rotation achievable for the first time. Nevertheless, there remained the need for large-scale offensive action from across the whole battlegroup at a crucial time in the political process.

Operation TELIC 9 has forged 2Rifles with a firm grounding for the future. The battalion has been proven in combat. It has been seen that you can take a light-role battalion, and with the right training, money and collective energy convert it to a mechanised protected mobility capability for complex combat in Iraq within the space of weeks. Yet 1RGJ and now 2Rifles have remained true to themselves, light in spirit, bold and agile. Being light, agile, quick thinking and confident were as important to the success of the tour as anything else. The riflemen of today are every bit as bold and brave as their forefathers. They are streetwise, confident and hardworking and in the swift and complex engagements where mounted and dismounted tactics were combined they were unbeatable. The corporate experience gained on Operation TELIC 9 is significant – real-time learning of hard lessons under fire.

Extracts From 'Letters from the Front'
October 2006–May 2007, A Company 1st Battalion The Royal Green Jackets/2Rifles, Basra
Major Alex Baring

Christmas and the New Year 2006–7
The frantic pace of life continues unabated. While the battlegroup is striving to achieve a degree of forward planning, events here move so fast that the programme ends up changing several times a day. New tasks come in from Brigade every night, often for the next day. But morale is still high; especially after a huge backlog of mail arrived the other day, including sackfulls of letters, Christmas presents, grub, etc …

The atmosphere in places like Al Quibla is pretty tense; it's one of the areas from which they occasionally launch rockets at us. Men with mobile phones appear at street corners to watch your progress. By day the locals have been seen releasing flocks of pigeons from roof-tops. They rise like a small cloud, advertising your presence. As you move along they release other flocks so that your movement can be tracked – like Apache smoke signals. Luckily, until they think of dousing them in luminous paint, the pigeon method is pretty useless at night. And the insurgents' flip-flops aren't so good in the mud either. But all this creeping around doesn't always get results.

'Forged Under Fire'

Sometimes the best way is just to go and sit on a road junction in one of 1 Platoon's armoured Bulldogs and wait until someone shoots at you. Then have a skilled rifleman shoot back. They probably won't make that mistake again. But let's hope they do …

Another 7 days have flown by; a week that will be remembered for 2 major contacts involving B Coy, which on our side sadly resulted in the injury of 2 soldiers. Both incidents occurred in the increasingly notorious Al Quibla area. No doubt we'll be seeing more of that place. Witnessing casualties arriving back at Basra Plalace from a contact is a moving sight: the Warrior or Bulldog vehicles arrive outside Battalion HQ at high speed, crews covered in dust and grime; there are shouts and commands as the injured man is lowered from the vehicle by many hands onto a waiting stretcher before being whisked into the Regimental Aid Post. Invariably the casevac helicopter arrives literally seconds later to complete the onward evacuation if necessary. The onlooker is torn between trying to help or just keeping out of the way. At least we know that the system works well …

Another hectic week, marred by the injury of two of our friends from C Coy, hit by a roadside bomb in the north of the city. The enemy is devious; and everyone is itching to smash them hard but it's not easy pinning them down. Their tactics are classic guerrilla: hit and run against vulnerable targets; and never take us on in a straight fight. We are trying to keep them guessing by varying our routes, timings and methods.

This week we launched our first joint 'strike' operation with the Iraqi Army. A Coy, as part of a battlegroup operation, was to raid a suspected militia house in the middle of sweet-smelling Al Quibla; with the Iraqis supplementing the outer cordon and providing their Strike Group (ISG) to storm the house. The Iraqis were not at the RV, but were eventually found; and they told us that the local militia had already threatened them and knew that we were coming. That put a whole new complexion on things. The operation had been compromised. Were we going straight into an ambush? The Iraqis said they were ready to go anyway (which way, we wondered). We waited for orders. Orders came: Go! No one can complain that the Army doesn't offer excitement. A Coy strike teams closed in on the target from holding positions north and south, expecting a volley of rocket propelled grenades from the rooftops at any moment. As 1 Platoon moved off kids were seen being pulled off the street by their elders, while others ran at full speed away from us – generally a surefire indicator of imminent attack. Sixty seconds later the target house, a modest dwelling behind a wall on a street corner, was surrounded by armoured vehicles and the Iraqi strike force went in. Not a shot was fired from within or without. The suspect was not at home; but a quick search of the building revealed an rocket propelled grenade rocket, 2 warheads and a pistol. Meanwhile, in the street outside 3 Platoon used ladders to scale nearby houses in order to dominate the high ground (they can get a machinegun onto a rooftop in 40 seconds from the time they stop their vehicles) … A difficult and frustrating week opened with 1 Platoon escorting our fortnightly resupply convoy out of the city, at night, along unfamiliar routes, with only intermittent comms and under sporadic rocket propelled grenade and automatic fire; all this just 24 hours after the arrest of a significant insurgent commander, which meant that the enemy was after our blood …

Anyway, back to the search. It is 0100, in a small hamlet on the outskirts of Basra. Dogs are barking. Recce Platoon have led the way in to the target on foot and gain entry into the building, using a sledgehammer a rifleman manages the remove the door, the hinges, and most of the wall in the process. In the background is the rising thunder of armoured vehicles as 1 Platoon Bulldogs sweep into position to cut off escape routes. Prepared for possible armed response, the strike group rapidly secures the building and occupants: two men, two women and two young children, all woken from sleep, all scared witless. The intelligence obviously wasn't that good. The search troops do their best to calm the women and children, handing out sweets brought along for such an eventuality (quote of the week 'to be honest, sir, straight from laser-dot on the forehead to jelly-baby at one in the morning doesn't really work'). The search is hampered by the revolting mess in every room, but quickly reveals two AK47s. Hopes are up, but some rapid questioning of the adult males suggests that they are unconnected to the insurgents; and most household in Iraq own an AK for 'home-defence' anyway. The section commanders wrap up the search (voice heard to the Sergeant Major: 'Sir, do you want me to put everything back as it was or should I tidy it up?'). Minutes later the company is back in the vehicles, moving at speed back to the Palace; to learn on arrival that plans have changed again, and that we must take over guard and Quick Reaction Force (QRF). But the week has ended on a high, with yet another huge delivery of parcels and letters. Absolutely fantastic …

One of the more violent Christmases any of us have experienced. A series of ops, some planned, some not, have blurred the days into one. It's difficult to remember what happened when. 1 Platoon spent the early hours of Christmas morning supporting a Basra City North battlegroup operation to flatten with explosives the old headquarters building of the corrupt and murderous Special Crimes Unit. C Coy, attached to 1 Staffords, played a leading role in the operation. The insurgent didn't like that at all, and have been trying hard to hit back at us. The day before yesterday they killed a sergeant from the Duke of Lancaster's Regiment with a roadside bomb close to Chindit Coy's base at the Old State Building; a sickeningly loud explosion that rang across the city and shocked us all. The whole battlegroup is now even more determined to strike the enemy; and we didn't have to wait long for our first opportunity. At 2300 intelligence located two target houses in the city. By 0415 that night A Coy and Recce were in position around one of the targets, a dilapidated bungalow surrounded by palm trees. 3 Platoon had done their party piece and silently scaled the adjacent

Cpl Howe indicates an en posn to Rfn Jones during Operation AREZZO.

Major Quentin Naylor.

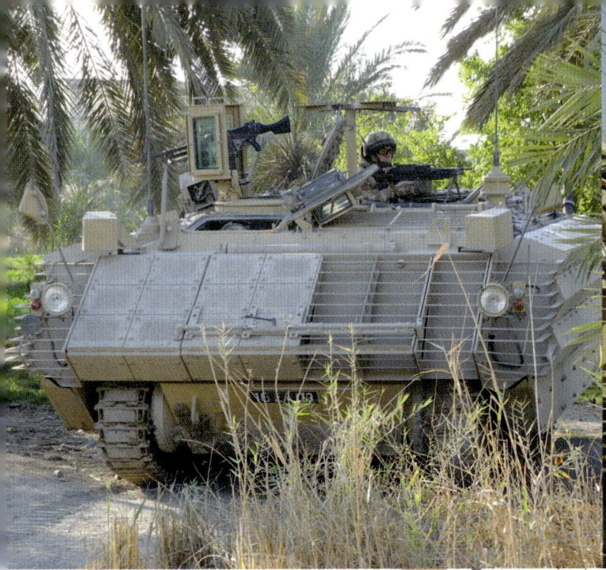
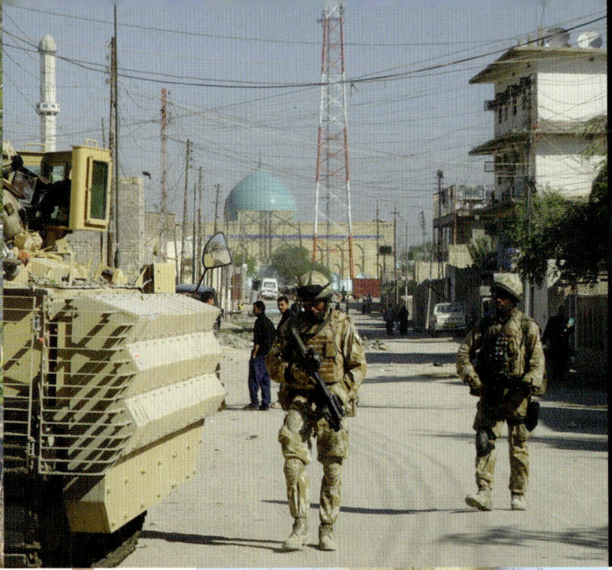
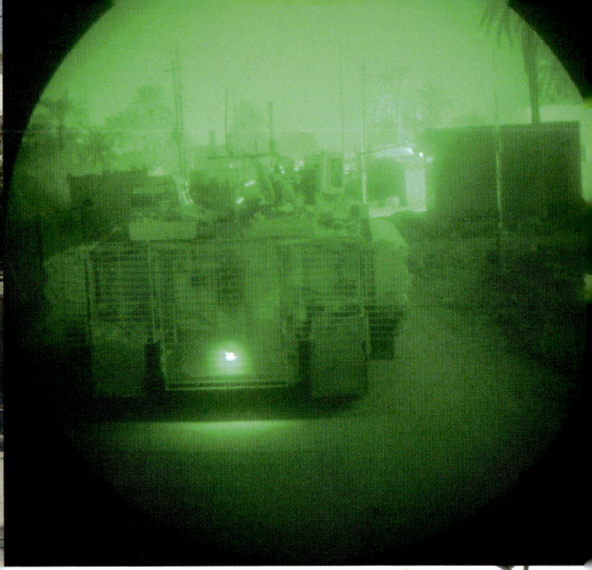
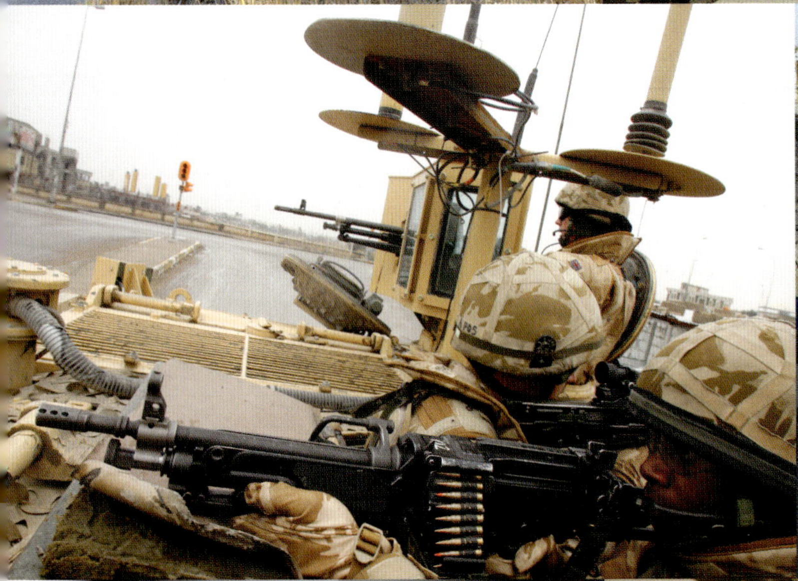
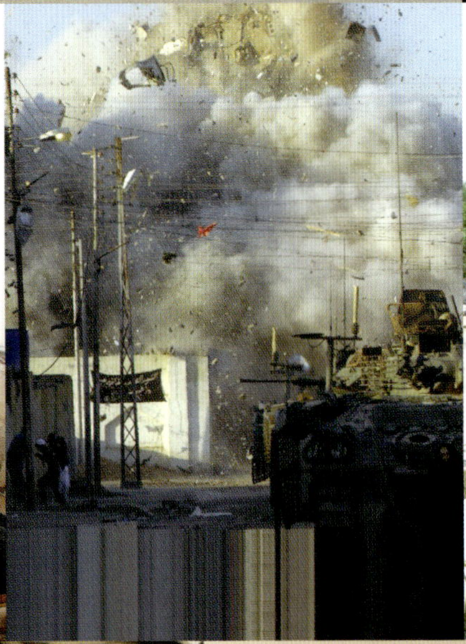
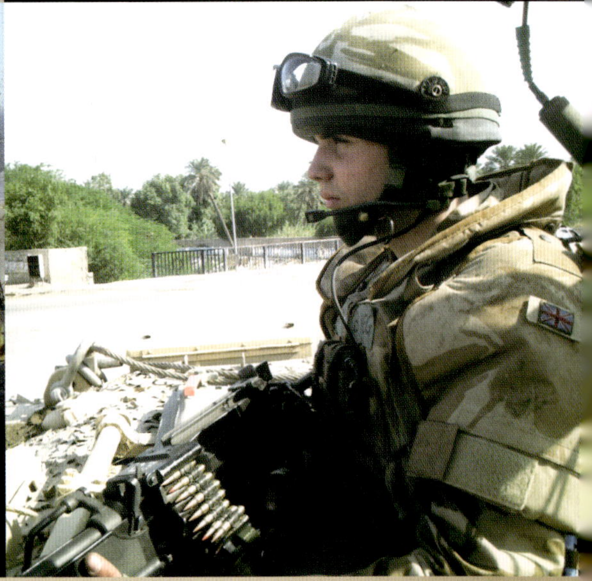
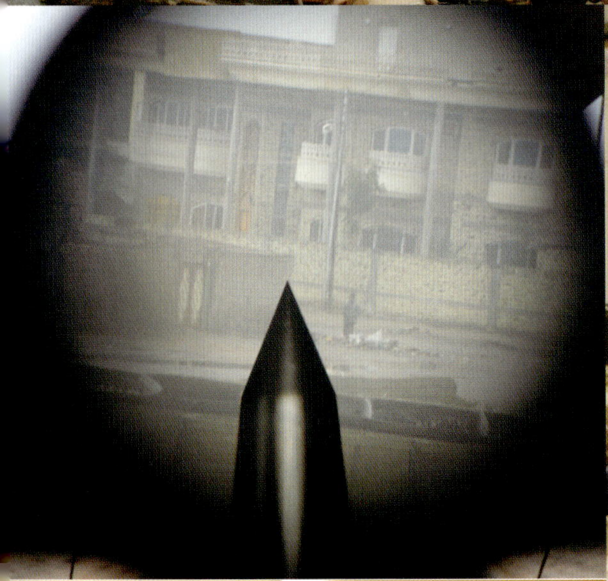
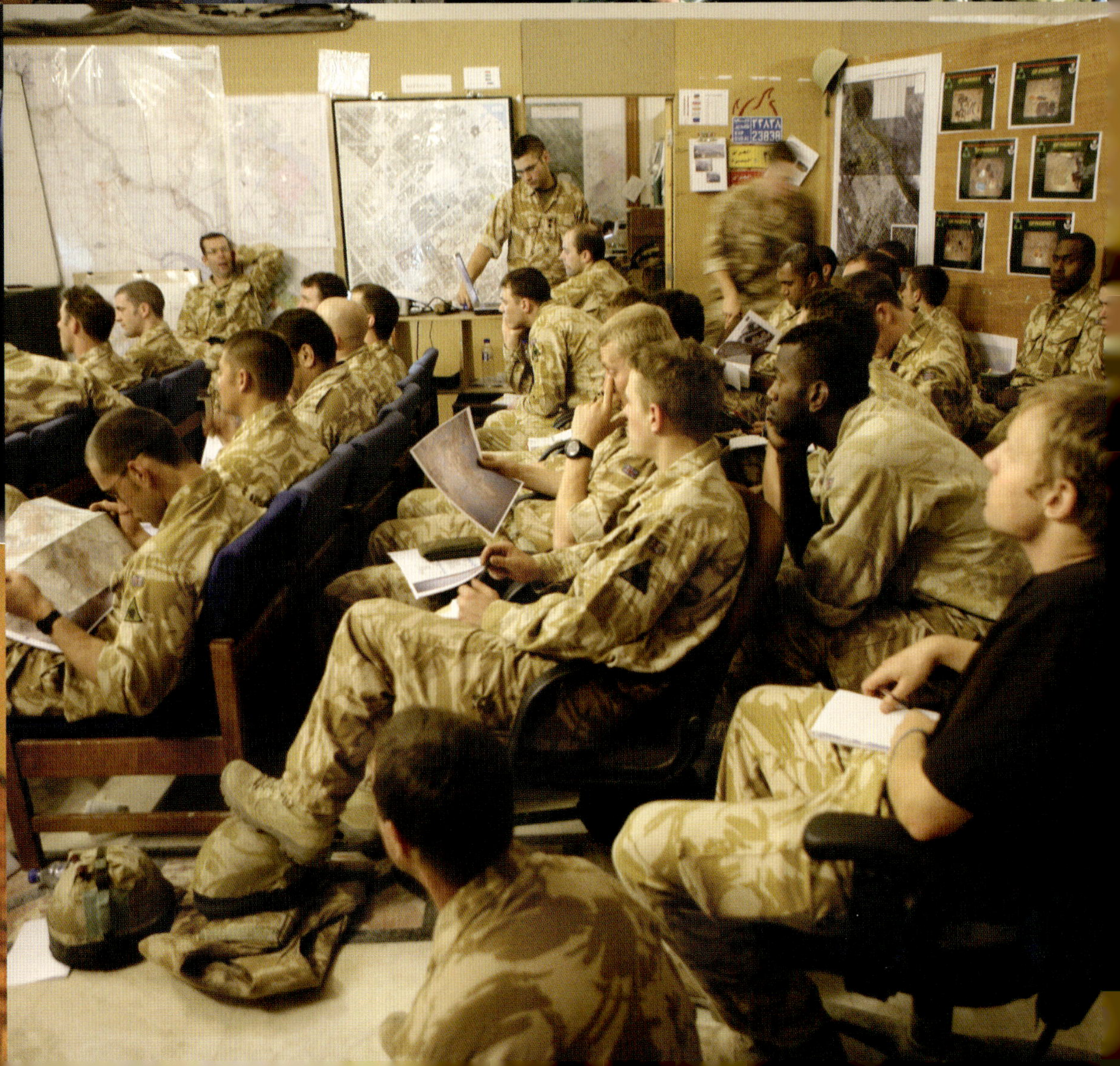
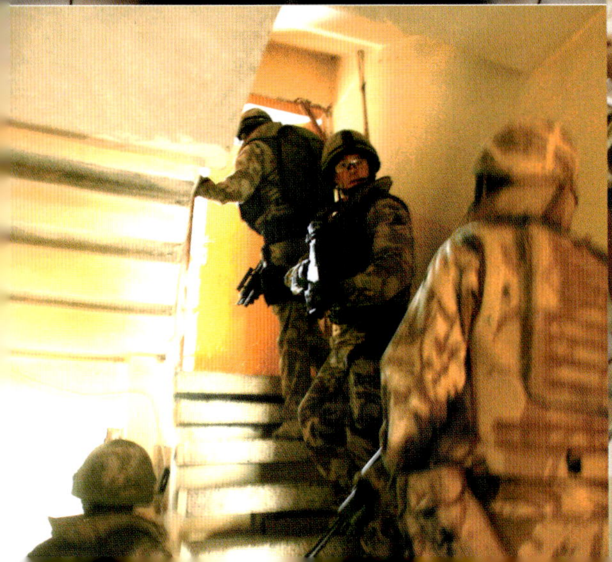

1. *Rfn Richardson provides top cover on a Rural patrol near Basra Palace.*

2. *LCpl Delana and Rfn Koro conducted dismounted checks near the Old State Buildings (OSB).*

3. *A Bulldog enters Basra Palace after a Strike Operation.*

4. *Contact in Al Saraji – Rfn Koro engages from top cover, LCpl Trollip, commanding, engages with GPMG.*

5. *Operation THYME 25 December 2006 – the destruction of the SCU HQ.*

6. *Rfn Lewin on top cover.*

7. *In the line of sight.*

8. *Cpl McAleese commands a house assault team during a strike operation.*

9. *B Coy orders group for Operation AREZZO.*

buildings and could be seen covering us from the rooftops. Being pretty sure of an unfriendly welcome this time, we decided to forego the sledge-hammer, opting instead for a 'small' demolition charge provided by some of our highly trained friends from 2 Platoon. In the early morning quiet, the explosion seemed enough to wake the dead; we were able to enter the building through the gaping hole in the wall and, to our great satisfaction, apprehend two suitably stunned and unpleasant looking men who just happened to be in possession of a range of weapons, military equipment, mobile phones and satellite photography of our bases. Cheeky buggers. Their phones were all ringing furiously, but too late for them; how sad. Meanwhile, Chindit Coy (supported by our own 2 Platoon), struck their target in the city centre: all hell broke loose as the insurgents tried – and failed – to prevent the raid, using roadside bombs, rocket propelled grenades and machine guns. In due course it became apparent why: Chindit had struck gold – two suspects plus a huge find of weapons ranging from small arms to rockets; a wealth of forensic evidence that will soon send some very unpleasant men to jail. It is worth mentioning that despite these violent flare-ups normal day-to-day life in Basra is pretty tolerable for the locals, and getting better (especially when compared to Baghdad). And we are still remarkably popular in most areas. People will smile, wave and return greetings; this morning I was offered a kebab by a street vendor despite having no money to pay for it. However, at the time of writing we are two hours away from the New Year, and expecting the odd flying festive offering from the other side of the perimeter wall. Apparently the insurgents are planning to take advantage of our drunken stupor by sending over a volley of rockets …

Best wishes for a Happy New Year, and roll on R&R! …

February 2007

So, farewell to The Royal Green Jackets. It's 1 Feb 2007 and we've now become the 2nd Battalion The Rifles. A short parade was held in Basra Palace to mark the occasion. Bugles played. Camera crews and photographers like wasps on a trifle (they really have no manners). Predictably some bright spark managed to imitate the whistle of an incoming mortar round as we stood to attention on the helicopter pad. But the joke's an old one, so no one moved. The hunt for insurgents continues. A and B Companies struck more target houses a couple of nights ago – the first Rifles operation …

The tour grinds on; the pace as hectic as ever; the danger ever present. Chindit Company lost a young officer to a roadside bomb just outside Basra Palace. Many of us in A Coy had worked with him, albeit briefly, when his Warrior platoon so ably led us into our target last week. He was a splendid chap. A small but moving ceremony was held for him before the helicopter arrived that night to take his body back to the Air Base. Some fifty soldiers from across the battlegroup gathered in the darkness by the helipad, in a narrow gap between the blast walls and the buildings. Stars shone above and the men stood still as a forest as the Padre, with the aid of a small red-filtered torch, read from the Bible in his Irish brogue. When he had finished, a green parachute flare from somewhere popped in the sky, casting weird swaying palm-tree shadows onto the wall that rose like smoke as it sank to earth. There being no song sheets, the Padre then sang 'Abide with Me', from beginning to end, on his own. As the last note faded the faint beat of rotors could be heard approaching in the distance, and soon the night was filled with noise and dust, and the stretcher was carried out to the waiting helicopter for the final farewell and the beginning of the long journey home …

March 2007

One of the busiest weeks of the tour. At last the enemy rocket teams have done something useful and have blown up one of our grotty old shower blocks; so hopefully we might get a shiny new one to replace it. But all the same, some light vengeance was in order. We had a fair idea where these creeps were operating from, so the Colonel tasked A Company at short notice to go and give them a call. We would get a Warrior platoon from Chindit Coy, and some extra Bulldogs from B Coy (for the benefit of my father, Bulldog as in the tracked armoured personnel carrier rather than inter-war biplane). Our first stop was a house in the Old Town, very close to where two Riflemen had been shot a few weeks ago.

0100: a suitably anti-social time. The Warriors lead us to the last street corner and the Bulldogs (still not planes) peel off down to the target. As 1 Platoon covers outwards across a darkened canal and the houses beyond, 3 Platoon deploys from the vehicles to gain entry. The front gates, springing backwards and forwards, resist the first few blows of a Rifleman's sledgehammer. We quickly go to Plan B: A Bulldog noses forward to pop the gates, which unfortunately bring down most of the wall with them all over the car parked inside. (I had waited an entire military career to be able to say 'you're only supposed to blow the bloody doors off' and didn't miss my chance.) The front door was easier and inside, to our surprise (!), an off-duty policeman and various others. But apart from that, some lurid propaganda posters, which are insufficient grounds on which to detain (though after 20 minutes of playing the 'bad cop – bad cop' routine they are left in do doubt that they are under observation and are not safe to operate with impunity). Undeterred, we remount and head on to the next objective – a suspected weapons cache located in the southern half of the 'Shia Flats', a grid system of tightly packed housing covering a square mile on the outskirts of Basra, considered for long as a no-go area. A militia stronghold, we don't go there in less than company strength, especially at night. And once you're in, don't lose track of which street you're on or you'll be going around in circles (or rectangles) all night having rocket propelled grenades or worse fired at you. As we approach, a single shot cracks above us – obviously someone is awake. And in; first left; first right, first left. parked cars: too narrow for Warriors, who are forced to keep going straight. From OC 1 Pl, 'Bulldogs might make it'. We stick to the plan, while Warriors find an alternative route. Down to the end, squeezing past cars, right turn, second alley, STOP! 3 Platoon leap out and smash in through the shutters of a small shop in a deserted bazaar; nothing inside. The clock is ticking. All is quiet so far. 3 Platoon crowbar into the shop on the right; fruit, veg, nothing. Bloody intelligence! We try one to the left – a clothes shop. 'JACKPOT!' Fantastic; but now the enemy will be mightily annoyed.

April 2007

It has been a sad week in Basra, for A Company and many others. A Kingsman from Chindit Company was killed by a sniper on Sunday as his patrol checked a bridge for roadside bombs. And on the afternoon of 2nd of April Rifleman Aaron Lincoln from 1 Platoon was shot and killed while on patrol in the city. His team was conducting a rapid 'follow-up' to an incident that had occurred minutes before, in which a Lance Corporal also from 1 Platoon, had been shot in the hand by a sniper. The platoon had been out patrolling one of the areas from which mortars are sometimes fired into Basra Palace. But their movements had been observed by a well-positioned gunman. The Lance Corporal was hit by a single shot as he scanned the area from a

The Royal Green Jackets

News from the Front: Operation Arezzo
(An afternoon with A Company 2Rifles in Al Quibla, April 2007)
Major Alex Baring

This week saw the battlegroup's eagerly awaited strike back against Jaysh al Mahdi (Mahdi Army); Operation Arezzo would kick the enemy where it hurts. The battlegroup operation would involve 3 Warrior Companies, 3 Bulldog Companies and a half squadron of tanks. The plan was simple: drive the whole battalion in broad daylight into the middle of the insurgent heartland of Al Quibla, raid some suspect houses then, instead of pulling back, simply occupy the roofs and wait for them to attack; and kill them. I'm pleased to say it worked a treat.

By about 1515, we were approaching Al Quibla from what we hoped was an unexpected direction, having met up with a half-squadron of tanks from the Force Reserve. The insurgents must have wondered what on earth was happening as we made the final turn towards Al Quibla, then headed straight into the middle of it.

It is 1530. With the tanks clearing the route ahead of us, we head on in our Bulldog Armoured Personnel Carriers to our target, a 3-storey terraced house situated on a main junction at the heart of Al Quibla. How satisfying to see the bewildered faces of the passers-by. We are obviously not expected. Our two Warriors seal the front entrance. Seconds later 3 Platoon arrive at the back and, using their trade-mark technique, 'nose' a small(ish) hole through the garden wall with the vehicle. The assault teams dismount, keeping close to the cover between the vehicle and the wall; then in. Inside, three men, women, children, sceaming.

This moment is always unpleasant. You think what it would be like if it was your home. It helps to concentrate on the intelligence brief. But the Riflemen are good; firm but controlled and very disciplined. Despite the week we've had there was no hint of temper or malice; just professionalism. While the women and children are made comfortable in one room, the men are questioned. The search reveals an AK, a pistol and some JAM (Mahdi Army) propaganda posters. These were not good people. Our search is only part of the mission: it also gives us a base from which to fight. As we searched, the recce platoon has gained access to a building across the main junction some 200 m to our South in order to give us some mutual support. Now a section from 3 Platoon push up onto the roof of the Alpha. Arcs are allocated among the troops; reference points identified.

The stage is set for Phase 2. Blood is in the water and the sharks are out there. The first nibbles come after about 45 minutes, right on cue. Children are chased from the street by their elders. Men appear on rooftops, pointing, then talking into mobile phones. We fire a warning shot. They duck out of sight. Next time it's for real. The Recce Platoon get a fleeting glance of two motorbikes, carrying an unbelievable 8 insurgents. Then, from further south in B Company's area, automatic fire; lots of it. A few minutes later a single round cracks over our heads. No firing point identified; and given the sniper threat, sticking your head over the parapet to look for one is not much fun. Then a burst. A policeman at a checkpoint on the street below falls from his car, fatally wounded. Our Warriors move to assist him. The incoming fire intensifies; the 'crack' of the bullet overhead, followed by the delayed 'thump' of the weapon firing. Then bursts. Crack-crack-crack-thump-thump-thump. From the east, then the north as well. Now our Riflemen start picking up targets and returning fire. Concise, accurate, deeply satisfying bursts. A gunman at the end of a wall, beyond a dusty football pitch; the wall disintegrates under a hail of tracer; it feels good. This is what Churchill meant when he compared war to Champagne. Muzzle flashes from the roof of a mosque some 300m away; more men directing fire from a rooftop. Our flat roof feels vulnerable; a heavy machinegun would cut through the concrete parapet. But the roar of automatic fire from our boys is invigorating. Empty cases tinkle onto the concrete roof. From Recce's building our star sniper, spots a man with an AK47 creeping up on 1 Platoon's Bulldogs, static around the target house; he stops him with a bullet to the chest. But the Bulldogs are looking after themseves pretty well:

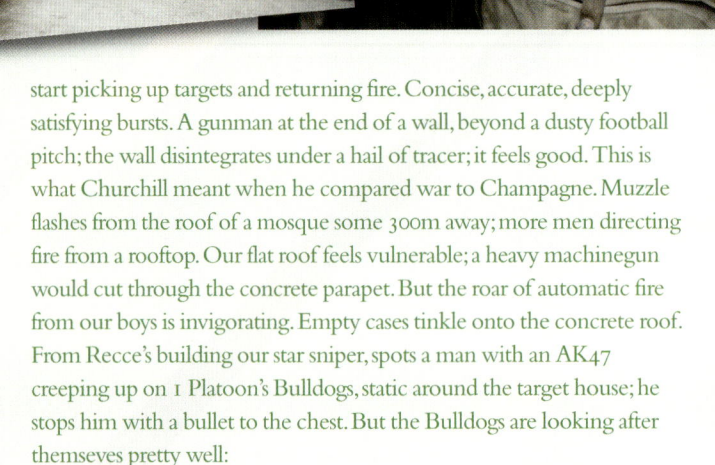

Our vehicles, hidden down an alley, are suddenly presented with clear but unsuspecting targets to their front. Ten rounds from the GPMG suffice. Meanwhile Recce have spotted a car full of armed gunmen – and drilled it full of holes. But by this stage they are drawing a lot of fire and are practically pinned down. It's probably time to go. The Bulldogs load up and head down a backstreet route to the RV; The commander at the front, faced with a deep sewage pit, orders his driver forward. He revs the engine, the Bulldog surges forward. It's deeper than it looks and a bow-wave of decaying human excrement surges up the front of the vehicle, engulfing the driver, who is not happy…

We think that 2Rifles battlegroup killed about 25 insurgents that day. And more good news was to come: two days later. Two 4-man Mahdi Army improvised explosive devices teams were killed by the Force Reserve. Very possibly the same who blew up the Warrior at the exact same spot last week. Couldn't have happened to nicer people.

Above left: Sjt Rafferty's Multiple from 6 Pl B Coy post Operation AREZZO. L–R: Rfn Beryy, LCpl Delana, Cpl McAleese, Sjt Rafferty, Cpl Sanday, Rfn Bagshaw; Top of Vehicle, L–R: Rfn Richardson, Rfn Willis, Rfn Strachan, Rfn Pearce, Rfn Gilmartin.

Above: Rfn Lewin post Operation AREZZO.

Below: Rfn Hudson – Bulldog Driver post Operation AREZZO.

doorway. His team returned rounds at the firing point, some 300 m away atop a derelict hotel. But by this stage he was bleeding badly and in need of medical treatment. Back under cover in the vehicle, a young rifleman rose to the occasion magnificently, applying a field dressing so tight that the wounded Lance Corporal had to protest – only to be told firmly 'no it isn't – I'm stopping the bleeding'. It was so well tied that the medics later left it in place. A few weeks ago this young riflman had seemed like a somewhat shy teenager. This tour is turning boys into men. As the vehicles sped the short distance back to camp, the other half of the platoon, working a few blocks away, was given a steer to the area of the firing.

Arriving at the scene, the patrol debussed and a team attempted to gain entry into a building but as they did so a series of shots rang out from behind them and Rifleman Lincoln fell to the floor, fatally wounded. His team-mates returned fire as best they could, but targets were fleeting and immediate casevac was required. Again the patrol was forced to pull off the ground; and minutes later were back in Basra Palace, where the medical staff did what they could in the few minutes before the helicopter arrived. Rfn Lincoln's stunned friends were in a terrible state but, with immense courage, and splendid leadership from their NCOs, put their helmets back on and went straight back out to support other patrols still dealing with the incident. An hour or so later we received the news that Rifleman Lincoln had died. Breaking the news later to the company, in a dimly lit corridor, was one of the hardest things I have ever done. Despite the fact that some must have guessed what I was about to say, there was an audible gasp. What do you say? I told them that Rifleman Lincoln had been incredibly brave – and that now they needed to be too; and that we needed to concentrate on our job to make sure that we all got through the rest of the tour; that generations of Green Jackets had overcome the same suffering in many different wars and that we were no different; and that we would do whatever it took to kill the bastards who shot him before we leave this place. I left it at that …

2nd Battalion The Royal Green Jackets/ 4th Battalion The Rifles

4Rifles, previously 2nd Battalion The Royal Green Jackets, deployed to Iraq, May–Dec 2007, assuming responsibility for the Basra Battle Group from 2Rifles, previously 1st Battalion The Royal Green Jackets. The report below comprises extracts from an article written by Major Tom Copinger-Symes, Second-in-Command 4Rifles, describing the battalion's experiences in Basra:

Commanding Officer's Foreword:

> *This has been written in Basra Palace, and covers something of our time there from May to July 2007. It has been written in between bouts of indirect fire and over a series of very late nights. Our perspective is quite different to what it was in February when we started training as 2nd Battalion The Royal Green Jackets and emerged as 4th Battalion The Rifles. Just before this article was despatched we held a Repatriation Service here in Basra Palace in stifling heat for our ninth fatality in the battlegroup, Corporal Eddie Edwards RTR. It was a sombre and emotional affair, but I was struck, as I have been since our first day here when we took our first fatality, by the remarkable resilience, good humour, camaraderie and fighting spirit of our riflemen and all those in the battlegroup. Our tour is not yet complete, but from where I sit our riflemen and officers are as tough and as good as they have ever been. This is something of their story so far …*

It was with a certain spring in our step that our deployment date approached. The Reception; Staging; and Onward Integration (RSOI) package was run in Kuwait, in an immense US facility called Camp Virginia, built to house 50,000 US troops as they transit through theatre. The RSOI package was primarily focused on acclimatisation training, which essentially involved runs under a selection of the Brigade's Physical Training Instructors; all delighted to have such a captive audience to entertain. We took the opportunity to run an all-too brief but very worthwhile package of integration training with our new Bulldog vehicles. For many iflemen it was the first chance they had to see these renovated Armoured Personnel Carriers in action, with the new Protected Weapon Station (PWS) and Remote Weapon Station (RWS) fitted. The RWS is an especially impressive piece of kit, an automated 7.62 mm or .50 cal machine gun slaved to a playstation screen and joystick that is controlled from under armour by the vehicle commander. With an excellent thermal imaging sight this had the potential to be a battle-winner in Iraq. Albeit that it would be another 2 months before we would actually get to use the new weapon system in anger this was a valuable chance to get some idea of its capabilities before using it in contact for the first time.

In mid-May the majority of the Battalion flew forward from Kuwait to Iraq, landing at the sprawling camp that is known variously as the Basra Air Station (BAS to the Americans); Basra International Airport (BIA to the Iraqis); or the Contingent Operating Base (COB to the members of Multi-National Division (South East), MND(SE). The COB is home to the vast majority of the division, as well as a large range of others including US State Department, UK FCO, private security contractors, and elements of the Iraqi Security Forces. It is a large camp by UK, not US, standards and adjoins the airport. It would be home to A Company, with the 2 R Welsh battlegroup for the duration of the tour, along with almost all of the Brigade.

4Rifles battlegroup was therefore the only major unit to be stationed outside the airport base; with only the Provincial Joint Coordination Centre (PJCC) as the other location in Basra City. The PJCC function is to liaise with various elements of the Iraqi Security Forces (ISF), in particular the Iraqi Police Service (IPS). With a protection force of a Rifle Platoon from 4Rifles, it was understandable that the Brigade Commander was keen to have a rifleman as the Chief of Staff, providing some much needed Infantry glue to the all-

The Royal Green Jackets

Arms organisation, as well as a natural link to the battlegroup, under whose protection and administrative oversight the PJCC naturally fell. Major Paul Harding was an obvious choice for the job, and he threw himself into the considerable task of pulling together the security, operation and administration of this isolated but strategically important little outpost in the heart of Basra.

Meanwhile, we began a fast-paced but enjoyable Relief in Place with our brother-riflemen in 2Rifles at the palace. It was a true pleasure to be taking over from friends; the usual frictions of handover were replaced with good humour and a real sense of common identity and purpose coupled with a sense of deep respect on our part for our predecessors, who had seen Basra deteriorate from a relatively benign operating environment to the maelstrom in which we found it in May 2007. A simple handshake on the evening of 20 May 2007 marked the Transfer of Authority (TOA) between Lieutenant Colonels Justin Maciejewski of 2Rifles and Patrick Sanders of 4Rifles.

As an isolated location, Basra Palace relies entirely on its air and land lines of communication in order to move men and materiel in and out. Much of this routine sustainment is done by helicopter, but with a threat from surface-to-air missiles and rocket propelled grenades there is little scope to fly by day and there are inevitable limitations on the amount of equipment that can be brought in by air. Hence the resupply of the palace relies predominantly on the few land routes. The convoy routes vary slightly, but there is little option other than to drive them along one of the major roads in and out of the city, where they run the gauntlet of insurgent attacks, ranging from improvised explosive devices to rocket propelled grenade and small arms fire to mortar fire.

The battlegroup has the unenviable task of protecting this incredibly vulnerable, painfully slow-moving behemoth. To do it we are typically given an additional two or three armoured infantry companies from the Manoeuvre battlegroup and we use a mixture of depth; route security pickets; intimate protection scattered through the convoy; and a strong vanguard, to keep the insurgents at arms length from the convoy and unable to target the soft-skinned vehicles. The level of logistic complexity in loading, unloading and marshalling the convoy is mind-boggling; and on every convoy at least one huge articulated vehicle breaks down, runs out of fuel, or simply drives off the road. Recovering them is a mammoth task. And this is all before the enemy gets a vote; it would be difficult to get such a convoy through Basingstoke; driving it through Basra is a significant challenge.

So this was what faced us on our very first operation, and we had it all that night: small arms fire; improvised explosive devicess; mortars; a 50 ton crane that broke down at the most dangerous point on the route and was only recovered by a REME Corporal siphoning fuel through a small hose; a Warrior that ended up in a ditch and could only be recovered by a Challenger Tank Recovery Variant; and drunken civilian contract drivers taking the wrong route. It was testament to the excellence of the training and the handover from 2Rifles that we got through that first night without serious injury and the convoy got through to Basra Palace unscathed.

Having got the convoy into the palace there remained two further tasks: first to run vital supplies from the convoy up to the PJCC and back; and second to extract the convoy back to the COB. Having resupplied the PJCC the convoy eventually set off back to the palace in the early afternoon; a mixture of Warrior, Bulldog and logistics vehicles. Coming down through the city the convoy slowed to turn a corner and was subjected to an extremely well-planned and effective complex attack: Cpl Jez Brookes, one of the R Coy Bulldog vehicle commanders, was shot in the head from behind as his vehicle slowed; and almost simultaneously the civilian tanker driver was hit by enemy small arms fire and his tanker was then hit by an rocket propelled grenade, causing a significant explosion.

Cpl Brookes was evacuated to Basra Palace immediately but there was nothing that could be done to save his life. The rest of the convoy managed to break through the ambush, but by this time a large crowd (from a JAM funeral very close by) had formed around the burning tanker, and insurgents seized the civilian drivers body from the cab. R Company continued to fight their way towards Basra Palace but the low-loader, which had been hit in the initial contact, collapsed with a buckled front axle as it drove over a narrow bridge, blocking the route and forcing the company commander to divert the rear end of the convoy to another bridge. They then fought to secure the immobilised low-loader. Attempts to recover the trailer proved ultimately fruitless, despite some incredibly brave attempts by a REME mechanic in an unarmoured Foden recovery vehicle. Whilst extracting, one of R Companys Bulldogs was struck by an improvised explosive devices, immobilising it and blowing the driver out of his hatch. The Quick Reaction Force dashed him back to the palace while the company commander, soon to be joined by a Warrior Platoon, secured the stricken vehicle. The Warrior crews did sterling work, recovering the Bulldog, still under fire, and the slightly battered packet finally made it back to the palace after a long and bruising introduction to the streets of Basra.

It was not a situation that any of us had hoped for on the first day of the tour, and there is little doubt that we were all shocked by the speed with which the situation unravelled so quickly and, of course, by Cpl Brookes's death. Sensibly, the decision was made to delay the extraction of the main convoy by 24 hours, and this gave us the chance to say farewell to Cpl Brookes before his body was taken out by helicopter that evening. We held the first of our mini-repatriation ceremonies by the helicopter landing site: an immensely moving little ceremony with the city and the Shatt al Arab silent in the background; service sheets lit up by head torches; the riflemen singing with rare passion; and the evening heat oppressive. Moving; incredibly effective as a means to say goodbye and to pay respect; and as Cpl Brookes's body was lifted away by the helicopter a great sense of release for all. Not that the grieving was finished, but at least some sense of closure and being ready to face the next challenge, the next day …

In our most recent convoy extraction the route security elements were hit by over thirty individual rocket propelled grenade attacks and fifteen other small arms attacks; we disrupted half a dozen improvised explosive devicess and were hit by the same number; we

Opposite: 4Rifles on operations in Basra, Iraq, 2007.

Left: Lieutenant Colonel Patrick Sanders, Commanding Officer 4Rifles, handing over Basra Palace to Colonel Sa'adi, commanding the Basra Palace Protection Force.

DON'T
RUN
GET
DOWN

suffered two gunshot wounds (in one a bullet grazed a soldiers head; in the other a soldiers weapon took the force of a bullet, saving his life but injuring his hand in the ricochet). Despite having already killed fourteen insurgents, we only finally gained the initiative by deploying Challenger tanks and Attack Helicopters onto the heaviest contact point. Nevertheless, and despite the inevitable breakdown serial en route, the convoy in this case over 100 articulated vehicles – was escorted, unscathed, through the mayhem. So convoy operations are extremely challenging and not conducted lightly or without very careful thought as to the necessity for them.

Immediately after having deployed into the city we sent our first platoon up to the PJCC as the guard force. Paul Harding was already doing a fantastic job to grip every facet of life at the site; with security being uppermost in everyone's minds. 10 Platoon deployed to the PJCC and quickly settled into the routine of guarding the site: a combination of sentry duty on the roof; controlling access; providing a close protection team for the commander; and generally enabling the full-time occupants of the PJCC, who are mainly Gunners to get on with their job. On 25 May 07 the death of the Basra JAM leader Abu Wissam Qadir (resisting arrest by Iraqi Security Forces) stirred up a hornet's nest quite unlike anything previously seen at the PJCC. At about 2200 hrs a substantial attack was launched against the PJCC building from over twenty different firing points from all points of the compass. 10 Pl battled for over 4 hours from the roof of the building to keep the attackers at bay; firing in excess of 9,000 rounds and resorting to cooking oil to keep their weapons firing. Jets were tasked in support, and the enemy only finally withdrew after one particularly effective air-strike convinced them that they had more to lose than to gain in the contest. 10 Pl had a number of lucky escapes, with one rifleman shot through the hand, and the platoon serjeant taking an AK47 round in the middle of his body-armour back-plate, leaving him with an impressive bruise and a lucky charm in the form of the bullet that he now wears around his neck.

Having experienced such a coordinated and intense attack on the PJCC, everyone's attention was rightly focused even more strongly on protection. Having been relatively free from indirect fire attacks previously, these began to intensify towards the end of May, with Rifleman Stephen Vause very seriously injured by a mortar round that landed on his sangar position on the roof of PJCC on 1 Jun 2007. Much of Paul Harding's focus as Chief of Staff was to ensure that the accommodation and work areas received additional Force Protection improvements. On the evening of 19/20 Jun 2007, Paul was killed instantly when hit by a mortar round at the PJCC – just as he adopted a fire position to give cover to an incoming resupply convoy escorted by B Company. His body was recovered to Basra Palace that night by the B Company convoy, which had to fight its way through a complex small arms and rocket propelled grenade ambush on the way. The brief service for Paul here at the palace was memorable; albeit nothing in comparison to his funeral at Winchester Cathedral, but with members of S Company coming back together to bid farewell their fallen commander it was an unforgettably moving experience …

The threat to Basra Palace has been increasing throughout 2007, from both direct and indirect fire. At any one time we have one of the Bulldog companies on guard, supported until recently by private contractors who guard the US compound, including the most vulnerable part of the palace perimeter. There are almost daily small arms and rocket propelled grenade attacks against the gates and sangars, and sentry duty is anything but dull. The threat from indirect fire (IDF) has also escalated significantly throughout the year; as the other UK bases in the city have closed and Basra Palace has become the easiest target of opportunity for the insurgent mortar and rocket teams. In July the amount of incoming indirect fire has almost doubled, with previous records for both number of attacks and total rounds fired being smashed – a very dubious distinction. In July we have been mortared or rocketed 101 times; with a total of 569 rounds fired. On 17 Jul 2007 we received 74 rounds of indirect fire in a single 24-hour period; this would have been a pretty serious week's worth of IDF until recently. Sadly many of the tools with which to affect the IDF threat lie outside the battlegroups control; and the Brigade is constrained by collateral damage considerations from maximising the potential for counter-battery fire. Thanks to the excellent work done by 2Rifles we are generally very well protected in all of the buildings, and most walkways are screened by hard cover.

As well as the harder end of the spectrum there is also still an immense amount of non-kinetic activity that is central to our operations. We manage over $2.5million worth of civilian infrastructure support projects. This activity is carefully coordinated with a matrix of contacts with key local leaders, whether tribal sheikhs, community figures such as doctors, or anyone else who can offer influence and insight.

Commanding Officer's End Note

The phrase be careful what you wish for springs to mind. In nine weeks we have suffered nine killed in action and forty-nine wounded. It has been an extraordinary experience, quite outside the parameters of what those with years of soldiering behind us had experienced previously on operations, but happily quite close to what we have prepared and trained for. And we have learned that the riflemen are extraordinarily good at it. They adapt swiftly, show great courage, have tremendous resilience and are bold in the face of the enemy. Through it all they maintain the characteristic sense of humour and banter that we have always thrived on it just gets a bit darker than usual! And above all their offensive spirit is second to none. They want nothing more than to deploy on patrol or battlegroup operations and when they encounter the enemy they pursue and harry him ruthlessly. Enemy casualties far outstrip our own and the militias, having been hit hard in our opening weeks, now avoid direct contact with our patrols, relying almost exclusively on improvised explosive devices and indirect fire. We have a long way to go before the tour is over. It is only mid July and we are here until December, so much can happen between now and then. The fighting spirit of our young riflemen is truly impressive and, despite the casualties that we have suffered, they remain desperate to get out on patrol again and again. It is our ability to continue the offensive that keeps the Riflemen going. Swift and Bold they most certainly are, worthy successors to their illustrious forebears.

Letter from the Second-in-Command
4Rifles Battle Group

Basra Palace, Iraq
16 July 2007

The headline news is that everything is going well; life in Basra Palace is comfortable enough; we are increasingly battle-hardened and streetwise; the boys are taking the knocks in their stride; and we are making good use of the opportunities to strike back; so we are in good shape. With all the reports of deaths and casualties it probably seems that everything must be pretty awful and tense and that we are suffering badly – actually we are in fine fettle and enjoying ourselves (at least some of the time!). Although it is all very foreign and some of it is straight from the movies, it is strange how much of it is actually very recognisable and everyday – it is as if all the violence and mayhem is laid down on top of an otherwise normal urban landscape and everyone does their best to get on with daily life ignoring the chaos and disruption as if it was a bad traffic jam that will ease before it's time for them to go home again. So what is utterly extraordinary and has taken me by surprise is the ordinariness of it all. By which I mean how we quickly and easily we have adjusted and accepted Basra as our new reality and apart from growing up a bit (and of course taking some casualties), everyone is pretty much the same as they were before they left Wiltshire.

Having stressed all the stoical stuff, we have lost some more really good guys which is of course hard to take, but the riflemen are displaying impressive resilience and, though it is inevitably shocking, they are into their stride now and sticking it to the Mahdi Army, or JAM as we know them, whenever we get the opportunity. It is undeniably serious business out here and the pace of life is pretty frenetic; taking over from 2Rifles, better known to you as 1RGJ, we stepped straight into the maelstrom, which took some getting used to as we were doing it at the same time as we were trying to learn the streets, and the enemy continued to up the ante in our first few weeks. So there's been plenty going on and not a lot of time or opportunity to dwell on any of it for too long. And some bits of it are undoubtedly enjoyable … by which I mean the satisfaction of doing the job well; wading through the treacle and dealing with the various threats as best you can and coming out the other end with as little damage as possible done to us and as much as possible to the enemy. It is definitely an art, albeit with a chunk of science thrown in, and there's a huge amount of experience to be gained and skills to be mastered. And we are learning how to take the knocks – it is something that has got to be learned I think.

The little repatriation services we run here at the palace before the bodies go up to the airport base are just wonderful. It's a pretty miserable business on the face of it, but they are incredibly effective at helping everyone cope, whether or not one is interested in the religious bit. It's very atmospheric: the evening heat (not much cooling breeze off the river now); the city silent but for the odd muezzin call; singing that would make a choirmaster faint but in the circumstances puts the hairs up and grips your throat; a simple body-bag with a Union Flag over it. There is a palpable lift to one's spirits at the same time as the helicopter flies off with the body – I was amazed at the sense of relief with the first one and it has been the same with the others. It's more difficult when we don't get the chance to say goodbye to them here at the palace usually because they have been casevaced to the airport base and died there, or if it's one of ours attached to another battlegroup as with Cpl Wilson. It just happens that all of our casualties have been real stars; good soldiers and characters all of them, which kicks everyone that little bit harder. You might remember Cpl Wilson turning up in the battalion in Paderborn from the Light Infantry; a maverick with massive talent and intelligence who was always bucking the system but with a wonderful twinkle in his eye. LCpl Brookes was with me in R Company; a typical Brummie and relentlessly positive – a dedicated and promising soldier. Cpl Rigby really was the outstanding corporal of his generation in the battalion; his twin brother, also in the battalion, not far behind him. Since then the list has got longer: we lost three of our 2 R Welsh boys all together the other night; two of them expecting babies back at home. And of course Paul Harding, having risen through the ranks all the way from Rifleman to Major… Anyhow, the Army has evolved over centuries to cope with exactly this, and it works: the little ceremonies and the eulogies and above all the relentless resort to humour. Whatever we do in the coming years we must not lose the culture, traditions and structures that we have evolved that carry us through these difficult times, nor the ethos that gets men to fight and die for their mates and their pride and their sense of honour.

It is of course much more fun when we get to go out and stick it to them. And when JAM have a go at us they tend to come off worse by a large margin, which is very satisfying. I had my first chance to command the battlegroup out on the ground the other night and it was fantastic, though just a tiny bit nerve-wracking. But it was great to be out and about at last and getting the chance to play with the train-set for once Colonel Patrick kindly stayed in and did my job in the Operations Room. It all went well and once I got over the pre-match nerves it was a huge amount of fun. It was only later on that it dawned on me the scale of what we had been engaged in and how far it was beyond anything I had ever done: three Armoured Infantry companies, a troop of Challenger tanks, and a Bulldog Armoured Personnel Company under command; 155 mm AS90 guns, and Apache Attack Helicopters firing in support; about twenty separate attacks ranging from Improvised Explosive Devices or improvised explosive devices (which can be massive) to small arms fire and rocket propelled grenade anti-tank rockets, to mortars; and nearly 100 civilian and logistics vehicles to shepherd through the centre of Basra amidst all the mayhem. Heady stuff and hard pounding, but good experience. Sadly the following night we lost three soldiers in one improvised explosive devices (plus another badly injured), which was pretty unpleasant. But the company involved, as well as everyone else in the battlegroup, was just magnificent: they gathered themselves together, got moving forward again, bounced straight through two more improvised explosive devicess (taking another four casualties) and pressed on with what they had to do, getting the convoy through without a scratch. And at the end of it they all came back in, sorted out their kit and had a brew and a fag and got their heads down to kip, ready to get up for work later that day.

Bizarre really, but I suppose that it shows that all the training does actually work and they are just as robust as their fathers and grandfathers, who did exactly the same thing in their time. It is fairly tasty for them here in camp too, with regular rocket and mortar attacks – four or five a day at the moment – and almost daily small arms and rocket propelled grenade attacks on our perimeter, so there's no danger of being bored.

So that's life in the madhouse; challenging, exciting, but great fun and the boys are simply magnificent.

Yours ever,
Tom

Maj T.R. Copinger-Symes

RGJ Battalion Postings and Operational Tours 1966–2007

	1st Battalion		2nd Battalion		3rd Battalion
1966–67	Germany, Berlin	1966–67	Malaya, Penang	1966–67	UK, Felixstowe
1966	*Borneo*	1966	*Borneo*		
1967–70	UK, Tidworth	1967–71	Germany, Münster	1967–68	Germany, Iserlohn
1967–68	*Cyprus (UN)*			1968–70	Germany, Celle
1969	*NI, Province wide*				
1970–74	Germany, Celle	1971–73	NI, Ballykelly	1970–71	UK, Tidworth
1971	*NI, Belfast*		*Province wide Ops*	1971	3rd Bn reduced to Representative Coy UK, Netheravon
1972	*NI, Belfast*			1971	*NI, Belfast*
1973	*NI, Belfast*			1972	3rd Bn Reformed
1974–78	UK, Dover	1973–75	UK, Catterick	1972–75	UK, Shoeburyness
1974–75	*NI, S Armagh*	1973–74	*Belize*	1972	*NI, Belfast*
1976	*Cyprus (UN)*	1974	*NI, S Armagh*	1973	*NI, Belfast*
1977	*NI, Belfast*	1974–75	*NI, Belfast*	1974	*NI, Belfast*
		1975–77	Gibraltar	1975–77	Germany, Berlin
1978–80	Hong Kong	1977–79	UK, Tidworth	1977–78	UK, Caterham
		1979	*NI, S Armagh*	1978–9	NI, Londonderry *Province wide Ops*
1980–81	UK, Hounslow	1980–86	Germany, Minden	1979–82	UK, Oakington
1981	*NI, S Armagh*	1981–82	*NI, Belfast*	1980	*Cyprus (UN)*
		1985–86	*NI, Belfast*		
1981–83	NI, Aldergrove *Province wide Ops*			1982–87	Germany, Celle
				1984–85	*NI, Belfast*
1983–87	UK, Tidworth	1986–88	UK, Warminster		
1984–85	*Falkland Islands*				
1986	*NI, Province wide*			1987–89	UK, Colchester
				1987–88	*Falkland Islands Coy*
1987–92	Germany, Osnabrück	1988–91	UK, Dover	1988–91	Gibraltar
1987	*NI, Armagh*	1989	*NI, Fermanagh*	1989–90	*NI platoons*
1990–91	*1st Gulf War Coy*	1991	*1st Gulf War Band*		
1991–92	*NI, Tyrone*	1991–92	NI, Omagh	1991–92	Dover, UK
			Province wide Ops	1991–92	*NI, S Armagh*

25 July 1992: The 1st, 2nd and 3rd Battalions merged into two battalions – the 2nd and 3rd Battalions redesignated as 1st and 2nd Battalions

	1st Battalion		2nd Battalion
1992–93	NI, Omagh *Province wide Ops*	1992–95	UK Dover
1993–96	Cyprus, Dhekelia		
1994	*Falkland Islands Coy*		
1995	*Falkland Islands Coy*	1995–97	NI Belfast *Province wide Ops*
1996–99	UK Bulford		
1996	*Bosnia*	1997–2001	Germany Paderborn
1999–2002	NI Belfast *Province wide Ops*	1999–2000	*Kosovo*
		2001	*Bosnia*
2002–2007	UK Weeton	2001–03	UK Warminster
2001	*Sierre Leone*	2003–05	NI Ballykinler
2002	*NI, Belfast*		*Province wide Ops*
2003	*Iraq*		
2004	*NI, S Armagh*		
2005	*Kosovo*		
2006	*Iraq*		
		2005–07	UK Bulford

1 February 2007: Formation of The Rifles – 1 and 2RGJ redesignated 2 and 4Rifles

List of Subscribers

This book has been made possible through the generosity of the following:

F.W. Abbott
Edmund J. Addington
Jonathan Agar
Capt Alexander Allen
Rfn Adrian Allen
D.J. Allen
WO1 (RSM) Jon Allen
Stuart (Tin Tin) Allen
Paul (Ollie) Alsop
D.J.L.F. Anderson
Edward Anderson
Herbert William Andrews
Mr P.M. Andrews
David L. Archer
R. Arnison-Newgass
Capt Mac Arnold
Martin (Gunner) Ash
Phil Ashby
Ross Ashe-Cregan
David Askew
William R. Asprey
Carl Atkinson
Nigel J.B. Atkinson
Alan (Zubes) Aubrey
Nicholas M.J. Austin
Tony (Pookie) Austin
Capt M.J. Aveston
Rfn Paul Axtell
Andrew Ayling
Hugh Babington Smith
Bill Bailey
Roy (Dan) Baillie
Nigel Baker
J.M.J. Balfour
Cpl Suren Ball
Bryan W. Balls
Chris Bannon
James Barber
Shaun Barber
Steven (Ronnie/Dog) Barker

CSgt Chris (Barney) Barnes
Sgt D.V. Barnett
Alvin L. Barrett
Titch Barrett
J. Barroll
Paul Barry
Rick (Baz) Barry
Rfn Betty Bates
Alec Bateson
Cpl J. Baylis
Tony Beach
Paul Beard
Paul Beaumont
Maj (Retd) Jim Beazley
Brian Peter Bebbington
Capt W.J.M. (Bill) Beckwith TD
Andy Beech
Corin Beeney
Bob Beesley
Charles Belcher
K.J. Belcher
David Benneyworth
Mark Benson
Richard Benyon
Brig A.E. Berry
Paul Biles
Steve Binfield
Mr W. Bingham
A.L. Bishop
Sandy Bissett
M.S. Blackman
Maj (Retd) C.D. Blackmore
Herbert Blackshire
Capt T.N.S. Blake
Lt Col G.P. Blaker
Cpl Jason Bloomer
D. Bloomfield
G.F. Blunden
Cpl Jon Bolam
Rfn Nicholas James Bonner

Simon P. Booth-Mason
Viscount Boringdon
Kenneth Bourn
William James Bourne
Jamie Bowden
Peter Bowring CBE
Thomas G. Bowring
B.D. Boyce
Derek (Des) Boyton
Capt J.R.O. Braithwaite
FM The Lord and Lady Bramall
WO2 A.J. Breach
Gary (Lofty) Brewer
Mike Bricknell
Capt Edmund Bright MM
R. Brimmer
LCpl Mike Bristow
WO2 Trevor Bristow
Rfn J.P. Brockhill
Rfn John Brockman
R.H.A. Brodhurst
M.J. Brogan
Capt Andrew Brogden
V.R. Brooke
Antony Brooks
N.I. Brooks
Sgt D. (The Whispers) Broughton
David Brown
WO2 John Brown
Cpl John Brown
Cpl M.D. (Fish) Brown
Mr Robert Brown
Lt Col P.D. Browne
Rfn Jim Browning
Pete Browning
John Brum
James R.B. Bryson
Cpl I.J. Bull
Spencer Bull
Mick Bullivant

Brig C.J.D. Bullock OBE MC
Cpl Tony Burbidge
Jason Burke
T.A.J. Burrows
Rfn Michael Paul Burtenshaw
Nick (Butch) Butcher
Mr Andrew (Buts) Butler
Brig Ed Butler CBE DSO
Robin Buxton
Rfn David Bye
Geoff Bye
Sgt J.A. Byrne
Mike J. Byrne
Maj (QM) Tom Byrne
Andrew Byron
Edward A.D. Cadogan
George Caldwell
Capt A.L. Campbell
Jamie Campbell
Lew Campbell
Andrew Candler
David Robert Cannon
Eddie Carbery
Maj Gen Sir Michael Carleton-Smith CBE DL
Michael Carroll
Mick Carroll
Alan Carter
D.J. Cassidy
Maj R.D. Cassidy MBE
S.P. Cassidy
Maj Peter Casson-Crook
W.G. Catlin
David Caws
Capt Howard Chaganis
Lt Col Peter Chamberlin
Rfn E. Chambers
K.T.T. Chambers
Cpl James Champion
N.J.L. Chance

187

The Royal Green Jackets

Dennis (Dutch) Chandler	T.R. Copinger-Symes	Malachy Doran	George Foulkes
Gerald Grant Chandler	Gerry Copp	T.J. Dove	Anthony (Herby) Fowler
Adam Chapman	Michael B. Copp	Tony Dowd	CSgt E.T.W. Fox
Maj Nobby Chapman	Cpl R.J. Corbett	Bob Dowling	Jim Fox
Col S.C. Chapman TD	Peter M.A. Corbin	John Dowling	Rfn L.H. Fox
Bugle Maj Steve Chapman	Mr David R.D. Cornell	Roger Downton	LCpl R. Foxley
Revd Tim Chapman	Jeff Cornell	Alan (Scripto) Draycott	Deborah J. Francis AGC (SPS)
John (Charlie) Charlton	A.J. (John) Cornford	Alastair Drew	Mr M. Francis
Nicholas Chavasse	Sgt Lou Costello	Dave Driscoll	Mr Thomas Frederick Francis
Charlie Chensee	N.J. Cottam	Gary Driscoll	Michael Frape
Gary Chester	Capt David Cotton	Pat Driscoll	Peter (Tich) Free
Capt S.E. Child	Robert Coulson	R. Drummond-Hay	Kevin Freemantle
John W. Clissold	Rfn Ginge Coulter	G.A. Duffy	Rfn French
Bob Churcher	John Cousins	Greg Dulson	Peter A. French
Justin A.D. Clark	Maj Gerry Coveney	R.A. Duncan	Lt Jono Froome
Pete Clark	Fred Cowan	William Duncan	Lenny Frost
Peter (Geordie) Clark	Rfn R.P. Cox	Rfn Gary Dunn	Richard Frost MBE
William Clark	Brian Cox	Ronald Dunn	Ray Gaffney
Rfn Brian Clarke	Mr J.W. Cox	M.L. Dunning	R.D. de V. Gaisford
Nobby Clarke	Johnny Cox	Maj Charles Dunphie	Jason W. Gard
Robert B. Clarke	WO2 Andy Coyle	Brig Christopher Dunphie	Alex Gardiner
His Hon. John Clay	Tim Crabtree	J.M.P. Durcan	Stuart (Percy) Gardiner
John Clayton	Martin and Charles Cracknell	Capt James Eadie	Rfn Geordie Gargett
J.S.M. Clennell	Rfn G. Crook	CSgt A. Easdon	H.E. Garratt
Pat Coffey	Frederick Crutch	LCpl Mark Eden	Mr G.M. Garrood
John Cohen OBE	Jim Cullen	Cleve (Super Soldier) Edmonston	Mr A.G.B. Garvey
Jack Colbert	J.R. Cunliffe	Maj G. Edwards MBE	Mr D.J. George BEM
James R.B. Cole	LCpl Currie	George Elliott	Dave George
Joe Cole	Leigh Curson	Terry Ellison	Col P.E. Gerahty CBE
John Cole	Andre (Dolly) Dalby	Trev Ellison	Mr R. Gerrard
LCpl Coles	P.C.J. Dalby	Cpl M. Emberton	Gary Gibbons
Bob Coles	Paul (Mr Teazy Weazy) Daley	Robert Etherington	Ian Gilder
Ian A.M. Coles	J. (Taffy) Daley	Mark Eustace	Capt M.A. Gill
LCpl John Coles	J.A. Daniell	Bill (Evo) Evans	Tony Gilley
Brendan Collins	Anthony Darell-Brown	Sgt Ernie (Bob) Evans	Rfn Thomas George William Glassett
Maj C.S. Collins	Capt (Retd) Brian Darvill BEM	James B. Evans	Maj (QM) M.F. Gleeson
Mr L.F.S. Collins	Kenneth Davidson	Mr E.J. Evelegh	T.F. Godfrey-Faussett
Martin J. Collins	Gareth N. Davies	Col Robin Evelegh	Brig D.H. Godsal MBE
Brian (Stud) Colloton	Glen Davies	Capt Brian Ewin	Michael Goodbun
Mr R.P. Colmaine	Chris Davis	Thomas William Fannon	Sir Philip Goodhart
T. Colton	John (Johnny Mc) Davis-McMullan	Brian Farndell	Robert Goodwin
Cpl S.A. Connal RAVC MBE	Bob Day	Rfn B. Farrell	Brig J.H. Gordon CBE
Ivor W. Connop	Maj David Day	Rfn Paul Farrell	Sir Brian Goswell
Terry J. Connor	Capt S.C. Day	Mark Farrer Esq. DL	Sean (Gracie) Grace
William F. Conroy	Maj T.E. de la Rue AAC	David Faulkner	Brendon J. Grainger
Richard Constant	Robin De Pree LRBR TD	Sgt J.A. Fenech	Ross Grainger
Maj R.A.M. Constant	Roland de Souza	Robert (Bob) Field	Rfn Thibault Grand
Robert Constant	Andrew Dee	Tony Finnigan	Ian Gray
Maj D.R. Conway	David Dee	Sgt J.L. Fitt	James Gray
George (Geordie) Cook	Leon Delana	Joe Flaherty	Maj Ken Gray
Lt Graham Cook	Ted Devlin	Rfn Paul M. Flaherty	Dave Green
Matthew Cook	Michael Dewar	Mr R.J. Flamson	LCpl Kyle (Groover) Greenfield
Peter Cook	Peter V. Dickins	B. (Fleckie) Flecknell	Maj John Green-Wilkinson
Moff Cooke	Gareth (Ginger) Dixon	Rfn Ian Fleming	Rob (Taff) Griffett
Lt Col M.D. Coolon	Ian Dobie	Gary Floodgate	Alan (Griff) Griffin
Tony Coombe	A.B.C. Dollard	Jason Fogden	John Griffith-Jones
Christopher M.J. Cooney	Tom Donaldson	Derrick Ford	Harry Grimes
Cpl Paul (Coops) Cooper	LCpl (Donny) Donnelly	Roger Forder	Sgt Neil Guerin
Tony Cooper	Malcolm Don Donnison	Steve Foster	John Guest
W.J.R. Cooper Esq.	Len Dooley	Maj M.E. Foster-Brown	Bond Rfn K. Gunn
Gary Cootes	Thomas Dooner	Mr Frank Foulkes (RGJ Enthusiast)	Maj Carol Gurney

List of Subscribers

J.F. Halford
Rfn David Hall
Paul Hallett
Nicholas Halsey
Alan Hames
Rfn B. Handley
Mr Ray Handley
Roger Handley
A.F. Hands MBE
J.E. Hankins
Maj Paul H.G. Harding
Peter (Hoggy) Hargreaves
Richard Hargreaves
Michael (Duke) Harley
John Harper
Lyndon Harper
Steve Harper
Martin Harris
Bryan (Evil Harry) Harrison
Peter Harrison
Brig Colin Harrisson CVO OBE
CSgt Darren Hart
T.M. Hartley
Geoffrey Harvey
Greig Harvey
A.K. Harwood
Robin D. Hastie Smith
John Hatchett
Barry Hatton
Mr F. Hawkins
Maj A.R. Hayden MBE
Rfn Gary Hayes
Richard M. Hayes
Vere Hayes
Nicholas Haynes
Capt John Hayter DL
H. Hayward
Capt C.P. Hazlehurst DL
Daniel Healy
John (Ted) Heath
Capt C.W. Heathcoat-Amory
Tim Heaton
Olly Heggs
John (Herbie) Helbert
Derek (Del) Hemsley
Dave Hemstead
Don Henchy
A.J.N. Henry
John Henry
Brig C.L.G.G. Henshaw CBE
Toby Heppel
Mr G. Heritage
Chris Hewson
Pete Hewson
J.E.G. Heyburn
Charles Heyman
S.J. Hibbert
Dr Ian Hicks
Mike Hicks
Ted Higginbottom
Roy (Skippy) Higgins

Maj (QM) B. Hill
Capt C.D.F. Hill
Christopher Hill
Jonathan R. Hill
Maj (QM) Mike Hill
Capt Roland A. Hill
Robert (Farmer) Hillier
Robert (Bob) Hilton
Sgt Terry Hissey BA (Hons)
Rfn Steve Hoare
R.L. Hobbs
Larry Hocking
Bernie Hodgson
Angus S. Hodson
Marc Hoffman
Paul (Dusty) Hoffman
Rfn Alan Hogg
J.A. Holden
Wayne Holdrick
Cpl Stanley Thomas Holland
Mr W.E. Holland
Buzz Hollis
Arthur E. Holloway
Steve Hooley
Peter Hopkins
Rfn Peter D. Hopkins
WO2 (Retd) Stephen Horsley
David Hough
John E. Houghton
Steve (H) Houghton
Derek Howard
J.B. Howell-Pryce
Keith (Dog) Hudson
John Eric Hudson
Ken Hudson
Rfn K.G. Hudson
Gary (Bluey) Hue
Tommy Huggan
Derek Huggins
Adrian Hughes
Billy Hughes
Rfn C. Hughes
Charles W. Hughes
Rfn J. Hughes
Mr David Humphries
Maj Danny Hunt
Derek Hunter
Cpl John J. Hynes
Phil Ibbotson
Paul Irby
Peter Irby
Terry Irvine
WO2 David Ivatt
Alan Jackson
A.J.R. Jackson
Alex Jackson
Bob Jackson
WO2 Bugle Maj John (Jacko) Jackson
Brig Jolyon Jackson
Mick (Flapper) Jackson
Mick (Jacko) Jackson

Capt P.N. Janes
Syd Jarman
David Jarrett
Ken Jeavons
Mr A.H. Jenkins
Mike (Jinks) Jennings
Phil Jephcote
Stephen Jessop
P. Jobson
Gen Sir Garry Johnson KCB OBE MC
Mick (Johno) Johnson
Col Neil Johnson OBE TD DL
Sgt Phil (Johnno) Johnson
Maj R.J.S. Johnson
T.J.S. Joll
D.F. Jolliffe
Alan Jones
Rfn Chris Jones
Capt Frank Jones
Rfn Frank Jones
Hume Jones
Capt R.T. Jones
Lt Col R.T.H. Jones MBE
Mr Allwyn Joseph
W.A. Joyce
Dave Judge
Anton Jeffery Karamath
Brig A.E.K. Karslake
J.H.R. Kellock
John L. Kelly
Richard (Ned the Med) Kelly
Kevin Kempton
Michael Kenevane
Stephen Kentish
Lt Col Roger Ker
Alan W. Kermarrec
Steve Keyes
David G. King
Ed Kingsbury
Andrew C. Kinnear
D.S. Kinrade
Gen Sir Frank Kitson
Maj J.F. Kitson
Nick Kitson
Keith Kneller
W.E.D. Knight
Brig Michael Koe OBE
Rfn Albert Koi
Peter A. Kotkowicz
Sgt Rory Lacey
Maj R.W.E. Ladds
Mr R. Laking
Capt Chris Lamb
Larry Lamb
Lt R.G.S. Lane
Rfn John Langan
Robert Langton
Robin Laugher
Maj P. Lawless
Capt Dave Lawn
Ray Lawrenson

Jon Lawton
P.J. Layton MBE
Sgt S.G. Le Couillard
Rod Le Couilliard
E.W. Leask
Michael L. Leavy
Mr Michael A. Lee
Martin Lee-Warner
William J. Lendrum
John Lengthorn
Mr Ian Lennock
Peter Leszczyszak
Cpl Doug Letteboer
Charles Lewer
Mr G. Liggins
Bryan M. Llywelyn
LCpl Martin Stuart Long
WO2 Reg Longhurst
Rfn Ian Longworth
Rfn John Longworth
Lonny Lonsdale
Derek Loombe
David Lowe
W.F. Lowry
George Luker
Roger C.H. Luscombe
Brig (Retd) Peter Lyddon
Mark Anthony Lydiat
Cpl W. Lynch
Sir John Maclure
Patrick Maclure
Rory MacSween
Stuart MacSween
Bryan Madden
Bob Maddocks
Mr P. Maguire
Garry John (Tich) Mahaffey
Mark Anthony Makepeace
Sgt W.L. Makepeace
MARK Mangham
Jackie Mann
Brig M.C.H. Manners-Smith CBE
Mick Mannion
Bugle Maj Patrick Mannion
Mr Peter Mansfield
Rfn Richard James Markham
Brian J. Marks
Julian D. Marks
Lt Col Richard Marriott
Simon H.C. Marriott
Dean Marsden
Dave (Boggy) Marsh
Tim Marsh
Mr Leigh Marshall
Leigh Marshall
Paddy Marshall
Bill Martin
Robert Martin
Graham Maskell
Sgt Peter Maslewski
Pete Mason

The Royal Green Jackets

Lee Massey
Capt R.L.S. Mather
Richard Matters
Alastair Maxwell
G.J. McCabe
Rfn E. McCallum
Bugler T. McCann
WO2 Bob McCartney
LCpl Pete McCartney
Col I.H. McCausland
WO2 D.J. McCreith
WO2 Peter McCreith
Bernard (Mac) McDonald
Chris McDonald
Rfn Aran (Mac) McGee
Mac McGlasson
Joe McGonigle-Napier
Andy McGrigor
Chris (Mac) McIver
Jonathan McIvor
P.R. McLaren-Smith
Cpl D.J. McLaughlin
WO2 Willie McLean
Jim (Ginge) McNeill
Michael (Mac) McQueen
John S. Measham
Steve Metcalf
Julian Meyrick
Mr and Mrs Ian Michie
LCpl Leo Midwinter
Lt Col Christopher Miers
Chris Mieville
Andy Mihalop
WO1 Barry Millard
Maj Gen G.H. Mills CB CVO OBE
John Mills
Steve Milsom
Rfn Milsted
Jonathan Rolf Milward
Rolf Milward
Don Mitchell
John M. Mitchell BSM
Kevin Mitchell
Patrick Mitford-Slade
Mick (Milo) Mizon
Brig J.N.B. Mogg
C.H. Molesworth-St Aubyn
Col W.B. Molloy RFD ED CLJ
Ged Monks
Maj Iain Moodie
LCpl A.J. Moore
Bobby Moore
Brian Moore
Dale (Rog) Moore
Robert M.J. Moore
Cpl Dave Moreland
Christopher Morgan
Rfn T. Morgan
Geoff Morrish
Darrell (Oz) Morrison
Norman Morrison

Bernie Morton
Chris Moss
M. Moss
Marty Mulligan
A.P. (Spud) Murphy
Dale Murphy
Michael Murphy
CSgt (Retd) David Murray
David R. Murray
Roy Murtagh
Azad Nandoo
George Nash
Mr C. Naude
Raymond Nelson
Gus Netzler
George J. Newman
David Nichol
David Nicholson
Colin Nufer
Geordie Oates
Michael G. O'Brien
Mick O'Connell
Sgt M.A. O'Connor
WO2 Ian O'Malley
Vic Osmand
WO1 D.L. Owen Esq.
Stephen Painter
David Vivian Paintin
David Pallett
Roy A. Palmer
Roy Kenneth Palmer
Mario V. Pampanini
David Paradise
Ian (Chalkie) Parfitt
Edward Parker
H.M. Parker
Maj P.H. Parker
WO2 Peter L. Parkinson
Cpl (Sparks) Parkinson
P.L. Parsons
Sgt C. (Snips) Parsons
Gen Sir Robert Pascoe KCB MBE
Mr Stephen Pascoe
Christopher Patey
Andy Patrick
Frederick (Pat) Patrick
Hugh Patterson
Col Rt Hon. Sir Geoffrey Pattie
David Payne
Cpl Herbert C. Payne
Ron Payne
Dennis Pearce
Rfn John Pearson
Gen Sir Thomas Pearson
Michael Peek
Capt Tristan B. Peniston-Bird
John Pentreath
D.R. Peppiatt
Rfn David Peppiatt
Capt Chris Percival QVRM
Rafael W. Perez

Rfn F.J. Perry
G. Peter
Richard Pett
Dave Phillips
Cpl L. Phillips
Rfn T. Phillips
John Pickford
Martin Pike
Sgt Gordon Pilcher
CLLR Chris Pines
Emma Pink
James Plastow
Maj Andrew Poë
Maj J.L. Poë
Rfn Dave Pomfrett
John Poole-Warren
Andy Porter
Maj H.R.M. Porter
C.F. Povey
WO2 Bugle Maj J.D. Powell
Mike (Enoch) Powell
Nick (Enoch) Powell
Richard Powlesland
Edward Poynter
Bob Pratt
George Price
Rfn Melvin Price
LCpl Sam Price
Brig Nicholas Prideaux
Capt William Prideaux
Andrew Pringle
Maj Paddy Proctor MBE
Andrew Purvis
CSgt Fred Purvis
C.J.L. Puxley Esq.
Gen Lord Ramsbotham
James Ramsbotham
Fred Ramsden
Henry Frederick Rawlins
Mick (Jungle) Read
Lt P.J. Readings
Doug Reed
G.D. Reid
Maj P.H. Reinhold RAMC
Lance D. Renetzke
Rfn Richards
David Richards
Sir Francis Richards
Peter Richardson
Elizabeth C.A. Riley
Lt Col (Retd) R.J. Rimmer
Rfn J. Ritchie
David J.M. Roberts
Mike Robertson
J. Robertson-Macleod
A.M. (Robbo) Robinson
Andy Robinson
Clive (Curly) Robinson
CSgt D.J. Roche
Mike Roderick
Mark A.A. Rogers

Mr C.N. Rodgers
Stuart Rolt
George A.D. Romans
Terry Roper MBE TD
Jim Rose
Sgt Reg Rose
Capt A.J.S. Ross
Alasdair Ross
Cpl Ian Rosser
P.J. Roszczyk
Bryan (Taffy) Rowlands
Chris Rumble
Terry (Squid) Rumble
Louis Rundle
Andy Russell
Rfn H.W. Russell
Maj R.K. Ryan TD
J. Sabini
Neil Saitch
Graham Sale
Graham Salsbury
Rachael Salsbury
M.C.E. Salter
Ken Salway
Lau Choon Sam
Lt C.A. San Jose
Lt Col P.N.Y.M. Sanders OBE
John Joseph Sandford
Cpl John (Paddy) Sands
Maj Gerald Sanford
Richard Savill
John Saxelby
C.E. Sayell
R.J. Schembri
Lt Col P.J.F. Schofield MBE
D.G. Scott
M.J. Scott
Michael Scott-Hyde
Mr and Mrs Mark Scrase-Dickins
Jack Seear
Jeff Seeney
Chris Selley
Spike Sells
Maj G.R. Seymour
Zareh (Shambo) Shamlian
Rfn Brian (Angel) Shanahan
Paddy Shanks
K.P. Sharkey
Rfn Paul Shaw
Maj Rupert Shaw MBE
P.J. Shelley
Philip Shelley
William Shipton
Bryn H. Shore
Joe (Medic) Shortall
Maj Shreeve
Sgt A. (Sibbo) Sibbons
Terry Sidhu
Cpl (Simmo Eastwards Ever
    Eastwards) Simmons
Sgt Graham James Simpson

List of Subscribers

John Sims
M.G. Slater
Gerald Slavin
Alan (Smudge 19) Smith
Cpl D.K. Smith
D.A. (Smudger 88) Smith
David (Smudger 70) Smith
WO2 David J. Smith
Derek Smith
George Smith
Brig Greg Smith TD DL
John R. Smith
John Robert Smith
K.J. Smith
Lt Kempley Smith
Brig (Retd) M. Smith CBE MC
The Hon. P.R. Smith
Mr Peter H.C. Smith
Mrs Philip Smith
Ronald Stephen Charles Smith
WO2 Roy Smith
Rfn R. (Smudger) Smith
Maj Tom Smith MBE
Col G.F. Smythe OBE
Col C.E.M. Snagge
Peter Snellin
Mr T. Sofuyi
Mr S.M. Solomon
Rick Sonnex
B.A. Southion RB
Andy Spalding
Geoffrey Sparrow MC TD DL
Michael Spence
Rfn Phil Spinner
Sgt D. Spooner
Stephen Squires
Maj Tommy St Aubyn
Maj (Retd) R.E. Stanger
Denis Staniforth
Christopher Staunton
LCpl Paul Steinmetz
J.D. Stephens
Robert H. Wilson Stephens
Jim Stevenson
John Stevenson
Col R.S. Stewart-Wilson MC
Aubyn Stewart-Wilson
Brig D.M. Stileman OBE
J.D.W. Stileman
Michael S. Stilwell Esq.
Albert Storey
Ian Strachan
Danny Stratford
Edward Strawson

Capt A.W. Strong
Sp Strype
Kevin Sturdy
John E. Sturgess
Glen (Pop) Sturman
Paul K. Sumner BEM
David Sunley
Kenneth J. Swann
Sir Michael Swann
Robert John Sweeney
Darren (Swifty) Swift
Mr S.P. Swift
Dave Swords
Lt Col Charlie Sykes PWRR
Mr Christopher Tebbutt
Jon Tate
F.J.B. Taylor
Brig John Taylor
Nick Taylor
Capt Sean E. Taylor
Ian (Titch) Tee
Glenn (Geordie T) Ternent
Donald Terrell
Mick Terrey
L.S. Thacker Esq.
Peter Thistlethwayte
Lt Clive Thomas
J.H. Thomas
Sgt Rod Thomas
WO2 Steve Thomas
Michael Christopher Thompson
Lt Col R.J. Thomson MBE
Robin Thorne
David Thornton
Alan (Prummie) Thorpe
Col John M.A. Tillett
Mr Peter S. Tilley
Cpl R.G. (Bob) Tilley
Roy G. Timms
D.J. Timms-Dolly
Simon Tomkinson
A. (REME Lad) Tomlinson
LCpl S. Trafford
Cpl Albert Trout
Jonathan Trower
Maj (Retd) L.R. Trower MBE
Catharine Trustram Eve
Luke Trustram Eve
Col The Hon. P.N. Trustram Eve OBE
Roy Trustram Eve OBE
Nigel Tubby
A.R. Turle
Mr K. Turner

CSgt (Retd) Keith Turner
Rfn W.J. Turner
Cpl Rick Twohey
Brendan Tyrrell
David (Tee) Tyrrell
David Tyrrell
R.J. Tyson MM
B.S. Ullah
Alexander van Straubenzee
Sgt C.R. Van-Son
Mr Philip Varney
Mr T.W. (Budgie) Venables
Rfn Bryn (Dodger) Viggers
Col Mike Vince
L.J. (Spud) Virot
Maj B.G.P. Vivian
Steven Voce
Bob (Rocky) Volier
Lt Col J-D von Merveldt
Charles Vyvyan
Maj Sir Hereward Wake Bt MC
Anthony Walker
Rfn John Walker
Lee Wall
Lt Gen Sir Christopher Wallace
Sgt Matthew Walsh
Roderick Walsh
Robert W. Walton
Joni (Small Waqa) Waqavonovono
Cyril Frederick Ward
John Ward
Stephen (Nasher) Wareing
Peter Warne
Maj Niall Warry TD
Steve Warsop
Julian Wathen
Rfn Roy (Muppet) Watkins
Edward Watson
Colin L. Watts
David Watts
Jonathan Wax
Edgar Wayman
Bruce Weatherill
Capt I.R. Weatherley PMICS
Keith Webster
Tim Welch
Vince Wellington
M.C. Wells
Capt W.J.D. Wells
Maj Valentine West
D.E. Westmoreland
Michael (Sticks) Weston
David Wheal
Rfn F.J. Wheeler

Mr G.H. Whitby
Rfn (Chalky) White
Dennis White
WO2 (CSM) Gary White
James White
J.A. (Tony) White
Murray Whiteside
LCpl I. (Boggy) Whittle
Sgt Wally Wickham
Alistair Wilde
Rfn S. Oscar Wilding
Rfn Waine Wilkins
Rfn Steve (Wiggsy) Wilkinson
William G.A. Wilkinson
Dave Willbourne
Rfn A. Williams
Capt Bill Williams MBE
Maj Dennis Williams MBE
Fred Williams
Keith Williams
Tony Williams
Lt Col E.I. Williamson TD AE
E.J.D. Willing
Brig H. Willing
George H. Willmott
Sgt Shane Willoughby
Paul Darling Wills
Albert Andrew Willsea
Brian Wilson
Jock Wilson
Mark Wilson
Mr S.L. Wilson
Andrew Wimble
Mr Derek Winckles MBE
Mr K.C. Winney
David Wood
Keith Woodcraft
John Woods
Michael Worrall
Henry Worsley
Gen Sir Richard Worsley
Cpl G. Wright
John Derek Wright
Bugle Maj Paul A. Wright
W.S.C. Wright
T. Wrighting
Philip Wroughton
David Wyatt
Chad Wyn-De-Bank
Rfn John Wynne
Capt (Retd) J.C.Y. Yang
J. Young
S.J. Young
Stephen Yow

Acknowledgements

Picture Credits

The Editor and publishers would like to thank all those who so generously contributed to the more than 500 images that appear in this book, and without whom the book would not have been possible. The images concerned are too numerous to attribute individually, but the following acknowledgments are essential:

British Film Institute 52T; Corbis 138R; Julian Calder 33, 42T, 44T, 67, 87 Bottom L/R, 88R, 88–9, 89L, 89R, 116; Matthew Cook 89–90T; Harriet Gosling/Henry Worsley 172–3; Ken Howard 38; Christopher Miers 106; Royal Highland Fusiliers Museum 138L; Soldier Magazine 127 Bottom R, 140 (inset); Bryn Parry 8, 54, 166; The Royal Green Jackets Museum, Winchester (Chairman Royal Green Jackets Museum Trustees: Lt Gen Sir Christopher Wallace) 7, 8, 9, 10, 11, 12, 13 (inset), 14, 15, 16, 18, 21, 23, 24, 32, 35, 37, 39, 41, 45, 49, 69, 71, 79, 86, 87, 98, 109, 116

Our grateful thanks for additional and vital assistance in sourcing images for this volume to: Ron Cassidy, Ken Gray, Vere Hayes, Bert Henshaw, RGJ Chronicle (special thanks to Stephen Edwards at Culverlands Printers, Winchester), The Rifles Officers' Club, 56 Davies Street, and also to Lizzie Shipton, Archivist, RHQ The Rifles, Peninsula Barracks, Winchester SO23 8TS

No image appearing in this book may be scanned or otherwise copied without the express permission in writing of the publishers, Third Millennium Information Ltd, acting on behalf of the copyright owners. While every effort has been made to identify copyright owners, the publishers will welcome any further information in writing to TMI Group Ltd, 2–5 Benjamin St, London EC1M 5QL

Swift and Bold: A Portrait of The Royal Green Jackets 1966–2007

© The Royal Green Jackets and Third Millennium Publishing Limited

First published in 2007 by
Third Millennium Publishing Limited,
a subsidiary of Third Millennium Information Limited.

2–5 Benjamin Street
London
United Kingdom
EC1M 5QL
www.tmiltd.com

ISBN 9 781905 942 69 7

All rights reserved

No part of this publication may be reproduced or transmitted in any form or by any means, electronic or mechanical, including photocopying, recording or any storage or retrieval system, without permission in writing from the publisher.

British Library Cataloguing in Publication Data
A CIP catalogue record for this book is available from the British Library.

Edited by Andrew Pringle
Designed by Matthew Wilson
Production by Bonnie Murray
Reprographics by Asia Graphic Printing Ltd
Printed by Butler and Tanner Ltd, Frome, England

Back jacket image: The memorial tablet to The Royal Green Jackets is in the National Memorial Arboretum, Alrewas, Staffordshire.

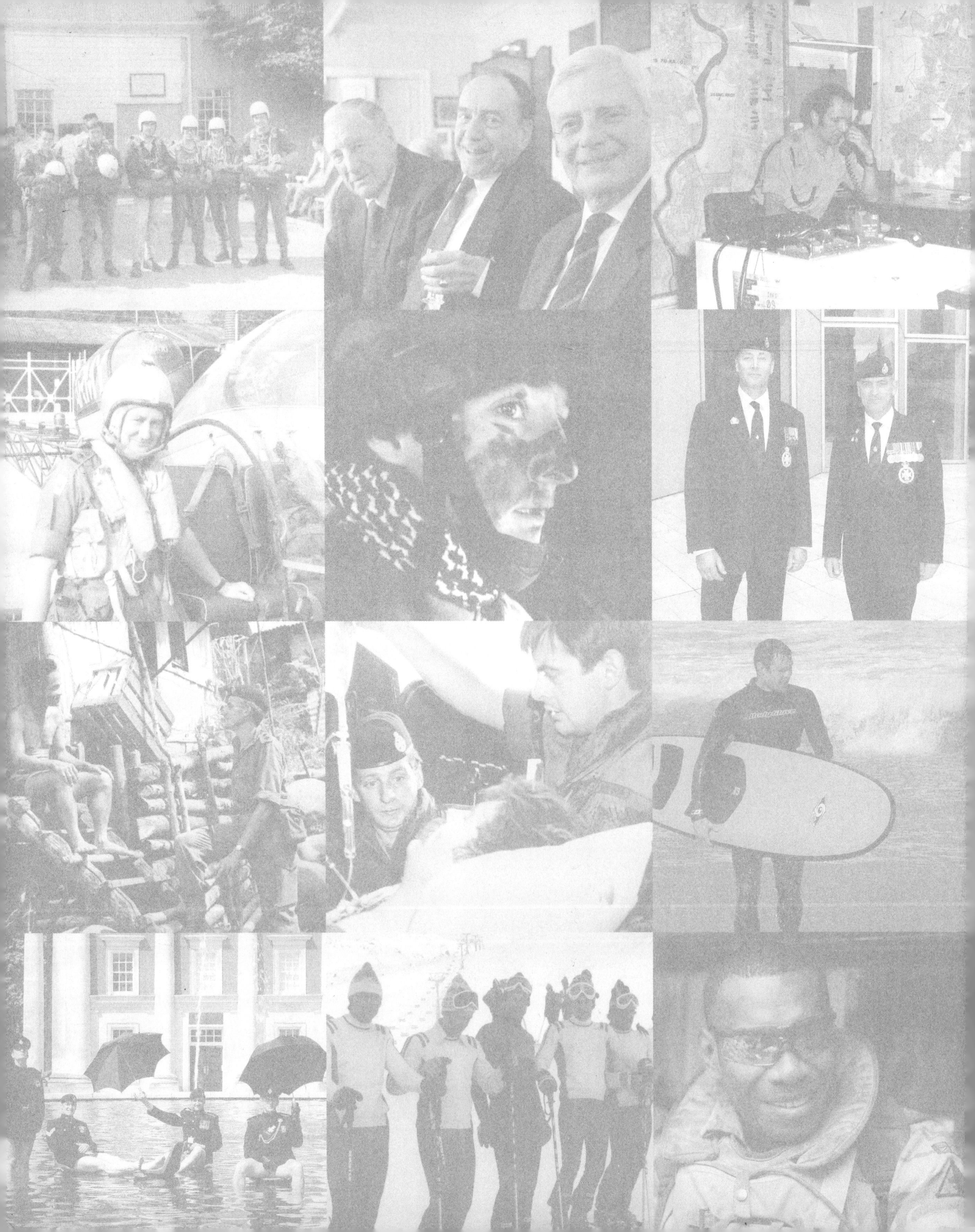